Drupal® FOR DUMMIES® 2ND EDITION

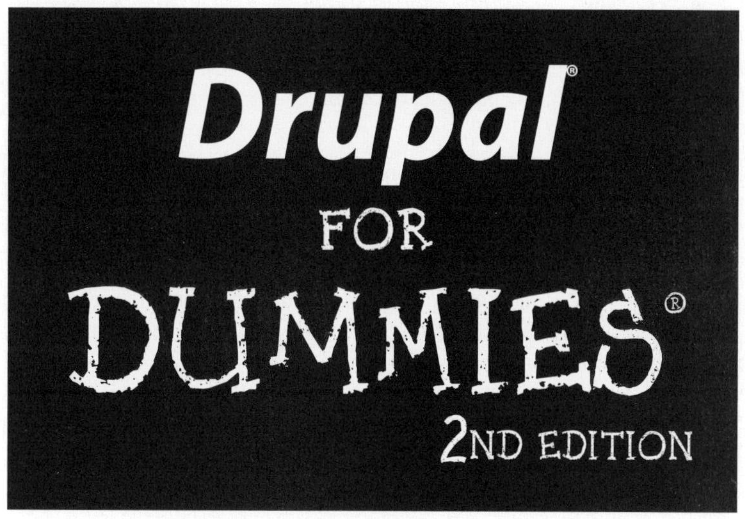

by Lynn Beighley and Seamus Bellamy

John Wiley & Sons, Inc.

Drupal® For Dummies®, 2nd Edition

Published by
John Wiley & Sons, Inc.
111 River Street
Hoboken, NJ 07030-5774

www.wiley.com

Published by John Wiley & Sons, Inc., Indianapolis, Indiana

Published simultaneously in Canada

For general information on our other products and services, please contact our Customer Care Department within the U.S. at 877-762-2974, outside the U.S. at 317-572-3993, or fax 317-572-4002.

For technical support, please visit www.wiley.com/techsupport.

Wiley also publishes its books in a variety of electronic formats and by print-on-demand. Not all content that is available in standard print versions of this book may appear or be packaged in all book formats. If you have purchased a version of this book that did not include media that is referenced by or accompanies a standard print version, you may request this media by visiting http://booksupport.wiley.com. For more information about Wiley products, visit us www.wiley.com.

Library of Congress Control Number: 2011937918

ISBN 978-1-118-08348-2 (pbk); ISBN 978-1-118-14749-8 (ebk); ISBN 978-1-118-14750-4 (ebk); ISBN 978-1-118-14751-1 (ebk)

Manufactured in the United States of America

10 9 8 7 6 5 4 3 2 1

About the Authors

Lynn Beighley has been a computer book author for a very long time, and this is her twelfth book. She's written about SQL, PHP, Flash, Photoshop, and Dreamweaver, and finds that they all have connections to Drupal. In fact, it's like "Six Degrees of Kevin Bacon" — she thinks maybe everything is connected to Drupal. Or perhaps Drupal is connected to everything. Either way, she loves it.

Lynn lives in a sleepy New Jersey town, and doesn't know anyone named Tony. She shares her slightly off-kilter 1920s home with her husband, Drew, and an 80-pound lap dog named Wroxton.

Seamus Bellamy has written only one other computer book so far — *Joomla! For Dummies* — and feels humbled in the face of his coauthor's massive body of work. During the time that Seamus should have been writing books, he instead frittered away his days pursuing a number of tangents — working in the security intelligence community, as a pub musician, and as a music and tech journalist. Most recently, his work can be found on a regular basis in *Mac|Life Magazine,* and *Maximum PC,* as well as online.

Seamus currently lives in Victoria, Canada. Like Lynn, Seamus knows no one named Tony. That said, during the late 1990s he did briefly share a house in Halifax with a fiddler named Anthony who ate nothing but fish sticks and ice cream for close to a year. That, however, is a story for another day.

Dedication

Lynn: For Drew.

Seamus: For my father, Jack. I wish you could have lived long enough to see me make a living doing what I love.

Authors' Acknowledgments

We'd like to thank Kyle Looper for giving us the opportunity to write a *For Dummies* book on such a great topic, and Jean Nelson for shepherding us through the process. We also thank the whole crew at Wiley who helped with this edition.

Publisher's Acknowledgments

We're proud of this book; please send us your comments at http://dummies.custhelp.com. For other comments, please contact our Customer Care Department within the U.S. at 877-762-2974, outside the U.S. at 317-572-3993, or fax 317-572-4002.

Some of the people who helped bring this book to market include the following:

Acquisitions, Editorial, and Vertical Websites

Project Editor: Jean Nelson

Acquisitions Editor: Kyle Looper

Senior Copy Editor: Barry Childs-Helton

Technical Editor: Johan Falk

Editorial Manager: Kevin Kirschner

Vertical Websites Project Manager: Laura Moss-Hollister

Vertical Websites Project Manager: Jenny Swisher

Supervising Producer: Rich Graves

Vertical Websites Associate Producers: Josh Frank, Marilyn Hummel, Douglas Kuhn, Shawn Patrick

Editorial Assistant: Amanda Graham

Sr. Editorial Assistant: Cherie Case

Cover Photo: ©istockphoto.com / Björn Meyer

Cartoons: Rich Tennant (www.the5thwave.com)

Composition Services

Project Coordinator: Kristie Rees

Layout and Graphics: Joyce Haughey, Corrie Socolovitch, Kim Tabor

Proofreader: Penny L. Stuart

Indexer: Christine Karpeles

Publishing and Editorial for Technology Dummies

Richard Swadley, Vice President and Executive Group Publisher

Andy Cummings, Vice President and Publisher

Mary Bednarek, Executive Acquisitions Director

Mary C. Corder, Editorial Director

Publishing for Consumer Dummies

Kathleen Nebenhaus, Vice President and Executive Publisher

Composition Services

Debbie Stailey, Director of Composition Services

Contents at a Glance

Table of Contents

Part III: Bending Drupal to Your Will 173

Part IV: Taking Drupal to the Next Level 217

Introduction

Welcome to the second edition of *Drupal For Dummies,* a book written especially for people who want to have their own websites but haven't a clue about how to start or where to begin.

Are you frustrated because the kid next door has five websites to your none? Are you tired of trying to find someone to build your site for you for free? Do you hear stories about how much a website has picked up your dentist's business? You need Drupal!

Or maybe you already have a website, but you have one problem: The guy who built it isn't around to help when things break. And he built it in Javanese HRH or some other gibberish you can't even remember the name of, much less decipher. Makes you want to scream.

Either way, you've found the right book. Help is here, within these humble pages.

This book talks about building a website from scratch, using Drupal — in everyday language. It doesn't assume you know how to create web pages. You don't need to know code, either; in fact, you can create your site without writing a single line of computer code. The language is friendly; you don't need a graduate education to get through it. The goal is to show you how to build your own site with the features you want, without coding, without deciphering technical jargon, and without pulling a single hair from your head in frustration.

About This Book

There are a couple of ways to use this book, depending on your preferences and experience.

If you're a content management, website, or Drupal newbie, you can start reading and working with Chapter 1 and keep going until you reach the index. Everything falls in sequence as you build experience and knowledge. We explain the concepts and give you practical instructions. Each of the 17 chapters in this book covers a specific aspect of building a website with Drupal — such as installing Drupal, building a basic site with a blog and forum, using images and video on your site, or building an online store.

But you don't have to memorize anything in this book. It's a need-to-know book: You can pick it up when you need to know something. Need to know how to put a YouTube video on your Drupal site? Pick up the book. Need to know how to create a contact form for your customers? Pick up the book.

This book works like a reference. Start with the topic you want to find out about. Look for it in the table of contents or in the index to get going. The table of contents is detailed enough that you should be able to find most of the topics you're looking for. If not, turn to the index, where you can find even more detail.

After you find your topic in the table of contents or the index, turn to the area of interest and read as much as you need or want. Then close the book and get on with it.

Of course, this book is loaded with information, so if you want to take a brief excursion into your topic, you're more than welcome. If you want to know the ins and outs of building an online store, read the whole chapter on storefronts. If you just want to know how to post a product on your site, read just the section on adding products. You get the idea.

This book rarely directs you elsewhere for information — just about everything that you need to know about Drupal is right here. If you find the need for additional information on related topics, plenty of other *For Dummies* books can help.

Conventions Used in This Book

As with other *For Dummies* books, we use certain conventions to keep things consistent and make it easier for you to read this book. Here are some of the conventions you'll find throughout this book:

- *Italics* appear on new terms that we go on to define.
- **Bold** shows the text you need to type. Also, we use **bold** on the steps you take in numbered lists.
- `Monofont` indicates code or a URL (web address), such as `www.dummies.com`.

What You Don't Need to Read

Aside from the topics you can use right away, some of this book is skippable. We carefully marked technical information with the Technical Stuff icon and put somewhat off-topic information in self-contained sidebars so that you can steer clear of them if you wish. Don't read this stuff unless you're into technical explanations and want to know a little of what's going on behind the scenes. Don't worry; our feelings won't be hurt if you don't read every word.

Foolish Assumptions

We're making only one assumption about who you are: You're someone who wants to build a website and has heard that Drupal is a good choice.

Macintosh and Windows users can all use this book.

How This Book Is Organized

Inside this book, you find chapters arranged in five parts. Each chapter breaks down into sections that cover various aspects of the chapter's main subject. The chapters are in a logical sequence, so reading them in order (if you want to read the whole thing) makes sense. But the book is modular enough that you can pick it up and start reading at any point.

Here's the lowdown on what's in each of the five parts.

Part I: Getting Started with Drupal

The chapters in this part present a layperson's introduction to what Drupal is all about, where to get it, and how to install it. This part is a good place to start if you don't have the Drupal software already installed for you. It's also a great place to start if you've looked at Drupal but have no idea what all those infernal links do.

The best thing about this part is that it starts at the very beginning and doesn't assume you know how to download and upload and extract and install software. It also suggests simple solutions on how to get started. In other words, this part is aimed at ordinary people who know almost nothing about how websites come to exist.

Part II: Your First Drupal Site

The goal of the chapters in this part is to show you how to build your first website quickly and easily. And it takes you beyond simply building a site, into fun stuff such as changing the appearance and building a site with a blog, forum, and user comments.

Part III: Bending Drupal to Your Will

After you get a basic website up and running, the chapters in this part show you how to add on to it and really control it. You find out all about safely allowing others to use your site and controlling what they can and can't do. You also spend time making your site even more your own by customizing colors, logos, and artwork.

Part IV: Taking Drupal to the Next Level

This part really takes your site to a whole new level. You discover how to pull content and data from other websites, and how to build a storefront. Those are just a few of the many new features you can add to your site using Drupal's modular design. You also discover how to use Drupal Gardens to create a site in minutes — without having to worry about web hosting or software installation.

Part V: The Part of Tens

This wouldn't be a *For Dummies* book without a collection of lists of interesting snippets: ten modules (or add-ons) for your Drupal site and ten sites you can visit to find out even more about Drupal.

Icons Used in This Book

Those nifty little pictures in the margin aren't there just to pretty up the place. They have practical functions:

Pay special attention to this icon; it lets you know that some particularly useful tidbit is at hand — perhaps a shortcut or a little-used command that pays off big.

Did we tell you about the memory course we took?

Hold it — technical details lurk just around the corner. Read on only if you have a pocket protector.

Danger, Will Robinson! This icon highlights information that may help you avert disaster.

Where to Go from Here

Yes, you can get there from here. With this book in hand, you're ready to build your own robust and useful website with Drupal. Browse through the table of contents and decide where you want to start. Be bold! Be courageous! Be adventurous! Above all, have fun!

Part I
Getting Started with Drupal

"Can't I just give you riches or something?"

In this part . . .

You want a website. But the kid next door doesn't know enough to build what you need — and the web design company wants to charge you an arm and a leg. Just when you're about to give in and pay too much, you overhear a conversation about Drupal, and how you can build a website with it.

But when you try it, you don't find it easy. The documentation is hard to follow, and you can't find anything in the Drupal interface.

If this has happened to you, you'll appreciate the chapters in this part. They provide a gentle introduction to building your first website with Drupal.

What if you don't even have Drupal and need to install it? Then the chapters in this part take you to the very beginning. That way your site will be up and ready to be enhanced by the great stuff in the chapters in Parts II and beyond.

Chapter 1
The Big Picture

In This Chapter

- Understanding open source software
- Comparing Content Management Systems
- Developing a website with Drupal
- Knowing Drupal's potential

At the dawn of time, if you wanted to create a fully featured website with forms, a blog, and a message board, you practically had to be a computer programmer — or at least have enough dirt on a programmer to bribe him into building a website for you. You needed to know how to write HTML (and possibly JavaScript and CSS), and to accomplish anything dynamic, you needed to know yet another language such as PHP or ASP. You probably would have needed to know SQL, the language that allows websites to store and retrieve information.

As the waters receded and the years wore on, web developers grew weary of having to build each and every site from scratch and began freely sharing code. If you knew some HTML and a few other things, you could use the work of other people to knit your site together. No longer did you need to write code every time you wanted a contact form or poll or image library on your website.

Today, we have entire robust and powerful web applications, supported by communities of web developers. Enter Drupal. Drupal is one of a class of web applications that do nearly all the work for you. You can build a site with Drupal without ever writing a single line of code. Indeed, that's the ultimate goal of Drupal: to free you from the inner workings of the code and instead let you focus on the layout and content of your site. There are other, similar applications you can use that also accomplish this, but Drupal is one of the best open source applications for quick, code-free website creation. In short, Drupal, just like RuPaul, makes looking good look easy.

Before we get into the installation and use of Drupal, we think it's helpful to start by introducing the features of Drupal. After all, there's no sense in installing it if you don't know what it does, right? The more you understand about what Drupal is, the better you can plan and use it to your advantage.

What Drupal Is

The official Drupal website, `http://drupal.org`, describes Drupal as "a free software package that allows an individual or a community of users to easily publish, manage and organize a wide variety of content on a website." This is a great description of this application. It's free, as long as you follow certain rules that we mention later in this chapter. Drupal allows for a wide variety of content, making it extremely flexible and customizable. The fact that more than one individual can publish and manage content makes it a Content Management System (CMS). We explain each of these important characteristics of Drupal in more detail a little bit later on.

Free

Drupal is distributed as *open source* software. This means that you can get a copy of the program and install it on your web server, modify the appearance of the pages and layout to suit your needs, and add your content to it without paying for the program. It seems too good to be true!

Software designated as open source essentially means it's "free," but it does have certain legal obligations associated with it. For example, if you were a programmer and made changes to the code itself and then provided the new code to other people, there would be certain rules you would have to follow under Drupal's license. You can learn more about open source licensing here: `www.gnu.org/copyleft/gpl.html`.

If you really like Drupal, or the great Drupal site you build helps your company make lots of money, you can contribute to the efforts of the many great programmers who have created this software by visiting `http://drupal.org/contribute`.

Flexible

Drupal sites are completely flexible. This means you can do things like

- **Modify the layout of your pages:** With the use of blocks, you can move your navigation links to anywhere else on your pages you wish. You can put all your content in one column or choose multiple-column layouts.
- **Remove or replace the default Drupal logo:** By default, your Drupal site will be branded with the official Drupal logo. You can easily remove it or replace it with your own logo.

- **Add and remove pages:** Drupal wouldn't be of much use to anyone if it were stuck with a specific set of pages. Drupal gives you complete flexibility to create as many pages as your site will need, as well as freedom to choose where page links will appear, and to delete those pages if they're no longer useful to you.
- **Hide content and pages from certain users:** You can, if you choose, allow only logged-in users (or even a subset of users) to see certain pages on your site. You can even hide content *within* a page from certain users. Sneaky!
- **Allow users to choose their own layouts:** You can let individual users choose their own layouts. When they log in, they'll see whichever layout they chose. This is a great way to make the visitors to your site feel welcome.

Customizable

One of the best things about Drupal is the ease with which you can customize your site's features. Drupal comes with lots of great features you can turn on or off with the click of a button. If you want to add a forum, poll, or blog, for example, you'll find they are features included with the Drupal application that you can easily include or exclude from your site. Your site can contain precisely what you want it to, and you can turn off features you don't want. Even if the rest of your life is an out-of-control mess, you can rest assured that your Drupal website will be exactly the way you want it.

What's better than free stuff? More free stuff! Beyond the features, or modules, included with the program, many web developers have created and made freely available *thousands* more modules you can download and install! We recommend you take a minute to check out the third-party modules here: `http://drupal.org/project/modules`. You'll find some great add-ons are in there. If you aren't already excited about the potential Drupal offers yet, you will be. For example, free modules allow you to integrate Facebook and Twitter information into your site, turn your site into an online store, or create photo galleries. We tell you about some especially useful and interesting third-party modules later in this book.

A Content Management System

At its heart, Drupal is all about *managing content.* Drupal belongs to a class of applications known as web *Content Management Systems* (CMS). These applications are designed to separate the content on a website from the presentation of that content. In other words, you can manage the text and graphics on your site through the Drupal interface as easily as you can create a Microsoft Word document.

After you set up your site, you don't have to worry about looking at HTML code and putting your desired text into some sort of web format. You can simply type in a text box on a form and click a button. BOOM! Your new content will show up on your site. That, friends, is what they call easy. Behind the scenes, Drupal handles the conversion of your text into a format viewable on the web. Drupal will also, in the case of a blog-style page, save any old content previously published and provide a link to it for your users.

But the real power of CMS applications is that you can give specific users the permission to easily post, edit, and/or delete content on your site, while at the same time, deny them the permissions required to change the layout or features of your site. You can even allow certain users to create content, but not allow it to be published on the site until you've had a chance to approve it. All this control allows your site content to be maintained, while your site structure remains safe from possible harm.

What Drupal Isn't

Drupal is a great application for creating a robust CMS website. But it's not perfect. You may encounter a few difficulties as you work with it:

- **Drupal isn't so easy to install:** Although the latest version of the CMS — Drupal 7 — introduces a great number of new, user-friendly elements, it can still be a tough nut to crack. Probably the most difficult part of building a Drupal website is installing Drupal in the first place. You have to understand its requirements, make a few decisions, and gather required information to get it installed correctly.

  Chapter 2 covers the ins and outs of installation.

- **Your site isn't automatically ready to go after you finish installing Drupal:** You go on from there to modify the configuration of the site, change the layout, and add your own content. You will also have to spend time deciding on the best site structure for your website.

  We show you how to customize your site, in great detail, in Part II.

- **You have only a limited capability to change the appearance or function of modules:** Any modules you use will have some configurable options, but there may be things you want to change that aren't configurable. This isn't unique to Drupal: It's the case with any open source CMS application you encounter. The developers of modules generally do their best to anticipate what you might want to configure, but they can't read your mind. Fortunately, the beauty of open source is that you have the code available to tweak until your specific needs can be addressed.

We don't discuss programming in this book, but after you get your site running, you may want to learn more about the code side of Drupal. In Chapter 17, we recommend some sites where you can get programming help if you choose to delve into the messy business of modifying the code.

- **Drupal's interface can be a bit confusing:** Drupal administration menus are not intuitive — which is why you bought this book, right? We show you where everything is and explain Drupal's language for its onscreen things throughout this book. Don't worry. We'll be gentle.

What Drupal Can Do for Your Site

From web polls to blogs and shopping carts, your site can be full of great features without any need for you to get into the actual web programming side of things. We're sure you'll agree that this is a very good thing. As you look through the features, think about creative ways you can use them for the sites you're building.

You won't have to build all these features at once; you can always add new features to and remove features from your site at any time.

Polls

A *poll* is a question posed to visitors to your site that users are allowed to answer on the site. Polls are great for getting your community of users involved in discussions. Drupal has a simple interface that allows you to create custom polls, such as the one shown in Figure 1-1. (Note that Figure 1-1 shows the default Bartik theme; in the figures we show in the rest of the chapter, we use the Garland theme because we think it looks nicer on the page.)

After a registered user has voted, he sees a tally of the current voting results (see Figure 1-2) and has the option of cancelling his vote. He can then vote again if he wishes. His vote counts only once.

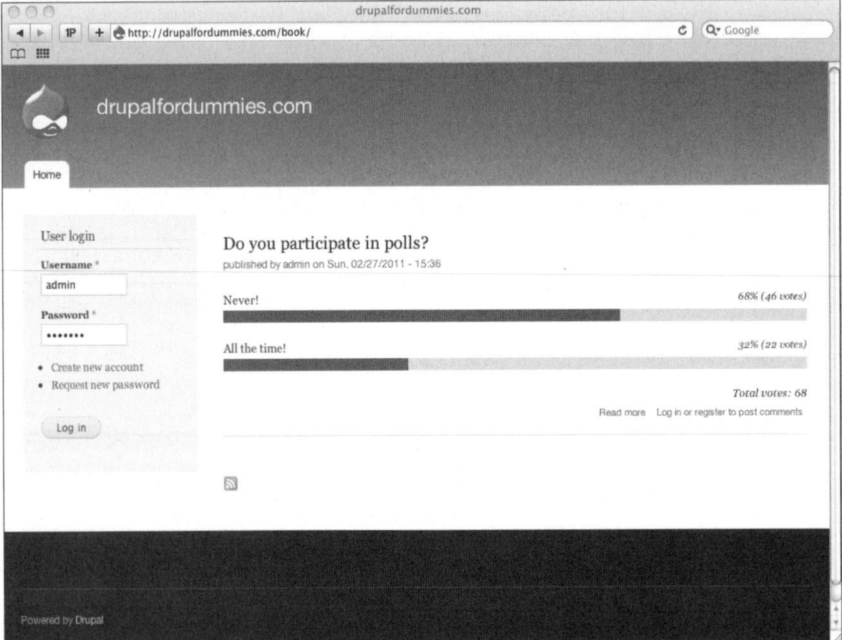

Figure 1-1: A poll.

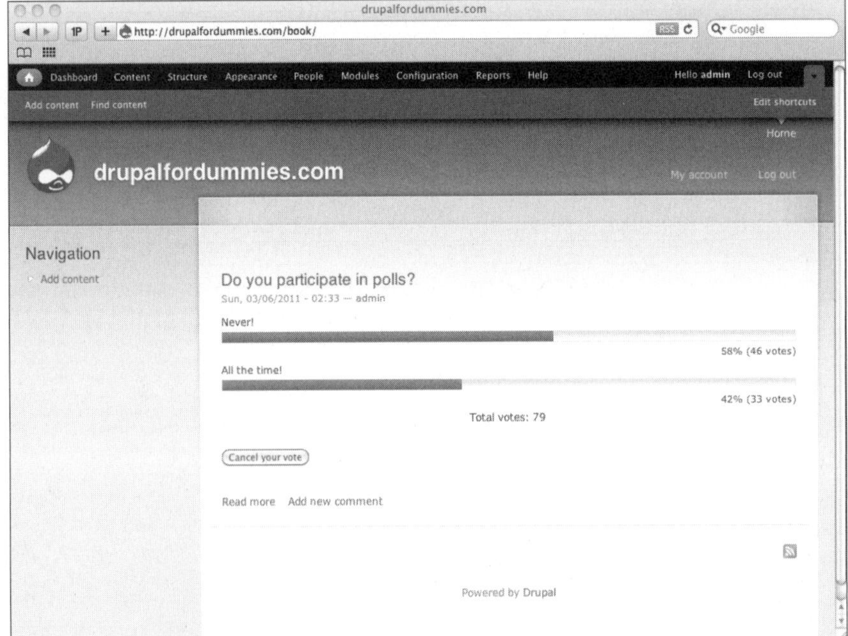

Figure 1-2: Poll results with Cancel Your Vote button.

Blogs

One of the primary reasons web Content Management Systems are extremely popular is the ease with which you can create blogs. Drupal provides full-featured blogging, complete with

- Automatic archiving of past entries.
- A simple-to-use interface for creating new blog entries.
- An optional comment system for site visitors to contribute their thoughts (see Figure 1-3).

Blogs aren't used just to document someone's daily activities. Companies use corporate blogs to keep the content on their sites fresh. Instead of having to create new HTML web pages every time they publish a press release, for example, they can blog the information.

Not only is it incredibly easy to create blog entries, but you also develop a history of all your blog postings over time. All this information, and any other content posted on your site (including forums, static pages, and comments), can be made searchable — an incredibly useful feature! It's also a built-in module you activate.

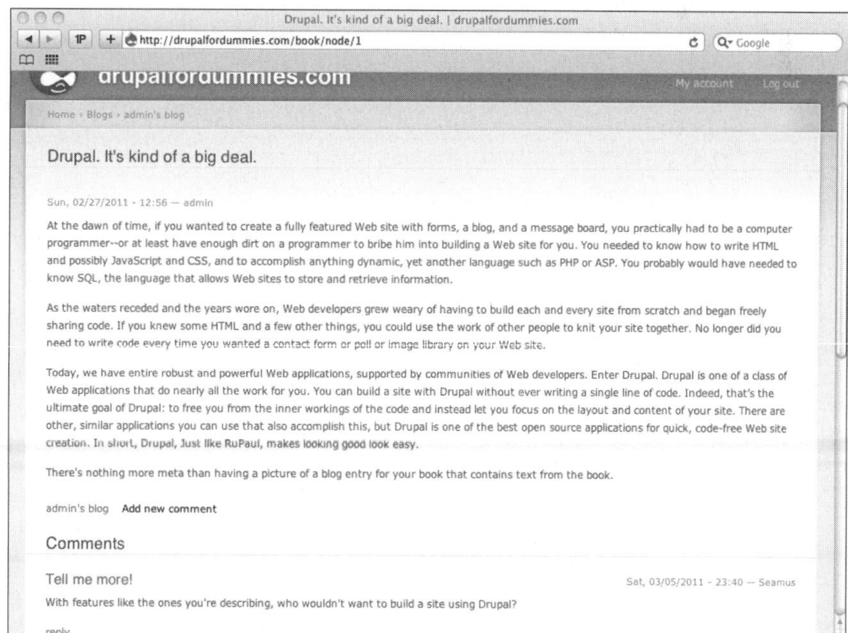

Figure 1-3: Blog entries with comments enabled.

Contact forms

Okay, the contact form may not be the most exciting feature of a website, but it is an important one: Your site visitors need a way to get in touch with you. In the past, if you didn't have programming skill, you might have used an HTML *mailto* link on a web page — and found that it never worked reliably. Drupal takes care of the contact form for you and creates a web form:

- The form sends the content to your e-mail address, or wherever else you tell Drupal to send it, when the form is submitted (see Figure 1-4).
- You can configure the form to send a custom confirmation message automatically to the e-mail address of the person who submits the form.

You can't change the fields in this form, but you can modify the text and add information, such as a contact address, a map and directions, and a phone number.

Figure 1-4: A contact form.

Forums

A *blog* (weblog) is generally used to share large amounts of information with your users — with the information flowing one way, from you to your site visitors. A *forum,* by contrast, is most often used to allow your site visitors to chat amongst themselves. If it's important to you to build community interaction and encourage communication among the users of your site, you should consider adding a forum.

A forum consists of a set of *discussions,* as shown in Figure 1-5:

- Inside each discussion is a set of topics (see Figure 1-6).
- Inside each topic, your users post their comments and replies to each other's comments.

  After you drill down into a discussion, you see all posts for that discussion. You also see a small icon indicating postings you have not read since you last visited the forum, allowing you to pick up on a conversation no matter how long you've been away.

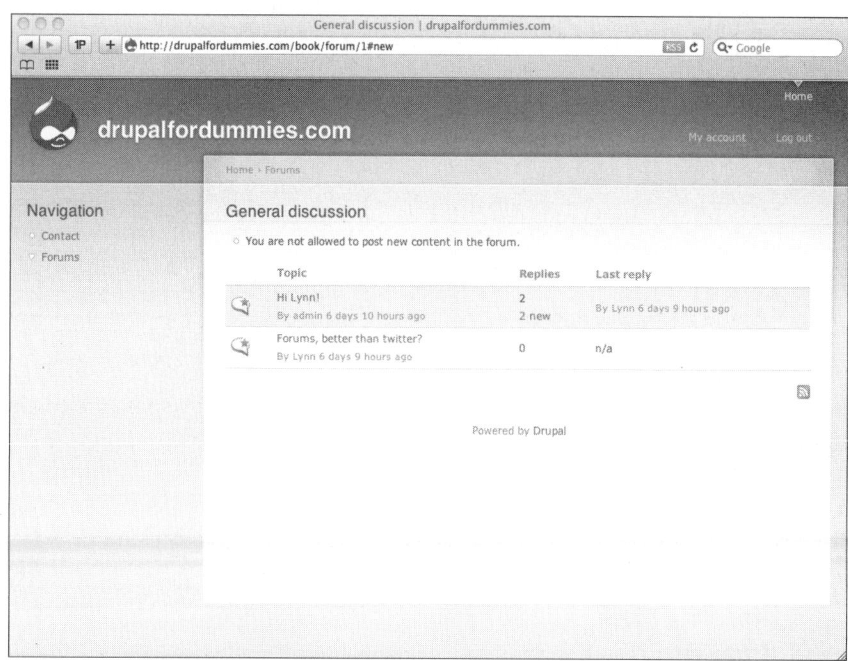

Figure 1-5: A set of Drupal user forums.

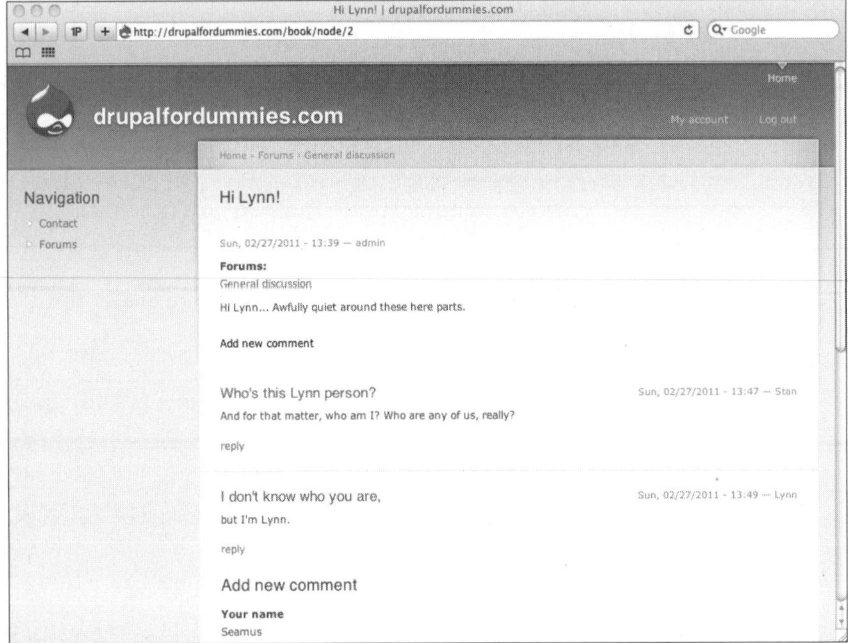

Figure 1-6: Topics within a discussion.

Like many of Drupal's features, the forum configuration settings give you a great deal of control over the permissions you give your users. You can either

- Maintain complete control over discussion topics.
- Allow your users to create topics.

You can even delegate specific people to be forum moderators and help you share the workload.

Assigning people to specific tasks on your site not only splits up the workload, but is also a great way to build a sense of community among the visitors and users of your site.

Examples of Drupal Sites

Are you excited about your website? Well, you should be! Using Drupal 7 isn't just a great way to build a site; it's also a superb venue for showing the world how creative you can be. The following are a few really slick-looking sites built using Drupal. Take a look and you'll see why we recommend them.

Drupal.org

It would smack of snake oil if Drupal's own site wasn't built using Drupal. Fortunately, `http://drupal.org` (see Figure 1-7) is built with the product it offers; you can see many of the features we mention earlier in this chapter — blogs, forums, and a search box — make the scene, along with quite a few more.

Zappos.com

Zappos.com (`www.zappos.com`), a major online retailer, has leveraged Drupal to create a robust online store. Although it customizes the Drupal code base, much of the core Drupal code is used.

Drupalmuseum.com and Drupalsites.net

These two Drupal sites exist to showcase other Drupal sites:

- Drupalmuseum at `www.drupalmuseum.com` (see Figure 1-8)
- Drupalsites.net at `www.drupalsites.net`

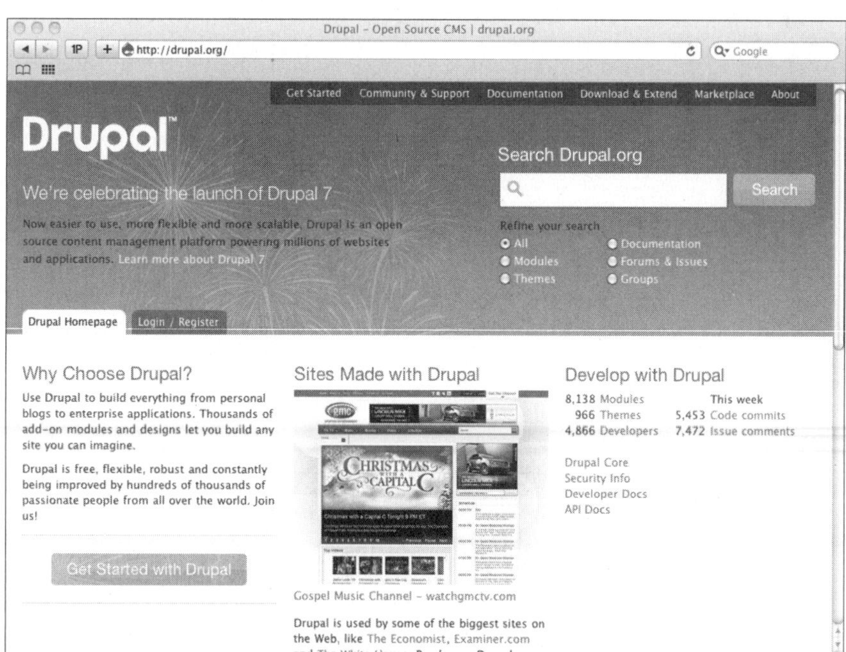

Figure 1-7: The home of Drupal.

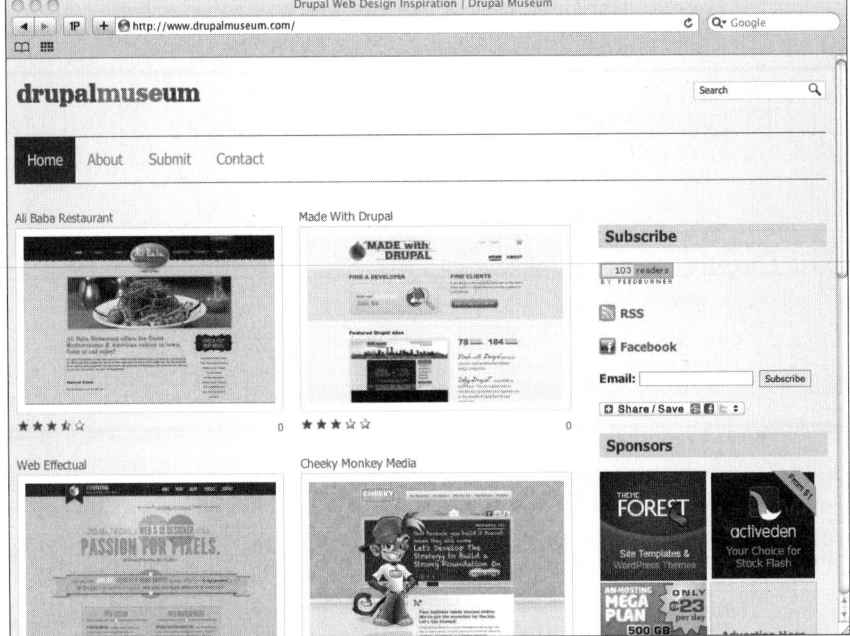

Figure 1-8: Drupal-museum.com features attractive Drupal sites.

Most of the featured sites have substantially customized their appearance, but the code behind them is all Drupal.

Chapter 2

Getting and Installing Drupal

In This Chapter

- Choosing your web server
- Downloading Drupal
- Gathering database information
- Installing Drupal on a web server
- Installing Drupal on a PC
- Configuring Drupal

We have to be honest. Installing Drupal is the worst part of the Drupal experience. If you're working on a Drupal site for your company and can get an IT person to install it for you, you're fortunate. But if you're stuck doing it yourself, prior to beginning, we suggest you turn on the calmest, happiest music you own. Turn down the lights, maybe light some candles. Find your happy place.

By comparison, once you've got it up and running, getting your site going will seem rather easy. Just push on through this part, keeping in mind that it does get simpler. And if all else fails, we offer some alternative suggestions that don't require you to install it yourself.

Feeling brave? Good for you! We're sure you can do it! But if you find yourself ready to give up (and you might), you can sign up for an account with a web hosting company that will do the dirty work of installing it for you. The downside of going through a web hosting company is that you won't get the latest, greatest version of Drupal, so we recommend you at least try to install it on your own. If you do give up, we offer you the names of a few web hosts that offer Drupal setup with the click of a button. You can also go the infinitely simpler route of signing up for Drupal Gardens (`http://drupalgardens.com`), which we discuss in great detail in Chapter 13.

To begin the installation, you need to decide where you want your Drupal site to be installed — and understand why you might not necessarily want to install it on that computer sitting in front of you. This chapter shows you the ins and outs.

Deciding Where Your Site Will Live

You're creating a website to share information with the people who browse to that site. The first decision you need to make is *where* (on what web server) your Drupal installation will run — because that governs if and how people can view it.

The term *web server* can mean either

- Web server software, such as Apache or Internet Information Server (IIS). These programs send web pages over the Internet to web browsers when users request them.
- The actual computer where the web server software runs.

In this book, when we refer to *web server,* we're talking about the computer, not the software.

Getting on the web

Obviously, the first thing you need is a computer to install Drupal on. But it also requires other resources.

Internet connection

Drupal needs to be installed on a web server for the rest of the world to see the website you create with it. Usually this means that you have an account with a web hosting company, such as GreenGeeks (`www.greengeeks.com`) or GoDaddy (`www.godaddy.com`).

If you download the Drupal software and install it on the computer sitting on your desk that has web server software installed, you will probably be the only person who can browse to your Drupal site. Unless your computer has been specifically configured for the Internet as a web server, it can't send your Drupal pages out to the web. You could develop and test a Drupal site on a desktop PC with web server software, but moving that site to a web server that can be reached on the Internet is not easy. You are better off developing your site on the web server of a web hosting company.

Other software

Drupal requires that other programs also reside on the web server computer before you can install it:

- **Operating system:** Drupal can run on common computer operating systems:
  - UNIX/Linux (only versions that can run Apache 1.3 or newer)
  - Mac OS X (or newer)
  - Windows 2000, NT 4.0, (or newer)
- **Web server software:** Drupal runs on either of these packages:
  - *Apache web server* (`www.apache.org`)

    With Drupal 7, we recommend using Apache 2.0 (or newer). Drupal 7 can run on versions as old as Apache 1.3.

    Apache is the only web server software option for UNIX, Linux, or Mac.
  - *Internet Information Services* (`www.microsoft.com/iis`)

    With Drupal 7, we recommend using IIS 7 (or newer). Drupal 7 can run on versions as old as IIS 5.

    IIS only runs on Windows.
- **MySQL 5.0 database software (or newer) (`www.mysql.com`)**

  With Drupal 7, you can use other database software, such as PostgreSQL and SQLite. In this book we use MySQL and recommend you use it as well, because other database software may require additional tricky steps that we don't have room to cover in this chapter.
- **PHP scripting language (`www.php.net`)**

  With Drupal 7, we recommend using PHP 5.3 (or newer). PHP 5.2.5 or higher will work with Drupal 7.

You don't have to worry about these requirements if you put your Drupal site on a web host that offers easy Drupal installation or if you use Drupal Gardens. We mention some great choices of Drupal-friendly web hosting companies in the next section and discuss Drupal Gardens in Chapter 13. Ask your web host which version of Drupal it offers.

Web hosting companies

Web hosting companies offer you access to a web server where you can install Drupal and make your site visible on the web. Some companies install Drupal for you or provide you with one-click install, saving you a bit of effort.

If you decide to skip installing Drupal yourself, consider getting an account with one of these or using Drupal Gardens.

The following list recommends a few web hosting companies we have worked with. Most of these use the programs Softaculous or Fantastico, which we walk through in this section.

- **GreenGeeks (`www.greengeeks.com`):** Offers great customer support and is committed to offering quality service with an eye toward environmental friendliness.
- **Site5 (`www.site5.com`):** Focus is on guaranteed performance and talented tech support. Winner of dozens of industry awards, including Best Shared Webhost.
- **CirtexHosting (`www.cirtexhosting.com`):** If you plan on uploading videos on your site and allowing users to stream videos online, then CirtexHosting is a good choice.

  CirtexHosting specializes in FFMPEG video hosting, which allows Drupal to convert videos into Adobe Flash videos online for your visitors to stream. Learn more about FFMPEG at `www.drupal.org/project/ffmpeg`.
- **GoDaddy (`www.godaddy.com`):** This is a very popular hosting service.

  GoDaddy doesn't use Fantastico, but its own installation script is very similar and very easy to use to get Drupal running.
- **Nexcess (`www.nexcess.net`):** You'll have to install Drupal manually if you use this web host. They pride themselves on being simple, affordable, and reliable.

Installing on a web host with Softaculous

Many web hosting companies offer super-easy Drupal installation using programs called Fantastico or Softaculous. If your hosting company uses Softaculous, this section shows you how it works.

The Drupal community doesn't recommend installing Drupal with third-party software such as Softaculous or Fantastico. Doing so can make upgrading difficult and can potentially cause problems with your databases that store all your site data. We suggest you use Softaculous just to create your first site quickly, as a way to help you learn how to use Drupal. Then we strongly recommend that you follow the instructions later in this chapter and install Drupal manually on your web hosting account when you are ready to build the actual site you want to present to your customers or site visitors.

Any of the web hosts that use Fantastico or Softaculous will have the correct versions of PHP, MySQL, and Apache installed. That means you *can* install Drupal manually; you don't have to use Fantastico.

To install Drupal with Softaculous, if your web host supports it, follow these steps:

1. **Locate the e-mail from your web host that has your username, password, and login information. Browse to your web hosted administration or control panel site (provided to you by your web hosting company) and log in.**

   You see a page of options for your new site (see Figure 2-1).

Figure 2-1: Website control panel with Softaculous icon.

2. **Click the Softaculous icon.**

   You may have to scroll down the page to find it. The Softaculous program opens, as shown in Figure 2-2.

3. **Click the Drupal link on the left side of the screen, located under the Portals/CMS section.**

4. **Click the Install tab near the top of the page.**

   Your screen now displays a form (see Figure 2-3). This is where you enter a number of options including a username and password for your new Drupal site. You also choose where on your site Drupal will run.

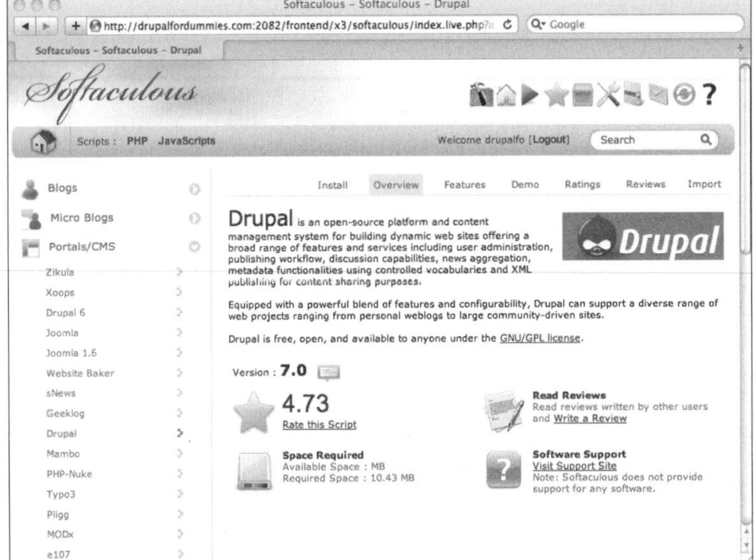

Figure 2-2: Softaculous application with Drupal link on left selected.

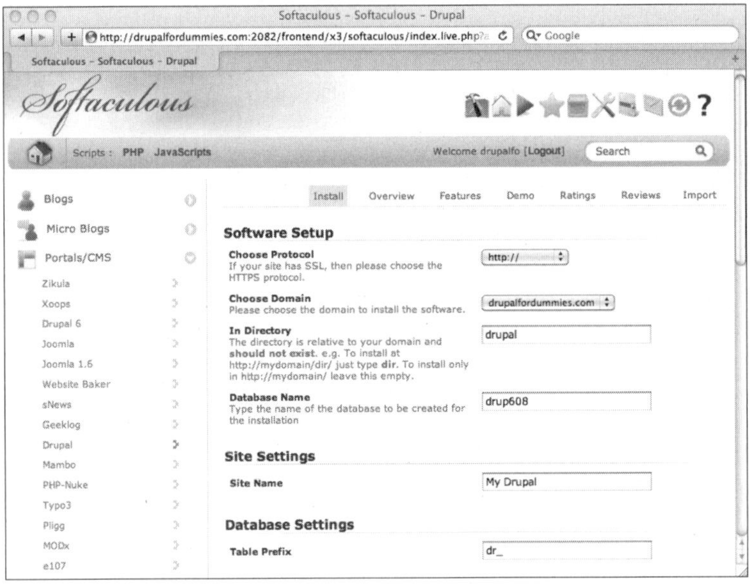

Figure 2-3: The first of three Softaculous screens for installing Drupal.

5. **Enter a directory where you want Drupal to appear on your website in the In Directory text box.**

   You can accept most of the default values on this form. The only thing you need to change is the In Directory text box. Suppose you have requested the domain `myshinynewdrupalsite.com` from your web host. If you want your Drupal site to be the first thing people see when they browse to `www.myshinynewdrupalsite.com`, leave the In Directory text box empty. If, however, you plan on having multiple sites or just want to play with this first Drupal site, you can put it in a directory on your site, such as **test**. Then, when people go to `www.myshinynewdrupalsite.com/test`, they see your Drupal site.

6. **Enter a username and password of your choice in the Admin Account section further down the page.**

   The username and password allow you to administer and customize your site.

   Choose a strong password; otherwise, you risk someone hacking your site.

7. **Enter your e-mail address and click the Install Drupal button.**

   A screen appears that gives you a bit more information about the databases Drupal will create. This is just for your information. (We talk more about databases and Drupal a bit later.)

8. **Click the Finish Installation button.**

   Your site is installing. It may take a moment, so don't bother reloading. You will see a confirmation screen when the installation finishes (as shown in Figure 2-4), and you will be e-mailed a confirmation that your site has been installed.

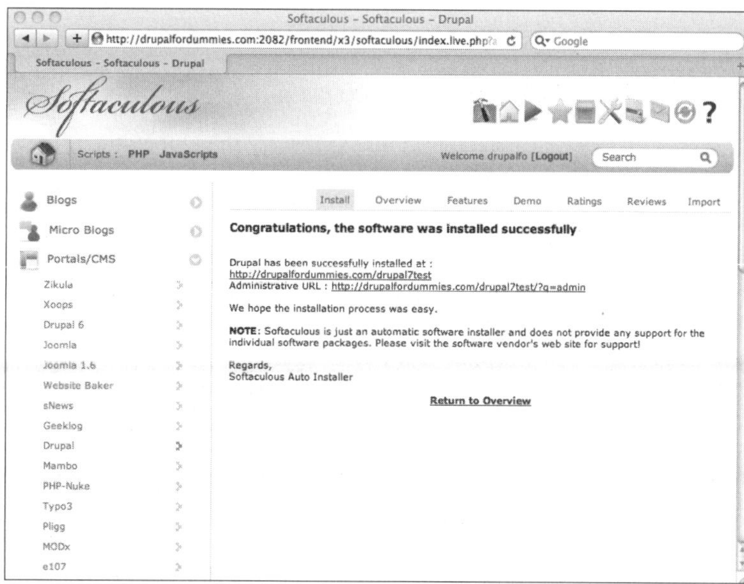

Figure 2-4: The second of three Softaculous screens for installing Drupal.

9. **Click the link to your site.**

   The link reads something like, "Drupal has been successfully installed at: `http://drupalfordummies.com/drupal7test`." Of course, the link will be to whichever domain you set up (for example, `http://myshinynewdrupalsite.com/test`).

You're finished with the installation. When you click the link, you see the main page of your new Drupal site (see Figure 2-5). If you want to log in, use the username and password you specified in Step 6 in the preceding step list.

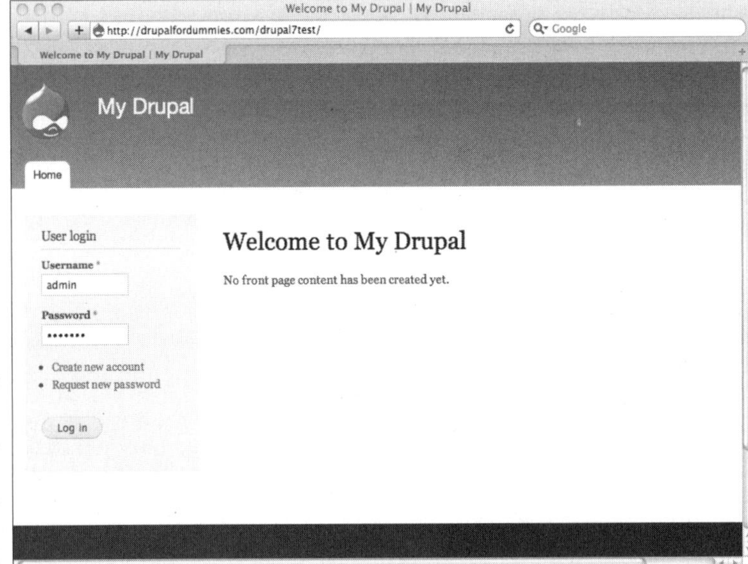

Figure 2-5: Your new Drupal website after installation.

Testing on your local machine

You can install Drupal on a computer in your office or in your home. You can't share your site with anyone on the web, but you can build a site and gain experience. This also allows you to experiment without worrying about

- Your site being hacked
- Embarrassing mistakes

You can't use Softaculous to install on your local machine. You have to do a manual installation. Follow the instructions in this chapter, beginning with the section "Installing Drupal on a Local Machine."

Obtaining Drupal

If you aren't using a web hosting company with Fantastico or Softaculous, you have to get a copy of the latest version of Drupal, copy it to your web server, and extract it yourself. The following sections show you how.

Downloading the package

Getting a copy of the Drupal software is free and easy. Follow these steps:

1. **Browse to `www.drupal.org` and click the green Get Started with Drupal button.**

   As we write this, the most current version of Drupal — and the version this text is based on — is 7.0. In general, this book applies to the 7.0 version or later.

2. **Click the Download the Latest Version link.**

   You will be taken to the Download & Extend page with a link where you can actually begin the download.

3. **Click the Drupal Core tab and scroll down to the Downloads list, and then click Version 7.0.**

   The file will be named something like `drupal-7.0.tar.gz` or `drupal-7.0.zip`. The `.zip` version is to the right, and you may find it easier to work with.

4. **Save this file to a directory you will remember.**

Uploading the package

When you download Drupal, it comes as a single, compressed `tar.gz` or `.zip` file, but it actually consists of many files and folders. All these files need to be located in a web directory on your web server. Here's how you can upload the single `.zip` file to your web directory on most web hosts. (In the next section, we show you how to uncompress it.)

Don't extract the `.zip` until you upload it. We recommend that you extract the files in the final web directory where you want them. Otherwise you may find it difficult to upload all the files and keep them in their appropriate locations in the Drupal directory.

The screen shots we show use a program called Fileman, but your web host may have a different program that handles file management. In general, these file manager programs do similar things. If you are familiar using an FTP program, feel free to use that instead.

To upload the `.zip` file from your computer, follow these steps:

1. **Locate the e-mail from your web host that has your username, password, and login information. Browse to the web host's site and log in.**

   You will see some sort of control panel with options for your new website. It may look like Figure 2-1, or it may look more like Figure 2-6.

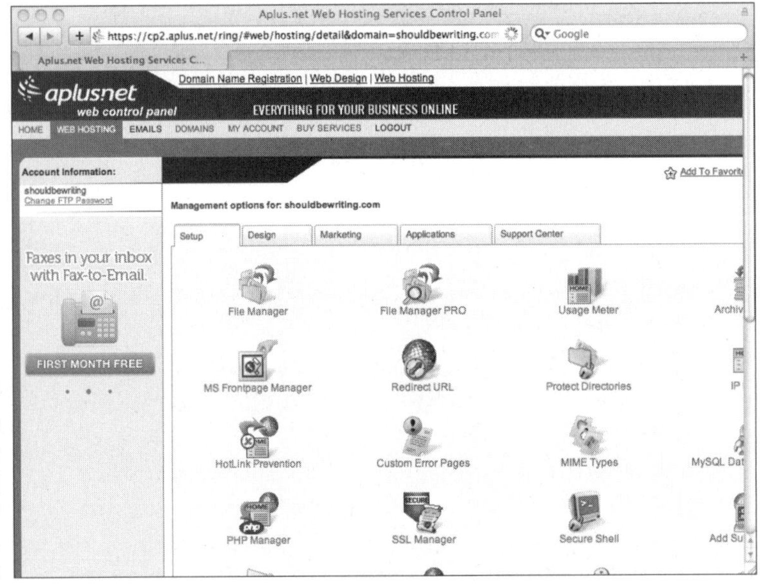

Figure 2-6: A web host control panel for your site.

2. **Find and click the link to a file manager.**

   You need a file manager so that you can select the Drupal `.zip` file and put it in the correct directory on your web host's site. After you click the file manager, you see a screen similar to Figure 2-7. This shows your files on your web host's web server.

3. **You should see a single folder or directory named `html`, `www`, `public`, or `htdocs`. Click its name to open it.**

   There may be several directories, but the one for your website should be easy to spot. This is where all your web pages belong — and where you need to install Drupal.

Not all web hosts name their web folders the same way. If you aren't sure which directory is your web directory, contact your web hosting company.

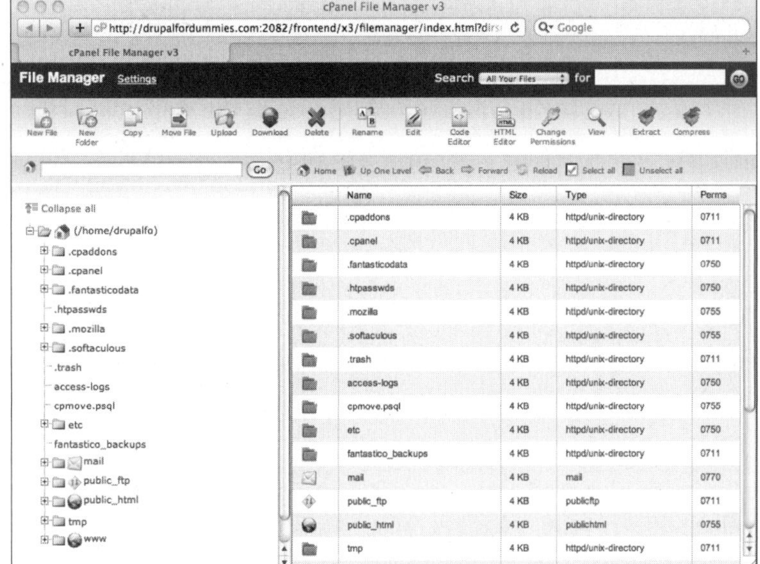

Figure 2-7: An example of a file manager application on a web host.

4. **Locate and click the Upload link on your file manager.**

   You should see an upload form with a Choose File or Browse button, as shown in Figure 2-8.

5. **Click Choose File or Browse and find the Drupal `.zip` file you downloaded. Click Upload.**

   Your file is now on your site. The following section shows how to extract it.

If you click one of the directories or folders accidentally and end up inside that folder in your file manager, look for the Parent Directory link near the top of the file listing and click it to navigate out of the folder you are in, and into the parent folder one level above.

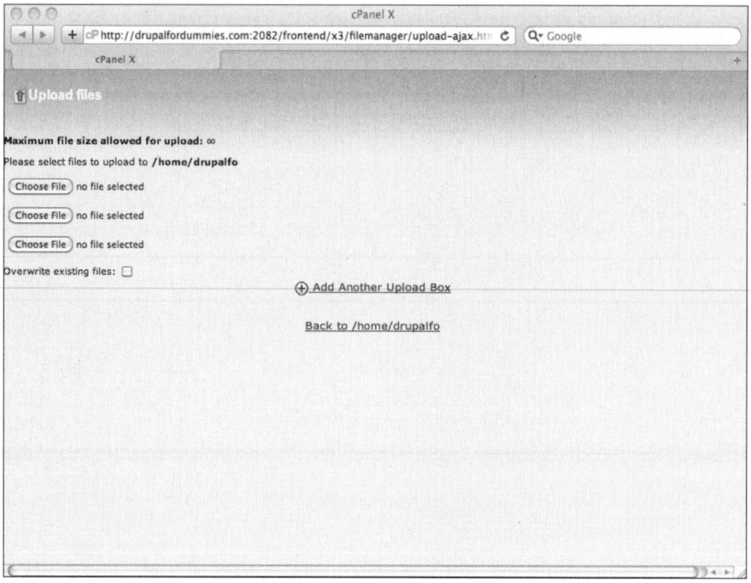

Figure 2-8: An upload form from a file manager.

Extracting Drupal

The file extension `.zip` indicates that the files are compressed into a single file. It's also a file compression type. Most file managers can extract your Drupal file for you. Here's an example of how it works. Your version may differ, so contact your web host for help if you can't find the same functions on your file manager.

1. **Find the Drupal `.zip` file you just uploaded to your web directory and select it, as shown in Figure 2-9. Select View to see the contents of the file.**

   You see a list of files stored inside your `.zip` file (look ahead to Figure 2-10).

2. **You should see an option to extract or uncompress your files, as shown at the top-right of Figure 2-9. Click the Extract button.**

   Doing so uncompresses your single `.zip` file into a folder with the same name (for example, `drupal-7.0`). This will take you back to the main directory. You'll see both the compressed file (for example, `drupal-7.0.zip`) and the uncompressed files in a new directory (for example, a folder named `drupal-7.0`).

   As things stand now, visitors coming to your website (for example, if your site is `www.myshinynewwebsite.com`) will only get to the Drupal site if they type something like **myshinynewwebsite.com/drupal-7.0** in the browser's address bar. This is not a great URL. You should move your Drupal files to your main site or to a different folder with a simpler name. Read on.

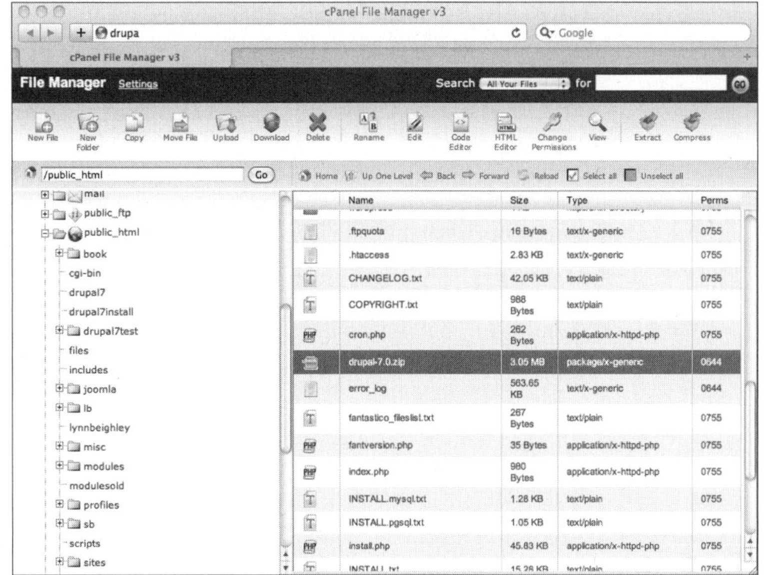

Figure 2-9: Select the Drupal .zip file in the file manager program.

3. **Select the new folder (for example, `drupal-7.0`) and click the Move command in your file manager.**

   You should see a form, like the one shown at the bottom of Figure 2-11, that asks you to type in a directory name. This will become the new name of the folder in which your Drupal files are stored. For example, if you type in **test**, and choose Move, the contents of your `drupal-7.0` directory will be moved to a directory named `test`. Visitors to your site will need to type your domain name and this directory to get to the Drupal site (say **myshinynewdrupalsite.com/test**).

If you want your Drupal site to be visible when people browse to your main site (for example, `www.myshinynewdrupalsite.com`), the process can be a little trickier. You first need to select the Drupal directory to see all the files and folders in it (see Figure 2-11). Everything in the folder needs to be selected. There's usually a Select all option somewhere in the file manager. With everything selected, type **/html** in the Move box, where `html` is the name of your web directory. (Remember, yours may be named `www` or `htdocs` or something else.) This moves all the files in the Drupal directory immediately under your main web directory.

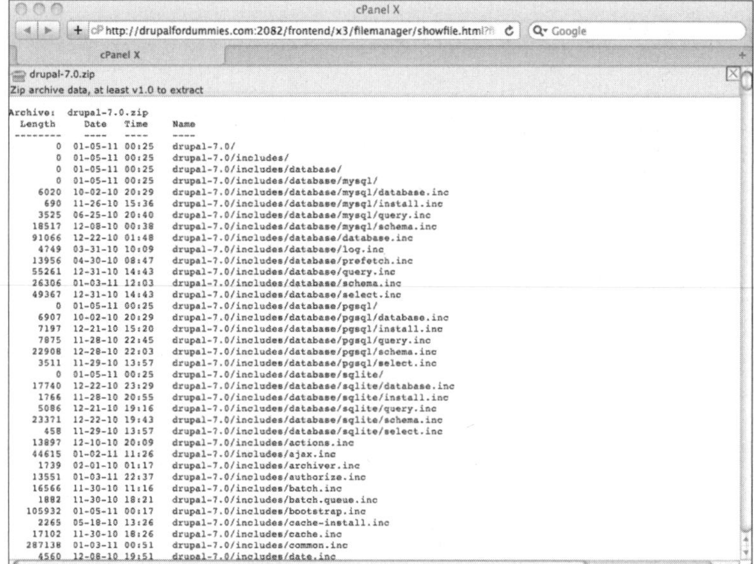

Figure 2-10: File manager showing the contents of the Drupal .zip file.

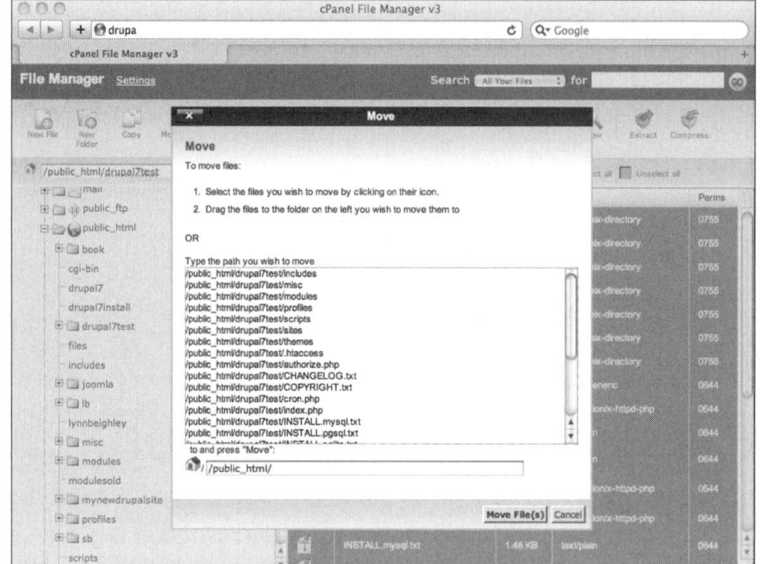

Figure 2-11: File manager with the Drupal directory selected and the Move command chosen.

Use this option with caution; it's painful to delete all those files if you change your mind later.

Setting Up a Database

Before we walk you through the Drupal setup script, there's one more major bit of work that needs to be done. You need to set up a database. It's not difficult, but like the last few steps, your own web host may have different software showing than what we demonstrate in the following sections, making things a bit confusing.

You should be able to find the same commands somewhere in your web host's particular interface, even if your setup doesn't match the screen shots in this chapter.

What a database is and why you need one

A *database* is a set of files that contain data, stored in a special format. You come in contact with databases all the time. For example, every time you look up something on Google, a computer program compares what you typed in the Search box to information stored in a database. The program that communicates with a database is called a *database server.*

Drupal uses a database to keep track of all kinds of data. Chapter 1 explains that Drupal can create a forum for your users, for example. All the postings your users type are stored in the Drupal database. And the people you allow to log in to your site have their usernames and passwords stored in your Drupal database.

To allow Drupal to save all this information, Drupal needs its own database that it can write information into and read information from. Fortunately, most web hosts provide an application that lets you create and manage the database your Drupal program needs. We show you how to create a database that Drupal can use for its data in the following section.

Creating a database for Drupal

Databases may or may not be located on the same computer as your website. Your web host may need to tell you where and how to create a database and what username and password you need to use to connect to it. The steps in this section assume that your MySQL program is located on the same machine as your Drupal files. This is the most common setup and is the case with all the web hosts we mention in the earlier section, "Web hosting companies."

Drupal needs a database, and you have to create one if you aren't using Fantastico. You may also have to create a database username and password. This varies tremendously from one web host to another, but here are the general steps to follow:

1. **Locate the e-mail from your web host that has your username, password, and login information. Browse to the web host's site and log in.**

   You will see some sort of control panel with options for your new website. It may look like Figure 2-1, or it may look more like Figure 2-6.

2. **Find and click a link that refers to MySQL as part of the name.**

   We'd like to be more specific, but this step varies too much from web host to web host.

   You're looking for a way to create a database. For example, look at Figure 2-6 and notice the MySQL link on the left. Clicking that causes a link to Databases to appear. And then clicking the Databases link gives you a form on the right where you type in the name of a new database.

3. **Type** drupal **as the name of your new database, and click the Add button.**

   Applications that allow you to create databases are fairly common, but if you don't find one, you may have to contact the technical support department of your web host. Other programs that allow you to create databases may be called things like *MySQL Databases* or *MySQL Database Wizard.* The whole point is to find an application that lets you create a database.

4. **Add a database username and password (if your web host didn't send any) by locating an application in your control panel that lets you add users to MySQL.**

   Make sure you keep this database username and password handy. You will need it when you install Drupal.

   We wish this step was easier to explain, but every web host is different. Some may have a simple link called Users that opens a form where you enter a username and password. Some web hosts send you a username and password just for MySQL. And some use the same username and password you were assigned to access your site's control panel. If you can't find them, consult your web host's help documentation and technical support.

Installing Drupal on a Web Host

After you've uploaded and extracted Drupal, and created a database named *drupal* for it to use to store its data, you're ready to begin the setup.

Browsing to your Drupal site

By now, you are probably eager to see your Drupal site. It's out there on the web, waiting for you to go through the setup. To reach it, browse to your domain and the directory where you installed it. For example, if your website is `www.myshinynewdrupalsite.com`, and you installed it in a directory called `test`, browse to `myshinynewdrupalsite.com/test`. You should see the Welcome screen, as shown in Figure 2-12.

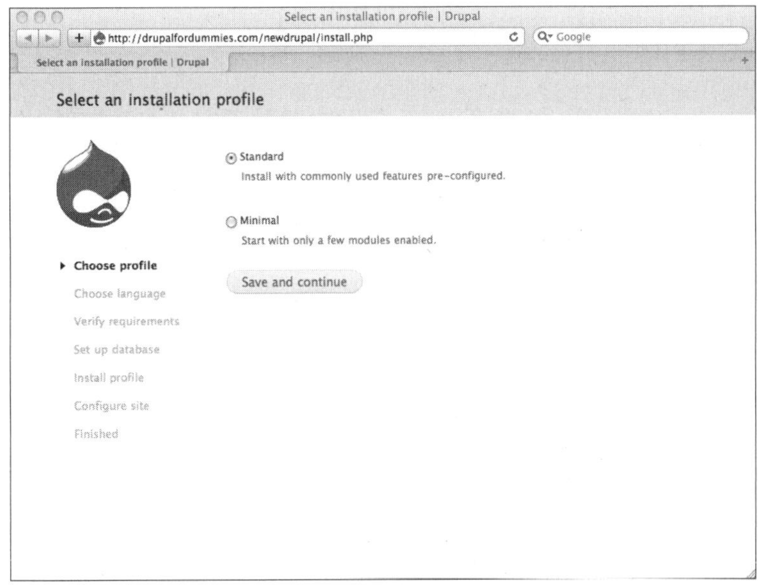

Figure 2-12: The first Drupal setup screen.

Running the setup

Drupal now takes you through a series of forms. Choose the Standard Install and click Save and Continue. Choose English (built-in) and click Save and Continue, shown in Figure 2-13.

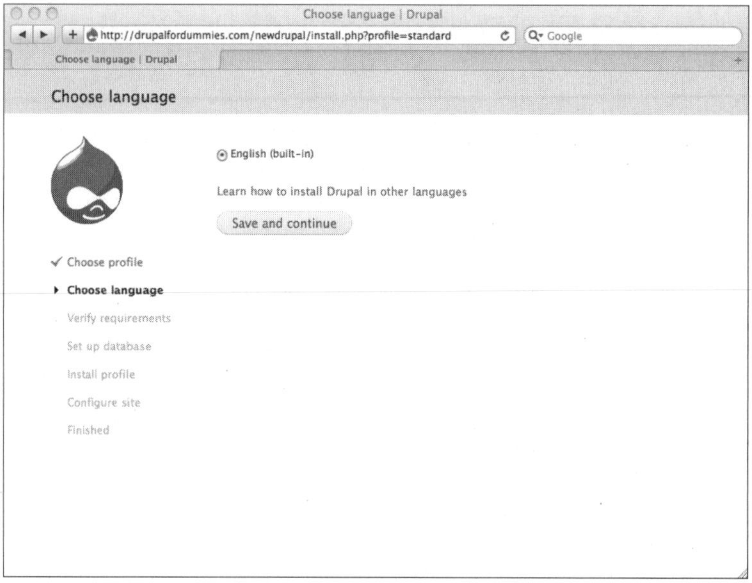

Figure 2-13: Choose Language screen.

Creating the configuration file

To create the configuration file, open the file manager on your web host's site, and copy and rename a file in the Drupal directory in the directory `sites/default/`. Follow these steps:

1. **Locate the e-mail from your web host that has your username, password, and login information. Browse to the web host's site and log in.**
2. **Find and click the link to a file manager.**
3. **Select the web directory and then the directory containing all the Drupal files.**
4. **Locate the `sites` directory and select it. Select the `default` directory.**
5. **Select the only file in this directory, named `default.settings.php`. Locate and select the Copy function in your file manager.**
6. **If your file manager asks you to enter a directory for the new file, type** ./settings.php **and click Copy.**

   Your file manager may simply make a copy of the file, and you may have a function that allows you to rename the file to `settings.php`.

Verifying requirements

Browse back to your Drupal site and reload the page. The error message should be gone, and you should see the Database configuration form shown in Figure 2-14.

Figure 2-14: The Database configuration screen of the Drupal configuration.

Setting up the database

Enter the name of the database you created earlier, **drupal**, in the Database Name text box. For the database username and password, enter the username and password we discuss in Step 4 in the section "Creating a database for Drupal." Click the Save and Continue button and cross your fingers. If everything goes well, your Drupal site is installed and you move on to configuring it (see Figure 2-15).

There's a very good chance that a problem will crop up as you're creating a database, adding a database username and password, or giving that username permission to communicate with the database you created. These are not trivial tasks and (okay) are probably the hardest part of the Drupal experience. It would take much of this book to explain the way databases, users, and database permissions work and to describe the most common setups for MySQL on popular web hosts. But don't despair . . . .

We *strongly* encourage you to read through the process we describe and contact your web host for help with these steps if you encounter any problems. You can also visit `www.drupalfordummies.com` and post questions on the forum, where other readers of this book can help you figure out how to solve your database problems.

Figure 2-15: Configure site setup screen.

Configuring the site

There are quite a few bits of information you need to provide on the Configure site form shown in Figure 2-15.

All this information can be modified later.

Here's the list of text boxes and options you fill out:

- **Site Name:** This text box is pre-filled with the domain name of your Drupal site. It's actually going to show up at the top of all the pages on your site.

  Change this to a title that makes sense for your current site. If you don't know what you want to call your site, you can name it later.

- **Site E-mail Address:** Drupal can automatically send e-mails when certain things happen, such as a new user signing up. The e-mail address you enter appears as the sender (the From address) on these e-mails.

- **Site Maintenance Account Username:** This is the username (yes, yet another username) that you use to connect to your Drupal administrative functions. You need this username to do anything to your site, from changing its appearance to adding new pages. Enter a username of your choice. Make this a name you will remember.

- **Site Maintenance Account E-mail Address:** Enter an e-mail address where you want to receive e-mails from the Drupal system.
- **Site Maintenance Account Password:** Enter a password to be used with your administrative login.

  Make it a difficult-to-guess password, but one that you will remember.
- **Site Maintenance Account Confirm Password:** Type the password again to confirm.
- **Default Country:** Select your country.
- **Default Time Zone:** Anything you do with Drupal that has a time associated with it will use this time zone. For example, if you post to a blog on the site, the time posted will use this time zone.
- **Check for Updates Automatically:** This is a nice feature to select. Drupal is an evolving application, and updates are released frequently. If you select this option, you will see a message when you log in as administrator anytime a new update is available. (We cover updating your Drupal application in Chapter 10.) You can opt to receive these notifications by e-mail.

After you fill out and submit the configuration form, you see a final screen that lets you know configuration is complete (see Figure 2-16). Congratulations!

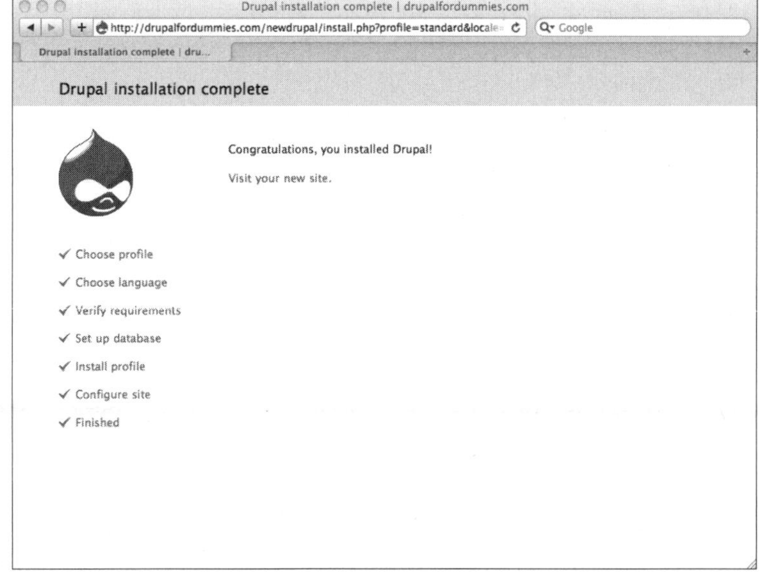

Figure 2-16: The final screen of the Drupal setup.

If you don't want to run Drupal on your own computer, you can skip to Chapter 3.

Installing Drupal on a Local Machine

Running Drupal on your personal computer can be helpful if you want to learn how to use Drupal without the expense of signing up with a web host.

Although installing Drupal on your local machine is similar to the manual installation we describe, you have the added steps of installing the correct Apache, MySQL, and PHP versions. If you are using IIS on a Windows machine, consult your documentation for information on using PHP applications — of which Drupal is one.

What you need

Drupal needs Apache, MySQL, and PHP. You have to install these first, and installing each one involves downloading the software, extracting it in the correct location, making any file configuration changes, and testing it. You should install MySQL (`http://mysql.com`) first, then Apache (`http://apache.org`), then PHP (`http://php.net`).

Walking through the installation of these three products is rather involved — and outside the scope of this book. Fortunately, some developers have put together applications that install all three of these packages at the same time for you. Read on.

Getting Apache, MySQL, and PHP

Several companies have taken the hard work out of installing these individual packages. Each of these companies provides its own single program that installs all three applications for you. We recommend these:

- **DAMP** may be your best option. It installs Apache, MySQL, PHP, and also installs Drupal. Find it at `http://aqcuia.com/downloads`.
- **XAMPP** (see Figure 2-17) describes itself as "an easy to install Apache distribution containing MySQL, PHP and Perl. XAMPP is really very easy to install and to use — just download, extract and start." It can be installed on Linux, Windows, and Mac OS X. The home page for XAMPP is located at `www.apachefriends.org/en/xampp.html`.

Figure 2-17: The home page of XAMPP.

- **WAMP** is a Windows option. Its home page is `www.wampserver.com`.
- **MAMP** (see Figure 2-18) is a great option created just for Mac OS X. Commercial and free versions of the software are available. The home page is `www.mamp.info`.

Figure 2-18: The home page of MAMP.

Finishing installation on a local machine

After you've got MySQL, PHP, and Apache running, whether individually or through XAMPP or MAMP, you are ready to set up a database and install Drupal.

To set up a database and install Drupal on a local machine, follow these steps:

1. **Locate and open the phpMyAdmin program installed by XAMPP or MAMP.**

   You may need to login with the username *root* and a blank password.

2. **Locate the Create a New Database text box on the right side of the phpMyAdmin screen.**
3. **Type** drupal **as the name of your new database, and click the Add button.**

The next order of business is to download the Drupal software and install it on your local machine under the web directory. Follow these steps:

1. **Browse to `www.drupal.org`.**

   Click Download & Extend on the upper-right side of the page just above the Search box.

2. **Click the Download button and scroll down the page to locate the table with the Download link; click it.**

   The file will be named something like `drupal-7.0.zip`.

3. **Save this file to a directory you will remember.**
4. **Double-click or right-click the Drupal `.zip` file to extract it.**

   It will be extracted as a single folder.

5. **If necessary, rename the extracted folder `drupal`.**
6. **Copy the `drupal` folder to your local web server directory.**

   Move this new folder to your local web server directory. This location depends on which package you used to install Apache. Consult the documentation for your particular package to find the web directory on your machine.

Now you are ready to run the installation. To reach it, browse to `http://localhost/drupal`.

Some server packages may require you to browse to `http://localhost:8888/drupal`. Check your server software's documentation.

Running the installation

Drupal will take you through a series of forms.

Enter the name of the database you created earlier, **drupal**, in the Database Name text box. For the database username and password, enter the username and password you chose, as we discuss in Step 4 in the section "Creating a database for Drupal." Click the Save and Continue button.

After you set up the database, you see the Configure Site page. See the earlier section, "Configuring the site," for details on filling out the options on this page.

Chapter 3

Essential Administration

In This Chapter

- Deciding where to begin
- Getting in and editing your account
- Creating basic content
- Becoming comfortable with Drupal terminology
- Configuring Drupal

After you install Drupal, you're ready for some less painful but equally essential tasks to get your site into shape. This chapter is fun — honest! You get to dive in and start shaping your website. You make changes and immediately get to see the results of those changes.

We cover some of the nitty gritty Drupal configuration settings that you need to know. We also introduce *Drupalese* — that is, we go over some of the language that Drupal uses and explain what it means in nontechnical terms. This is especially important because these terms are used frequently in the rest of the chapters. Understand them here, and you won't be in the dark later. Sound good? Of course it does. Let's get down to work!

Setting a Strategy for Your Drupal Site

It's never too early to think about the purpose of your site. In our case, we created the drupalfordummies.com site to support this book and give readers a place to discuss information in the book and Drupal in general. One of our goals for the site was to help create a sense of community.

In this chapter, when you see screen shots of drupalfordummies.com, they are early ones, taken when the site was first being put together. We were still considering the site configuration options that Drupal 7 offers and which choices made the most sense for this particular site. With every decision we made, we made a point to consider the site's purpose and audience.

You can see the finished product, complete with a blog where we share our personal Drupal experiences and forums that allow site visitors to discuss topics covered in the book, at `http://drupalfordummies.com`. Pretty cool, huh? Before we could build these features into drupalfordummies.com, we had to become familiar with the Drupal administrative menus and take care of some initial administrative tasks. As we made our preliminary site strategy decisions, we had to keep in mind our eventual objective: a website designed to help us build a community for readers of this book. Throughout this chapter, we talk about how our personal site goals influenced the administrative decisions we made.

Working With Your Account

After installing Drupal and doing some initial configuration of your site, you can browse to your new Drupal website and take a look at the current default home page (see Figure 3-1).

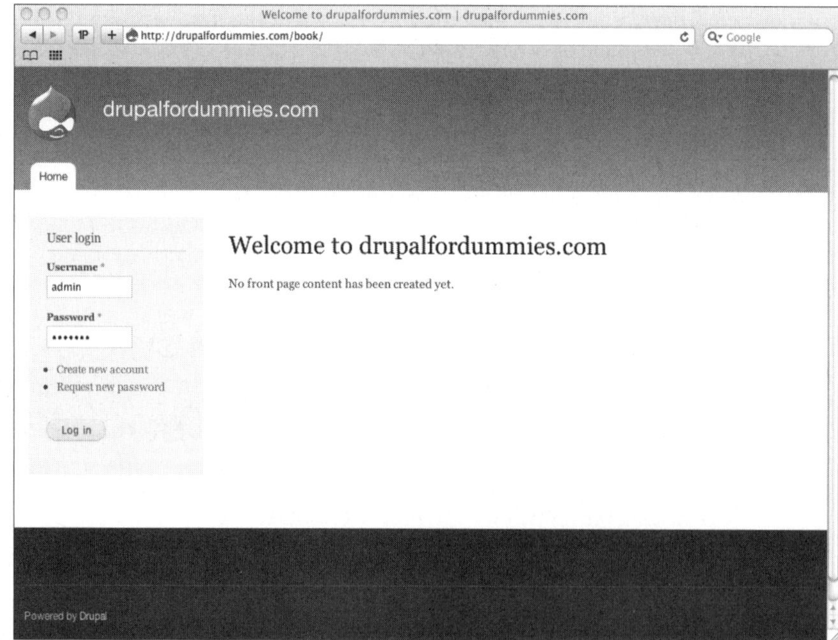

Figure 3-1: Your new Drupal site before any administrative changes.

There's not much to see yet. It's still a default Drupal installation and needs lots of work. To do everything in this chapter, begin by logging in with the administrative username and password you set up in Chapter 2.

Logging in and logging out

Everything begins by logging in. Type the administrative username and password that you chose when you installed Drupal (refer to Chapter 2) and click the Log In button. Note that a menu bar appears at the top of your browser window, as shown in Figure 3-2.

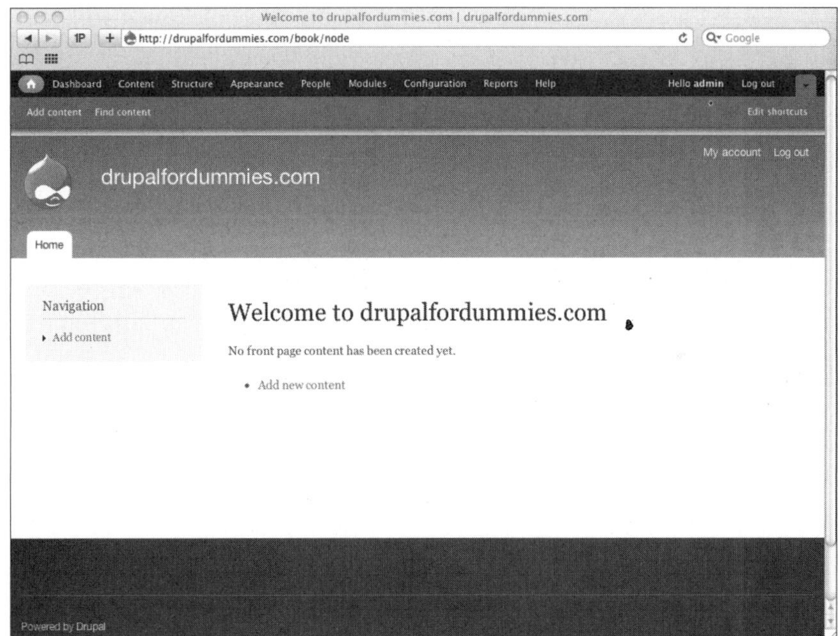

Figure 3-2: Logging in to Drupal presents new interface options.

This menu bar contains the following links:

- **Dashboard:** New for Drupal 7, the Dashboard provides Drupal site administrators with an at-a-glance information interface for everything that is going on with their site. You can see if new people have registered with your site, review new posts, forum entries, and see how many people are currently visiting your site. At this point in the life of your site, the Dashboard looks pretty vacant. This will change as you populate your site with content and visitors begin to, well, visit. As with most Drupal features, the Dashboard is highly customizable.

- **Content:** As the name suggests, clicking this link will open a pane that details all the content present on your site, no matter whether that content is published or unpublished.
- **Structure:** When logged in as an administrator, the Structure link will allow you to change the layout and ordering of your site. This is done by manipulating Blocks, Content types, Menus, and Taxonomy (we discuss all of these topics in later chapters).
- **Appearance:** With the Appearance tab, you can review the various themes that come preinstalled with the Drupal web application. From here, an administrator can enable or disable themes and even install new ones.
- **People:** Once opened, the People pane will allow you to peruse, edit, and set the permissions of the user accounts associated with your Drupal site.
- **Modules:** The Modules pane allows administrators to manage all of the modules contained within the Drupal application. The Modules pane also allows administrators to install new modules, and uninstall any they feel don't add value to their websites.
- **Configuration:** Clicking this link gives site administrators access to a wide variety of options including the ability to automate site maintenance tasks, web services, regional settings customizing the site's information, the number of posts allowed per page, and how the Drupal installation handles media files such as photos and video.
- **Reports:** From here, you can brush up on site information, check for available updates for your Drupal installation and its various modules, or consult a recent event log and a number of error logs to ensure that you're always aware of any hiccups visitors to your site may be encountering.
- **Help:** Best. Feature. Ever. If you're ever stumped on how to proceed with your Drupal site, design, maintenance, or even just some of the jargon used in the application, the Help pane will see you sorted out in short order. Covering a wide variety of topics and even offering links to additional free help located around the World Wide Web, the Help pane is indispensable. (But since you bought our book, you won't need to use it all that often, right? Right.)
- **Log out:** This does exactly what you think it does — logs you out. Make sure to log out if you plan on leaving your computer unattended in a public place for any length of time. All users see this link.

Editing your account

In addition to the links described in the previous section, the menu bar also contains a Hello *Youraccountname* link. (In the case of our site, the link reads Hello admin).

Here, we use admin as the name of our Drupal site administration account strictly for illustrative purposes. In reality, this is a horrible security practice. When choosing a username and password for your site administration account, be sure to pick something that's both original and complex — but not too complex: There's nothing more embarrassing than getting locked out of your own site!

Click the Hello *Youraccountname* link and it takes you to your personal settings. When you click on it, you see your basic account information. Locate the Edit link in the middle of the screen and click on it to edit your personal settings, as shown in Figure 3-3.

Even though you are logged in as the administrator, the account settings shown on this page are the same ones any registered user will be able to control. When a user clicks the My Account link and then the Edit tab, he will be able to make changes to his personal account.

The settings are:

- **Username:** You can change your current username here.
- **E-mail Address:** This is the e-mail address for the current user.
- **Password:** If you want to change the password for this account, enter it here.

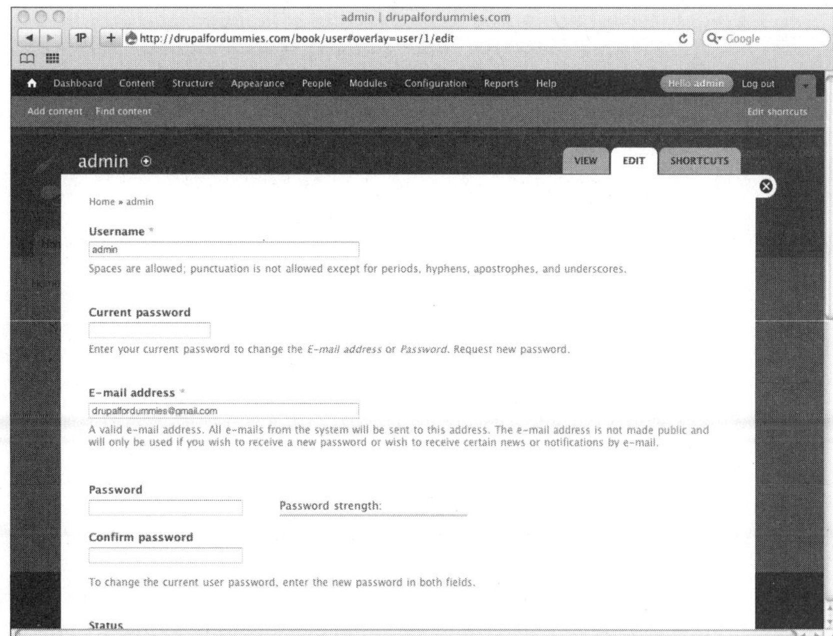

Figure 3-3: The Edit tab of the Account information page.

- **Password Strength:** If you decide to change the password for the account, this meter gauges how strong the password is. A red rating means that your password protection is so lax that your dog could hack into your account. A green rating means that it'd take a crack squad of ninjas to break through your account's security.
- **Confirm Password:** Type the new password again to confirm.
- **Status:** You can change the status here from Active, which allows you to post on the site, to Blocked, where you can't. There isn't any reason to change this setting in this drop-down list. Another section of the site that we talk about later allows you, as an administrator, to manage the setting for any user on the site.
- **Roles:** You have two choices here: Authenticated User (which is anyone who holds a site account), and Administrator. It you have an administrator account, you're an authenticated user by default.
- **Picture:** With this option, a user can upload a photo to associate with her account.
- **Administrative Overlay:** This option is turned on by default. Deselecting it will force administrative pages such as those accessed via the administrative menu bar to open as regular web pages (as opposed to the slick-looking tabbed overlay shown in Figure 3-3 and Figure 3-5).
- **Locale Settings:** If you did a manual install of Drupal (see Chapter 2), you set the time zone. No matter what the site time zone is set to, when you are logged in, you see the time zone selected here. If you've picked up house and home to move across the country, you can also elect to change your current time zone with this feature as well.

Embracing Drupal Terminology

Drupal has its own jargon beyond basic web terminology. A few Drupal expressions that you'll encounter often are:

- **Basic page:** A type of content primarily used for information that doesn't change very often. By default, this type of content does not allow for comments. For example, a Contact page would be a basic page.
- **Article:** A type of content primarily used for news. This type allows registered users of the site to add comments. By default, visitors to your site can make comments about articles.

- **Blog entry:** A type of content that refers to an entry made to a multi-user blog page. Primarily used for news. By default, visitors to your site can make comments about blog entries.
- **Menu:** In Drupal, a *menu* means a collection of links.
- **Dashboard:** A Drupal site's administration overview page.
- **Theme:** This is a set of styles, graphics, and layouts.

Creating Content for Your Site

In the earlier section, "Logging in and logging out," we talk about the various functions of the Dashboard, and how they allow you to administer your Drupal site. It's time to put those functions to work.

Account settings are important, but let's be honest: They're not very interesting. We spend the first two chapters of this book showing you how to set up and administer your site. If you feel comfortable with that, you're ready to make a visual change to your Drupal site. In the following sections, we get you started adding content to your site and changing its theme. (We cover content creation in much more detail in Chapter 5, and discuss changing and customizing themes in Chapters 7 and 11, respectively.)

Creating an article

To add your first article to the home page of your Drupal site, follow these steps:

1. **If you aren't logged in to the site, log in with your administrator username and password.**
2. **Click the Add Content link on the left.**

   You see The Add Content overlay appear, showing links for Article, Basic Page, and Blog Entry.
3. **Click the Article link.**

   You see a form that allows you to create an article (see Figure 3-4). There are lots of other options and settings on this form, but we won't discuss those until Chapter 5.

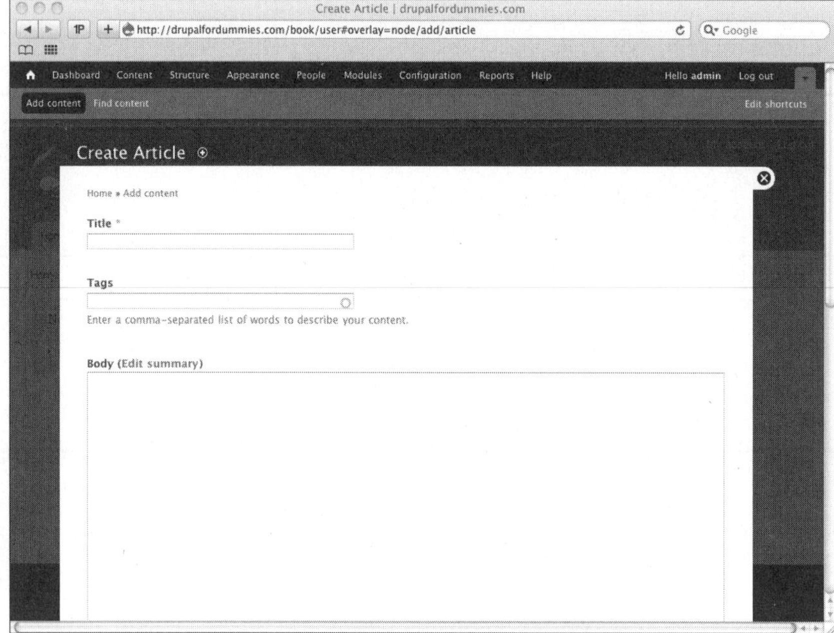

Figure 3-4: The Create Article page.

4. **Type something in the Title and Body text boxes. Scroll down to the very bottom of the page, and click the Preview button.**

   You see a preview of your article (see Figure 3-5).

   Your article will not yet appear on your website. This just gives you an idea of what it will look like when it is published — and gives you the chance to make changes before it appears on your website.

   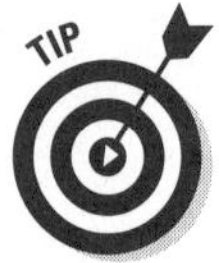

   You can use the Preview button again and again as you write, add to, and edit the article. Preview your article as often as you wish without saving it. It won't appear on your website until you click the Save button.

5. **After you've made any additions or changes to it, and when you are happy with it, click the Save button at the bottom of the page.**

   That's it! You see a confirmation message in green (see Figure 3-6) that your article has been published, but that message won't show up on the site when you reload, and anybody else visiting your site will not see the green text.

To see your new article, reload the browser. Your article is visible to anyone who browses to your site, whether or not they are logged in.

By default, your article has a Comment link. Only registered users can add comments.

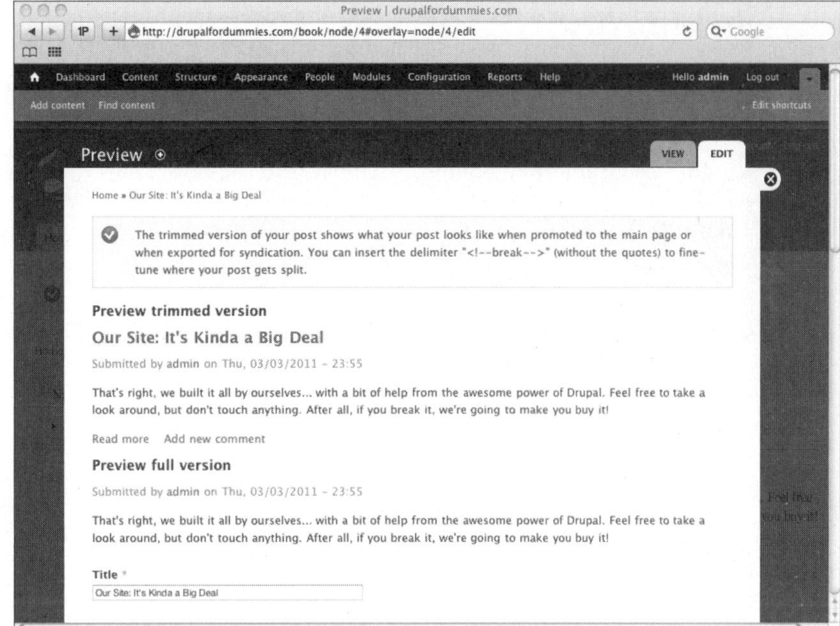

Figure 3-5: A preview of your first article.

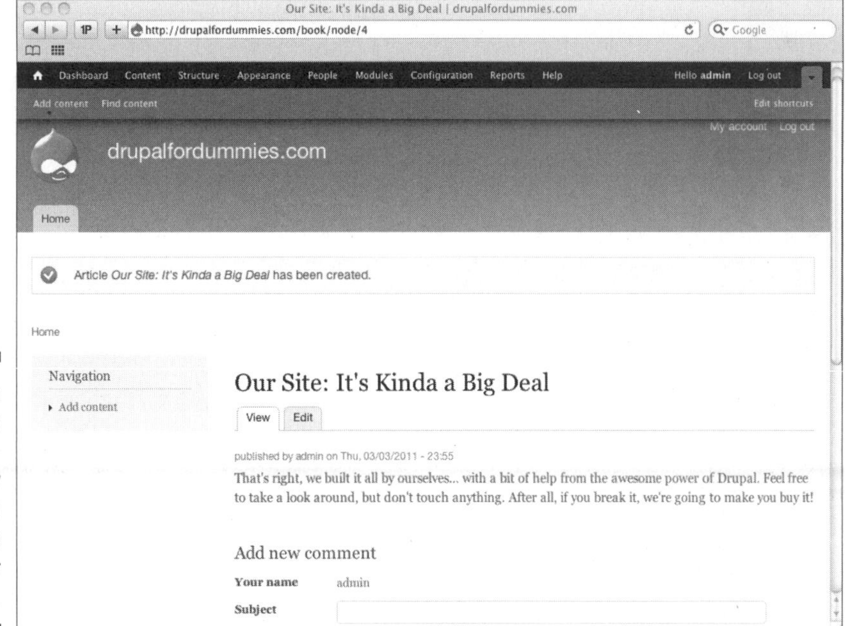

Figure 3-6: The article you created now appears on the home page of your site.

Changing the default theme

Like Doug Floyd once said, "You don't get harmony when everybody sings the same note." The same can be said for having a website that looks the same as every other Drupal site on the Internet. While we describe how to customize your site in greater detail later in the book, here we discuss one fun thing you can change on your site, conveniently located right in your Dashboard:

1. **From the Dashboard menu bar, choose Appearance.**

   This opens the Appearance overlay, where your Drupal installation's themes can be viewed.

   By default, Drupal is set to use Bartik 7.0. Here we want to change it to something else.

2. **Scroll down and find the Garland 7.0 theme. Click the Enable and Set Default link (see Figure 3-7).**

   The Appearance page reloads, with a green notification bar. Click the Home icon located in the left side of your Dashboard menu bar. Your site has changed to a new theme (see Figure 3-8). Only the appearance has changed. The content is still there, and the layout is even the same.

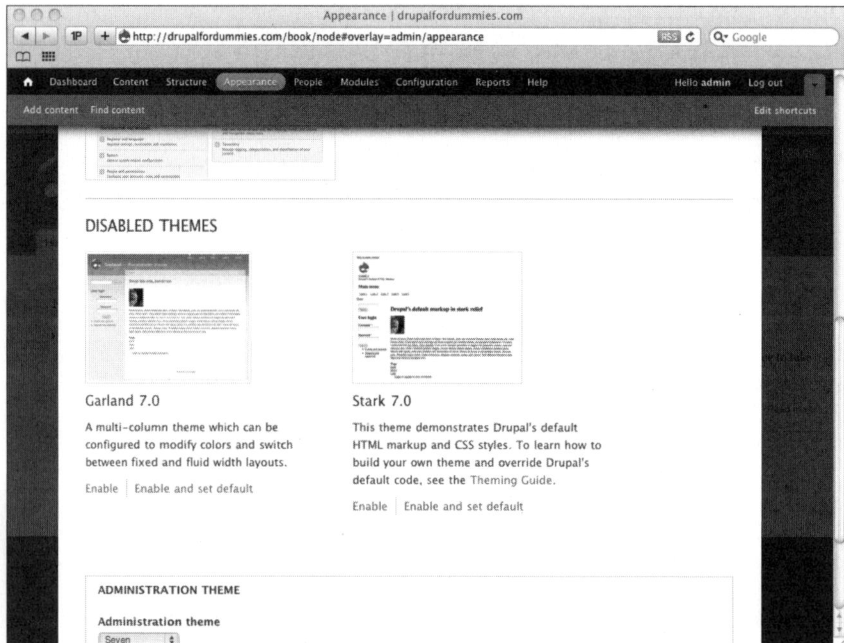

Figure 3-7: Changing the default theme to Garland.

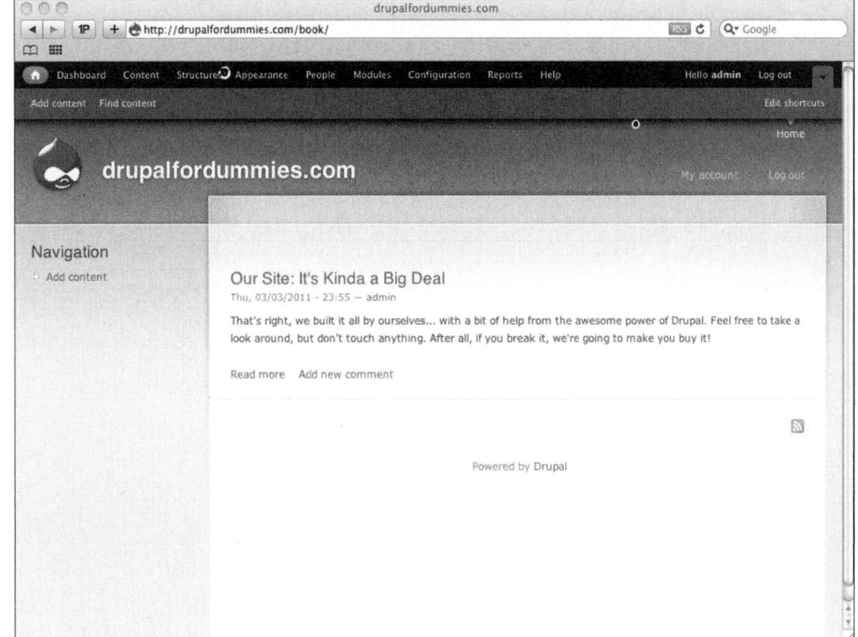

Figure 3-8: Drupal site using the Garland theme.

If you don't like the new theme, you can return it to the Bartik theme by selecting Set Default to the right of the Bartik theme on the Themes page. Or try one of the others. You can change it back if you don't like it.

Configuring Your Site

You may not have manually installed your Drupal site, choosing to go the Softaculous route instead. If so, the name of your site is still "Drupal." It's time to change that, as well as a few other important configuration options.

Perusing the Configuration menu

We begin by looking at all the options under the Dashboard's Configuration menu. To get there, log in with an administrator account and click Configuration on the menu bar.

Here are the configuration options you are most likely to use at some point:

- **Actions:** Suppose you wanted Drupal to send you an e-mail whenever someone comments on your article. Sending that e-mail to you is a type of *action.* Clicking this link allows you to create new actions.
- **Clean URLs:** Many Drupal URLs look like this: `http://drupalfordummies.com/?q=node/1`. Enabling the Clean URLs option makes them look like this: `http://drupalfordummies.com/node/1`.
- **Date and Time:** Here's where you can change the default time zone for your site.

  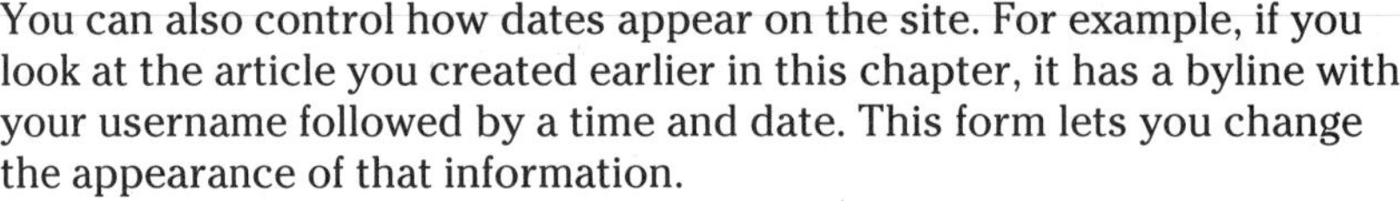

  You can also control how dates appear on the site. For example, if you look at the article you created earlier in this chapter, it has a byline with your username followed by a time and date. This form lets you change the appearance of that information.
- **File System:** These settings control where files uploaded by users are kept and how Drupal handles those uploads.
- **Image Toolkit:** You can control the quality of images and how they are handled if you add an image gallery or similar feature on your site.
- **Site Information:** Here you can find a number of text boxes in which you can enter information that will, if you wish, appear on every page of your site. (We explain this feature in more depth in the following section.)
- **Maintenance Mode:** If you want to work on your site but don't want anyone to see the changes — or log in while you're making them — you can take your site offline here. In this mode, visitors see a message about the site being unavailable. You can still see the site when you log in with your administrator username and password.

Setting your site information

There are quite a few settings in the Site information form you should fill out. This is where you can put your own name on the site, as well as additional information that appears on every page of your site. Where the information appears on your site may vary, depending on the theme you have chosen to use.

To customize your site information, follow these steps:

1. **Log in with your administrator username and password, and click Configuration on the Dashboard menu bar.**

   You see the form shown in Figure 3-9.

   If your administration overlay looks different from the one we use for this book, don't panic. If you're using a different theme (for example), your screen won't look like ours. Don't let that throw you; all the same form fields are on all versions.

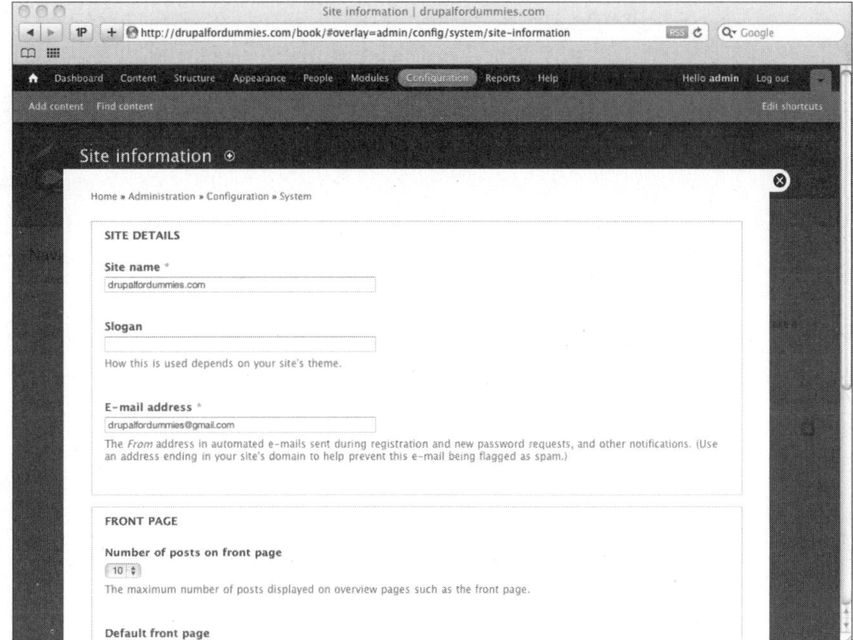

Figure 3-9: Site configuration settings.

2. **Enter your site's name in the Site Name text box.**
3. **Enter a slogan for your site in the Slogan text box.**
4. **If you don't have an e-mail address in the E-mail Address text box, enter one now.**
5. **Scroll to the bottom of the screen and click Save Configuration.**

   Look at the top of your page. Instead of the word "Drupal," the name you entered is displayed. In our case, our site now has a title (see Figure 3-10).

Later in this book, we show you how to make the slogan appear on the site.

At this point, your site should begin to look like *your* site, not the default Drupal site. It only gets better from here on out!

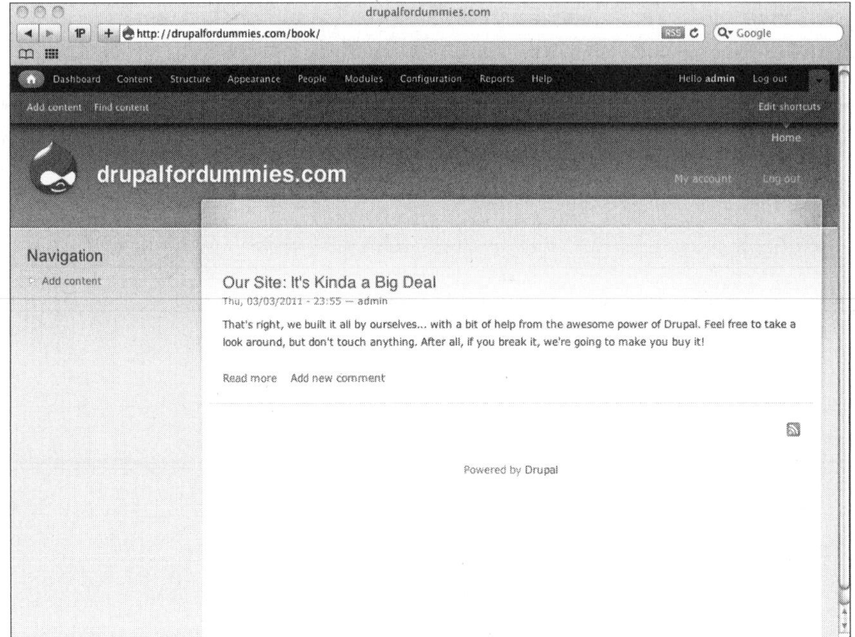

Figure 3-10: Site with a title.

Chapter 4

Tackling User Management

In This Chapter

- Securing your administrator account
- Controlling site registrations
- Keeping tabs on your users
- Understanding roles

When the business of installing and configuring Drupal is complete, people can visit your site. You need to consider how these visitors to your site will be treated. Part of this consideration involves the decision of whether to allow users to register on your site and, if so, the privileges they get as registered users. Will you be a giving and permissive site administrator, or rule your domain with an iron fist? The choice is yours.

This chapter is about making your own administrator account a bit more secure, managing whether your visitors can register and log in, how that process takes place, and the privileges both unregistered and registered users get on your site.

Managing Your Administrator Account

The *administrator account* is the username and password you set up when you installed Drupal. This account is your key to the kingdom: The administrator account allows you complete control over everything on your site.

Editing administrator settings

To change settings for your administrator account, log in and click the My Account link, found on the right side of your site's home page. You will see basic information about how long your account has existed under the View tab (see Figure 4-1).

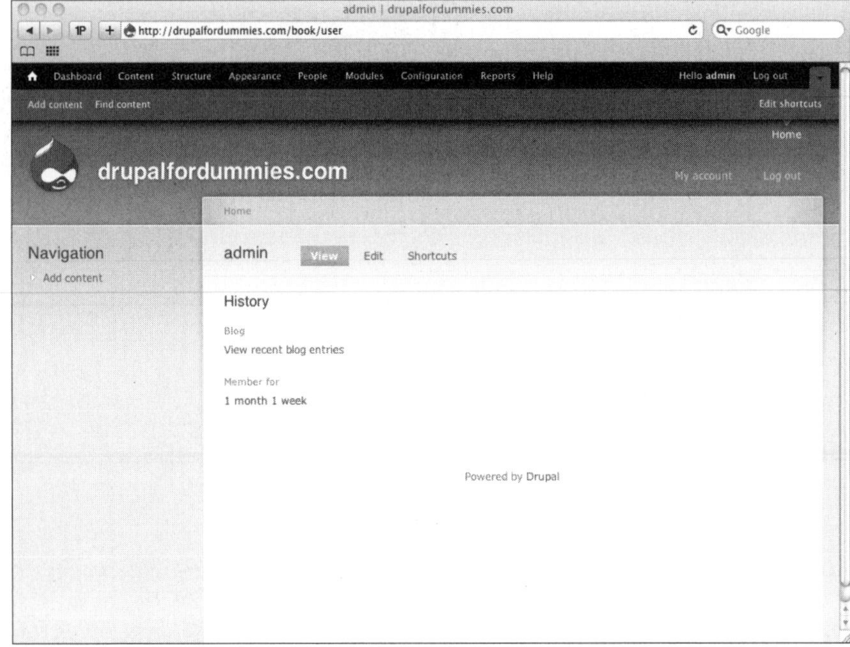

Figure 4-1: The View tab under the My Account page.

You can't configure anything on this page; it simply states your history. To configure the settings of your account, click the Edit tab (see Figure 4-2).

Initial user setup

Drupal allows three types of users by default when you first install it:

- Unregistered users are visitors to your site who don't log in.

  By default, unregistered users can view the content on your site, located in pages, articles, and comments, but they can't contribute any content themselves. If they try to comment, they will be told they must log in to do so.

- Authenticated users have set up their own usernames and passwords on the system.

  By default, authenticated users can view all the content and are allowed to add comments.

- Administrators (that's you).

  By default, an administrator account is created as part of a Drupal installation. An administrator has full access to create or change anything within a Drupal installation.

These are the standard, default Drupal settings for unregistered and registered users, but you can change these settings to your liking.

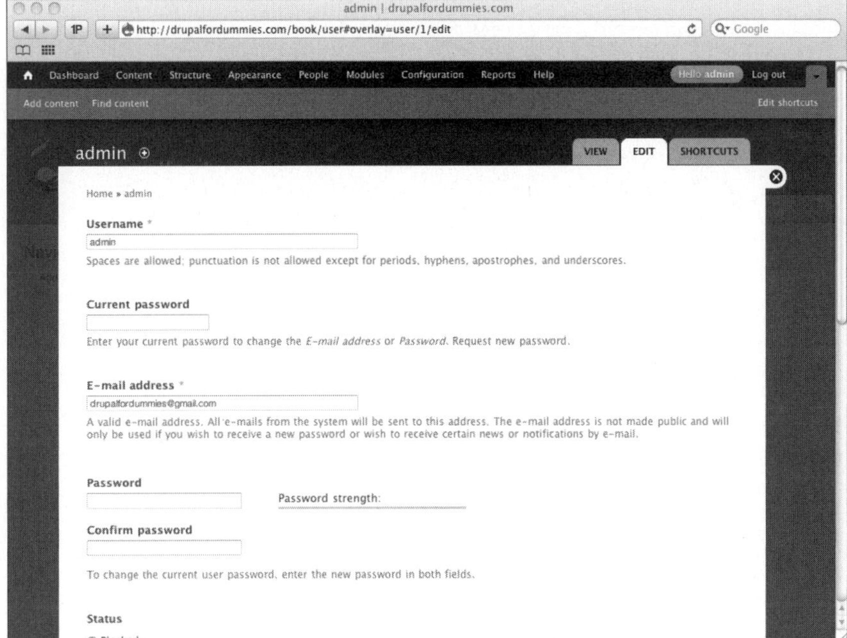

Figure 4-2: The Edit tab of the My Account page.

The account settings overlay opens up to reveal a much longer page with options for you to change your *status* (which we explain in a moment), username, e-mail password, and account password. There are also sections for Theme configuration and Locale settings (see Figure 4-3).

The My Account page and account settings overlay show up for all registered users on your site. They can control their own passwords and, by default, control the same options that your administrator account can change here. For a closer look at the My Account page's contents, please refer to Chapter 3.

Maintaining security

Your administrator account controls everything, and we mean *everything,* to do with your Drupal site. Keep your administrator account safe at all times:

- If you started with a simple password, consider changing it to something with at least seven characters, using letters, numbers, and special characters.

  Changing your password is easy. Click the My Account link, then the Edit tab on the right. Type in your new, stronger password, and type it again. Then click the Save button. For an even higher level of security, it's a good practice to change your password on a regular basis.

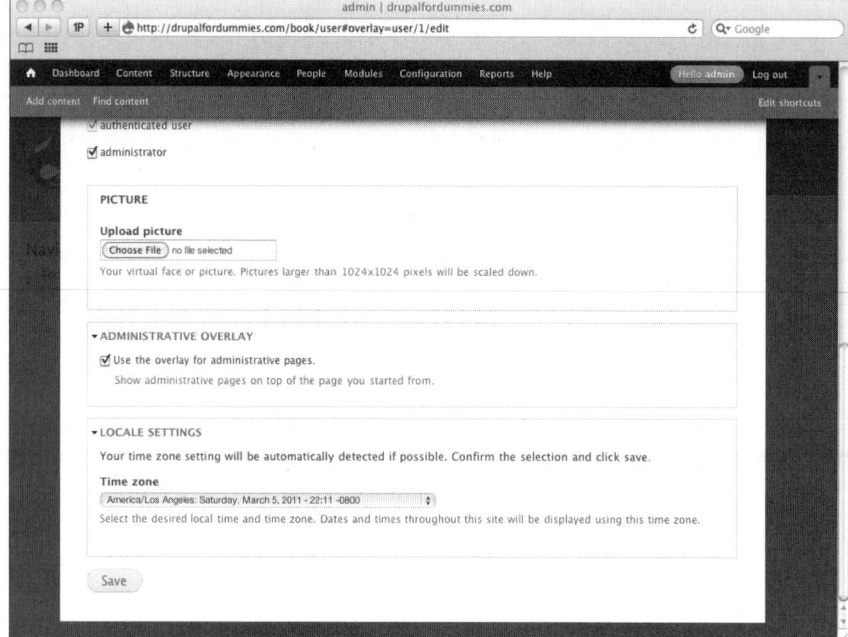

Figure 4-3: The bottom half of the Edit tab under the My Account page.

- Consider changing your username if you've used something predictable (like "admin") or your first name.

  Change your username on the Edit tab of the My Account page. You can use your full name (for example, Lynn Beighley or Seamus Bellamy) as your username. This is a nice choice because when you post to your site blog or write comments, your full name will appear as the author.

Allowing Public Registrations

As Drupal is set when you first install it, anyone can register for an account on the site without having to be approved by you. You can set up your own user account and see how user registration currently works:

1. **If you are currently logged in, click the Log Out link at the bottom of the left menu.**

   You see a login form on the left. Under that are two links: Create New Account and Request New Password.

2. **Click the Create New Account link.**

   You see the User Account page with the Create New Account form, as shown in Figure 4-4.

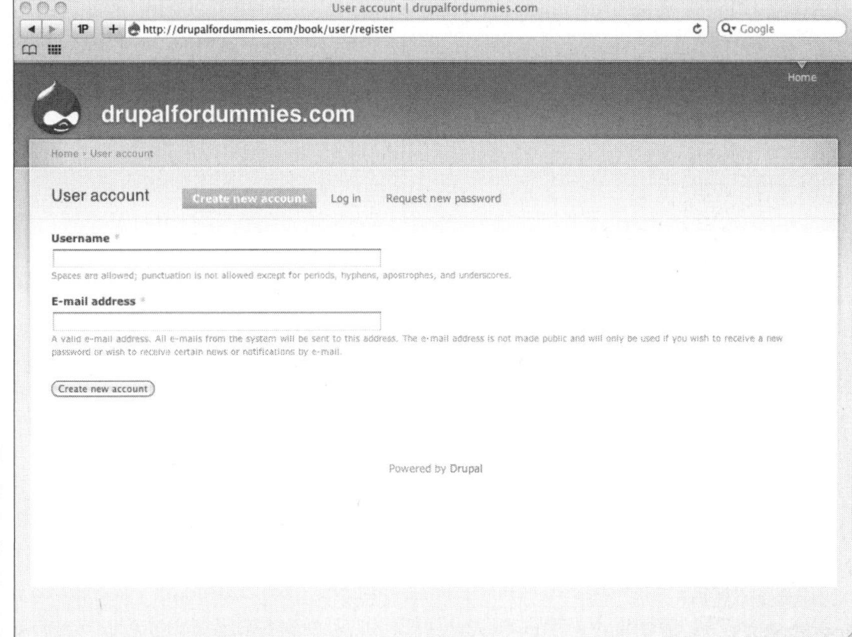

Figure 4-4: New user account request form.

3. **Enter a username and a valid e-mail address, and then click Create New Account.**

   You will receive an e-mail at that address in a few minutes, as shown in Figure 4-5.

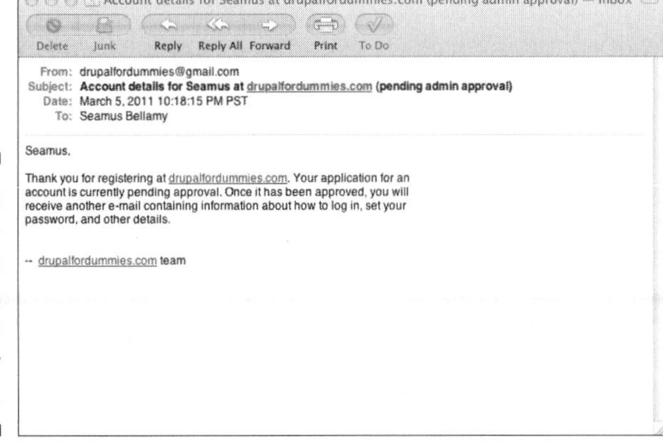

Figure 4-5: The confirmation e-mail users receive when they register.

Use a different e-mail address for your test user account than the address you used with your administrator account. Drupal identifies users on the site by e-mail address; only one user to an e-mail address is allowed.

The text of this e-mail is up to you. (We show you where you can change it in the "User e-mail settings" section, later in this chapter.)

To complete the account setup process, an administrator will have to set the new account to Active. For more information on working with user permissions, please refer to the later section, "Adding, Editing, and Deleting Users."

Now that you have a registered user account in addition to your administrator account, take advantage of it to see how the site looks to your registered users. You should also preview your site completely logged out as you work through the chapters of this book.

Sensible registration guidelines

If your site is configured to allow users to create their own accounts, the site administrator (you) won't necessarily know when a new user registers. However, there are a couple of settings that can help you control new registrations:

- You can control how you're notified when users register.
- More important: You can control whether new users have to be approved by you first.

To control user registrations and a few other settings involved with new user creation, you have to use the People overlay (see Figure 4-6).

To get to the Account settings page, log in with your administrator username and password. From your Dashboard menu bar, choose Configuration➪People➪Account Settings.

You may have noticed that the Dashboard menu bar prominently displays a People link. Everyone loves a good shortcut; sadly, clicking People will open a list of your site's registered users instead of the Account Settings page that we're working with in this section.

Scroll halfway down the page, and you'll find a set of radio buttons under the heading of Registration and Cancellation. These radio buttons control how users are registered to the site. The options are

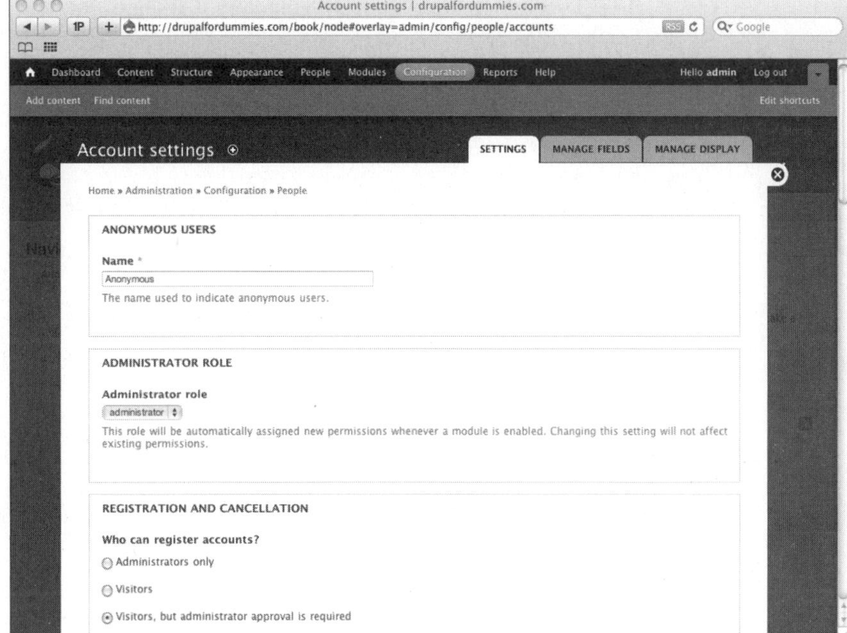

Figure 4-6: The Account settings section of the People overlay.

- **Administrators Only:** If you select this option, you must create new accounts yourself. The link that invites visitors to create a new account won't show.

  To create new accounts, you will need to use the Add User form that we discuss in the section "Adding, Editing, and Deleting users."

- **Visitors:** If allowed by the site administrator, this setting will allow users to register for a user account without undergoing a review process. Under this setting, registrants have to:
  - Provide the system with a username and e-mail.
  - Receive an e-mail from the system with a temporary password and a link to log in.

- **Visitors, but Administrator Approval Is Required:** This is the default setting. Drupal will send an e-mail to your administrator account password asking you to approve the new user registration. If you follow the link in the e-mail and approve the user, he will be able to log in. If you don't approve the user, Drupal throws away his information.

We recommend using the administrator approval required setting, at least until you finish designing your site.

The next option on the page is a check box that asks whether you want to require e-mail verification when a visitor creates an account. This option, which is selected by default, causes the new registering user to get an e-mail like the one shown in Figure 4-5.

Leave this option selected. It prevents users from registering with a fake e-mail address. They have to use the password provided in the e-mail they receive, which proves that they have access to a real e-mail account and aren't spammers who want to fill your site up with spam advertisements.

The next section on the page, titled When cancelling a user account, provides administrators with a number of options for what should be done with they decide to cancel a user's account. The following options are offered:

- **Disable the Account and Keep all of Its Content:** This option cancels the user account, but preserves all content created by the account, such as articles, blog posts, or forum postings.
- **Disable the Account and Unpublish all of Its Content:** This option cancels the user account and sets all the site content created with the user account to unpublished.
- **Disable the Account and Make Its Content Belong to the *Anonymous User*:** This option cancels the user account and preserves all content created with the account, by assigning it to an anonymous user account. The anonymous user account is an arbitrary authorship assigned to site content that has no user associated with it. It may also refer to users who are not logged in to the site.
- **Disable the Account and Its Content:** Poof! Like magic, all traces of the user account and any content disappear from your site.

A user with administrator privileges can override any of these options, even an option you've set as the default.

User e-mail settings

The last section of the Account Settings page contains a pane titled E-mails. From here, you can customize the e-mails that get sent out to users by Drupal when certain things happen on your site. For example, here is where you can change the text sent to people who register. The E-mails pane handles more than just site registration e-mails. Figure 4-7 shows the list of situational e-mails that Drupal handles. The Subject line and Body of each e-mail type can be altered by an administrator. This is great news for Drupal site administrators who want to provide a personal greeting to their site's new users.

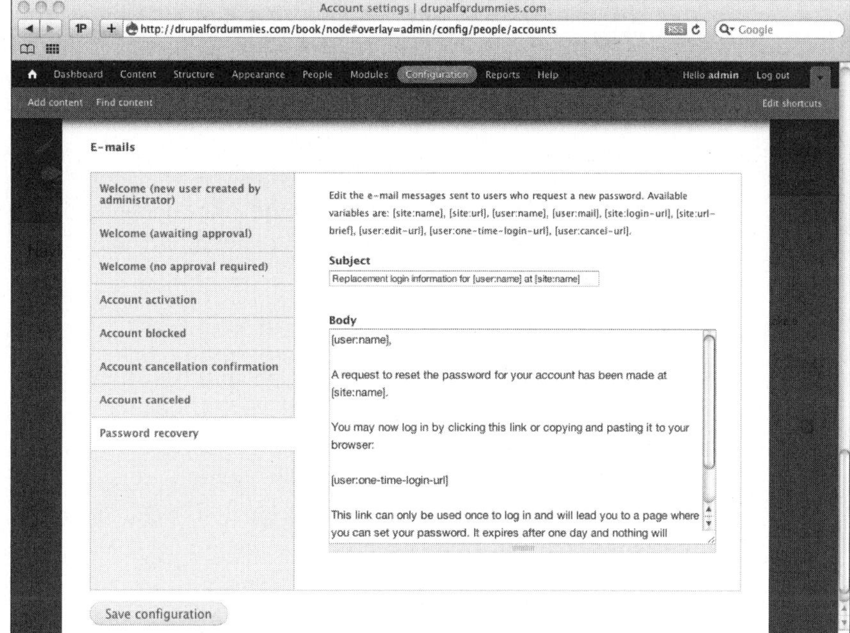

Figure 4-7: User e-mail settings on the User management page.

To look at or edit any individual e-mail form, click its title.

Take a close look at the e-mail listed under Welcome, awaiting administrator approval. It starts with the word `[user:name]`. Any time you see a word bracketed like this in these e-mails, the word is a stand-in. Because this e-mail is meant to go to any new registering user, Drupal uses `[user:name]` and then replaces it with the appropriate username when it sends an e-mail to a specific user.

If you edit these e-mails, pay special attention to any words that are placeholders. These are the most commonly used:

- **`[user:name]`:** The username of the e-mail recipient.
- **`[site:name]`:** The site name that you set in the site configuration settings discussed in the preceding chapter.
- **`[user:one-time-login-url]`:** A URL that takes the new user directly to the Edit tab of the My Account page where he can change his password.
- **`[user:mail]`:** The e-mail address of the e-mail recipient.

There are seven e-mails you can modify here:

- **Welcome (New User Created by Administrator):** If you select the first option under the User Registration settings (shown in Figure 4-7), this is the e-mail that gets sent to the user.
- **Welcome (Awaiting Approval):** If you select the Visitors, But Administrator Approval Is Required option under the User Registration settings (shown in Figure 4-7), this e-mail is sent to the user. This is the e-mail you received, shown in Figure 4-5, when you created the user account earlier in this chapter.

  Edit this e-mail to let the user know how long the approval will take.
- **Welcome (No Approval Required):** Sent to users if you select the Visitors option under the user registration settings.

- **Account Activation:** If you are using the Visitors, But Administrator Approval Is Required option under user registration settings, this message gets sent to the user when you approve his account.
- **Account Blocked:** If you block a user account, this e-mail informs him that he won't be able to log in to the site.

  We show you how to block users in the section "Adding, Editing, and Deleting users."
- **Account Cancellation Confirmation:** Should a registered user decide to cancel the account, this is the e-mail sent.
- **Account Canceled:** This e-mail is sent to a user to confirm that his or her account has been canceled.
- **Password Recovery:** Visitors who aren't logged in see a link to request a new password. After they enter the appropriate username or e-mail address, this is the e-mail they are sent. It contains a link to a page on which they can reset the password.

There is one more section on this page: Personalization. We discuss this section in Chapter 9, where we show you how to add a forum to your site.

Assigning user permissions

By default, logged-in registered users can add comments to your postings, but unregistered users can't. This setting, and many other settings, is controlled by the Permissions form. The form can be found by clicking the People link located in the Dashboard menu bar. Once the People overlay opens, click the Permissions tab found in the upper-right part of your screen (see Figure 4-8).

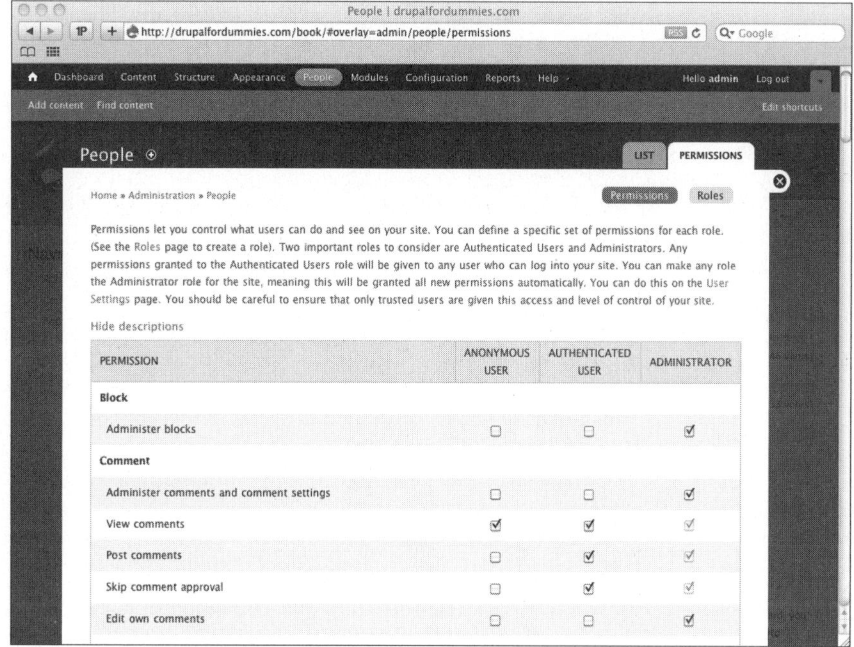

Figure 4-8: The Permissions form controls what users can do.

Drupal calls users who are logged in to the site *authenticated.* From this point on, we use *authenticated users* to mean users who are logged in to the system, and *anonymous users* to refer to users who are not logged in.

Along the top of the table on this page, are the table headings Anonymous User, Authenticated User, and Administrator. Anything you select under Anonymous User will only apply to anyone who visits the site without signing in. Anything selected under Authenticated User will only apply to users who sign in. What about Administrator? If you answered anything selected under this category of user will be applied to administrative accounts, treat yourself to a cookie for getting the correct answer.

There are lots of options here, but for now we only discuss a few of them.

It seems odd, but if you select an option in the Anonymous User column but not in the Authenticated User column, only the people who haven't logged in will have that privilege. Generally, if an anonymous user can do something, an authenticated user should be able to do it as well. Make sure both check boxes are selected when the Anonymous User check box is selected.

Most of these permission settings are covered in detail elsewhere in the book, as we show you more Drupal modules. You should know about these permission settings right now:

- **Comment:** This section controls whether users can view, create, or administer comments.
  - *Administer Comments and Comments Settings:* If this is selected, users can edit or delete comments.
  - *View Comments:* Controls whether users can see comments.
  - *Post Comments:* If this is selected, users can post comments, but they have to be approved by you first.
  - *Skip Comment Approval:* If you want users to have the ability to post comments to your site without prior approval, select this. In general, it's a good idea to not allow anonymous users to comment on your site. If you decide to allow it, make sure this setting is selected for you to view what they've written first. Spammers frequently take advantage of comments to advertise their wares.
  - *Edit Own Comments:* Have you ever been in a situation where you say something that you wish you could take back? If you answered yes, you'll want to turn this feature on. It allows site visitors within the user group to change or delete posted comments.
- **Node:** Nodes contain all the content on a Drupal site. We discuss only a few of these permissions that will be familiar to you at this point. Be cautious about granting permission for most of these.
  - *View Published Content:* This is probably the one permission you will always grant. This allows visitors to see content on your site. They can't do anything except view it, so it's safe to give to anonymous users as well.
  - *Article*: *Create New Content:* You may recall that the text we entered that appears on the front page of drupalfordummies.com is an *article.* This permission allows users to add their own articles to the site. You probably won't do this.
  - *Article: Edit Any Content:* Granting this allows users to edit articles posted to the site. For example, with this selected, a user could change the text posted to the front page of drupalfordummies.com.
  - *Article: Edit Own Content:* If you allow users to enter articles, you may want to enable this to allow them to edit only articles they have created.

   - *Blog: Create New Content:* This permission allows users to create blog entries. This option is only available if the Blog module is enabled.
   - *Blog: Edit Any Content:* Granting this permission allows users to edit any blog entries posted to the site. This option is only available if the Blog module is enabled.
   - *Blog: Edit Own Content:* If you allow users to enter blog entries to your site, you may want to enable this to allow them to edit only the entries they have created. This option is only available if the Blog module is enabled.

- **User:** This controls the administration of users.
   - *Administer Permission:* If selected, users can edit the page we are discussing right now. It is never a good idea to give users that much authority.
   - *Administer Users:* You will allow your users to do all the things we talk about in the section "Adding, Editing, and Deleting Users." This is probably not something you'll want to do.
   - *View User Profiles:* Allows a user to view other users' profiles.
   - *Change Own Username:* If you select this, users will be able to change their usernames by using the Edit tab of the My Account page, as shown in Figure 4-2. It makes no sense to select this for an anonymous user, but you may want to allow authenticated users to change their usernames.

You can see many more permissions available here, but until you have an understanding of these modules and features (for example, blocks and filters), you shouldn't modify the permissions for them. You can always come back to this page and tweak permissions later. In general, it's best to start with as few permissions as possible and add more only as needed.

Adding, Editing, and Deleting Users

Drupal gives the administrator (you) complete control over the registered user accounts on your site. This means you can add new users, edit all user information, and delete users.

Adding users

To add a new registered user to your site, log in as the site administrator and click People, located in the Dashboard menu bar. Once the People overlay has opened, click the Add User link on the left side of the screen. You will see the Add User form (see Figure 4-9).

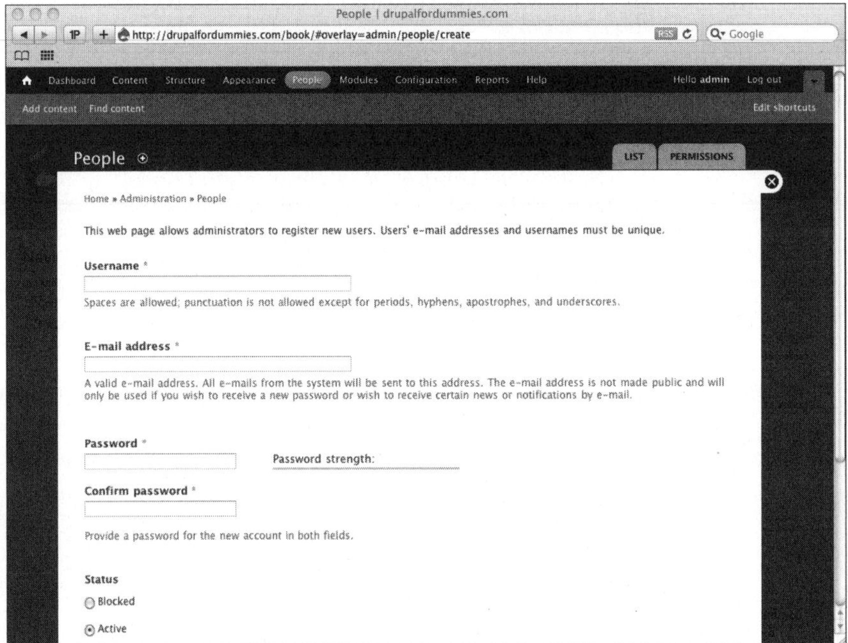

Figure 4-9: The Add User form.

With the Add User form, administrators can enter a username, e-mail address, password, for anonymous users who want to be registered as authenticated users on the site. If you set the status to Active, the new user can log in — and if you select the Notify User of New Account check box, an e-mail will be sent to the e-mail address you entered for this new user. The e-mail will inform him that his account has been created and explain where he can log in.

Editing user information

Before you can edit user information for a particular user, you need to see a list of your users to select the correct account. You can see a list of your site's authenticated users by turning to the Dashboard menu bar and clicking People. By default, the People List will open (see Figure 4-10).

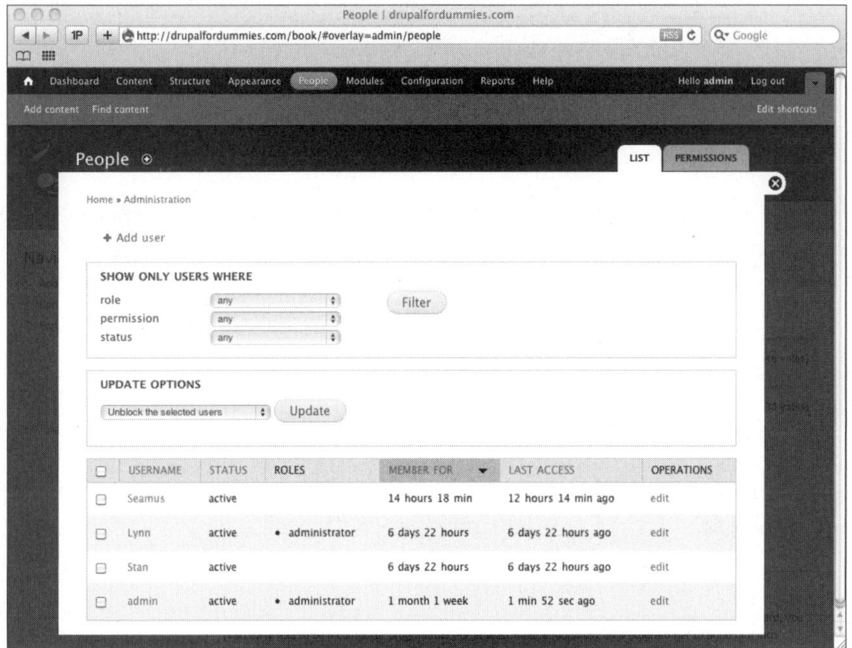

Figure 4-10: User management page with list of users.

Over time, your user list will get longer and longer. The table that lists your users can be sorted using the links at the top. For example, if you click Username, the list will be alphabetized by username, A to Z. If you click it again, it will be ordered from Z to A. You may also find it useful to sort by the Member for heading if you are looking for a user who has just joined.

The section with the Filter button (as shown in Figure 4-10) allows you to view only users who satisfy particular criteria. You can choose to view a list of users based on the permissions or role you have granted them. Or if you need to see just your blocked users, use the Status option.

To edit an individual user account, click the Edit link in the Operations column. You will then be on the Edit tab of the My Account link for that user (see Figure 4-11).

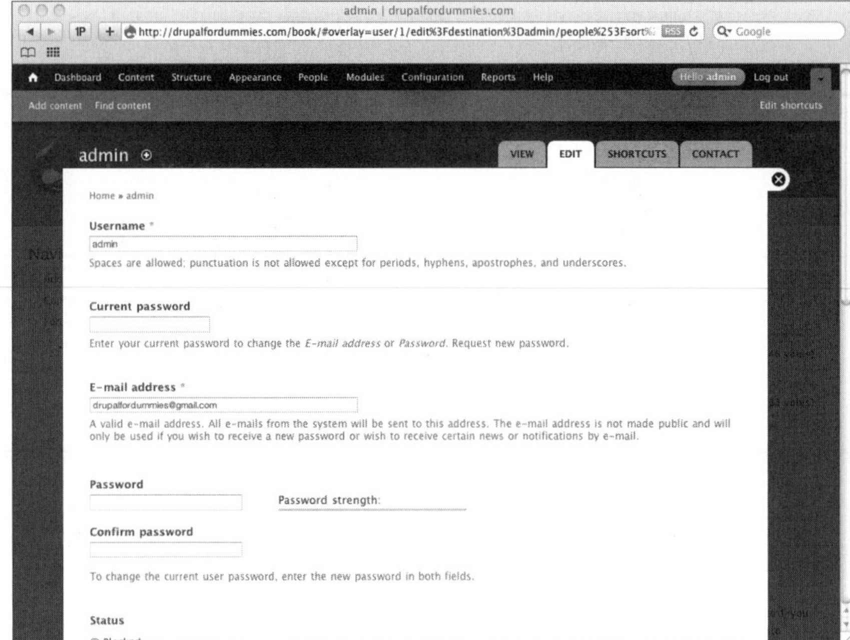

Figure 4-11: The Edit tab the adminis-trator sees.

For each registered user, Drupal keeps track of a username, password, e-mail address, a status (active or blocked) and locale. It also keeps track of roles, which we discuss in the next section. This is information that you, as administrator, can change. Drupal also records information such as the last time a user logged in and any comments a user has made; you can't edit that information.

The Edit tab you as administrator see is basically the same as the Edit page the user sees, with a few exceptions:

- The status section isn't available to the user. Only the administrator can control a user's status.
- Administrators can choose to use the overlay setting. Normal users, by default, cannot.
- The administrator can specify which *roles* (explained later in this chapter) the user has.

If you're ever asked to reset a user's password, this is the place to do it. But Drupal provides the Request new password link on your home page. This link sends the user an e-mail with a link that provides the user with single-use access to her account so that she can log in and change her password herself.

Canceling user accounts

To cancel a user account, follow these steps:

1. **Log in as the site administrator and from the Dashboard menu bar click People.**

   You will see the list of users (refer to Figure 4-10).

2. **Select the check box next to the user account(s) you want to cancel.**
3. **In the section Update Options, select Cancel the Selected User Accounts from the drop-down list.**
4. **Click the Update button.**
5. **On the confirmation page, click one of the following options to delete all the users you've selected:**
   - Disable the Account and Keep Its Content
   - Disable the Account and Unpublish Its Content
   - Delete the Account and Make Its Content belong to the *Anonymous* User
   - Delete the Account and Its Content

Understanding User Roles

Drupal allows you to create new user types with permissions other than those of anonymous or authenticated users. Drupal refers to such special groups of users as *user roles.* For example, imagine that you want to allow a group of people permission to create new articles, but you don't want your average authenticated user to have permission to do this. The way to do this is to assign user roles to the group.

Creating roles

To create a new role, log in as administrator, and then from the Dashboard menu bar choose People➪Permissions➪Roles (see Figure 4-12).

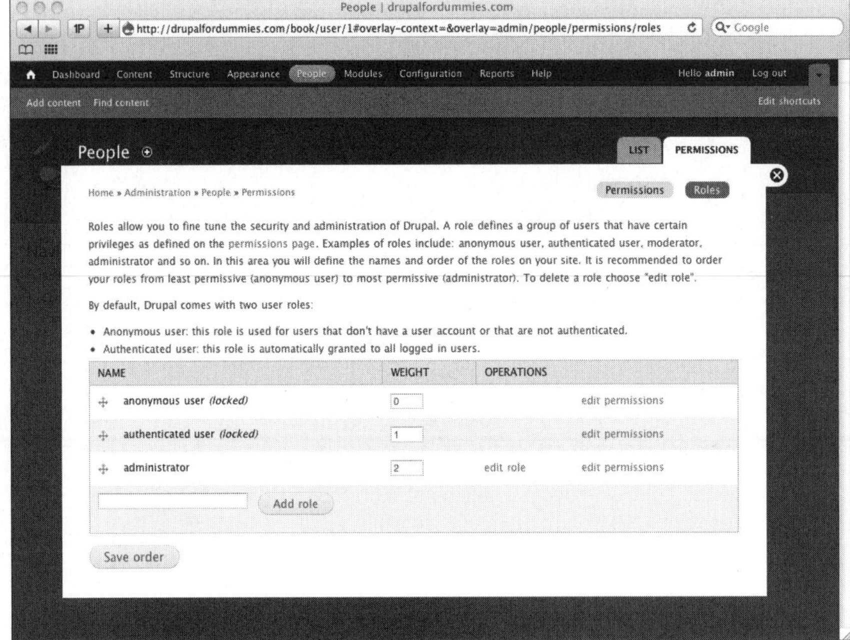

Figure 4-12: Adding a new role on the Roles page under People.

To create a new role, type a name for your role in the text box and click the Add Role button.

At this point, you have a new role, but it has exactly the same permissions the authenticated user role has. In our example, we created the Drupal Warlord role to allow people with that role permission to create articles on the site and strike fear into the hearts of anyone who would dare to use another Content Management System. First, the new role doesn't have any permissions, and second, we haven't assigned this role to any users. To fix the first part, and modify a new role to have the right permissions, click the Edit permissions link that appears to the right of the role name. You see a page much like the Permissions page you saw earlier (refer to Figure 4-8), only with a single column (see Figure 4-13). You can add the appropriate permissions here.

Although you can edit permissions for your new roles by clicking the Edit Permissions link, it's actually better to click the People link located by default in the Dashboard menu bar. When the People overlay opens, click the Permissions tab found at the top-right of your screen. This page lets you see all your roles and permissions at once, making it much easier to ensure your new role has the basic permissions that an authenticated user has in addition to the new permissions (for example, *Article: Create New Content,* which our Drupal Warlords need).

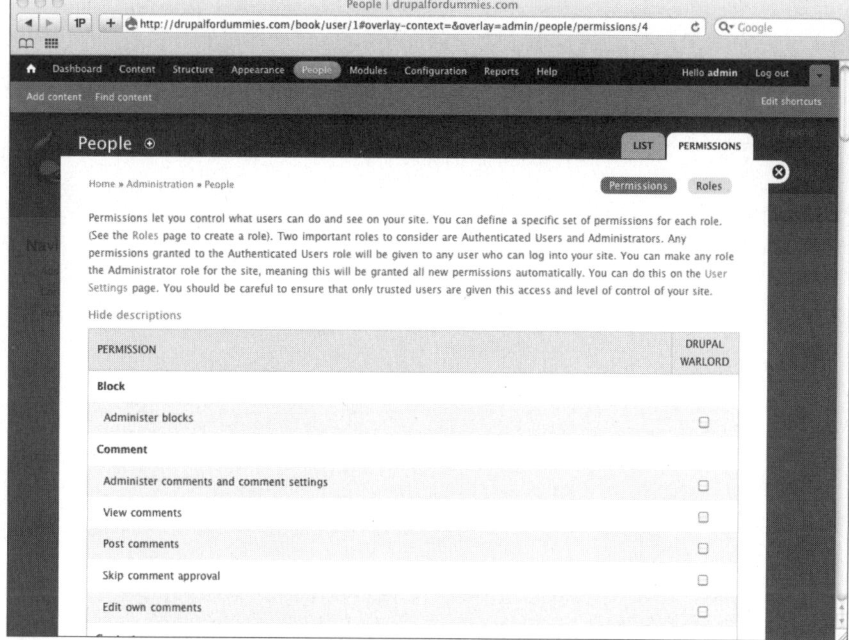

Figure 4-13: Permission editing for a new administrator-created role.

Assigning roles to users

Users can have as many roles as you want to give them. There are two ways to give users an additional role. To assign roles, follow these steps:

1. **Navigate to the Dashboard menu bar and click People.**

   The list of your site's authenticated users opens.

2. **Select the check box to the left of the user you are assigning the new role to.**
3. **Click the drop-down list under the Update Options section and select your new role from the list.**

or

1. **Navigate to the Dashboard menu bar and click People.**
2. **Click the Edit link to the right of the username in the list.**

   Because you created a new role, Drupal displays a Roles listing in the Account information section of the Edit page. Only the administrator can see this section. By default, all users are authenticated, so you can't deselect the check box.

3. **Select the check box next to the name of your new role and click the Save button at the bottom of the page.**

Part II
Your First Drupal Site

The 5th Wave   By Rich Tennant

"As a website designer I never thought I'd say this, but I don't think your site has enough bells and whistles."

In this part . . .

You discover how to take control of your new site, which includes creating and publishing content, changing the appearance of the site, and building menus. You find out how to post more images to your site. And to top it all off, you discover the secret to Drupal: modules.

Things are a tad more complicated here, but the rewards are great. By the end of this part, you'll have built a site with lots of fun features.

Chapter 5

Creating Content: Basic Pages and Articles

In This Chapter

- Understanding nodes
- Beginning content creation
- Organizing your content
- Writing articles
- Creating basic pages

What's the point of creating a website without content? The primary reason to have a website is to communicate. You need content to get your message across, be it to sell something, to teach something, or to build a community. This chapter is all about content creation and organization.

The term *content* in this book refers to text, images, sound, video, and what's in other such media files that are intended to communicate information to site visitors. In this chapter, we focus on creating basic pages and adding text and image content to the pages of your site.

Understanding Drupal Nodes

Drupal has several types of content. In this chapter, we discuss two types: basic pages and articles. Each basic page or article you create for your Drupal site is stored as a structure called a *node*. Think of a node as a block of content, be it a basic page, article, or blog posting.

Don't confuse a Drupal page with a web page. Drupal uses the expression *basic page* to describe a block of content that doesn't allow comments and is largely static. And while you can view a *basic page node* (for example, a page that contains directions to your office or contact information) as though it were a single web page, you can do the same with an article node or any of the Drupal content types discussed in this book.

Making basic pages

At this point, your site has a home page. Chances are you need additional content on your site for things such as contact information and information about your company or group. Drupal *basic pages* contain information you want on your site that

- Must be kept available to visitors.
- Doesn't need to be on the main page of your site.
- Doesn't change very often.

Examples of appropriate information for Drupal basic pages include directions to your office; contact information; background information about your company; Frequently Asked Questions (FAQs); legal terms and policies; and biographies of your management team.

Content on a Drupal basic page doesn't allow visitors to add comments. If you want to allow your site users to comment, you need to create an article instead of a basic page. We cover articles later in this chapter.

Accessing content creation

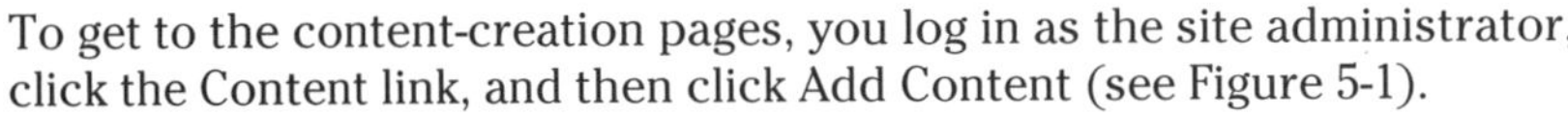

To get to the content-creation pages, you log in as the site administrator, click the Content link, and then click Add Content (see Figure 5-1).

You can also go directly to the content creation page by clicking the Add Content link under the Dashboard menu bar.

You see a menu allowing you to create a basic page or an article — along with some text to help you understand the difference between an article and a basic page. The important differences between the two are:

- Articles allow user comments; basic pages do not.
- Articles appear on the home page of your site. Both articles and basic pages are created as unique pages on your site with their own URLs.
- Articles are best for content that changes over time, such as news. Basic pages are best for static content.
- Articles can use tags and images. You add tags and images using text boxes on the Create Article form. These text boxes are not present on the Create Basic Page form.

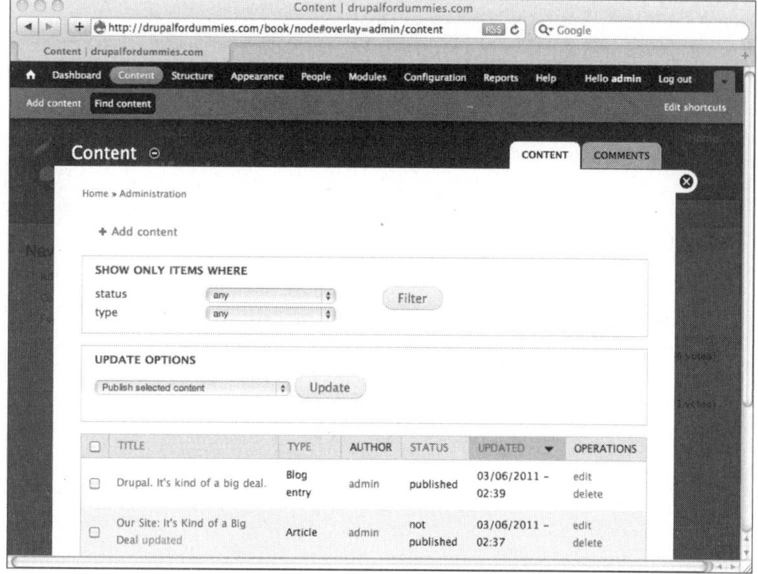

Figure 5-1: The Create Content section of the administrator site.

Adding a page

You create a new basic page by clicking the Page link under the Create Content section. Follow these steps:

1. **Log in to your site as administrator.**
2. **Click the Content link on the top of the page.**
3. **Click the Add Content link.**
4. **Click the Basic Page link.**

   You see the Create Basic page form.
5. **Enter the title of your basic page in the Title text box.**
6. **Enter some sample content in the Body section of the form.**

   Figure 5-2 shows sample content for a contact page.

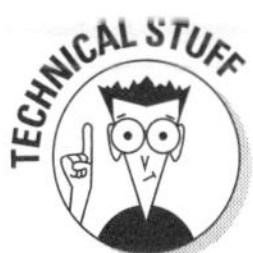

   We've used some HTML code in this sample. This code turns our e-mail addresses into links on the basic page we're creating. Don't let this throw you. You don't need to use HTML in your basic pages, but you can if you want. We discuss this in more detail in Chapter 6.

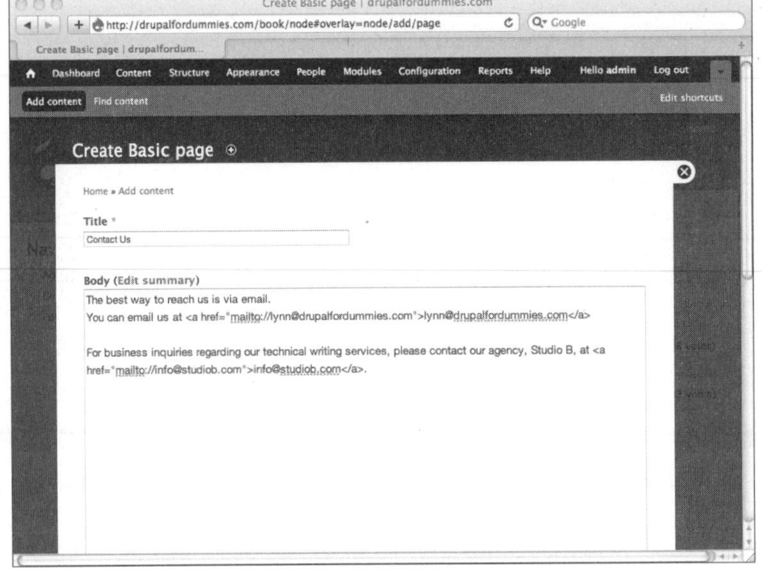

Figure 5-2: The Create Basic Page form with the Title and Body text boxes filled out.

7. **Scroll to the bottom of the form and click the Preview button.**

   If you click Save, your basic page will be published to the web automatically. Clicking Preview allows you to see what your basic page will look like before it's published.

   Figure 5-3 shows you a preview of the new basic page we created. If you want to change anything, scroll down and make your changes in the Create Basic page form. The same two buttons, Save and Preview, are at the bottom of the page.

8. **When you are happy with the content on your new basic page, click the Save button.**

When you save your new basic page, you see your new page with a status message, "Page *Contact Us* has been created." (See Figure 5-4.) The status message appears only once after you save your new basic page. You won't see it again when you visit the basic page later, and your site visitors will never see it.

The title you gave your basic page will appear near the top of your new page, along with part of the title bar at the top of the browser when the page is viewed.

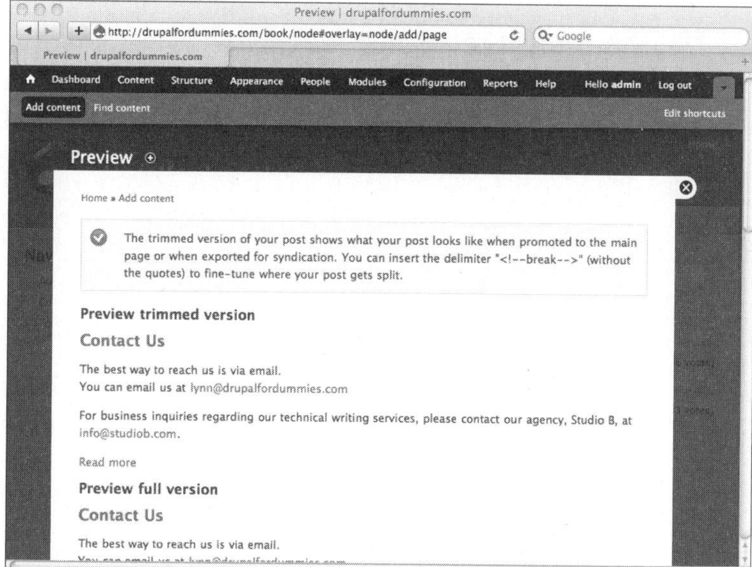

Figure 5-3: The Create Basic Page form with a preview of the page.

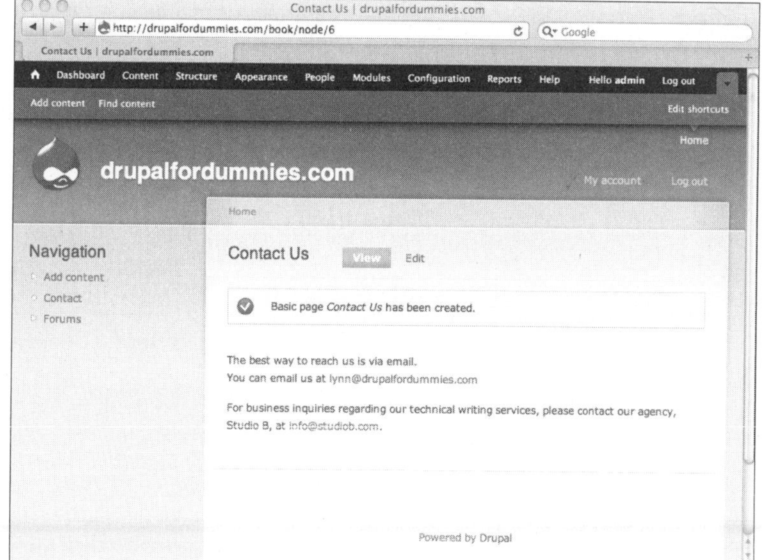

Figure 5-4: You see your new basic page with a status message after you save it.

Editing a basic page

When you view a basic page you create, your basic page has an Edit tab (refer to Figure 5-4). Site visitors will not see this tab. It exists to allow you, the site administrator, to make changes to the content on your basic page. In the example we created, we left out a comma that we now want to add. We can go back and edit the basic page to fix this. To edit your basic page, follow these steps:

1. **Log in to the site as the administrator.**
2. **Click Content on the Dashboard menu bar.**

   You see a list of pages, including the new one you just created (see Figure 5-5).

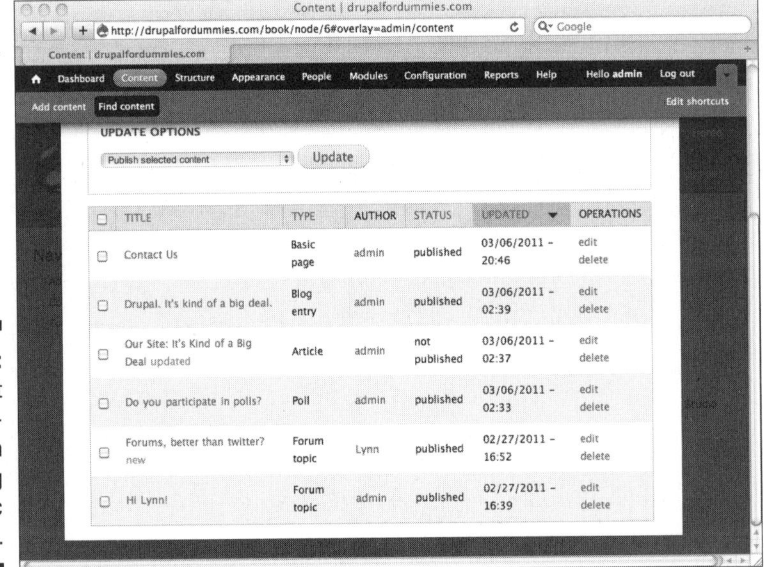

Figure 5-5: The content management section with a listing of basic pages.

If you ever create a basic page and click the Preview button, but never click the Save button, the basic page will not be saved. Make sure you save the page before browsing elsewhere.

3. **Click the Edit link next to the basic page you want to edit.**

   You see the same form you used to create the basic page, but this version has two tabs: a View tab and the currently selected Edit tab (see Figure 5-6).

Only you, as the administrator, will see the Edit and View tabs. Site visitors will not see them.

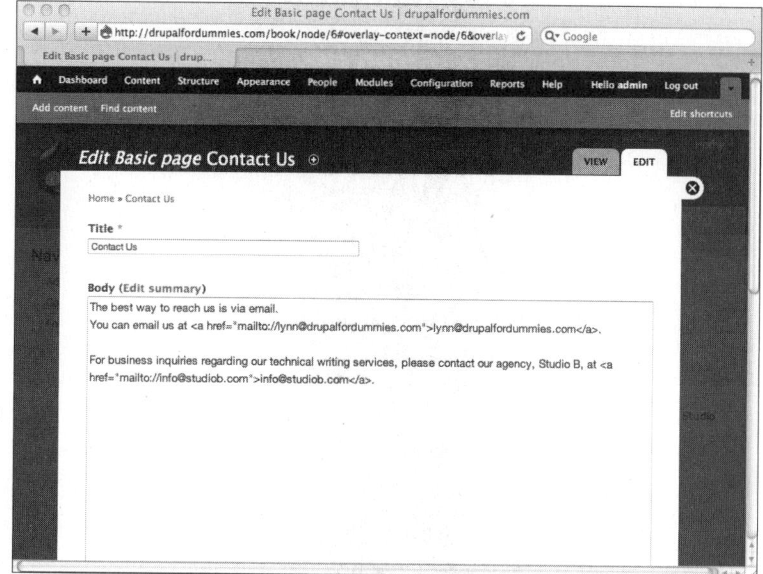

Figure 5-6: Edit tab on your basic page.

4. **Make your desired changes and click Save or Preview until you're happy with your changes.**

Deleting a basic page

Deleting a basic page is done from the same content management section shown in Figure 5-5. To delete a basic page, follow these steps:

1. **Log in to the site as the administrator.**
2. **Click Content on the Dashboard menu bar.**

   You see a list of pages, including the new one you just created (refer to Figure 5-5).
3. **Select the check box to the left of the title of the basic page you want to delete (see Figure 5-7).**
4. **Choose Delete Selected Content from the Update options drop-down list and click the Update button.**

   You're asked to confirm the deletion. Click the Delete button to delete your basic page.

You can delete as many basic pages as you want at the same time by selecting the check boxes next to all the basic pages you want to delete.

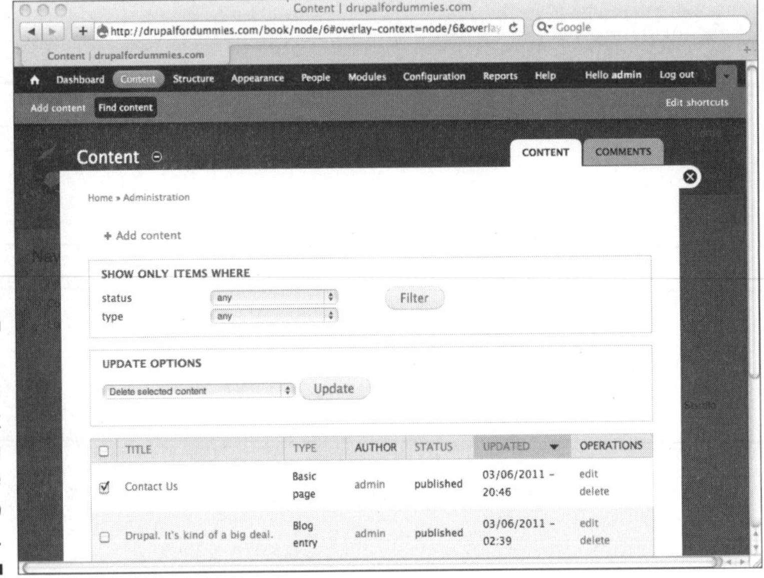

Figure 5-7: Select the check box next to the basic page you want to delete.

Accessing your basic page

If you go to the home page of your site, you won't see a link to your new basic page. Even though your basic page exists on the web, your site doesn't give visitors a link to get to it.

Later in this chapter, you add a basic page to a site menu that will contain links to pages you create and will show up on every page of your site.

For now, you can get to your basic page by clicking the page title on the Content page (refer to Figure 5-7).

To see how your basic page will look to visitors to your site, follow these steps:

1. **Click the page title on the Content page.**
2. **Copy the URL from the address bar in your browser by pressing Ctrl+C or ⌘+C.**

   The URL will be something like `http://drupalfordummies.com/node/6`. (The number at the end of the URL might be different.)
3. **Log out of the site.**
4. **Paste the URL in the browser's address bar by pressing Ctrl+P or ⌘+P, and then press Enter.**

   You will see the page as site visitors will see it.

Writing an Article

If you're jumping around in the book, FYI: We create a Drupal *article* in Chapter 3. This bit of content appears on the home page of our site by default. It also allows logged-in users to comment on it.

Even though an article can allow user comments, it doesn't necessarily have to. You may want your article to contain news from your company, but may not be interested in user feedback on that news. Sometimes comments can clutter up a site and are better left for pages other than the home page.

You can have more than one article on the home page and turn off comments. Follow these steps:

1. **Log in to your site as administrator.**
2. **Choose Content⇨Add Content⇨Article.**

   The Create Article form appears (see Figure 5-8).

   The Title text box for an article posted on the front page behaves differently from the Title text box for a basic page. A basic page title is the actual title on a page and appears both at the top of the page and in the title bar of the viewer's browser. The title of an article appears directly above the article, but the page the article is on has its own title.
3. **Add a title and body for your new article in the Title and Body text boxes, respectively.**
4. **Add tags to your article by typing in the Tags text box. Separate each tag from the next with a comma.**

   Tags are keywords or topics associated with your article. They are a way to organize your articles. They give visitors quick access to a list of all articles about a particular topic. For example, if you have a site all about dogs and you have an article on beagles, you can add the tag *beagle.* Then, when beagle fans click the word *beagle* (which appears under your published article), they see a list of all articles with the same tag.
5. **Scroll down and click the Comment Settings link.**
6. **Select the Closed radio button to turn off comments for this article.**
7. **Click the Save button at the bottom of this page to publish your new article to the front page.**

   Your new article will appear above any you created earlier and won't have a Comment link (see Figure 5-9).

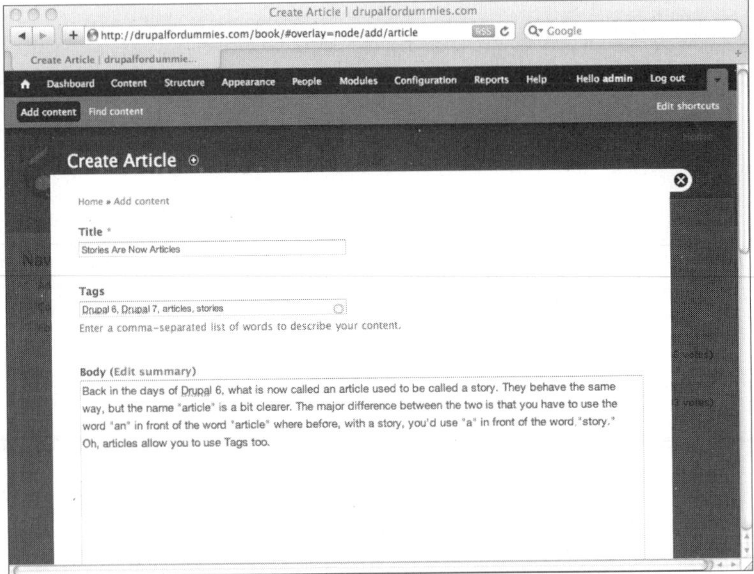

Figure 5-8: Create Article form.

Editing and deleting articles

You edit and delete articles exactly the same way as you edit and delete pages. Follow these steps:

1. **Log in to the site as the administrator.**
2. **Click Content on the Dashboard menu bar.**
   - To edit, click the Edit link next to the article you want to edit.
   - To delete an article, select the check box next to the article you want to delete. Choose Delete Selected Content from the Update Options drop-down list and click the Update button.

Ordering your content

The default behavior of an article is to show up on the home page. New articles are at the top; older ones move to the bottom of the home page. However, say you create an article that you want always to appear at the top of the home page. You can accomplish this by setting the article as *sticky*. Follow these steps:

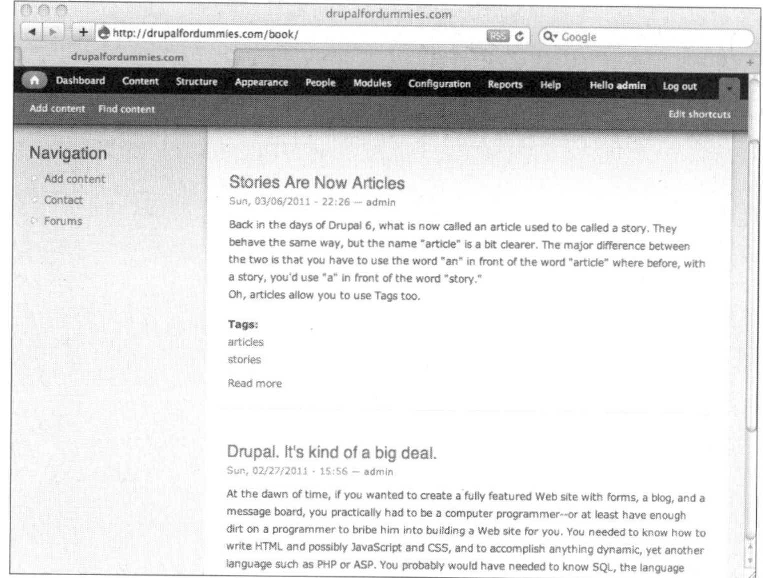

drupalfordummies.com
http://drupalfordummies.com/book/
Google
drupalfordummies.com
Dashboard Content Structure Appearance People Modules Configuration Reports Help
Hello admin Log out
Add content Find content
Edit shortcuts
Navigation
Add content
Contact
Forums
Stories Are Now Articles
Sun, 03/06/2011 - 22:26 — admin
Back in the days of Drupal 6, what is now called an article used to be called a story. They behave the same way, but the name "article" is a bit clearer. The major difference between the two is that you have to use the word "an" in front of the word "article" where before, with a story, you'd use "a" in front of the word "story."
Oh, articles allow you to use Tags too.
Tags:
articles
stories
Read more
Drupal. It's kind of a big deal.
Sun, 02/27/2011 - 15:56 — admin
At the dawn of time, if you wanted to create a fully featured Web site with forms, a blog, and a message board, you practically had to be a computer programmer--or at least have enough dirt on a programmer to bribe him into building a Web site for you. You needed to know how to write HTML and possibly JavaScript and CSS, and to accomplish anything dynamic, yet another language such as PHP or ASP. You probably would have needed to know SQL, the language

Figure 5-9: Home page with two published articles.

1. **Log in to the site as the administrator.**
2. **Click Content on the Dashboard menu bar.**
3. **Select the check box next to the article you want to always appear at the top of the page.**
4. **Choose Make Selected Content Sticky from the drop-down list in the Update Options section (see Figure 5-10).**
5. **Click Update.**

If you no longer want your article to be sticky, reset this option by choosing Make Selected Content Not Sticky from the Update options drop-down list.

Managing article length

If you create a particularly long article, Drupal automatically shortens it for you and provides a Read More link if users want to read the entire article. Instead of showing a long post that takes up the entire screen, and making users scroll down to see any other content on the page, Drupal displays the first few sentences of the post. To see a shortened article, look at Figure 5-11.

When your post is really long, it can use up all of your screen real estate. The first post on the home page is fairly long, but it doesn't bump down the other posts on the page. Figure 5-12 shows what this page would look like with the first post left untruncated.

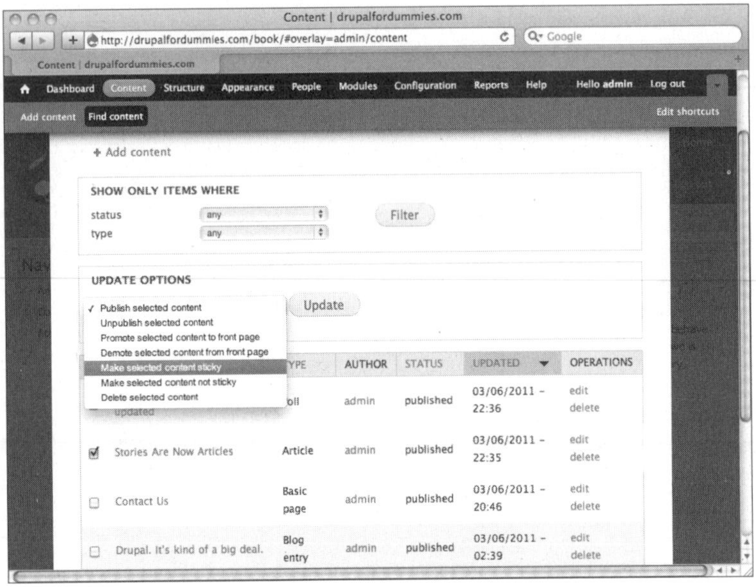

Figure 5-10: Setting an article as sticky.

There's nothing inherently wrong with having a long post, except it forces the visitors to your site to scroll down the page if they want to see additional content — and they might not bother. Therefore, it may be better to truncate the visible part of your post.

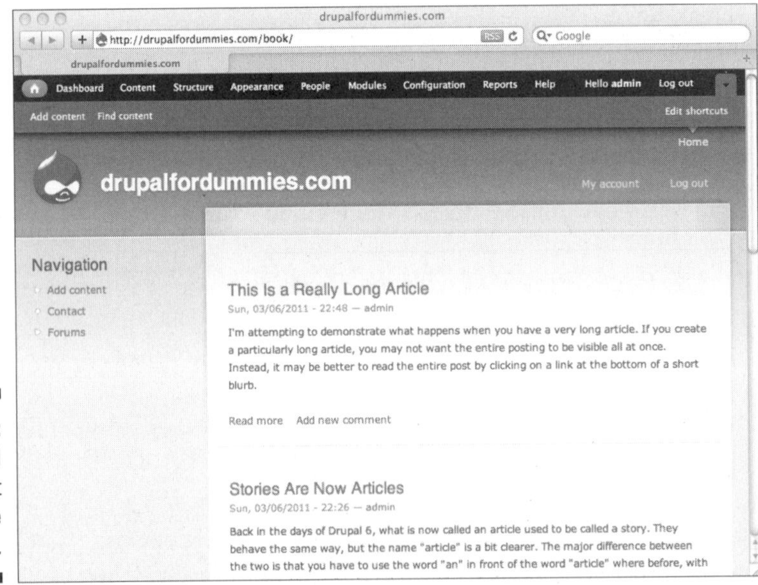

Figure 5-11: Truncated article post on the home page.

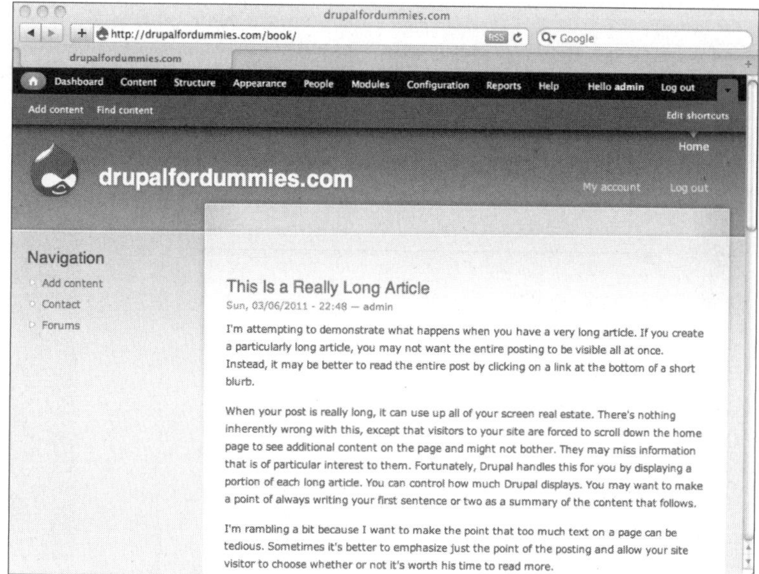

Figure 5-12: Home page with long first article.

You can control how many characters Drupal displays when it truncates your articles. Follow these steps:

1. **Log in to the site as the administrator.**
2. **Choose Structure➪Content Types.**
3. **Click the Manage Display link to the right of Article and click the Teaser tab on the upper right.**

   The Article Manage Display settings form appears (see Figure 5-13).
4. **To change how many characters are displayed, click the Settings button to the right of Trim Length.**
5. **Change the value from the default 600 characters to whatever you choose.**

   To force Drupal to display entire articles rather than truncate them, choose Default from the Format drop-down list.
6. **Click Update and then the Save button on the bottom left.**

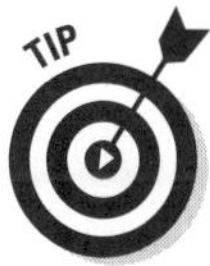

When you change the Trim Length of trimmed posts setting, it will also have an effect on articles that you have already published. Old articles will automatically be shortened to the new setting.

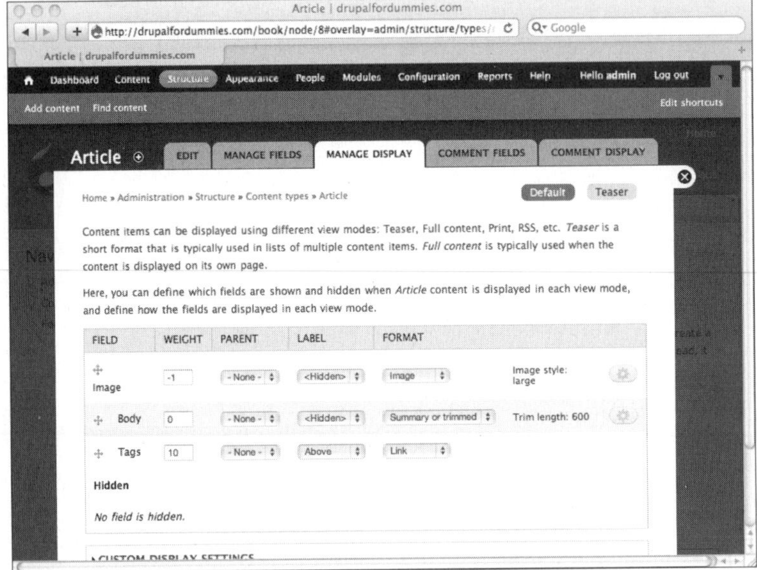

Figure 5-13: The Manage Display form.

Setting Menu Options for a Basic Page

If you haven't created a basic page, now is a good time to do so; if you have, choose Content➪Find Content and click the Edit link next to your basic page. You see the Menu Settings tab near the bottom of the form. Click this tab to open the Menu Settings form (see Figure 5-14).

These settings allow you to put a link to your basic page in a menu that will appear on every page of your site.

Giving your node a menu link title

Your basic page already has a title. In our example, the page title is Contact Us. The Menu Link Title text box is where you specify what text to use to link to your page. In our case, Contact Us is appropriate. Most of the time, your page title will be the perfect text to use as the link. It's possible, however, that your page title is too long to be a good link title, and this is how you can reword it to be more succinct.

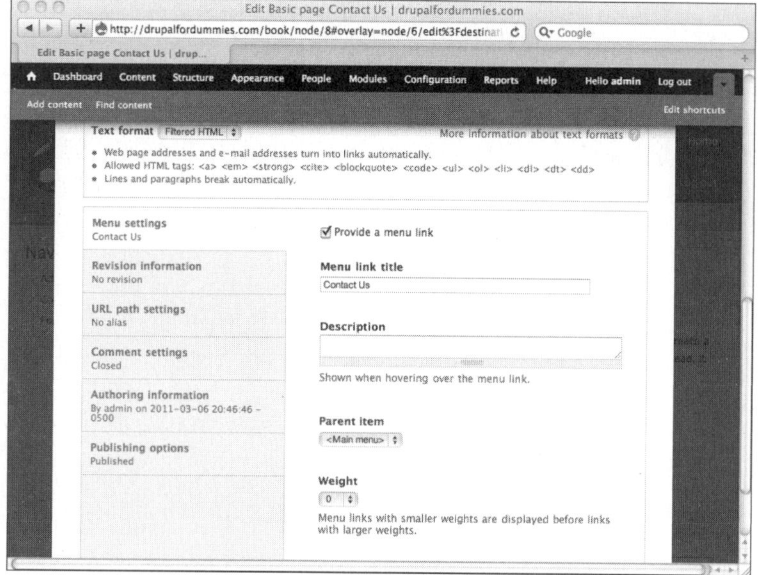

Figure 5-14: Menu settings in page editing form.

Choosing a parent item

The menu in which you want to put your current page link is called the *main menu.* The main menu appears on every page of the site. By default, it currently displays the Home link. When we add this link, it will appear as a new menu item to the left of the Home link, just under the site header (see Figure 5-15). Your new link will appear after you complete this form and save your page.

Choose the option <Main Menu> from the Parent Item drop-down list. This puts your new link to your page in the main menu.

Setting the link weight

The Weight setting controls where in the menu your link appears. If you choose –50 from this menu, your link will be at the left (or at the top if the menu is displayed vertically) of the main menu. Choosing 50 will make your link appear on the right (or at the bottom) of the menu. In our case, it makes sense to choose a higher number (that is, "heavier" weight), so the Contact Us link will always be the last one in the main menu.

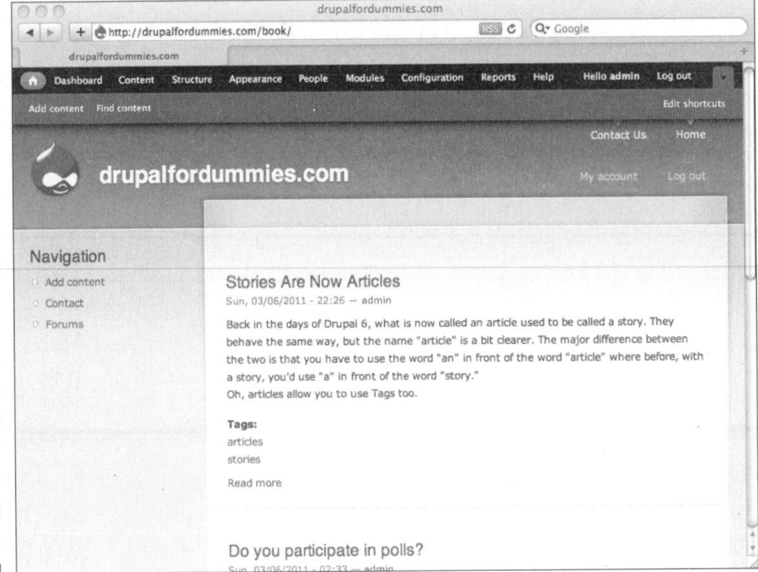
drupalfordummies.com
http://drupalfordummies.com/book/
Dashboard
Content
Structure
Appearance
People
Modules
Configuration
Reports
Help
Hello admin
Log out
Add content
Find content
Edit shortcuts
Contact Us
Home
drupalfordummies.com
My account
Log out
Navigation
Add content
Contact
Forums
Stories Are Now Articles
Sun, 03/06/2011 - 22:26 — admin
Back in the days of Drupal 6, what is now called an article used to be called a story. They behave the same way, but the name "article" is a bit clearer. The major difference between the two is that you have to use the word "an" in front of the word "article" where before, with a story, you'd use "a" in front of the word "story."
Oh, articles allow you to use Tags too.
Tags:
articles
stories
Read more
Do you participate in polls?

Figure 5-15: The main menu appears under the menu bar with a link to the Contact Us page.

When you're choosing a weight for your menu items, consider the big picture. Will your site have several links? Does it make sense to put the About Us link in front of the Contact Us link? Make a list of links and assign a weight to each one before you actually create them. If you know you want Contact Us to always be the rightmost link, give it a weight of 50. If you know you want your Products link always to appear on the left, because people will see it first, give it a weight of –50.

When you create or edit an article node, you also have a Menu Settings section on the form. It works exactly the same way as it does for Drupal basic pages.

There are lots of additional options for managing the content you create, and we discuss them in Chapter 6.

Chapter 6

Managing Your Content

In This Chapter

- Controlling HTML in your content
- Controlling revision information
- Managing comments
- Modifying authoring information
- Choosing publishing options
- Including images in your pages

Drupal offers you a number of options that allow you to customize the appearance of your content. This chapter shows you how to leverage Drupal's options to refine your content further. You see how to include HTML code, images, and even Flash movies in your posts. Also, we discuss the comment system and how to control the appearance and behavior of comments. We also show you how to temporarily hide posts while you continue to work on them and how to control who can see them when they are published. Along the way, we offer information about a few other optional tweaks to the presentation of your content that Drupal gives you. There's a lot of good stuff in this chapter to help you fine-tune your nodes.

The tweaks and settings discussed in this chapter apply to both basic pages and articles. They also apply to other node types, including polls, blog posts, and forum posts (discussed in Chapter 9).

Finding the Settings

Most of the settings we discuss in this chapter are located on the form used to create or edit content. You access them by clicking the links under the large Body text box (see Figure 6-1).

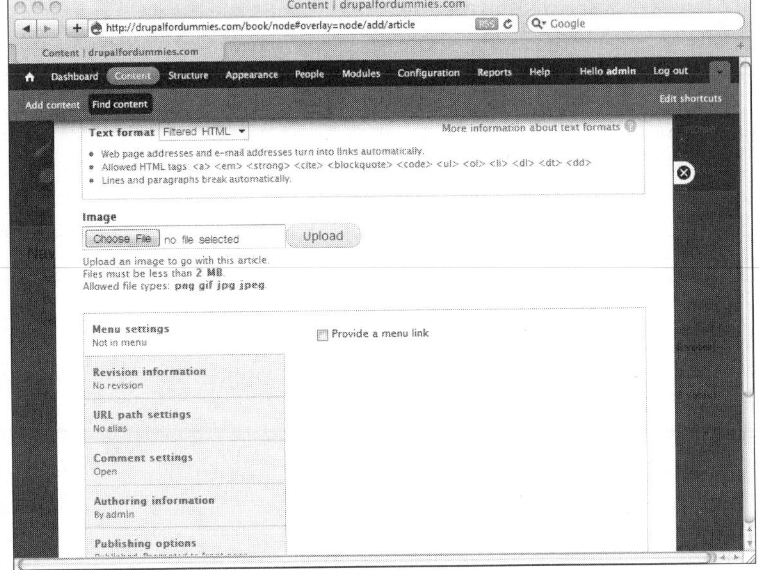

Figure 6-1: Content editing page, with option links below the Body text box.

You get to the content editing form for any of your basic pages or articles by logging in as administrator and clicking Content on the Dashboard menu bar. Locate the content you want to edit and click the appropriate Edit link. The options we discuss in this chapter are also accessible when you first create content by clicking the Add Content link and choosing Page or Article.

The options and links are Text Format, Menu Settings, Revision Information, URL Path Settings, Comment Settings, Authoring Information, and Publishing Options.

Handling HTML Content

If you aren't familiar with HTML, you're in luck this time: You don't need to know how to code in HTML to create links with Drupal.

To see that you don't need to know HTML, consider the text in these two versions of the Contact Me page node we created: one with HTML and one without.

- **With HTML code, the page text reads:**

```
The best way to reach us is via e-mail. You can send e-mail to us at
<a href="mailto://lynn@drupalfordummies.com">lynn@drupalfordummies.com</a>.
For business inquiries regarding our technical writing services, please
contact our agency, Studio B, at <a href="mailto://info@studiob.com">
info@studiob.com</a>.
```

- **Without HTML code, the text reads:**

```
The best way to reach us is via e-mail. You can send e-mail to us at
lynn@drupalfordummies.com. For business inquiries regarding our technical
writing services, please contact our agency, Studio B, at info@studiob.com.
```

Both versions give you the same end result, e-mail addresses that are hyperlinks (see Figure 6-2). The first version, with HTML tags, is a little tricky to type and definitely not as easy to edit if (for example) an e-mail address were to change.

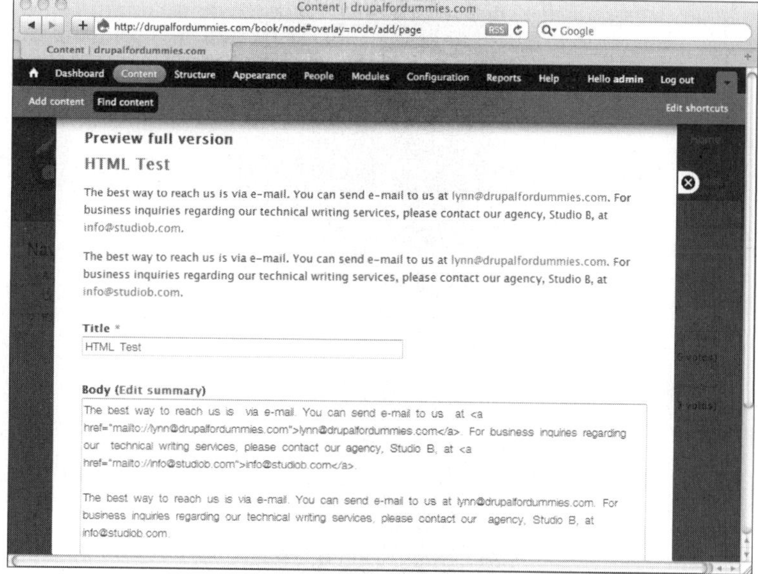

Figure 6-2: Hyperlinked e-mail address automatically created by Drupal.

Drupal does the dirty work for you. This also applies to web addresses and URLs. To create an HTML link, you would ordinarily have to type

```
<a href="http://drupalfordummies.com">http://drupalfordummies.com</a>
```

Instead, Drupal automatically converts `http://drupalfordummies.com` into a link.

HTML requires tags to create paragraph and line breaks. Drupal handles this for you, behind the scenes, so you don't need to include `<p>` or `<br>` tags in your content.

This automatic formatting takes some of the work out of your content creation. When you create or edit your content by typing text in the Body text box of a basic page or article, it's very readable.

Choosing a Text format

Choose from the Text format section when you create or edit content (see Figure 6-3). If you don't want to use any HTML, choose the Plain text option. If you know HTML, you can use it in your posts. Drupal offers you two choices: Filtered HTML or Full HTML.

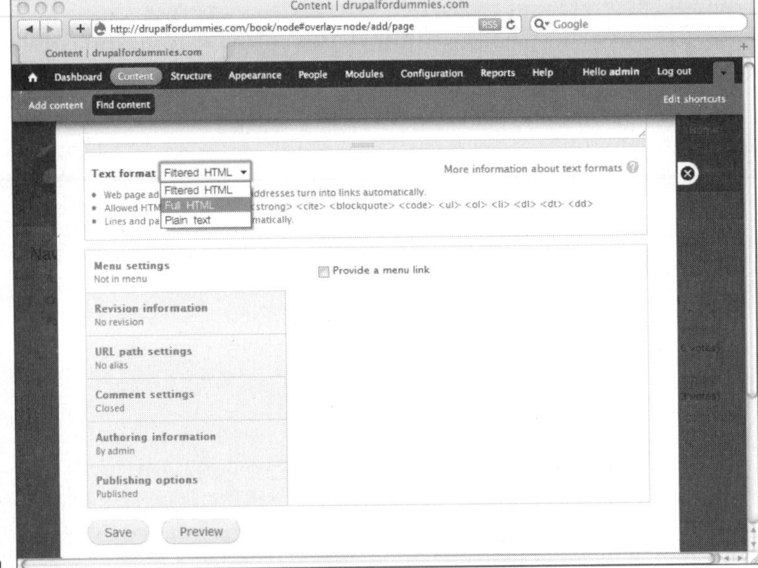

Figure 6-3: The Input format settings available when you create or edit content.

By default, Filtered HTML is selected.

Using filtered HTML

Filtered HTML allows you to use only certain tags, as listed in Table 6-1.

Table 6-1 Tags Allowed by Filtered HTML

HTML tag	Function
<a>	Create a link from words in your text, such as <a href="http://drupalfordummies.com">Drupal for Dummies</a>.

HTML tag	Function
<em>	Italicize.
<cite>	Italicize.
<strong>	Boldface.
<code>	Display as computer code.
<ol>	Start an ordered (numbered) list of items.
<ul>	Start an unordered (bulleted) list of items.
<li>	Identify an item in a numbered or bulleted list.
<dl>	Start a definition list.
<dt>	Define a term in a definition list.
<dd>	Create a definition in a definition list.

Using full HTML

When you choose Full HTML from the Text Format drop-down list, you can use any HTML tag you want. When you edit or create a basic page or article, you decide which HTML tags to use.

Only choose the Full HTML option if you have to. If you ever give another user the capability to edit posts (as discussed later in this book), remember: Keeping your content filtered prevents inadvertent code mistakes or the inclusion of tags that give the content an appearance inconsistent with other content on your site. Even worse, Full HTML allows JavaScript and other script tags to run in a page, potentially opening your site to hackers.

Adding Menu Settings

The Menu settings available when you create a new post give you an easy way to add a link to your content from one of the site menus. Chapter 8 discusses Drupal menus in more detail, but here's an overview.

When you select the Provide a Menu Link check box, a form appears. The Menu Link Title contains the link text, for example, Contact Us. If you add a description in the Description text box, that text will appear when the mouse cursor is over the link. You can set up multiple menus on your site. The Parent Item controls which menu the link should go in. The Weight setting controls where in the list your new link belongs. Links are displayed in order of weight, with the lower numbers showing up first. If your menu is horizontal, the lower weight is on the left, higher weight on the right. If the menu is vertical, the lower weight is at the top, and the higher weight is at the bottom.

Controlling Revision Information

Things change. Maybe you made a mistake, leaving out some important bit of information. Maybe something new happened, making the current content inaccurate. Drupal allows you to revise your content and keep track of both the original version and all the revisions you make.

To create a revision, follow these steps:

1. **Log in to your site as administrator.**
2. **Click Content.**
3. **Choose a basic page or article you created earlier and click the Edit link.**
4. **Make a change in your content.**
5. **Scroll down to the Revision Information link and click it. (See Figure 6-4.)**
6. **Select the Create New Revision check box and type something in the Revision Log Message box that explains changes you have made to the content.**
7. **Click Save.**

Your revision has been saved, and you will now see a new Revisions tab that you can click to see all saved revisions (see Figure 6-5).

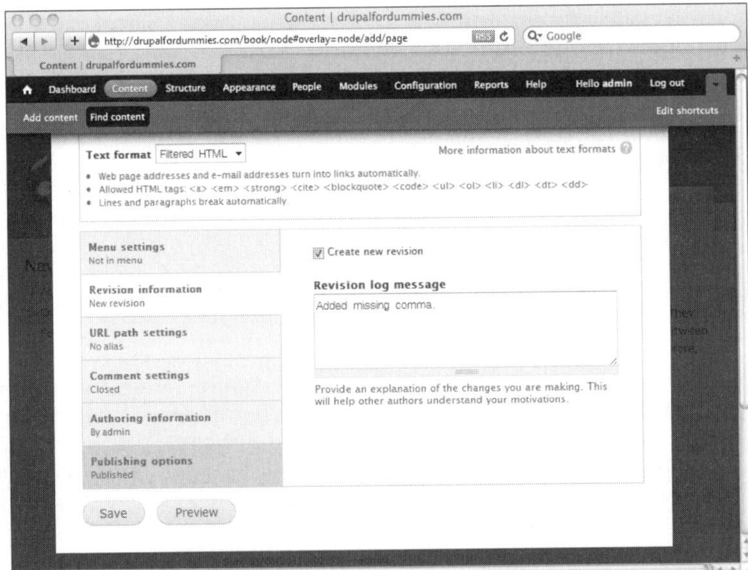

Figure 6-4: The Revision Information settings available when you create or edit content.

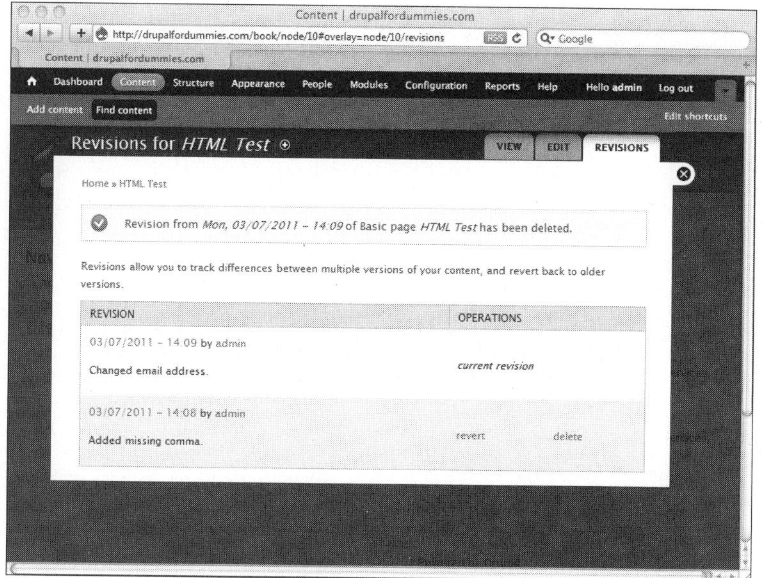

Figure 6-5: Revision history of content.

Next time you edit the content, you will see the current revision. If you want to edit the current revision but not create a new revision, don't use the revision settings when editing. To go back to the original version, click the Revert link on the Revisions tab.

Revisions are great for keeping track of changes to the content:

- If you need to make a temporary change to content on your site but eventually want to go back to the original, you can create a revision and then click Revert when you no longer need the latest change.
- When more than one person works on the same site, the Revisions feature can record when someone else changed something and why.

Managing Comment Settings

You can allow users to submit their thoughts about your content by allowing comments. When you create or edit content, you use the Comment settings (see Figure 6-6) to control whether registered users can add comments.

When you open comments, a link appears at the end of your post. When comments are posted, a link to view the comments is visible, as shown in Figure 6-7.

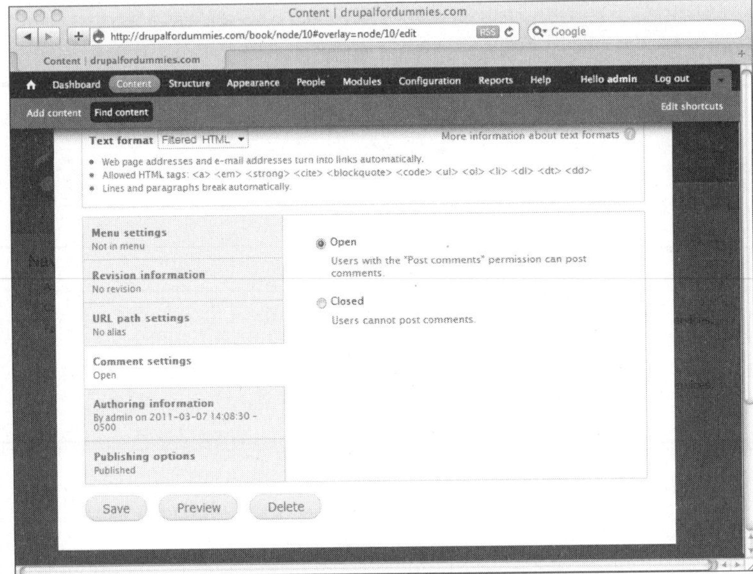

Figure 6-6: The Comment settings available when you create or edit content.

Drupal. It's kind of a big deal.

Sun, 02/27/2011 - 15:56 — admin

At the dawn of time, if you wanted to create a fully featured Web site with forms, a blog, and a message board, you practically had to be a computer programmer--or at least have enough dirt on a programmer to bribe him into building a Web site for you. You needed to know how to write HTML and possibly JavaScript and CSS, and to accomplish anything dynamic, yet another language such as PHP or ASP. You probably would have needed to know SQL, the language that allows Web sites to store and retrieve information.

Read more admin's blog 1 comment Add new comment

Figure 6-7: Posts with comments allowed and comment links.

To view comments on a post, click the Comment link or the title of the posting. Doing so opens the article or basic page node in its own page, with the comments visible and a link for users to add a new comment (see Figure 6-8).

The administrator (or users with sufficient permissions) will see links for deleting or editing the comment. Users can also reply to comments.

Considerations of allowing comments

A primary difference between basic pages and articles is whether comments are permitted by default. Basic pages don't allow comments by default; articles do. The Comment settings control this capability in two ways by default:

Comments

Tell me more! Sun, 03/06/2011 - 02:40 — Seamus

With features like the ones you're describing, who wouldn't want to build a site using Drupal?

delete edit reply

Add new comment

Your name

admin

Subject

Comment *

Figure 6-8: View of a single post with comment.

- When you create a basic page, comments are closed by default.
- When you create an article, comments are permitted.

Every node you create (for example, each basic page and article) has the option of allowing users to comment. For some types of content, this doesn't make sense. Our Contact Us page doesn't need to allow comments. But some content you create may be appropriate for allowing user comments.

A setting under People⇨Permissions allows you to permit anonymous users (site visitors who are not logged in) to post comments. Do not allow anonymous users to post comments. You leave yourself open to spammers. It's best to allow only authenticated users (people who are logged in) to post comments.

Closing comments

If you close comments for your post, no comments will be allowed. The Add New Comment link won't appear on the page. If you edit a post and change the Comment settings from open to closed, all the current comments will be visible, but no new ones can be added.

Hiding comments

When comments already exist on a post, and you edit the Comment settings, you will see a third option, Hidden. If you select Hidden, the existing comments will not be displayed. They will not be deleted; they will show up again if you choose Open or Closed.

Changing Authoring Information

Every time you post an article, Drupal includes information about when the content was posted and who posted it. (Refer to Figure 6-7.) The poster's username (in this case, `admin`) appears onscreen, along with the time and date the article was posted.

By default, articles include this information and basic pages do not.

You can fine-tune your control over this with the Authoring information section when you create or edit your article (see Figure 6-9).

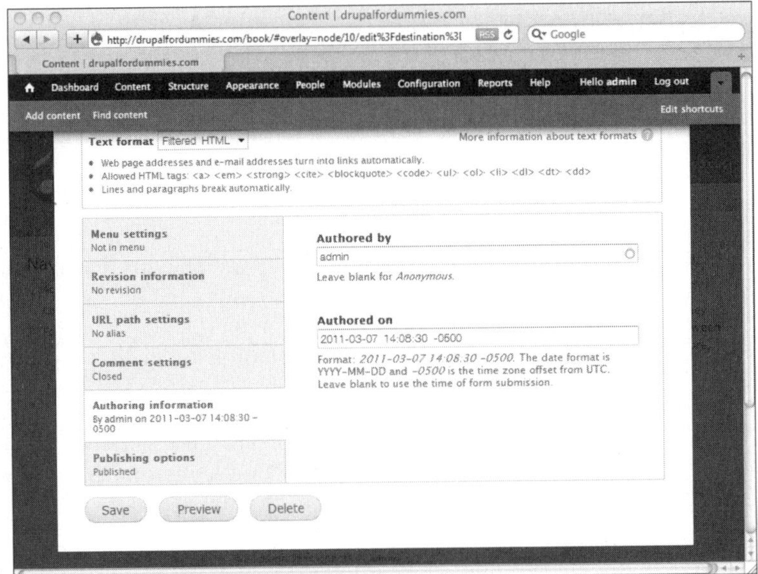

Figure 6-9: The Authoring information settings available when you create or edit content.

By default, your username will appear in the Authored By text box. You can change it or leave it blank if you don't want an author name to appear.

The Authored On text box allows you to change the date of the posting. The date is in the format *year-month-day hour:minutes:seconds*. When you save your post, Drupal takes that date and reformats it to a date in a format like 07/21/2011 – 11:46.

To change the format of this date, follow these steps:

1. **Log in as an administrator.**
2. **Choose Configuration➪Date and Time.**

   It's located in the Regional and Language links near the bottom of the page. The Date and time configuration page appears (see Figure 6-10).

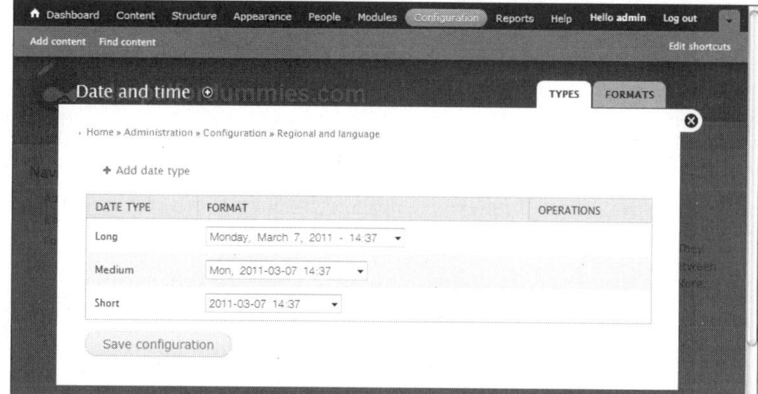

Figure 6-10: The date and time configuration formatting page.

3. **Locate the Short Date Format drop-down list, in the bottom half of the page, and select a new format.**

   This is the format used as the Authored on Date.
4. **Click Save Configuration.**

You can fine-tune the appearance even further by clicking the Formats tab on the top right. This causes a form to appear, where you can precisely customize the date by clicking Add date format (see Figure 6-11).

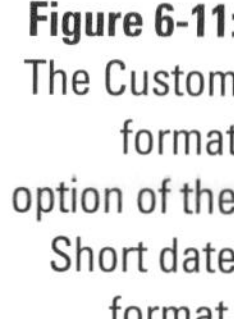

Figure 6-11: The Custom format option of the Short date format.

If you are determined to create a custom date format, we recommend visiting this page: `www.tizag.com/phpT/phpdate.php`. Scroll down to the heading "Reference" and use the information there to build your date.

Publishing Options

When you write articles, they appear on the home page when you click Save. When they are published, basic pages and articles can be visited directly by anyone. But you don't have to automatically publish your content to the web. You may want to write content but publish it at a later time. The Publishing options section lets you control what happens after you create content. This section is available when you create or edit your article (see Figure 6-12).

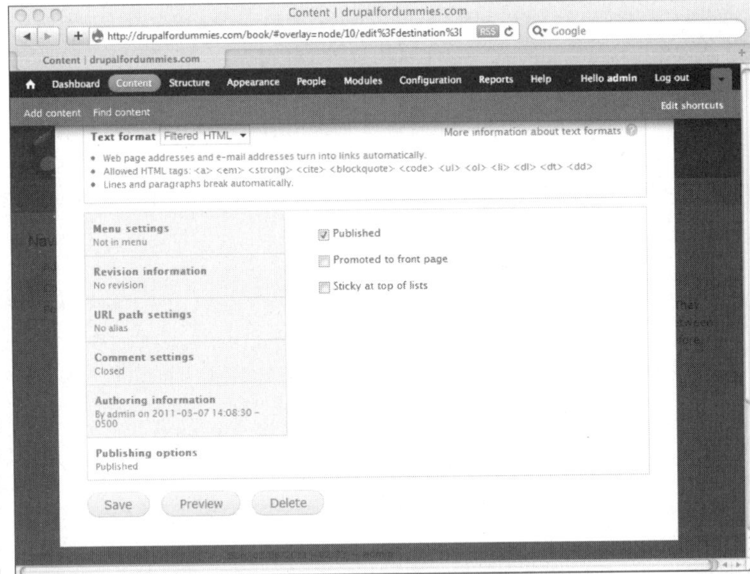

Figure 6-12: The Publishing options available when you create or edit content.

The options you select here control what happens when you click the Save button.

Publishing

By default, for both basic pages and articles, the Published check box is selected — which means your content will be made live on the web when you click Save.

If you deselect the Published check box and click Save, your content is saved but not actually published. No one but you, logged in as administrator, will be able to see it. You have three options:

- To access unpublished content, log in as administrator, and click Content. You see all of your content with the publishing status listed next to it. If it's unpublished, it shows a Status of *Not Published* (see Figure 6-13).
- To publish your content without any changes, select the check box next to its title, choose Publish Selected Content from the Update Options drop-down list, and then click Update.
- To make changes to the content before publishing, click the Edit link, make your changes; under Publishing Options, select the Published check box, and finally, click Save.

Promoting to front page

Articles appear on the home page by default; basic pages do not. But if you select the Promoted to Front Page check box, you can change this behavior regardless of node type.

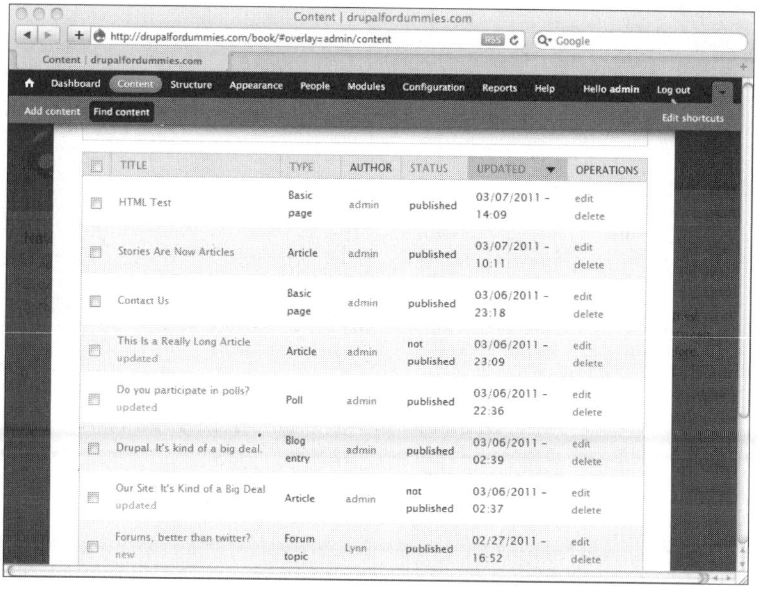

Figure 6-13: The Content page lists the publication status of all content.

Making content sticky in lists

When you create a new article and post it to the home page, it ends up as the one on top. Articles are ordered from newest to oldest. This check box accomplishes the same thing as modifying the "stickiness" in the Content page. (Chapter 5 explains how to use the Content page to set an article as sticky, so that it always appears at the top of the home page even when newer articles are published.)

Previewing your content

The Preview button lets you take a look at your post before you actually publish it. (See Figure 6-14.)

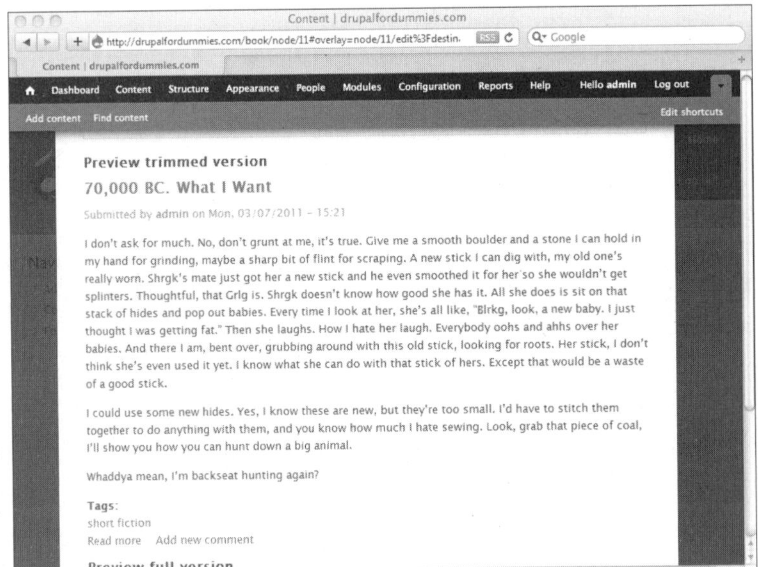

Figure 6-14: The preview of a post.

You may have noticed the View tab (top right) that sometimes appears as you're editing your posts. It gives you a look at your published posts. It only shows up after you've published a post, and it lets you see what the post will actually look like on your site, as opposed to Preview, which only gives you a view of the content in the Administrative interface and will not save your work.

By default, when your post is published, only 600 characters appear. Visitors have to click Read more to see the rest of your post. Chapter 5 explains how to modify the number of characters from 600. But suppose you want to only change this for a single article, and not for every article you write. You can control this on a post-by-post basis.

To create a custom summary, follow these steps:

1. **Log in as an administrator.**
2. **Open an article you have posted to the home page in Edit mode.**
3. **Click the Edit Summary link.**

   This opens a new Summary text box.
4. **Copy (press Ctrl+C or ⌘+C) the text of your post that you want to appear as the summary.**

   Generally, you want to copy the first few sentences of your post.
5. **Paste the text into the Summary text box by pressing Ctrl+P or ⌘+P.**
6. **Click the Preview button.**

   Your page changes to show your Summary and Body text (see Figure 6-15).
7. **Click Save to save your content.**

   Your home page now reflects the new blurb length.

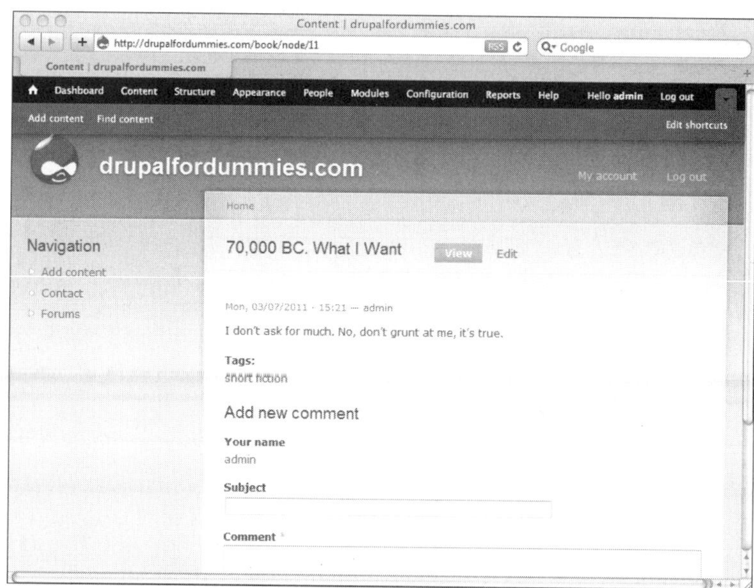

Figure 6-15: The front page now displays a summary.

If you edit an existing posting and use the Edit Summary text box, make sure you click Save to republish your content. You may have to reload the home page to see the changes.

Depending on your content, you may want to write a specific blurb to show up on the home page. You can create a summary of your content in the top box and keep all your content together in the bottom box.

Adding Images

You may be eager to include images in your pages. Drupal 7 has made it very easy to upload and include an image in your article or basic page. The downside is that you don't have any control over the layout of these images, and you can only include one image per post.

To use HTML to add an image to your content, make sure you're logged in as an administrator, and then follow these steps:

1. **Create a new article by selecting Content⇨Add Content.**
2. **Enter a title such as** Posting an Image.
3. **In the Body section, enter some text.**

   Try to enter a few paragraphs so you get a sense of how the image will look onscreen.
4. **Scroll down to the Image section under the Body text box.**
5. **Click Choose File to locate the image.**

   The Upload File dialog box appears, as shown in Figure 6-16.

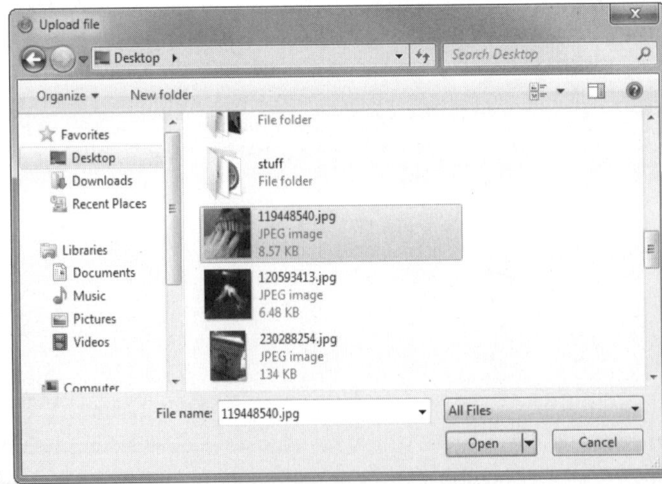

Figure 6-16: The Upload File dialog box.

6. **Browse to the desired folder, select the image, and click the Open button.**

   Your image must be a `.jpg`, `.jpeg`, `.gif`, or `.png` image and can't be larger than 2MB. Also keep in mind that Drupal will resize your image to fit on the web page if it's very large.

   The image you want to use must be stored somewhere on your computer. You can't use an image from the web without first downloading it. And, in general, using images you've downloaded from the web can get you into legal hot water.

7. **Click Upload to save the image to your website.**

   You see a thumbnail of your image, as shown in Figure 6-17. Add in descriptive text in the Alternate text box.

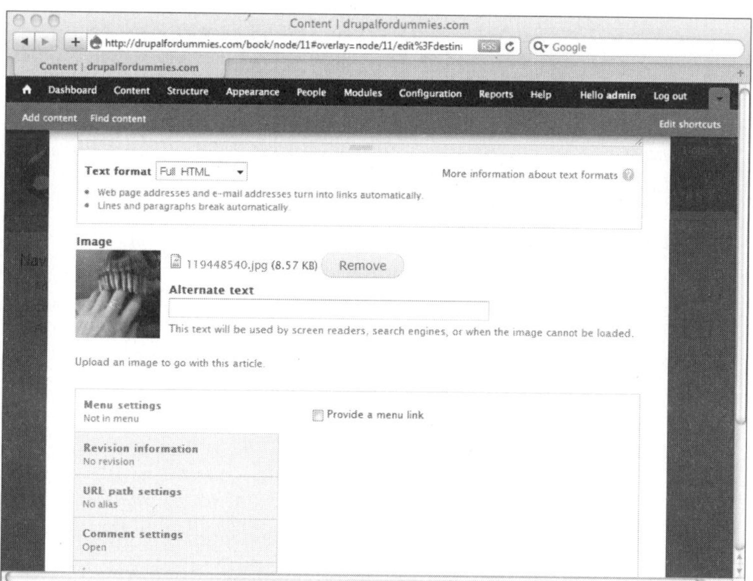

Figure 6-17: Thumbnail preview of uploaded image.

8. **Preview to see the image with your content, and then click Save to view it on your home page.**

   Figure 6-18 shows the image on the home page.

If you edit an existing post and use the Edit Summary text box, make sure you click Save to republish your content. You may have to reload the home page to see the changes.

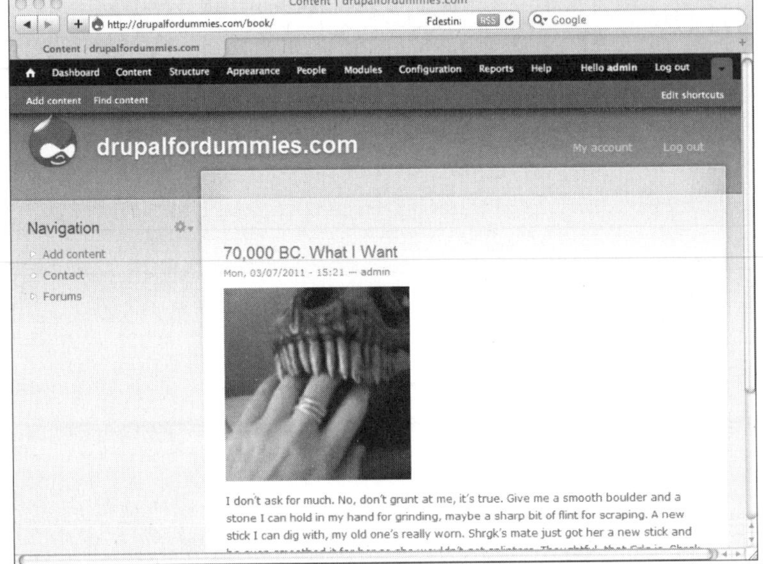

Figure 6-18: Home page with an article containing an HTML-coded image.

Chapter 7

Changing Themes

In This Chapter

- Changing themes
- Configuring themes

In Drupal, the look and layout of the site is dependent on a set of files collectively called a *theme*. A Drupal theme is a bit like a skin or a Windows desktop theme. In Drupal, a theme controls the appearance of the fonts, how many columns are displayed, background colors, and the appearance of logos, buttons, and menu items.

When you first install Drupal, its default theme is called Bartik. While it's a perfectly nice theme, you aren't obligated to continue using it, nor should you be. After all, who wants a website that's identical to everything else on the Internet? Not only is it good to know how to change themes, but it's also fun to see your site change appearance with just the click of a button. In this chapter, you see how to change from the default theme to another preinstalled theme. We show you where you can preview and download even more themes (for even more suggestions, see Chapter 17). You find out how to swap quickly between themes while you're developing your site. Finally, you discover how to configure your theme.

Changing Themes

Getting and changing Drupal themes is one of the simplest administration tasks in Drupal. To change the look of your site, you can choose to enable preinstalled themes by changing a simple administrative setting.

Enabling a theme

Before you can use a theme, you must *enable* it — that is, set it so you can turn it on easily whenever you want to use it.

In addition to the default theme, Bartik, Drupal provides you with a number of preinstalled themes. They are installed but not enabled.

To enable and view the other preinstalled themes, follow these steps:

1. **If you aren't logged in, log in to your site with your administrator username and password.**
2. **From the Dashboard menu bar, click Appearance.**

   The Appearance overlay opens, listing the themes available for use on your site.
3. **Click the Enable link next to each theme in the list you want to use.**

   The Bartik theme is enabled by default.
4. **To select a theme, click the Set Default link or the Enable and Set Default link next to one of the themes.**

   For example, if you select the Garland theme, your site looks something like Figure 7-1.
5. **Scroll to the bottom of the page and click the Save Configuration button.**

Close the Appearance overlay to see your site with the new default theme you selected.

Enabling a theme doesn't make it the *active* or *current* theme. A theme must be *both* enabled and selected as the default before it'll load on-screen as your website opens.

The default theme

By default, Drupal uses the Bartik theme. Take a moment to look at it. Every page on your site uses it.

The Bartik theme has two columns:

- The left column contains a form for logging in and user-specific site navigation. When you aren't logged in to the site, the login form appears in the left column.

  When you are logged in as the administrator, you see the administration Dashboard.
- The larger right column contains all the site content.

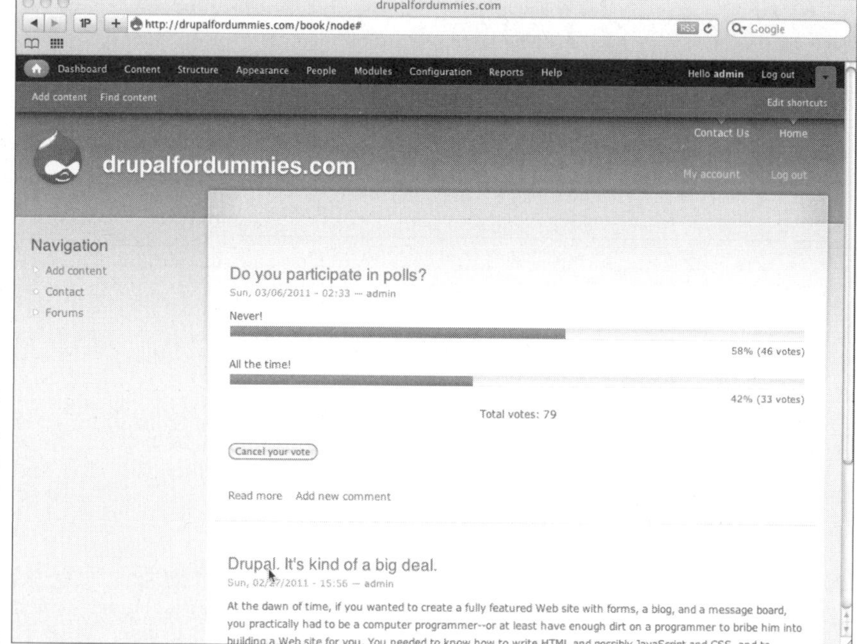

Figure 7-1: A site with the Garland theme enabled and set as default.

Setting an administration theme

While the theme you set as default is the active theme for the entire site, you can also set a different theme that appears only on the site administration pages when you're logged in as an administrator. This allows you to tinker with the site theme and layout while retaining the capability to reset the site theme should something go horribly wrong with the design. Trust us — having stuff that still works as it should when everything else goes wrong is a very, very good thing. You want this.

To set a different theme for the site administrator pages, follow these steps:

1. **From the Dashboard menu bar, click Appearance to open the Appearance overlay.**
2. **Scroll to the bottom of the overlay and locate a pane titled Administration Theme.**
3. **Choose your preferred theme from the drop-down list.**

   You can also enable this theme when you post or edit content by vselecting the Use Administration Theme for Content Editing check box.
4. **Click the Save Configuration button.**

You now have a theme selected that only appears when you're logged in as the site administrator.

Configuring Themes

Themes have settings associated with them. You can change settings for all themes or manage individual themes. A custom theme may have special settings that only apply to it. The following sections show you the general or global theme settings — and common settings for individual themes.

Global theme settings

To work with the global theme settings, log in as administrator and click (you guessed it) the Appearance link on the Dashboard menu bar. When Appearance overlay opens, click the Settings tab found at the top right of the overlay (see Figure 7-2). Notice the list of themes, as well as the words Global Settings. These are all the currently enabled themes. Global Settings will be opened by default.

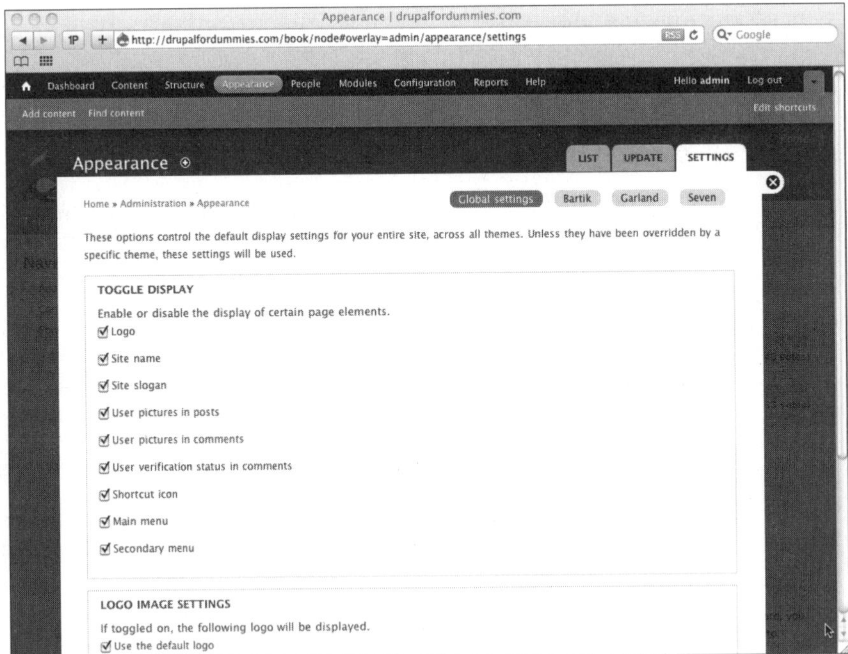

Figure 7-2: Specifying your global settings for themes.

The theme settings let you choose

- Elements, such as how many columns or rows, that will appear on the site.
- User information that appears in various content sections.

- Whether the default Drupal logo appears.

  You can select to use an alternative logo here: Just deselect the Use the Default Logo check box. Doing so opens the options that you use to link to an online image or upload an image file to your Drupal installation.
- A *favicon,* that small shortcut icon that appears in the URL address bar in users' browsers when they visit your site. The default favicon is a tiny Drupal logo.

Toggle display settings

Of all the settings you can control, by far the most powerful are the appearance or absence of the elements. Here's the common element settings that you can turn on and off and what they do:

- **Logo:** Simply enough, this check box controls whether your site has a logo. By default, it is the Drupal logo, unless you specify another one in the logo image settings section further down on this page.
- **Site Name:** Select this check box if you want the site name to appear.

  To set your site name, log in as administrator and on the Dashboard menu bar, click Configuration. When the overlay opens, click the Site Information pane. Whatever you type in the Site Name text box appears as the site name.
- **Site Slogan:** Also set on in the Configuration overlay's Site Information pane, the site slogan text is an optional field that shows up on all pages of your site, typically under the site name, depending on the theme.
- **User Pictures in Posts:** This controls whether the picture of the user who made a post appears in that post.
- **User Pictures in Comments:** If selected, the picture of each user appears next to any comments he makes. Both this setting and the User Pictures in Posts setting depend on whether you have allowed users to have picture support.
- **User Verification Status in Comments:** If selected, a registered site user's name and a link to his or her account will appear whenever the user makes a comment on site content. Additionally, when turned on, this setting will also turn on a mark indicating that anonymous site users leaving comments on the site have not been verified as registered users by the site administrator.
- **Shortcut Icon:** This check box controls whether visitors see a favicon in the address bar. By default, it is the Drupal logo, unless you specify another one in the shortcut icon settings section further down on this page.

- **Main Menu:** Deselecting the Main Menu check box hides your primary links from the user. In general, always leave this checked.
- **Secondary Links:** This is also one you typically leave selected. When it's deselected, the secondary links don't appear.

Logo image settings

Just under the Toggle display section are the logo image settings. To use the logo that comes with the default theme you're using, just leave the check box selected.

If you want to use your own logo, deselect the check box, then either

- Type a URL for your logo image in the Path to Custom Logo text box (for example, `http://yourwebsite.com/images/yourlogo.jpg`).
- Click the Browse button next to the Upload Logo Image text box to locate the file on your local machine. Doing so uploads the logo to the web server where Drupal is located.

When you use a URL or path to your logo, you may not have control over that image. If, for example, you're using an image from a web server you don't control, the owner can choose to delete that image at any time, leaving your site logo-less — and (worse) with a broken image. If, however, the logo resides on the same web server as your Drupal software, there's generally no reason why you shouldn't use a URL path.

Shortcut icon settings

Shortcut icons, also known as favicons, aren't the same as image files you may be familiar with. Icons are a specific type of image file that uses an `.ico` extension.

To create a shortcut or favicon, you need a special image editor. Most major image-creation programs don't offer support for this file type.

If you have a favicon, these settings work the same way as the logo image settings described earlier. Deselect the Favicon check box and either enter a path to your favicon or upload it.

If you don't have an icon and don't want to use the Drupal logo as your shortcut icon, deselect this check box. Icons aren't as popular as they once were, and many sites don't bother to use them at all.

Specific theme settings

If you aren't still looking at the Appearance overlay's Settings tab, return there via the Dashboard menu bar by clicking Appearance and then selecting the Settings tab. Notice the other enabled themes listed after the Global Settings link. Take a moment to click these and notice the settings you can control.

When you are on one of these theme-specific settings pages, you can control the options for just that theme. For example, if you click Bluemarine and deselect the Primary Links check box, the primary links don't show up when Bluemarine is the default theme.

If you let users override the default theme, they see their chosen theme displayed as you configure it here. Even if Bluemarine is not the default (for example) but they choose it, they see the Bluemarine theme, complete with your configuration settings for Bluemarine.

Chapter 8

Building Blocks and Managing Menus

In This Chapter

- Understanding regions, menus, and blocks
- Using regions
- Using blocks
- Creating and administering menus

Themes are customizable. A theme can be modified, for example, to put the primary menu on the left side of the web page rather than across the top. In this chapter, we extend the discussion of themes and take a closer look at how they can be manipulated from their default appearances. If you're a control freak, you're going to love this stuff.

We also discuss menus in more detail in this chapter — in particular, secondary menus and custom menus. (Chapter 5 covers primary menus.) Finally, we discuss creating a dynamic menu that changes when you post new content.

Understanding Blocks, Regions, and Menus

You need to understand three Drupal terms before diving in to this chapter:

- **Region:** A location on your web page. For example, the Header region is located at the top of all your site pages. It usually contains a logo and the title of your site.
- **Block:** A container that holds a chunk of code. Drupal organizes menus and other chunks of code into blocks. This makes them easier to move around as you redesign the look of your site.

- **Menu:** If you've spent any amount of time on the Internet, you probably have a pretty good idea of what a menu is: a set of links to web pages. In Drupal, that basically describes a menu — but those links can also point to *nodes* (a fancy word for Drupal content) such as articles and basic pages. When a link to an article or basic page node is chosen from a menu, a web page opens with the article or basic page node content presented as though it were an actual web page.

Think of it this way — *menus* are stored in *blocks,* and blocks are placed into specific *regions* on your website.

Using Regions

To see where regions are located, look at Figure 8-1. You can see the *Header, Left Sidebar*, and *Right Sidebar* regions.

The regions your site has depend on which theme you use. Figure 8-1 is using the Garland theme. In the Garland theme, a Header region is at the very top of each page of your Drupal site. The Left Sidebar region is on the left and contains the administrative menu functions as well as the login. The Right Sidebar is empty.

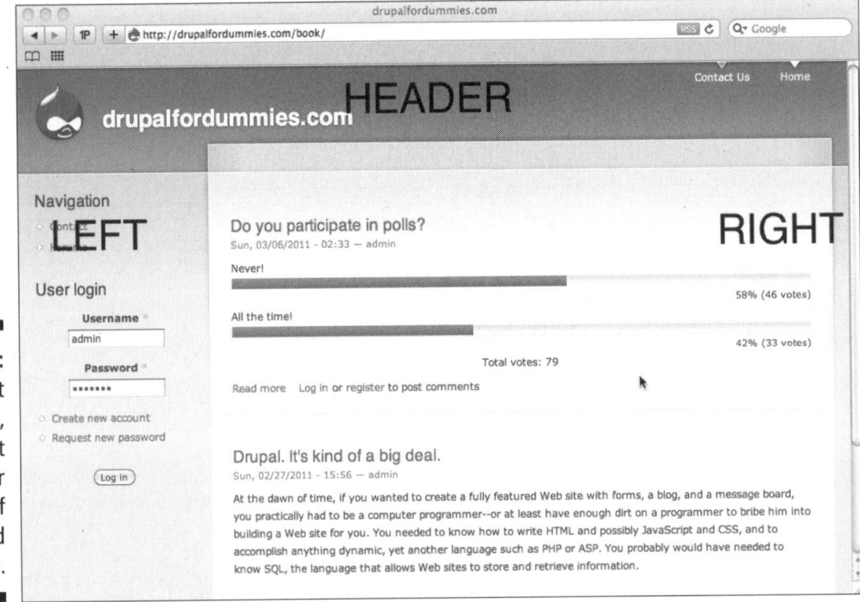

Figure 8-1: Header, Left Sidebar, and Right Sidebar regions of the Garland theme.

The Garland theme has two more regions — the Content region and the Footer region — visible when you scroll to the bottom of the web page, as shown in Figure 8-2.

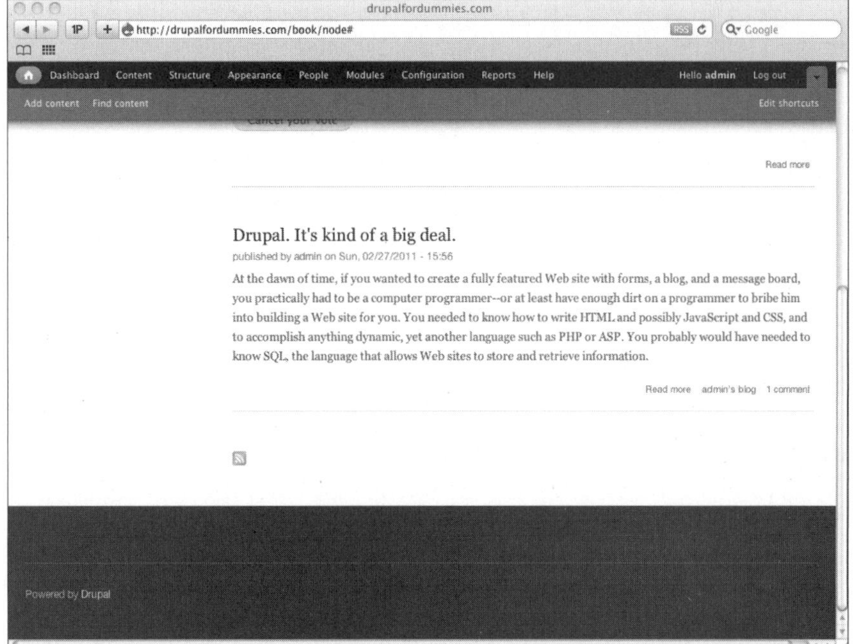

Figure 8-2: Content and Footer regions of the Bartik theme.

The Content region is where articles and basic pages appear. The Footer contains a default *Powered by Drupal* link and any other footer content you add.

In Chapter 3, we configure the Site Configuration➪Site Information page. The *drupalfordummies.com* name we set in the Site information page appears in the Header region in Figure 8-1.

Understanding how themes work with regions

The Bartik theme has 17 regions: Header, Help, Footer, Page Top, Page Bottom, Highlighted, Featured, Content, Sidebar First, Sidebar Second, Tyiptych First, Triptych Middle, Triptych Last, Footer First Column, Footer Second Column, Footer Third Column, Footer Fourth Column, and (finally!) just plain Footer. To keep things interesting, not all themes have the same number of regions. Some have fewer than you see in Bartik; some have many more.

To see which regions your current theme has, follow these steps:

1. **Log in as administrator.**
2. **From the Dashboard menu bar, click Structure.**
3. **Click the Blocks link.**

   When the overlay opens, look at the top right of the page, and you'll see tabs for all of the themes you have installed and enabled on your Drupal site.
4. **Click the tab of the theme for which you want to see the regions.**

   For example, we clicked the Bartik tab. The Bartik blocks page opens.
5. **Click the Demonstrate Block Regions (Bartik) link.**

For your efforts, you are rewarded with a regions map of your theme, illustrating all of the places you could possibly jam a block into, as shown in Figure 8-3. Pretty snazzy, huh? You can look into the regions of all the installed templates on your site the same way — just click the tab for the template and then click the Demonstrate Blog Regions *(Theme)* link.

At this point, it's a good idea to enable a few different themes. To find out how, refer to Chapter 7.

Figure 8-3: Block regions of the Bartik theme.

Programmers who build Drupal themes may create additional regions beyond those we cover here. If you use a custom Drupal theme, you may have more or fewer regions to work with.

Exploring the regions

Each of the common theme regions controls a different section of each page on your site.

The following figures use the Garland theme because it contains all five regions: Left Sidebar, Right Sidebar, Header, Content, and Footer.

Header

The Header, shown in Figure 8-4, contains the site logo and the site title.

Figure 8-4: The Header region of the Garland theme.

In the Garland theme, the Header region also contains the primary menu. You can tell that the primary menu is in the Header because the Contact Us link is present. Other themes may place the primary menu in a different region.

Content

The Content region is in the middle of the page, just below the Header (see Figure 8-5). It displays Story and Article content created by you and other authorized site users.

The most central region in a theme is usually Content. As you no doubt guessed, it's where you put the main content on each page of the site.

Footer

The region at the very bottom of the website is the Footer (see Figure 8-6).

The Footer usually contains a copyright statement. Sometimes it will contain a small Drupal logo or link and RSS feed logo.

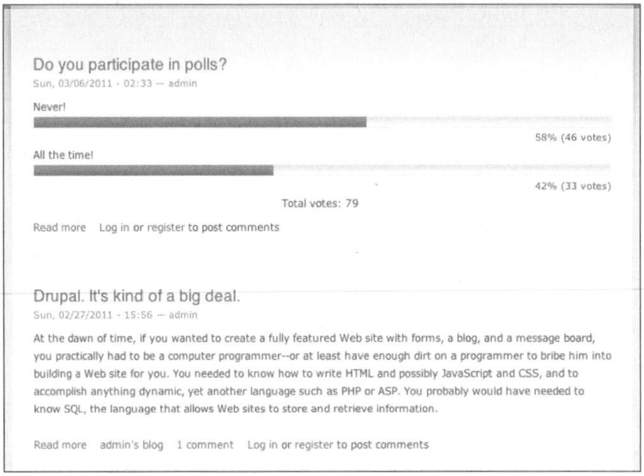

Do you participate in polls?
Sun, 03/06/2011 - 02:33 — admin
Never!
58% (46 votes)
All the time!
42% (33 votes)
Total votes: 79
Read more Log in or register to post comments

Drupal. It's kind of a big deal.
Sun, 02/27/2011 - 15:56 — admin
At the dawn of time, if you wanted to create a fully featured Web site with forms, a blog, and a message board, you practically had to be a computer programmer--or at least have enough dirt on a programmer to bribe him into building a Web site for you. You needed to know how to write HTML and possibly JavaScript and CSS, and to accomplish anything dynamic, yet another language such as PHP or ASP. You probably would have needed to know SQL, the language that allows Web sites to store and retrieve information.
Read more admin's blog 1 comment Log in or register to post comments

Figure 8-5: The Content region of the Garland theme.

Powered by Drupal

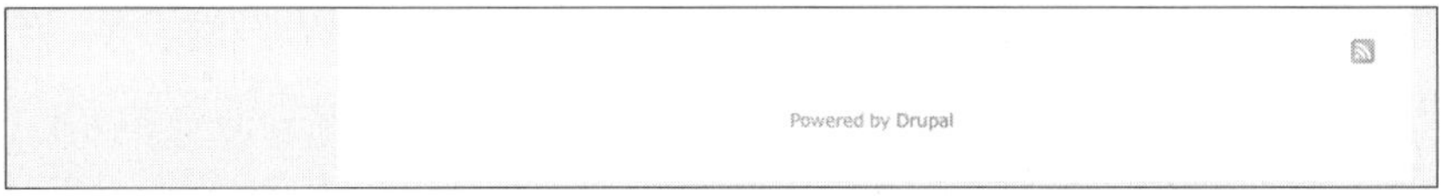

Figure 8-6: The Footer region of the Garland theme.

Left Sidebar

In this theme, the user login module appears in the Left Sidebar (see Figure 8-7).

The username of the logged-in user is displayed at the top of the Left sidebar region. If the site visitor isn't logged in, the login form is displayed in this region.

Right Sidebar

In Garland, the Right Sidebar is empty. It serves as a space between the Content region and the right side of the browser window. Normally, should a region be left empty, it will not be visible.

Configuring regions

A useful feature of most Drupal themes is the capability to customize where various page elements (such as blocks containing navigation) appear on the page. For example, you can move the User login from the Left Sidebar region to the Right Sidebar region. To do so, follow these steps:

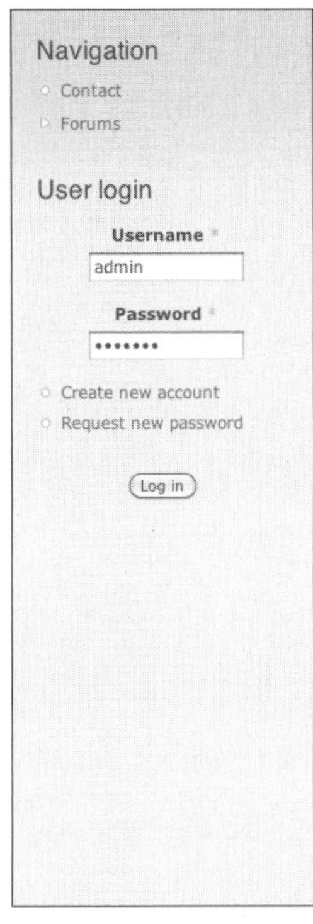

Figure 8-7: The Left Sidebar region of the Garland theme.

1. **Log in as Administrator.**
2. **Change to the Garland theme by clicking Appearance on the Dashboard menu bar.**

   You see the Appearance overlay open.
3. **Scroll to Garland and click the Set Default link. (See Figure 8-8.)**
4. **Click the Save Configuration button.**
5. **From the Dashboard menu bar, choose Structure⇨Blocks.**

   You see the Block configuration page (see Figure 8-9).

   This page allows you to move blocks from one region to another. Because the User login form is contained in a block, when you move that particular block to another region, the User Login form moves.
6. **Look at the table on this page and locate the block you want to move. Click the drop-down list next to it and choose another region.**

   For example, we selected Right Sidebar from the User Login drop-down list. The User Login label moves down to the Right Sidebar section of the table.

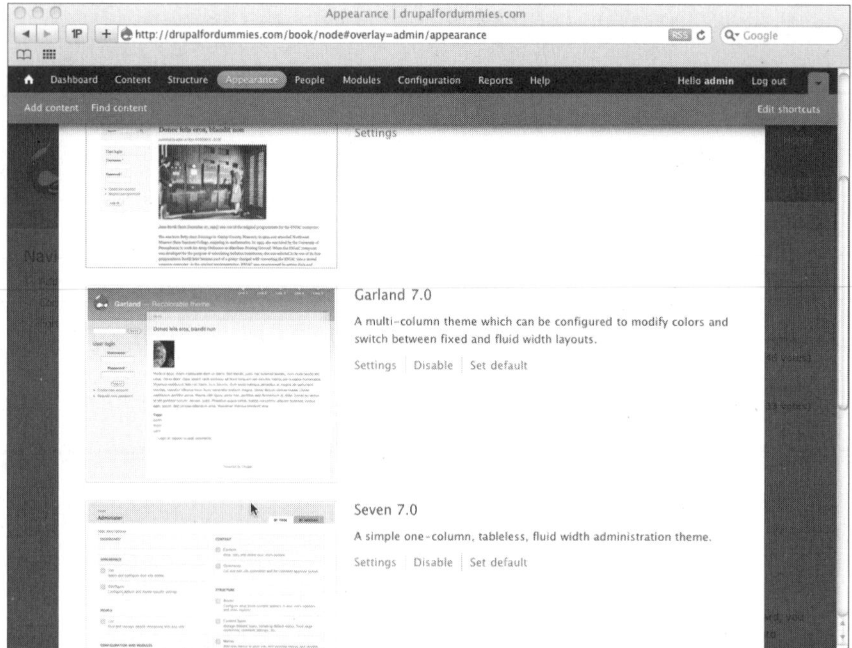

Figure 8-8: The Garland theme in the Appearance overlay.

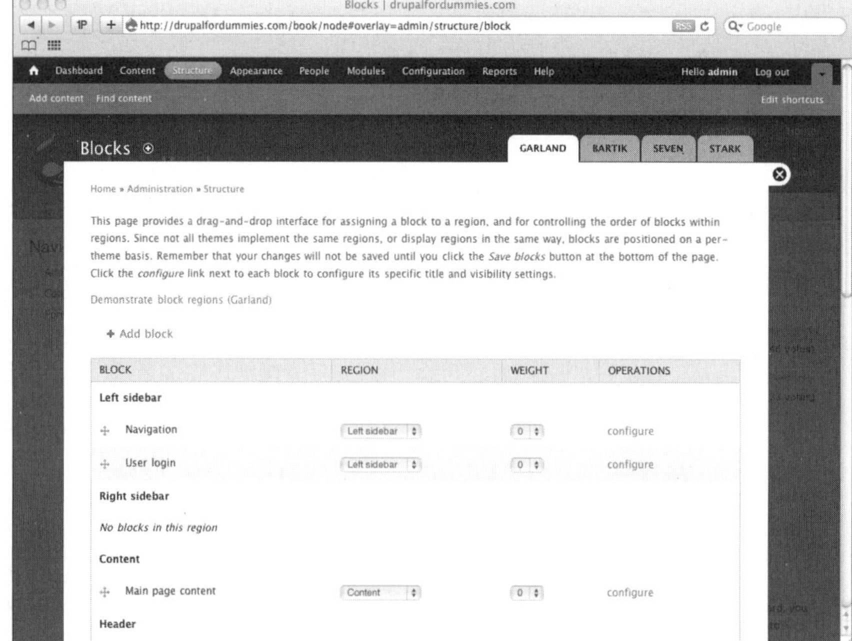

Figure 8-9: The Block configuration page for the Garland theme.

You can also simply grab and drag the cross icon down into another section of the table.

7. **Scroll down and click Save Blocks.**

In our example, the login form now appears in the Right Sidebar region. To see your changes, log out of the site and then browse to the home page. To change it back, log in as administrator, return to the Block configuration page, and drag the User Login back up into the Left Sidebar section. Easy like pancakes!

See the tabs for your other enabled themes near the top of this page? If you click one of the other themes and move blocks around, you see those changes reflected on the website only when you make that theme the default. This means you can change the block settings without changing themes. Because this page changes your theme *temporarily* when you click a different theme, you can preview how the page will look when you move blocks. That's why the Blocks configuration page displays the label for each region.

You move any of the built-in blocks in a given theme from one region to any other in the same way — by using the drop-down list or dragging the block into the region where you want it.

In the Block configuration page, the order of blocks matters. Suppose you have three blocks under the Left Sidebar region. The order they're in will be the order in which they appear on all your web pages. You can order the blocks within a region by dragging them above or below other blocks in the same region. For example, if you want the User Login block to appear as the bottom item in the Right Sidebar region, drag it under any other blocks in the list.

Administering Blocks

At this point, you have seen the User login block and moved it, but that isn't the only block you can move. All the preinstalled themes have the same nine other built-in blocks we describe below. Also, you can create your own blocks and move them to any region you want. This can come in handy for posting images to the Right Sidebar, for example.

Using the built-in blocks

Standard built-in blocks appear in all of the preinstalled Drupal themes. You can see a few of them in Figure 8-10, where we've opened the Bartik theme's Blocks administration overlay.

The default built-in blocks are

- **Navigation:** The Navigation block contains the administrator links when you are logged in as administrator, and the My Account and Log Out links for logged-in users. It also displays the username (see Figure 8-11).
- **User Login:** This block contains the User Login form. It's only visible when a visitor to the site has not yet logged in; if a visitor is logged in, the block is not visible. This block also contains Create New Account and Request New Password links (see Figure 8-12).
- **Powered by Drupal:** This little block, shown in Figure 8-13, contains a link to Drupal.org when you click it.

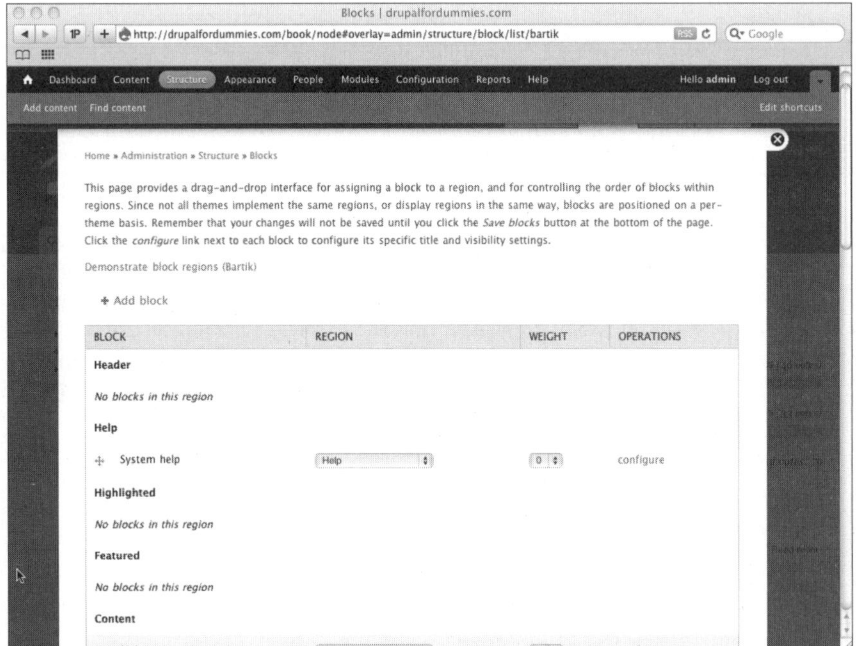

Figure 8-10: The built-in blocks shown with the Bartik theme.

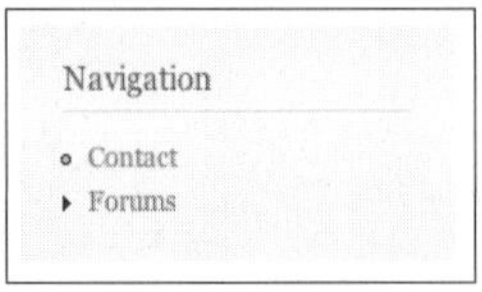

Navigation

- Contact
- Forums

Figure 8-11: The Navigation block.

Figure 8-12: The User login block.

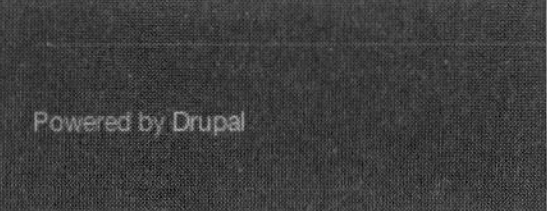

Figure 8-13: Powered by Drupal block.

- **System Help:** This block contains a search text box that provides users with a means for tracking down tips on using Drupal.
- **Main Page Content:** As its name suggests, this block displays the main or central content of a given page.
- **Search Form:** The search form block is for — you guessed it — entering site search queries for site-specific content.

In most themes, the following blocks are disabled by default (see Figure 8-14):

- **Active Forum Topics:** This block becomes available only if the Forum module is enabled.
- **Management:** This block contains all of the links already available via the Drupal Management menu.
- **Most Recent Poll:** This block is designed to inform site visitors of the most recent poll posted on your site. This block becomes available only if the Poll module is enabled.
- **Main Menu:** When enabled, this block offers users another access point to the links usually located at the top of your site.
- **New Forum Topic:** When enabled, this block will alert users to new forum topics. This block becomes available only if the Forum module is enabled.
- **Recent Blog Posts:** This block displays recent user blog posts on your site. This block becomes available only if the Blog module is enabled.

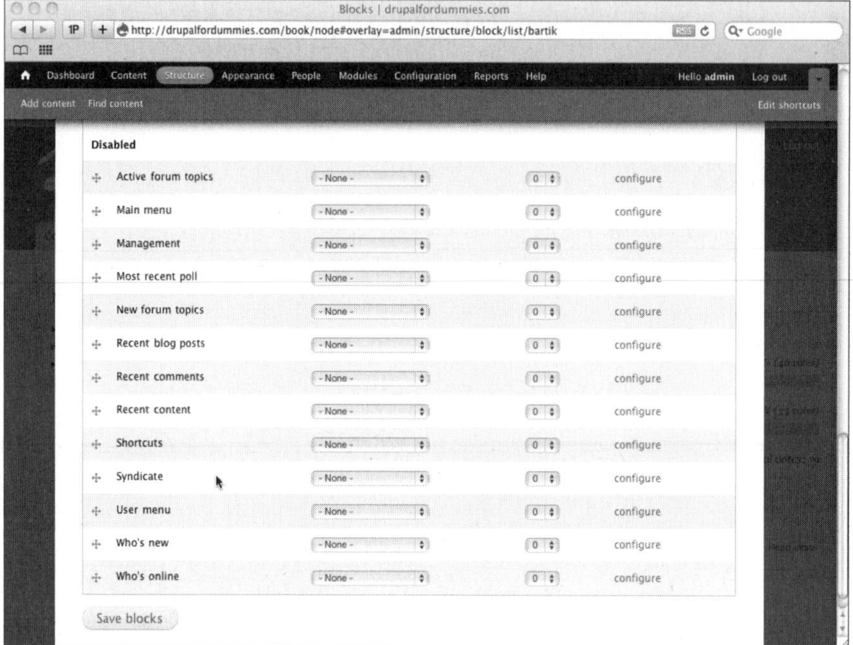

Figure 8-14: Bartik's disabled blocks.

- **Recent Comments:** This block provides site visitors with an overview of recent comments posted to your site.
- **Recent Content:** This block provides site visitors with an overview of content posted to your site.
- **Shortcuts:** This block lists links to internal and external links, allowing your visitors to navigate easily to areas of interest on your site and elsewhere on the Internet.
- **Syndicate:** This block adds a logo and a link to the XML version of your site pages, which allows users to grab and use the syndicated content from your site. We discuss this in detail later in the book in Chapter 14.
- **User Menu:** This displays a number of options for registered site users, offering items like account access and if enabled, the capability to manage their account settings.
- **Who's New:** This displays usernames and links to profiles of the newest registered users of the site.
- **Who's Online:** Shows a summary of how many people are currently using the site, divided into registered users and people who aren't logged in. It also shows a list of the registered users and links to their profiles.

Creating custom blocks

You can create your own blocks and put content in them. For example, using a bit of HTML wizardry, you can create a block that provides a link to a Twitter account.

Log in as an administrator, and then follow these steps to create a custom block and add content to it:

1. **Choose Structure⇨Blocks.**

   You see the Block configuration page, as shown in Figure 8-10.

2. **Click the Add Block link near the top of the Blocks overlay.**

   The Add Block overlay appears, as shown in Figure 8-15.

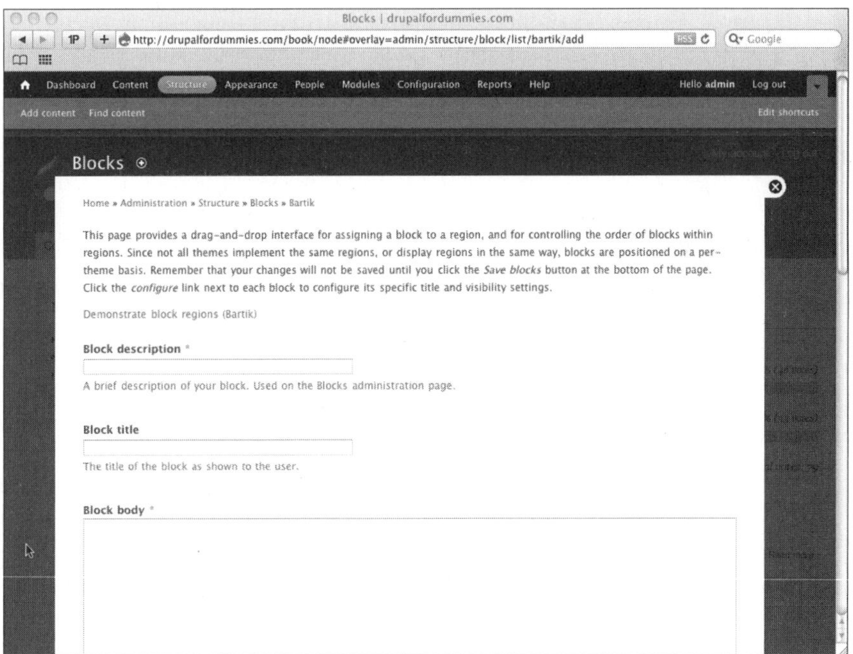

Figure 8-15: The Add block form.

3. **In the Block Description text box, enter a meaningful description.**

   For example, we enter the description **Twitter**. Only you will see the description. It is used on the List tab of the Block configuration page where you drag your custom block to the region where you want it to appear.

4. **(Optional) Enter a title in the Block Title text box.**

   The Title shows up on all your pages just above whatever content you put in the body. Here's where we enter the title **Follow us on Twitter.**

5. **In the Block Body area, enter any content you want for the body.**

   The same rules apply here as with other types of content, such as articles and basic pages. For this example, you can enter the HTML code to display a brief message and Twitter address. If you want to, you could also enter text here.

6. **If you used any HTML code in your body content, click the Input Format link and select the appropriate setting.**

7. **Click the Save Block button.**

   Your new content block has been created, as you see as soon as the Block overlay opens again (see Figure 8-16).

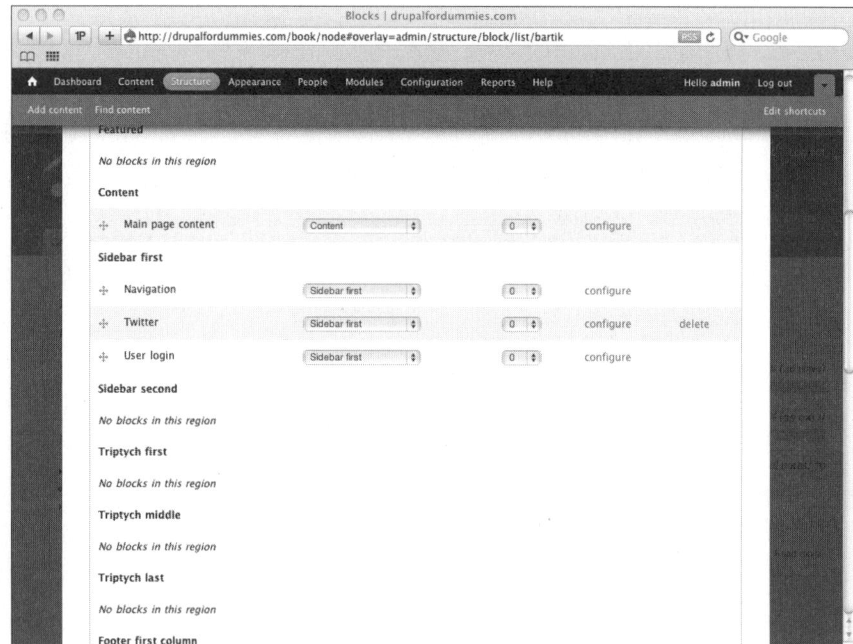

Figure 8-16: Your new custom block now appears in the list of blocks.

8. **Drag your new block to the region of your choice and click Save Blocks.**

Don't forget that the order of blocks in each region also matters.

Editing and deleting custom blocks

Our new block is listed in the Blocks overlay under the List tab, as shown in Figure 8-16. To edit a custom block, click the Configure link. Doing so opens the same form as the Add Block link; your content is visible and editable.

If you want to delete your custom block, click the Delete link next to it.

Changing block visibility settings

When you create a custom block, there are visibility settings at the bottom of the Add Block form. These settings can also be applied to the pre-built blocks. To see them, click the Configure link next to a block. You see the block visibility settings, as shown in Figure 8-17.

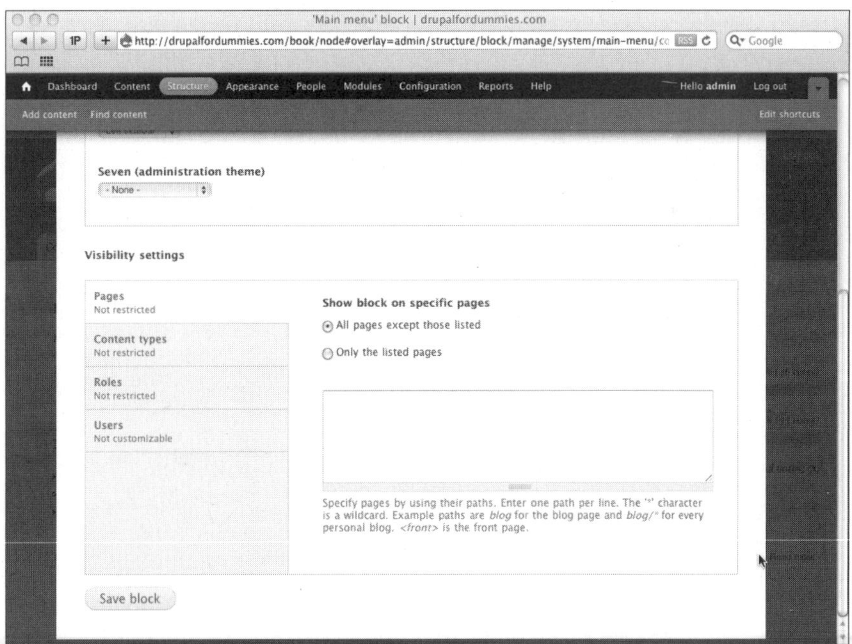

Figure 8-17: Block visibility settings.

The visibility sections are:

- **Pages:** This first option allows you to display your block on specific pages of your site. It requires you to enter the path to the pages on which you do or do not want the content to appear.

Before you can enter paths in here, you need more pages on your site. (We discuss how to add additional pages to your site in Chapter 5.)

- **Content Types:** This option allows you to display your block on pages that display information of a certain type: Article, Basic Page, Blog Entry, Forum Topic, or Poll.
- **Roles:** If you want to allow only registered users to see your block, this is where you control that. Leave everything deselected if you want both signed-in and guest users to see your block.
- **Users:** These settings control whether registered users can choose to hide a block from view when they visit pages on your site. The first option gives them no control. The second lets them hide the block, but it is visible at first. The third lets them hide the block but lets them show it if they wish. If you let them control the visibility, a check box with the block name will appear on their My Account⇨Edit page.

Editing pre-built blocks

There aren't many things you can change about Drupal's pre-built blocks. If you click the Configure link next to any of them, you will see a form that allows you to enter a title for the block. Doing so will override any title the block currently uses. All of them also provide you with the visibility options.

Seven of the pre-built blocks have many other options, and none of them are very exciting:

- **Active Forum Topics:** This option lets you control how many active forum topics are listed in this block.
- **New Forum Topics:** This option lets you control how many new forum threads appear in the New Forum Topics list.
- **Recent Blog Posts:** This option lets you control how many recent blog posts appear in the Recent Blog Posts list.
- **Recent Comments:** This option lets you control how many comments by recent site users appear in the Recent Comments list.
- **Recent Content:** This option lets you control how many recent content items appear the Recent Content list.
- **Who's New:** This option lets you control how many users' names appear in the Who's New list (see Figure 8-18).
- **Who's Online:** You can control which users' names appear in this block based on how long it's been since they last clicked a link on your site. This option also controls how many users to list (see Figure 8-19).

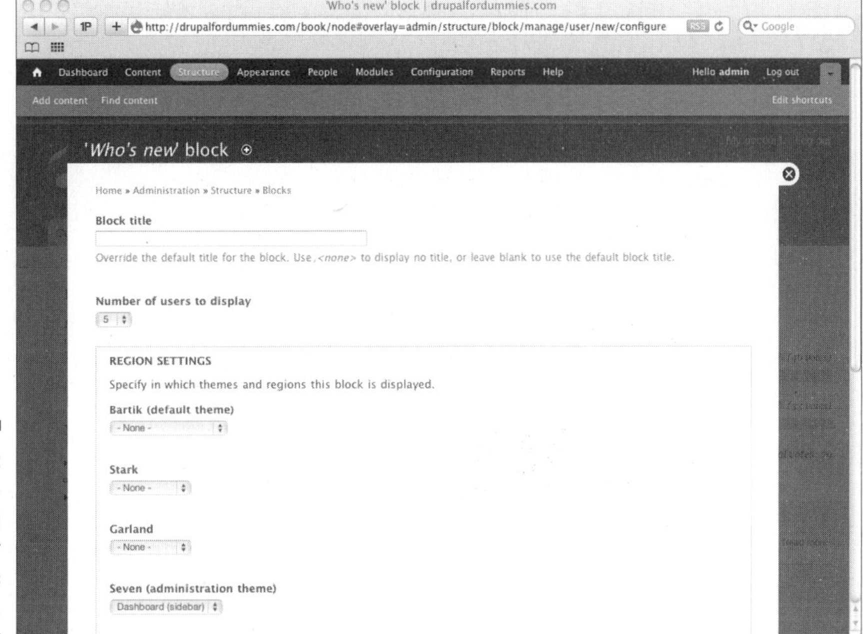

Figure 8-18: Special configuration options for the Who's new block.

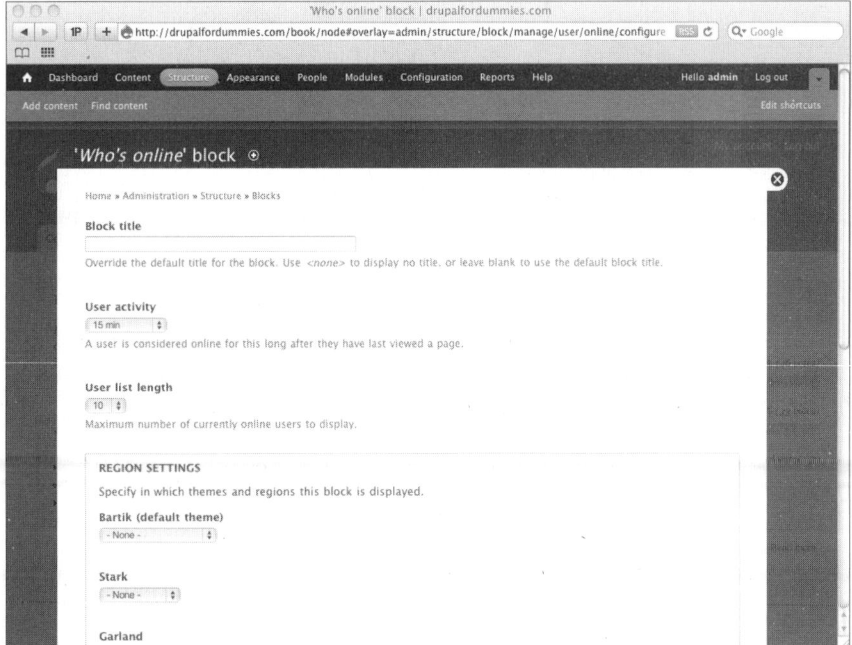

Figure 8-19: Special configuration options for the Who's online block.

Managing Menus

Drupal offers you four menus you don't have to create: the Main menu, Management menu, Navigation menu, and the User menu (see Figure 8-20).

- **Main menu:** On many sites, the main menu showcases links to significant content, and is often located in the top navigation bar.
- **Management menu:** This menu contains links to the site's administration pages and can only be utilized by users' administrative permissions.
- **Navigation menu:** This is the menu used on many sites to show links for site visitors. Some modules add links to this menu automatically.
- **User menu:** The User menu shows links related to a registered user's account, as well as the Log Out link.

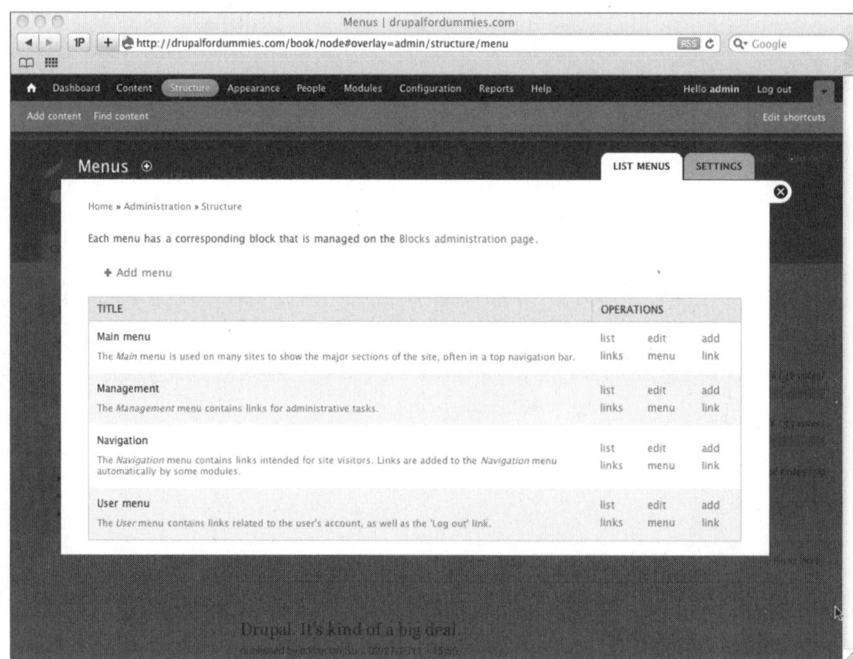

Figure 8-20: The four Drupal menus.

At this point, you know how to put a page node in the Main menu when you create or edit it. Our Contact Us page is in this menu, and a link to it appears on every page of our site. But instead of going through the process of editing a page to add it to the Main menu, you can add more links directly. To work with menus directly, choose Structure⇨Menus from the Dashboard menu bar. You see the options shown in Figure 8-20. There are two tabs on this page:

- **List menus** lists all the menus.

  From here you can edit an existing menu or create a custom menu.
- **Settings** controls the overall structure of your menus.

It's best not to make any changes to the Navigation menu. We're not saying that the Earth will careen out of orbit into the sun or anything if you do, but if you change the Navigation menu, you run the risk of being unable to get to particular sections of your site — such as the My Account link, Log Out link, or any administrative functions.

Adding an item to a menu

To add an item to a menu, follow these steps:

1. **From the Dashboard menu bar, choose Structure⇨Menus.**
2. **Click List Links in the row of the menu to which you want to add an item.**

   For our example, we click List Links in the Main Menu row. You see a list of links in the menu. In our case, we only see the Home and Contact Us links (see Figure 8-21).

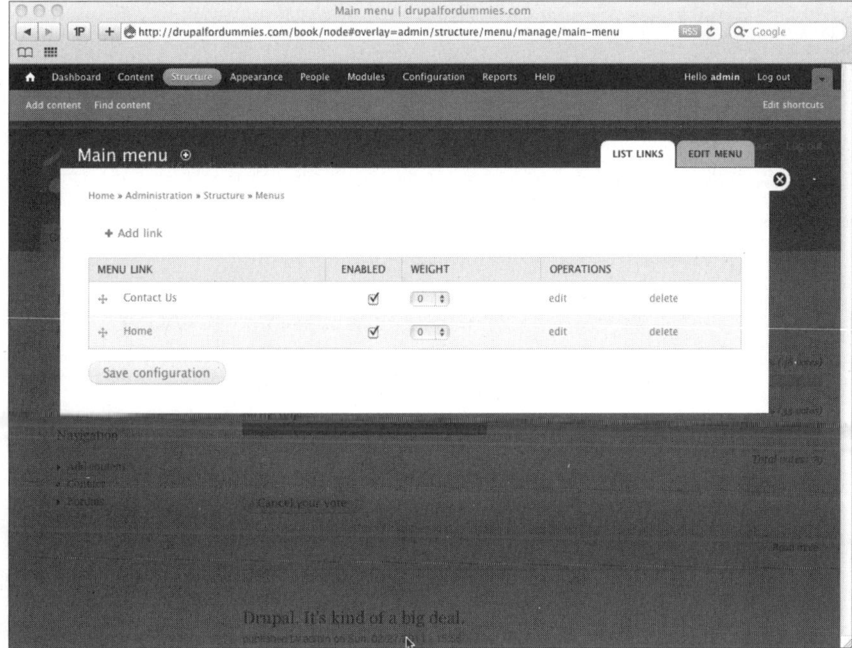

Figure 8-21: The list of links in the Main menu.

3. **Click the Add Link icon.**

   You see the Add Item form (see Figure 8-22).

4. **In the Menu Link Title text box, enter the text you want used for the link.**

   For example, you could type something like **About Us** or **Products**.

5. **Enter the URL or path to your basic page or article in the Path text box.**

   You can also use external links (for example, `www.dummies.com`).

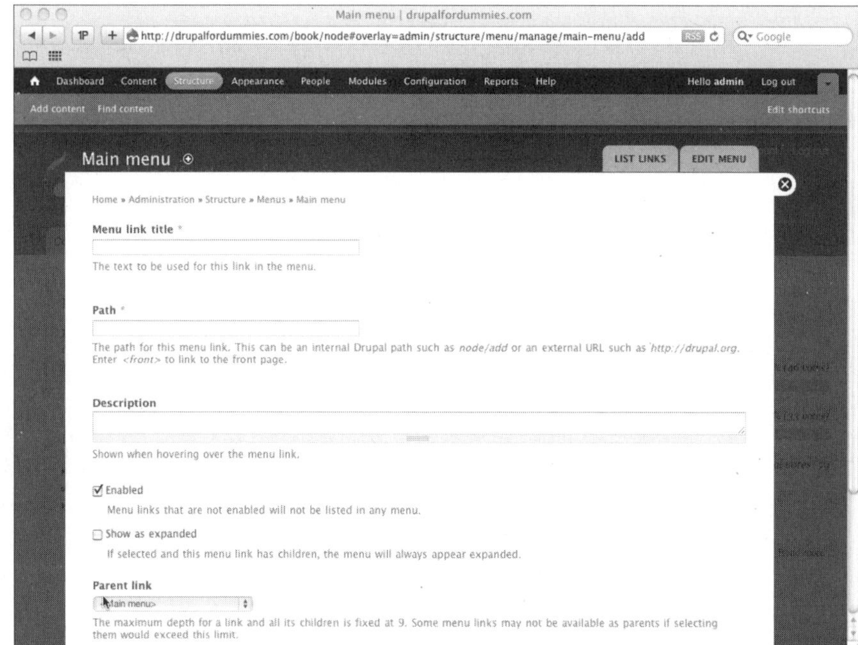

Figure 8-22: The Add Item page to create a new menu link.

To get the correct URL for a basic page or article node, follow these steps:

a. Open your site in another browser window.

b. From the Dashboard menu bar, click Content.

c. Locate the article or basic page to which you want to link and click its title.

d. Click in the address bar of your browser and copy the URL to that page by pressing Ctrl+C or ⌘+C.

The URL will look something like `http://drupalfordummies.com/node/10`. This is what you paste into the Path text box.

6. **(Optional) Enter a description of the page you're linking in the Description text box.**

   This description will appear when a mouse cursor passes over the link.

7. **(Optional) If you want to hide the link temporarily, deselect the Enabled check box.**

8. **For now, leave Show as Expanded, Parent Item, and Weight settings as they are.**

   You use these when you create child links.

9. **Click Save.**

   You return to the List Items form.

You should already see your new Main menu item on your pages.

You can change the order of the Main menu items by dragging them up or down in the list on the List items page.

Editing and deleting links

Just as with the block menu, you have to delete links on the List Links page. To edit a link, click the Edit link. You are presented with the same form you used to create the link.

Adding a menu

Drupal allows you to create custom menus. They are put in blocks automatically; you can move those blocks to various regions on the site in the same way as you would a custom block.

To create a new menu, follow these steps:

1. **From the Dashboard menu bar, choose Structure⇨Menus.**

2. **Click the Add Menu icon.**

   You see the form shown in Figure 8-23.

3. **Enter a title for your menu in the Title text box.**

   Type something like **Product links** or **My links**. This title will appear in the same listings with Main menu, Navigation menu, and the rest of the menus that came with your Drupal installation by default (or were created by little old you).

4. **(Optional) Enter a description of your menu in the Description text box.**

   This is a good idea if anyone else will be working on your site with administrative privileges.

5. **Click Save.**

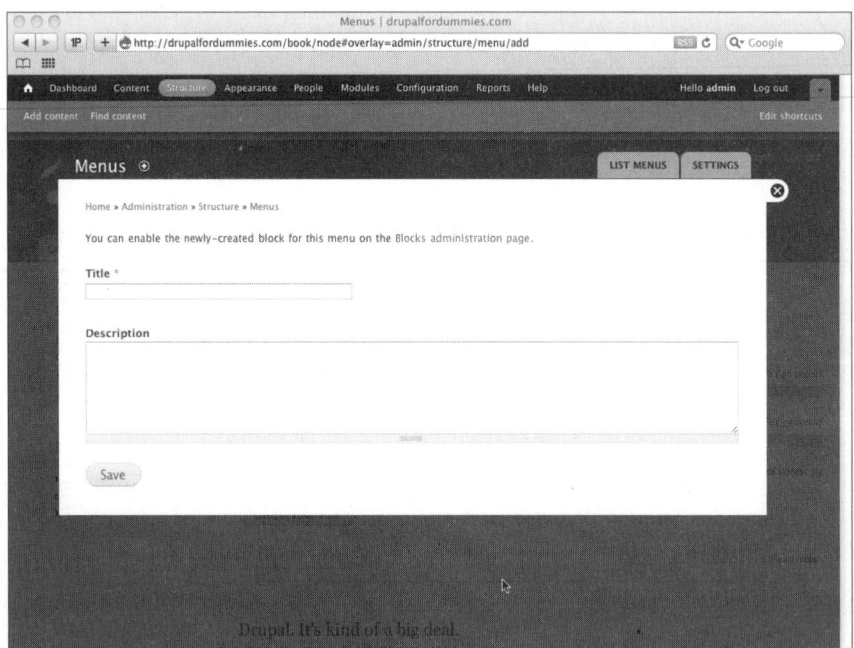

Figure 8-23: The Add menu form.

In Drupal, a menu exists inside a block. Before your new menu can be seen on your site, you have to enable its block via the Blocks administration page.

You add links to your menu in exactly the same way you add them to the Primary menu, as described earlier in the chapter.

With custom menus and Block Visibility settings, you can create a custom page that contains and shows its own content and menu. Create as many custom blocks and menus as you need, put them in the Content region, and make them visible only on the necessary page. It's a bit of work, but it allows you increased control over your page than just a single article or basic page node can have.

Chapter 9

Using Modules to Create a Site with a Blog and Forum

In This Chapter

- Using modules
- Building blogs
- Managing forums
- Moderating comments

A Drupal *module* is a plug-in program that extends Drupal's core functionality. Think of a module as an add-on application that allows Drupal to do more things; for example, the blog and forum we talk about in this chapter are modules. Drupal comes with a large number of modules preinstalled, but there are many more available online. As with new themes, new modules have to be downloaded, placed in a directory on your web server, and then enabled.

In this chapter, you take a close look at modules. You see how to build a site complete with a blog and a forum. Along the way, you discover how to upload and activate modules and where to find new ones.

Understanding Modules

You may not realize it, but you're already using modules. Drupal itself is composed of a set of modules, known as the *Core modules*. To see what we mean, log in as an administrator and choose Modules from the Dashboard menu bar (see Figure 9-1).

Modules preinstalled with Drupal are called Core modules. The two types of Core modules are

- **Optional:** These are modules you don't have to enable for Drupal to run, but they are also some of the most useful ones. A few of them are enabled by default (so your "option" is to turn them off or leave them on).

- **Required:** As you might guess, these modules have to be enabled for Drupal to run. They're the heart and soul of Drupal. You can't disable or delete them.

The easiest way to tell which module is required and which is optional is to look at the check box next to the title of each module that was installed with Drupal. An optional module may appear checked or unchecked, depending on whether you wanted that module enabled or disabled. A required module will always be checked and cannot be altered — it's enabled by default.

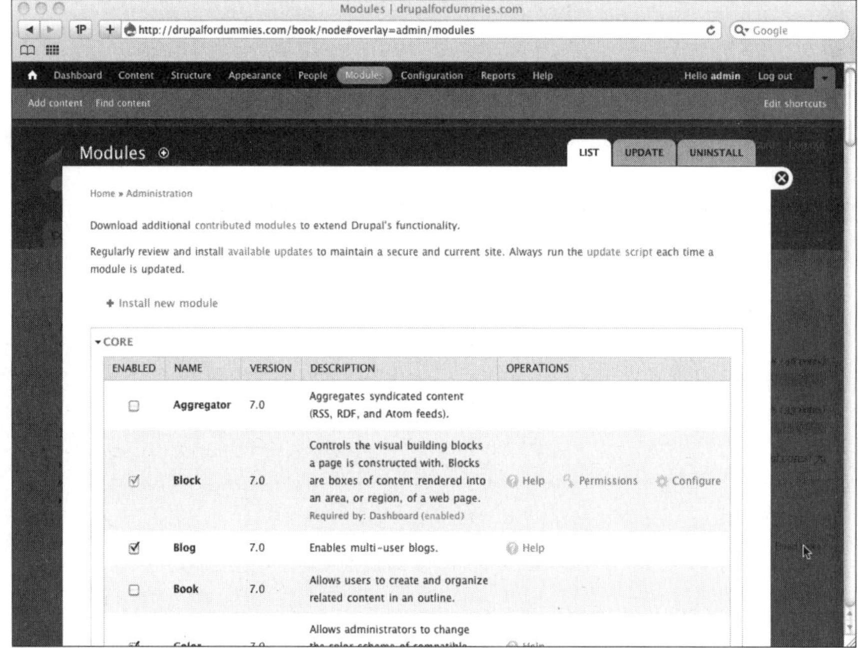

Figure 9-1: The Modules menu displays all the preinstalled modules.

Understanding the required modules

Take a look at the Modules list and notice the required Core modules. There are eleven of them:

- **Block:** These modules are chunks of code that hold content and menus; you can place them in the regions around the main content area. (In Chapter 8, we show you how to add and remove blocks from the various regions.) The regions displayed in your site depend on the theme you're using; they control where you can place Block modules.
- **Comment:** This module allows users to comment on and discuss the content published to your site.

- **Field:** The Field module is responsible for storing, loading, editing, and rendering field data. This module makes it possible for Drupal to display fields that the user can edit and interact with.
- **Field SQL Storage:** This module stores the data captured by the fields that the user accesses via the Field module.
- **Filter:** Before Drupal displays content on your site, it removes and modifies certain kinds of code or content that could allow your site to be compromised by hackers. The Filter module scans and removes potentially harmful content. It also turns web-page addresses into clickable links.
- **Node:** Content types, such as a story, page, poll, or blog post, are organized into *nodes,* discrete units that can be viewed either alone on a single page or on the same page with other nodes. This module is responsible for managing nodes.
- **Options:** This module defines the check box, selection, drop-down menus, and other input methods for the Field module.
- **System:** This module manages all the important site configuration settings that you, as the administrator, control.
- **Taxonomy:** Simply put, the Taxonomy module allows you to tag and classify your Drupal site's content.
- **Text:** The Text module defines how text behaves on your Drupal site. This module works in conjunction with the Field module.
- **User:** If you couldn't log on to your website as the administrator to manage it, your site wouldn't be very useful. The User module contains the code that allows users to log in, the administrator to set up and manage accounts, and unregistered users to request accounts.

Some of the required modules allow the administrator to modify specific settings.

Block module

In Chapter 8, we show you how to use the Block module settings to control in which regions Drupal displays various content. It's worth taking another look at the Block module interface. There are two ways to access the Block module interface:

- From the Dashboard menu bar, you can choose Structure⇒Blocks.
- From the Dashboard menu bar, you choose Modules. Then you scroll down until you find the Blocks column and click Configure, as shown in Figure 9-2.

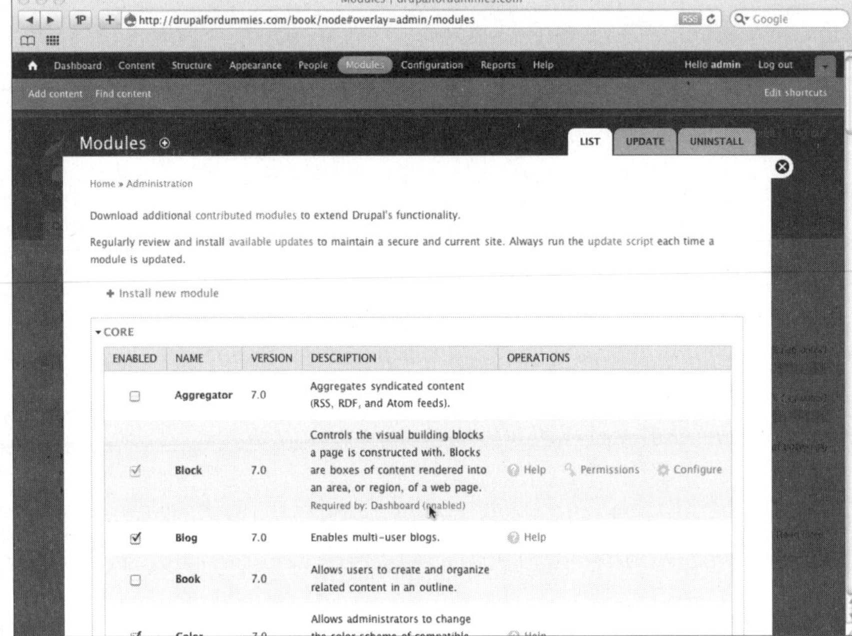

Figure 9-2: The Blocks module as seen in the Modules overlay.

If you access Blocks via the Modules overlay, click the Help link in the Block column. This displays some useful rules that may come in handy when you're working with blocks.

Filter module

The Filter module is responsible for three types of content filtering:

- **Filtered HTML:** This filter removes HTML code when you choose to restrict certain HTML tags. The filter also attempts to find and correct faulty code. For example, if the HTML is missing a close-table tag, `</table>`, this filter adds it. The HTML corrector applies only when HTML code is allowed. You can also restrict all HTML tags and this filter will remove them.

  By default, Drupal filters out potentially harmful content. This includes JavaScript events, JavaScript URLs, and CSS styles. Even when you allow HTML, this kind of coding will be removed. Drupal also removes PHP scripts.

- **Full HTML:** This filter converts carriage returns and line feeds into HTML tags.

Any time you create text content, Drupal scans it and looks for carriage returns or line breaks. When you type text into a text box to create a story or posting, the Filter module converts your carriage returns and line breaks into HTML style line breaks. Without this, your carriage returns won't show up in the browser when you publish your story. This all happens behind the scenes, so you can type away without worrying about the HTML side of things.

- **URL Filter:** When you're creating content and you type a URL (for example, `www.drupalfordummies.com`), after you publish it, Drupal turns it into a clickable link. This also applies to `mailto` links (for example, `<mailto://lynnbeighley@gmail.com>`).

Node module

Because nodes contain every bit of the content on your site, the Node module controls how content is created and submitted. You use the administration links for the Node module to manage content types, edit and delete submitted content, and manage how posts to the front page behave. The only settings you can change for the Node module itself are how the roles can interact with content. These settings are found on the Permissions page at Administer⇨User Management⇨Permissions. (They're discussed in Chapter 4.)

System module

The System module contains the code that runs Drupal. To get an idea of all the areas under the umbrella of this module, choose Modules⇨System, and locate the column on the page titled System (see Figure 9-3).

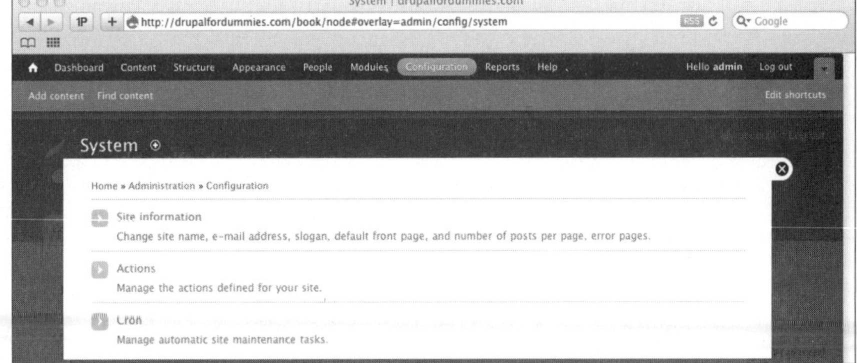

Figure 9-3: The System module configuration overlay.

Some of the settings here you've seen already; many are covered in detail in Chapter 10. The System module controls, among other things, these:

- **Site Information:** Settings for the entire site, such as site name, e-mail address for automated e-mails to users.
- **Actions:** Tasks that Drupal can do automatically when something happens. You can add custom actions, as described in Chapter 10.
- **Cron:** Allows Drupal to do routine site maintenance automatically.

User module

The User module controls everything to do with roles, user accounts, and access rules and permissions.

You may have noticed that many of the modules listed on the Modules overlay have a Permissions link. The Permissions link controls who can change the settings associated with the associated module. In general, unless you trust your authenticated users or article editors implicitly, you should never give anyone permission to control anything under the Core modules.

Looking at the optional modules

A number of optional modules are installed with Drupal. Some of these are enabled by default; most are not.

Here's a quick look at most of them:

- **Aggregator:** This module allows you to grab content from other sites and publish it on yours. You can add, edit, and delete RSS, Atom, and RDF feeds from other sites. (More about this in Chapter 14.)
- **Blog:** A module that allows you to create blog entries. This is the module you use later in this chapter to create your own blogs.
- **Book:** An organized set of web pages. They can be organized like a book's table of contents — especially useful if you want to publish anything structured, such as a manual or user guide.
- **Color:** Some themes have settings that allow users to choose their own colors. This module has to be enabled for such settings to work.
- **Contact:** Rather than publishing a page with an e-mail address for your visitors to contact you, this module lets you create a contact form. Visitors can fill out and submit the form.
- **Content Translation:** This module helps you translate your published content into different languages.

- **Database Logging:** This handy module keeps track of system events — such as user postings or people trying to browse to a nonexistent page on your site — and keeps a record of when anything changes.
- **Forum:** Like a bulletin board, a forum allows registered users to post content and other users to respond.
- **Help:** This module controls online help documentation.
- **Menu:** With this enabled, administrators can add links to and edit all of the menus on the site.
- **Image:** Provides a few basic tools for manipulating images on the site.
- **OpenID:** You can allow users to log in to your site with accounts from other service providers. They don't have to create new accounts on your site. For more about OpenIDs, visit `www.openid.net`.
- **Path:** The Path module lets you create simpler and shorter URLs for pages on your site.
- **PHP Filter:** This allows PHP code to be included in content created for your site.

  This module can cause security risks unless used by an expert.
- **Poll:** Creates a question and a set of responses for your users to choose.
- **Search:** This module allows visitors to search through content posted on your site.
- **Statistics:** If you want to know more information about visitors to your site, this module can provide it. You can find out where your visitors are coming from and which pages they visit the most.
- **Tracker:** This creates a block displaying the newest content.
- **Update Manager:** It's always a good idea to keep your Drupal software, modules, and themes up to date. This module checks for available updates and lets you install them via Drupal's web interface.

Setting Up Your Blog

It seems everyone has a blog these days. A blog is a relatively simple way of getting your message out to the interested public. People read blogs, and a well-written blog may make the difference between a customer buying from you or going to your competitor.

As you probably figured out in the preceding section, setting up a blog in Drupal begins with enabling the Blog module.

Enabling the Blog module

To enable the Blog module, follow these steps:

1. **On the Dashboard menu bar, click Modules.**
2. **Scroll down to the Blog module (see Figure 9-4).**
3. **Select the check box next to the Blog module.**
4. **Click the Save Configuration button at the bottom of the page.**

   The page reloads, and you see this message: `The configuration options have been saved.`

With the Blog module enabled, you have access to a new content type called Blog entry. Pretty easy, huh?

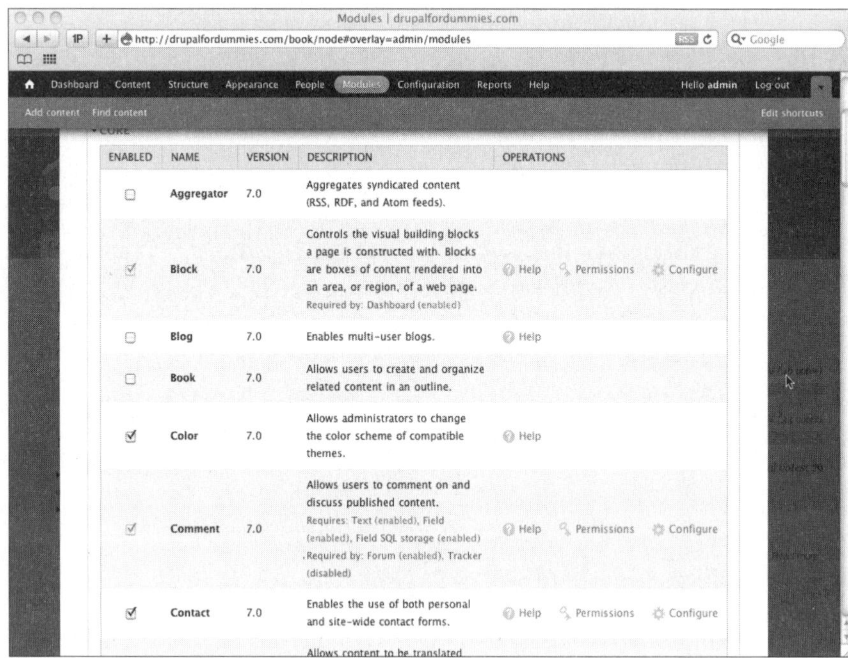

Figure 9-4: The Blog module in the Modules Overlay.

Creating your first blog entry

To create your first blog entry, follow these steps:

1. **Choose Add Content from the Dashboard menu bar or from the Navigation menu of your Drupal page.**

   The content creation overlay opens.

2. **Click the Blog Entry link.**

   You see the form shown in Figure 9-5.

3. **Enter a title in the Title text box and the text of the blog entry in the Body area for your first blog entry.**
4. **When you're done, scroll down and click Preview.**
5. **If you're happy with the preview of the blog post, click Save.**

By default, your blog post is published to your site home page. Browse to your home page and take a look.

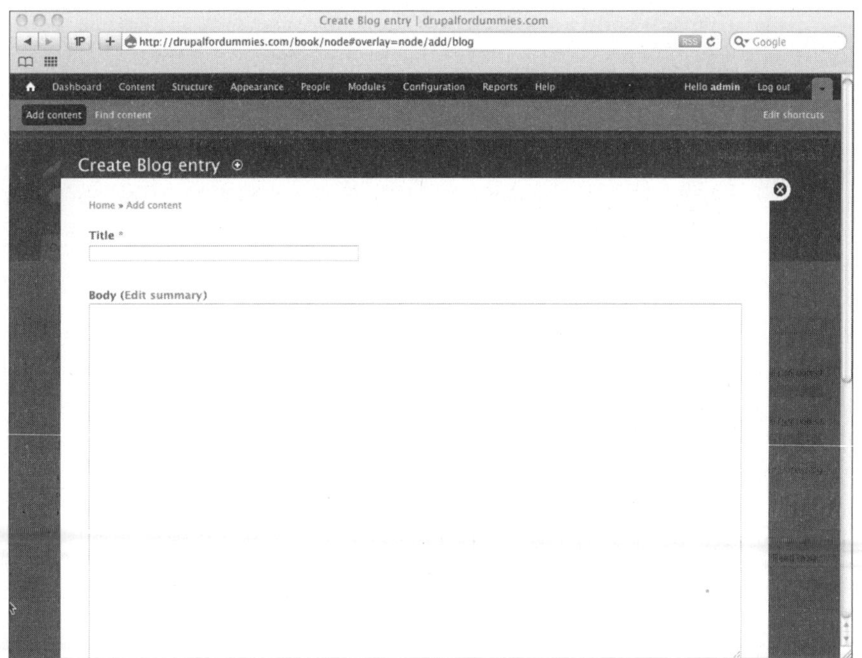

Figure 9-5: The Create Blog entry form.

Changing blog-entry settings

Creating your blog entry probably feels very familiar to you. It's very much the same as creating an article or basic page. If you scroll down the Create Blog entry form, you see the same optional sections (see Figure 9-6):

- **Menu settings:** In general, you should not change the Menu settings. The Blog module creates a specific area where all blogs are stored. Using the Menu Link Title and Parent Item creates a link to just this specific blog entry, not to your entire blog.
- **Revision Information:** If you want to make changes just to this blog entry but want to keep the old version, use Create New Revision.
- **URL Path settings:** Allows you to specify an alternative URL for your blog entry.
- **Comment settings:** Decide whether you want to allow comments, and use these settings accordingly. They apply to just this blog entry, not all.
- **Authoring Information:** Your name and the time and date are automatically populated. If you have several people contributing to the same blog, you can customize each entry here.
- **Publishing options:** These control where this single blog entry will appear.

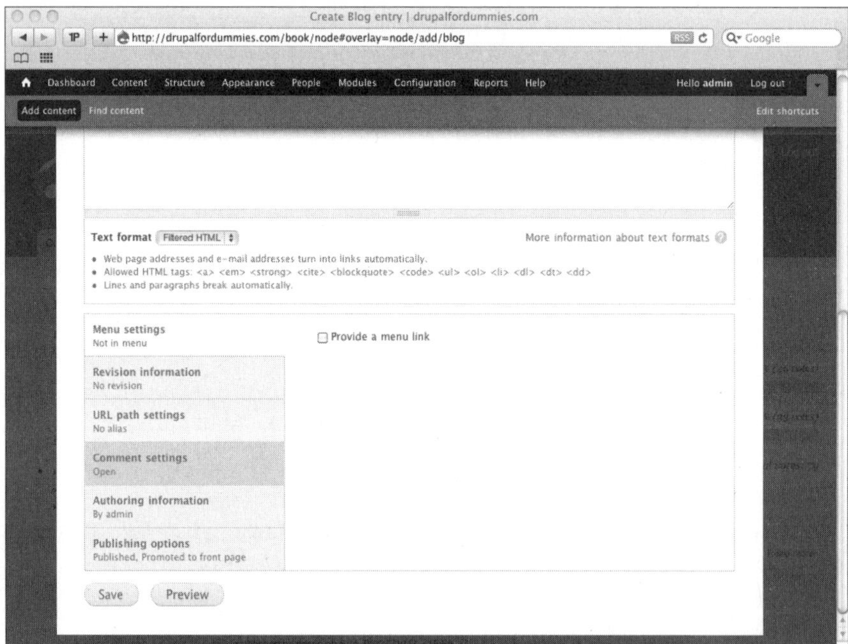

Figure 9-6: Settings on the Create Blog entry form.

With the possible exception of Revision Information, it's a bad idea to use these settings very often. Blog entries should be consistent — and when you change the settings for one, you have an entry that no longer fits in with the others. Instead, you should change the overall configuration of your blog. In the next section, we show you how to apply some of these options to the entire blog, not just to a single entry.

Configuring your blog

There are a number of other blog configuration tasks you should know about. Some accomplish the same things as the settings on the Create Blog entry page, only they apply to every entry in your blog. And some — such as creating a link directly to your blog and adding it to a menu — help visitors locate your blog.

Removing blog postings from the home page

You may prefer not to clutter up your home page with blog entries, especially if you post frequently. To control where your blog postings show up, follow these steps:

1. **From the Dashboard menu bar, choose Structure➪Content Types.**

   The Content Types overlay opens.

2. **In the Blog Entry column, click the Edit link.**

   This takes you to a form that controls how your blog entries behave.

3. **Scroll down and expand the Publishing Options settings (see Figure 9-7).**
4. **To remove future blog postings from the front page, deselect the Promoted to Front Page check box.**
5. **Click the Save Content Type button.**

Although you have made sure new blog postings won't make it to the front page, the blog entry you created earlier is still there. This is easy to fix. Follow these steps:

1. **Browse to the front page of your site.**

   You see your first blog post.

2. **Click the title of the entry.**
3. **Click the Edit tab.**
4. **Scroll down to Publishing options and expand this section, and deselect the Promoted to Front Page check box.**
5. **Click Save.**

   Your blog post is no longer on the front page.

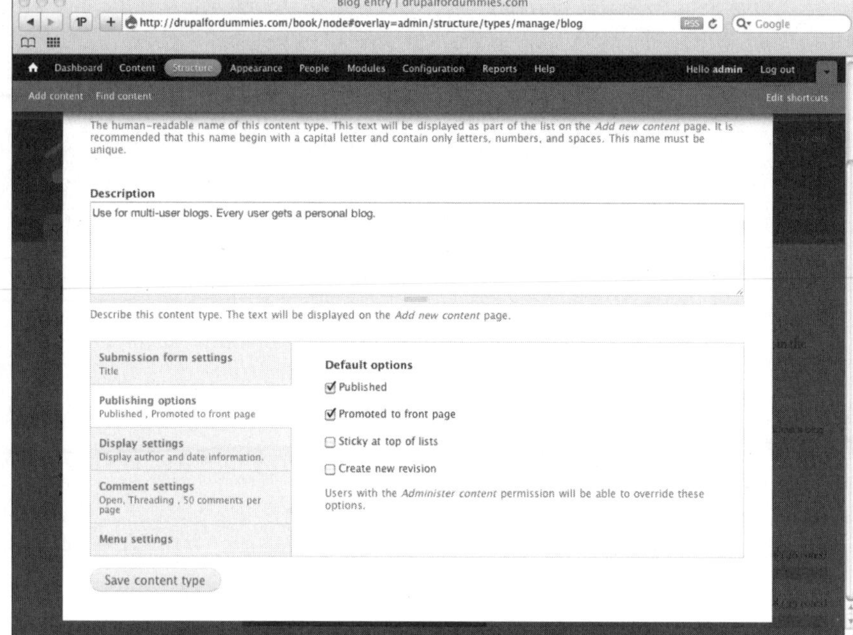

Figure 9-7: The Workflow section of the Blog Entry Settings form.

Browsing directly to the blog

You have removed your post from the front page, but it still exists. As things stand now, though, you have no easy way to get to it. But Drupal puts all the blogs on your site in the same place, and it's easy to get to. The first blog you create is located under your site at `directory/blog/1`. For example, ours is at `http://drupalfordummies.com/book/blog/1`.

You can also find your blog by choosing My Account. You see your account settings and a link to View recent blog entries (see Figure 9-8). Clicking this link takes you to your main blog page. In our case, this is `http://drupalfordummies.com/book/blog/1`.

The Blog module creates one blog per authorized user with the appropriate permission settings. This means that you, as the administrator, can create a single blog with as many blog entries as you want. Your blog is associated with your username. Later in this chapter, we show you how to allow other authorized users to create blogs, but for now, we focus on the single blog we have created.

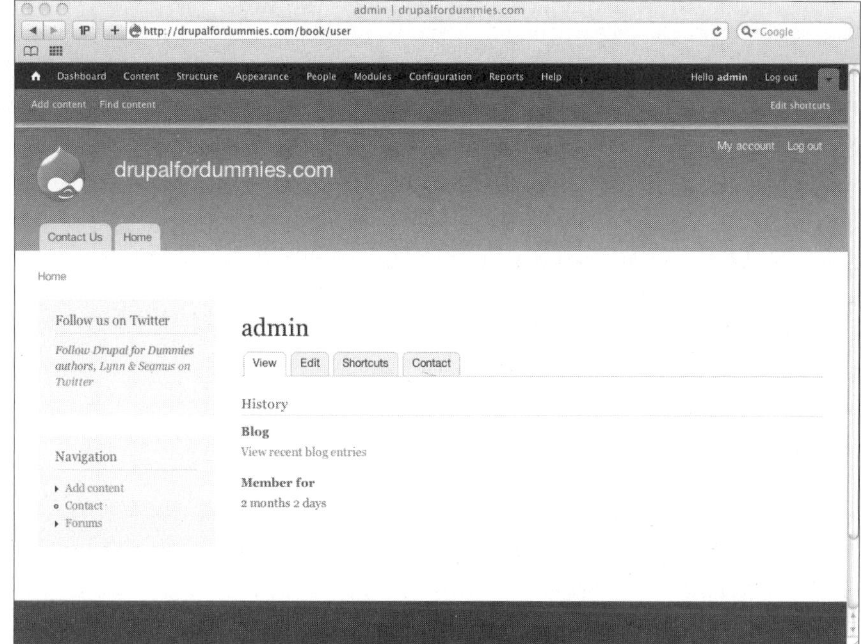

Figure 9-8: A link to your blog is under the My Account link.

Creating a link to your blog

If you click the link to your blog under your My Account page, you're taken to the blog's main page. Copy the URL from your browser's navigation bar.

To add a link to your blog to the Primary Links menu, follow these steps:

1. **From the Dashboard menu bar, choose Structure⇨Menus.**
2. **Locate the menu you want to show a link to your blog in, and click List Links from that menu's column.**

   For this exercise, select List Links from the Navigation menu row. The Navigation Menu Links overlay opens.
3. **Click the Add link.**
4. **In the Menu Link Title text box, enter the text you want for your link.**

   In our case, we enter **Drupal For Dummies Blog**.
5. **In the Path text box, enter the URL of your blog.**

   In our case, it is `http://drupalfordummies.com/book/blog/1`.

6. **(Optional) Enter a description of the blog entry in the Description text box.**

Entering a description is a good idea. When visitors to your site move their mouse cursors over the link, they see this text. It also provides search engines a little more information about your site and can improve your ranking in search results. (Every little bit helps!)

7. **Click Save.**

You're now back on the List items page.

Did it work? There's only one way to find out. Close the Menu Link overlay and navigate to your front page. Behold! A link to your blog now resides in the Navigation menu! (See Figure 9-9.)

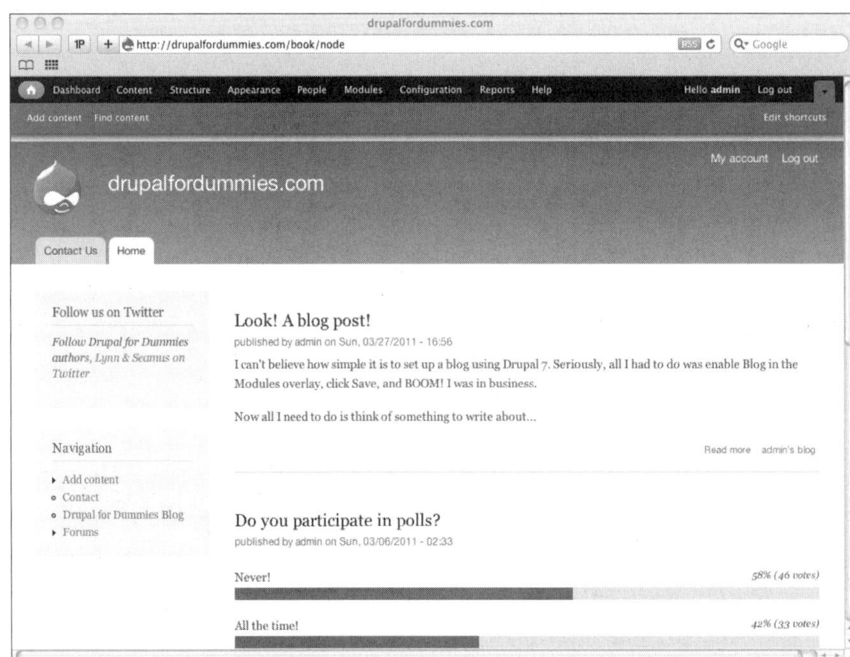

Figure 9-9: A link to the Drupal For Dummies blog in the Navigation menu.

Adding more blog entries

There are two ways to add more entries to your blog. The first is the same technique you use to create your first entry (refer to the earlier section, "Creating your first blog entry") — that is, by choosing Create Content➪Blog Entry.

The second is by clicking the Post New Blog Entry link on your blog page. This link will be visible to you only when you're logged on and viewing your own blog.

Editing and deleting blog entries

Editing a blog entry is much the same as editing any other content. When you're logged in and viewing one of your blog entries, you will see an Edit tab. Click this tab, make your desired changes, and then click Preview or Save when you're satisfied with the changes.

To delete an entry, click its Edit tab and click the Delete button.

You can also edit and delete your blog entries by choosing Content from the Dashboard menu bar and locating the entry you want to change in the list. Don't forget to use the filtering options in the Show Only Items Where section if you have a lot of content.

Creating multiple blogs

We mention that blogs are associated with user accounts; that is, one user can have one blog. By default, only the administrator can set up a blog. But if you want to allow a trusted group of users to create their own blogs, you can. In order to do so, you need to either create a new user role for your site, or modify an existing one, so that registered site users who you want to empower with the ability to create a blog can do so.

For more information on how to perform either of these tasks, refer to Chapter 4, where we cover working with user roles and permissions.

Setting Up a Forum

Forums are great for creating a user community. People can get help from others, provide you with feedback about your content, and simply socialize. Your forum can be as tightly or loosely controlled as you wish. You can control the categories allowed on your forum. To see an example of a forum, browse to `http://drupal.org/forum`.

Enabling the Forum module

Just like setting up a blog, creating a forum begins by enabling the Forum module. To enable the Forum module, follow these steps:

1. **From the Dashboard menu bar, choose Structure➪Modules.**
2. **Scroll down to the Forum module listed under the Core – Optional section (see Figure 9-10).**

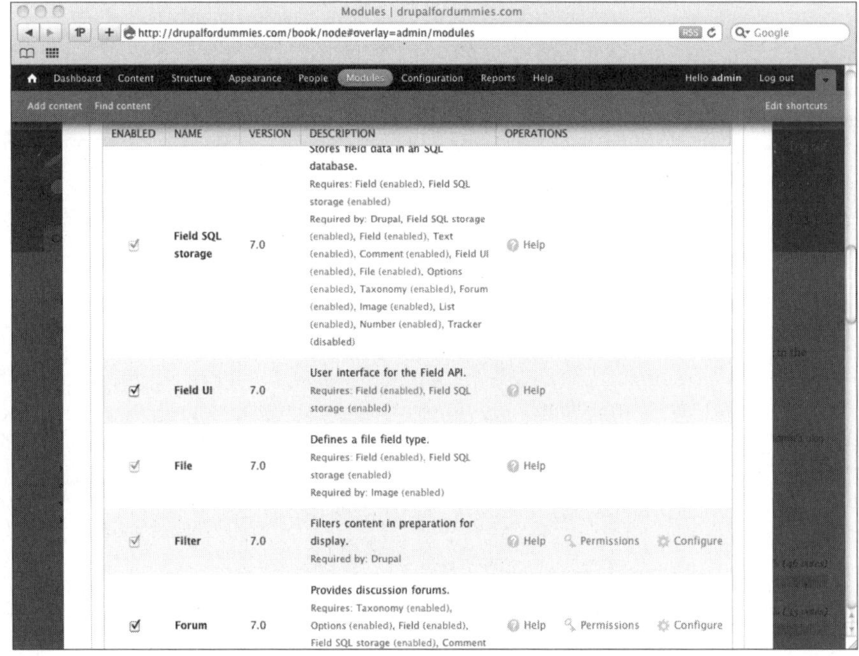

Figure 9-10: Enable the Forum module optional section of the Modules overlay.

3. **Select the check box next to the Forum module.**
4. **Click the Save Configuration button at the bottom of the page.**

   The page reloads and displays this message: `The configuration options have been saved.`

You might notice that under the Create Content link, there is a new link to create a Forum topic. You can't actually create forum content until you set up your forums.

Organizing the Forum module

Take a look at a section of the Drupal.org forum shown in Figure 9-11.

In this figure, a number of minor headings are grouped underneath a major heading called Support. A major heading, such as Support in this example, groups discussion threads of a similar nature. These groupings are called *containers*.

Inside each container are the actual *forums*. For example, under Support, the forums are Post installation, Before you start, Installing Drupal, and Upgrading Drupal.

If you click one of these forums, you're presented with a list of *topics*.

So containers hold forums, and forums hold topics. Note that containers are optional. If you want, you can create forums and not put them in containers at all. As an example, look at Figure 9-11 — and imagine that the container (Support) is missing: The page would consist of no more than a list of forums.

To help you decide whether you need containers, consider how many forum topics you want and whether they can be easily categorized. If you're creating only three forum topics, for instance, you probably don't need containers.

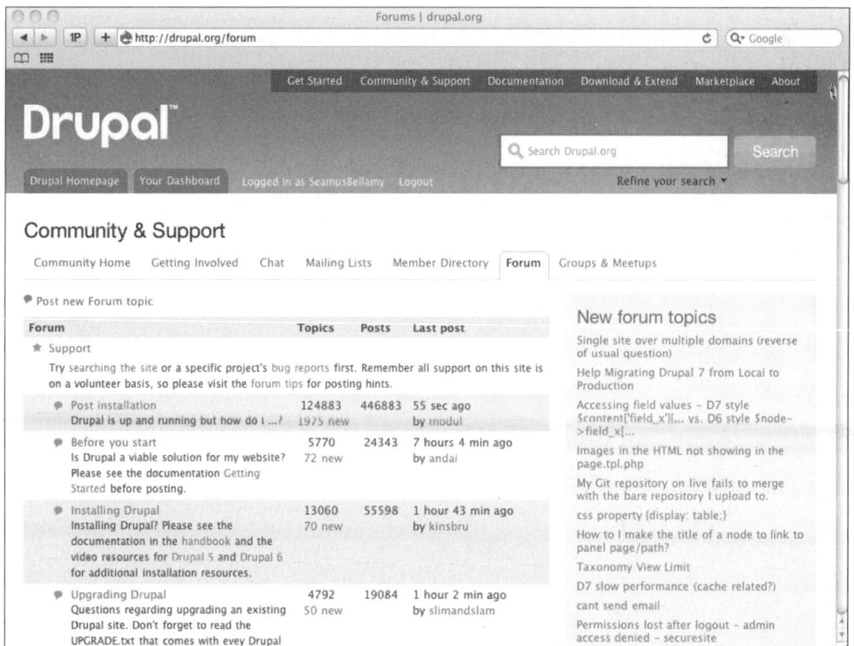

Figure 9-11: Part of the Drupal.org forum.

Configuring your Forum module

In this section, we show you how to create containers and then how to create forums both with and without containers. Finally, we show you how to add existing forums to new containers, move forums to different containers, and remove containers.

Creating containers

To create a forum with containers, follow these steps:

1. **From the Dashboard menu bar, choose Structure⇨Forums.**

   This opens the List tab of the Forum settings page. Because you don't yet have any containers or forums, you see this message: `There are no existing containers or forums.`

2. **Click the Add Container link.**

   This opens the Add Container form, shown in Figure 9-12.

3. **Enter a title for your first container in the Container Name text box.**

   For this exercise, we enter **Drupal Help**.

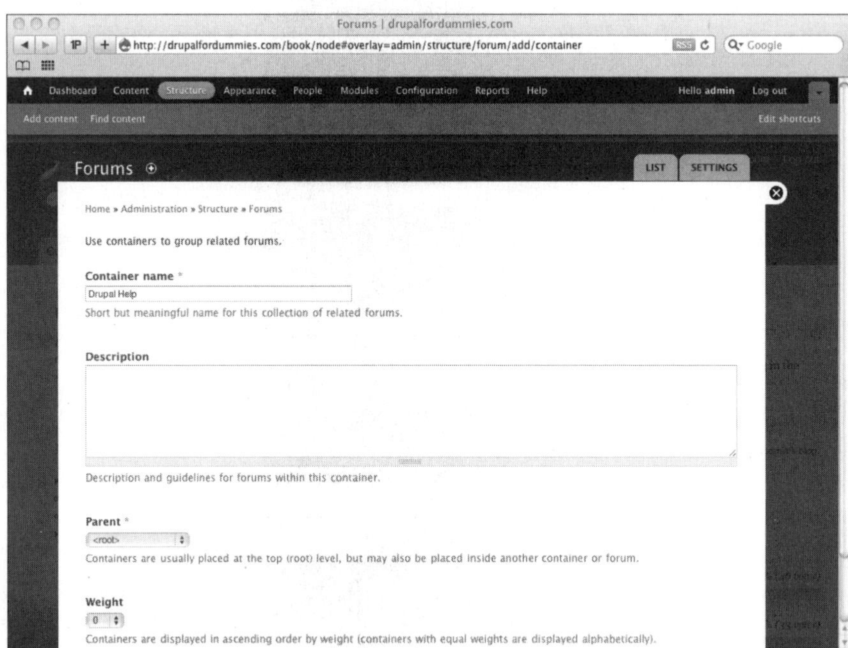

Figure 9-12: The Add Container form.

4. **(Optional) Enter a description of this container in the Description text box.**

   This text shows up under the container title. While including a description is optional, it's a good idea to do so because it provides site visitors with information about what sort of forums the container, er, contains.

5. **Click Save.**

6. **Add more containers by repeating Steps 2 through 5 until you have all the containers you need.**

   For this example, we created three containers: About the Book, Drupal Help, and Drupal Sites.

When you finish, all your containers will show up under the Structure⇨Forums⇨List tab. From this page, you can:

- Re-order your containers by dragging them in the list.
- Edit container information by clicking Edit.
- Delete a container by clicking Edit container and then the Delete button.

Creating forums

To create a new forum, follow these steps:

1. **From the Dashboard menu bar, choose Structure⇨Forums.**

   This opens the List tab of the Forum settings page.

2. **Click the Add Forum link.**

   This opens the Add Forum form, shown in Figure 9-13.

3. **Enter a title for your forum in the Forum Name text box.**

   If you're using containers, the topic should fit under one of these. In our case, we create a forum called *Look at my site*. It's a place where visitors to our site can post the Drupal sites they build and get comments and praise.

4. **(Optional) Enter a description of this forum in the Description text box.**

   This description will appear on the forum page. The description is optional, but it does help your visitors understand what should be posted in this forum.

5. **If you're using containers, choose the appropriate one from the Parent drop-down list. Leave this selection as `<root>` if you're not using containers.**

   For this exercise, we select a container named Drupal Sites from the Parent drop-down list.

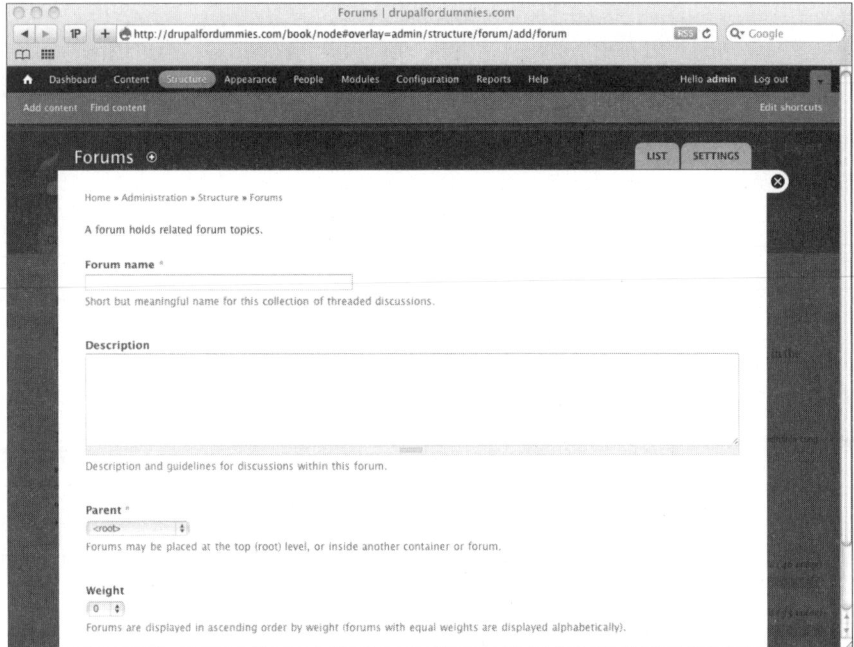

Figure 9-13: The Add Forum form.

6. **Click Save.**
7. **Add more forums by repeating Steps 2 through 6 until you have all the forums you need.**

Changing forum and container organization

After you create your forums (and optionally, your containers), you can move forums from one container to another — or take them out of containers entirely. You have two ways you can change the container a forum is in. To do it the first way, follow these steps:

1. **From the Dashboard menu bar, choose Structure⇨Forums.**
2. **Click the Edit link next to the forum or container you want to change.**
3. **Change the Parent drop-down list to the new container or select `<root>` to leave the forum out of all containers.**
4. **(Optional) Modify the name or description of this forum to be more appropriate for the new container.**
5. **Click Save.**

The second way of moving forums around is a bit easier — but it doesn't give you the chance to change the forum name or description. To use this method, follow these steps:

1. **From the Dashboard menu bar, choose Structure➪Forums.**
2. **Click the small cross icon to the left of the forum you want to change, and drag it under the new container.**
3. **If you want to take the chosen forum out of all containers, drag it to the top of the list.**

When you remove a container with forums in it, they don't get deleted. Instead, they end up located outside of any containers.

Viewing your forums

After you have created some forums and containers, you may want to take a look at them. To view them, you need to create a forum topic. Follow these steps:

1. **From the Dashboard menu bar, choose Add Content➪Forum Topic.**

   This opens the Create Forum Topic overlay (see Figure 9-14).

   By now, this form should seem very familiar. With the exception of the Forums drop-down list, it's pretty much the same as the article, basic page, or blog content creation forms. The settings we discuss in earlier chapters (including Menu Settings, Input Format, and Publishing Options) apply to this forum topic post as well.

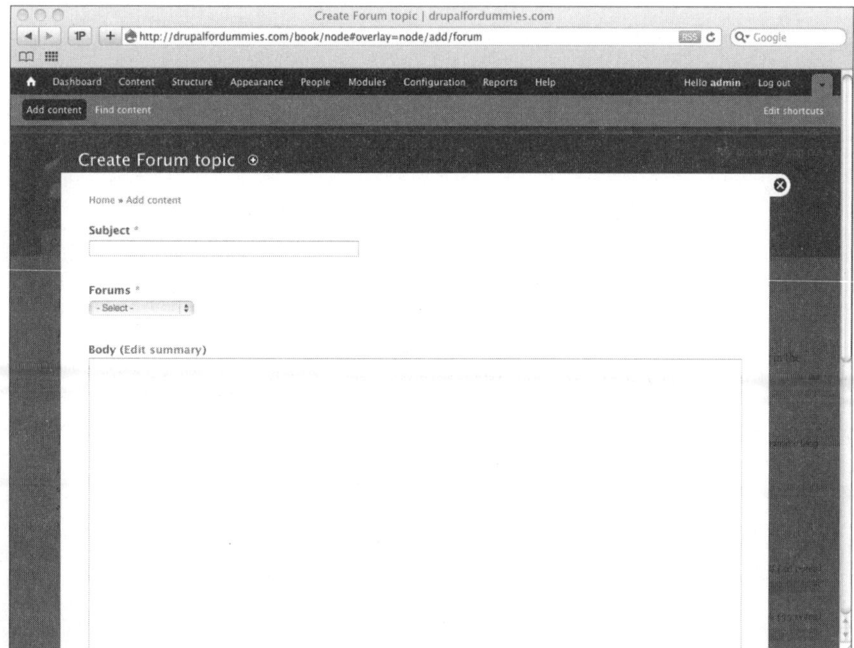

Figure 9-14: Create Forum Topic overlay.

2. **Enter a subject and body in the Subject and Body text boxes that make sense for posting in one of the forums you created.**

   In this example, we create a post that shows off a new Drupal site.

3. **Choose the appropriate forum from the Forums drop-down list.**

   We chose Look at My Site from the Forums drop-down list.

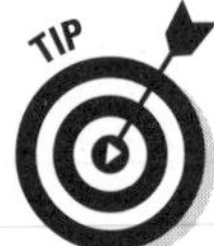

   You can tell the containers from the forums in this list. The forums all have a dash in front of their names to indicate they're underneath containers in the hierarchy.

4. **When you're finished, click Save.**

To see your containers and forums, browse to `/forum` under your domain name. In our case, it's `http://drupalfordummies.com/book/forum` (see Figure 9-15).

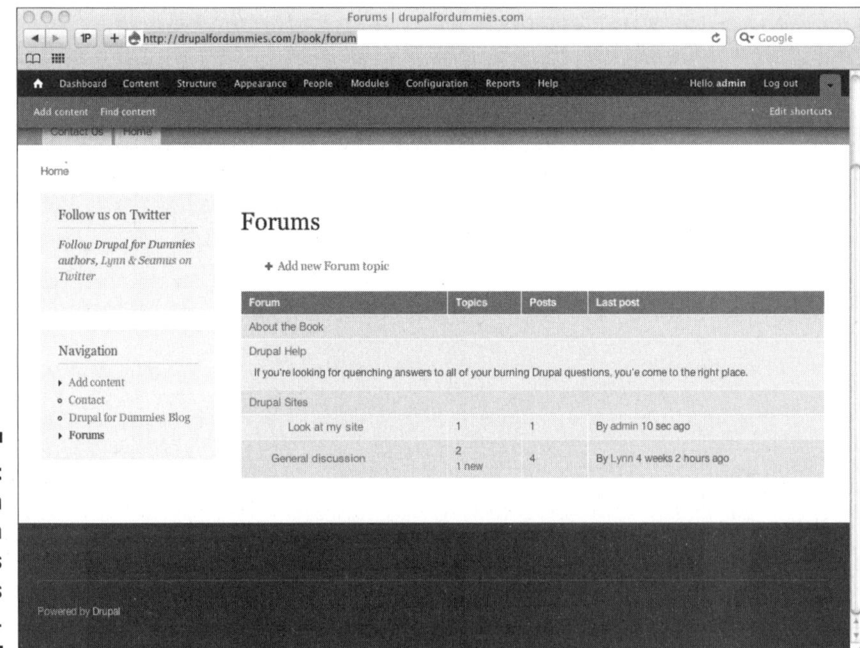

Figure 9-15: The forum page with containers and forums shown.

After you're on your main forum page, you can see posted forum topics by clicking forums that contain posts. In Figure 9-16, you can see that a post exists under the forum Look at My Site.

To see the individual forum topic posts, click the forum title. In this case, when we click the forum Look at My Site, we end up on the forum topic list shown in Figure 9-16.

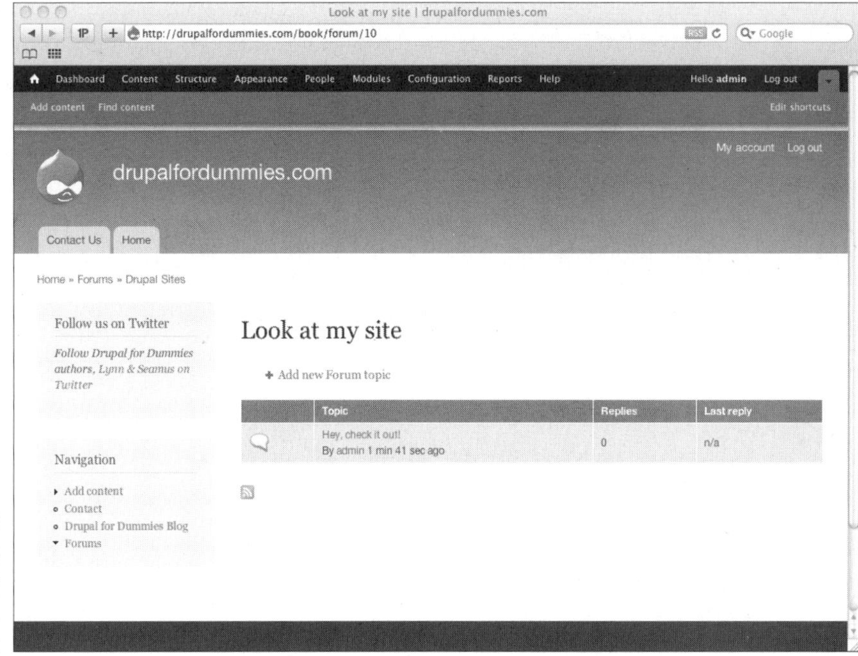

Figure 9-16: An individual forum topic.

Although we went to the trouble of creating this topic by choosing Create Content⇨Forum Topic, the easy way to create new forum topics is to drill down into the forum and click the Add New Forum Topic link, as shown in Figure 9-16.

Unlike containers and forums, forum topics exist to allow discussion. To view a forum topic and reply to it, click the link to the topic. In Figure 9-16, clicking the Hey, Check It Out! link takes you to a page where you can comment on this topic.

By default, only the administrator can create containers and forums. Signed-in users can create forum topics and add a comment to a forum topic thread.

Changing forum topics settings

You have some control over the behavior of your forum topics. To access the forum topic settings, choose Structure⇨Forums and then click the Settings tab (see Figure 9-17).

On this page, you can control the following:

- **Hot Topic Threshold:** When a topic reaches a certain number of postings, a small graphic is displayed, indicating that it's popular. This setting controls how many posts it takes to become a hot topic.

- **Topics per Page:** You can limit the number of topics shown on a page here. If the total number of topics is greater, a Next link will appear.
- **Default Order:** This is the order in which topics will appear on the page.

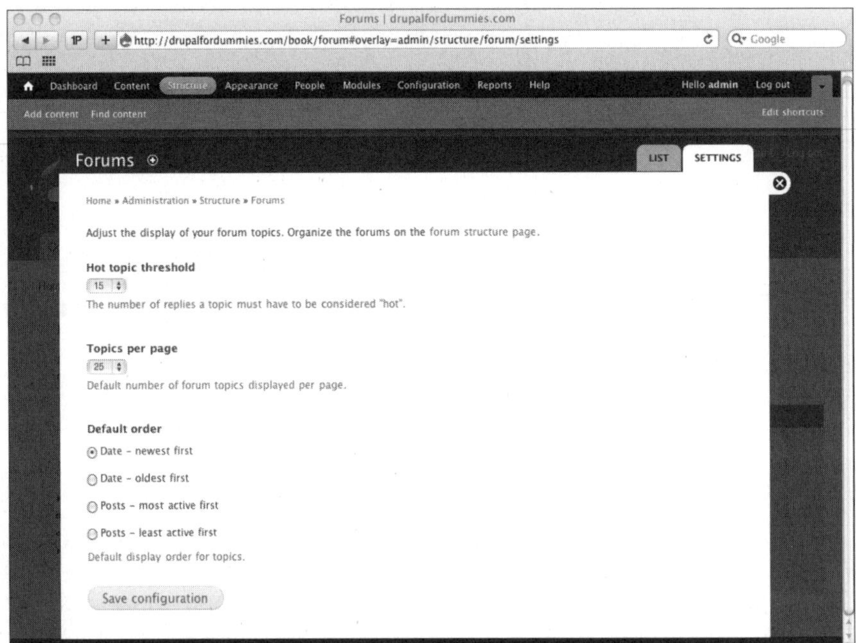

Figure 9-17: Settings for forum topics.

Managing forum permissions

Registered users can comment on forum topics. But right now, you're the only one who can post forum topics. Because the point of having a forum is to elicit discussion from visitors to your site, you will want to allow other people to post forum topics. This is controlled by the permissions settings for the Forum module. Using the Dashboard menu bar, select People and then click the Permissions tab. When the Permissions overlay opens, you see a number of permission options related to how users interact with your site's forums. The forum permission topics are

- **Administer Forums:** Grants permission to create, edit, and delete containers and forums.
- **Forum Topic: Create New Content:** User is permitted to create new forum topic.
- **Forum Topic: Edit Own Content:** User can edit only forum topics she has created.

- **Forum Topic: Edit Any Content:** User can edit all forum topics, not just his own.
- **Forum Topic: Delete Own Content:** User can delete only forum topics she created.
- **Forum Topic: Delete Any Content:** Grants permission to delete all forum topics, not just ones created by this user.

If you trust your authenticated users not to abuse the privilege, allow them to create new forum topics, delete their own forum topics, and edit their own forum topics. Doing so makes for a much more vibrant online community that will keep your users coming back for more, time and time again.

Managing the Comments Module

The commenting system used by the Forum module — and by all the other content types — is contained in a separate module, the Comment module. By default, authenticated users can comment on any content on your site that allows comments.

Every time you create content, be it a basic page, article, blog entry, or forum post, you can select whether to allow comments. The option is located on each content creation page in a section called Comment settings. There you can decide if no comments are allowed, new comments are allowed, or existing comments can be read, but no new ones added.

Moderating comments

Sometimes you might prefer to moderate comments. This means that the comments people make aren't immediately published; instead, they're kept in a list for you to approve and *then* publish or delete. To turn on comment moderation, follow these steps:

1. **From the Dashboard menu bar, choose People and click the Permissions tab.**
2. **Under the Comment section of the Permissions list (located near the top of the list), deselect the Skip Comment Approval check box under Authenticated User (or any other user group whose comments you want to approve before they appear on the site).**
3. **Click the Save Permissions button.**

   Now each time anyone from a targeted user group posts a comment, she will see this message: `Your comment has been queued for moderation by site administrators and will be published after approval.`

Approving or deleting comments

This comment will not be published until you approve it. To go through the list of comments waiting for you to moderate, follow these steps:

1. **Choose Find Content from the Dashboard menu bar, and then click the Comments tab.**

   The Comments overlay opens, as shown in Figure 9-18.

2. **Hover your cursor over the Subject line.**

   The text of the comment appears. Alternatively, you can click the comment link to view the comment.

3. **Click your browser's Back button to return to the Approval queue.**
4. **If you approve a comment, select the check box next to it.**
5. **From the Update Options drop-down list, select Publish the Selected Comments.**
6. **Click the Update button.**

You can select multiple comments and delete them by selecting the check boxes for the comments you want to delete, selecting Delete the Selected Comments from the Update Options drop-down list, and then clicking the Update button.

Figure 9-18: Approval queue with comments to be moderated.

Part III

Bending Drupal to Your Will

"Jeez – I thought themes just defined the look of the website."

In this part . . .

There has to be more to Drupal than what you've seen so far. And there is. The chapters in this part take you deeper into Drupal administration. You dive into all those hidden-but-important nooks and crannies of the administration menus. You turn on more modules to help you keep tight control of your site. And you discover how to customize existing themes to make it truly yours.

Chapter 10

Advanced Administration

In This Chapter

- Getting new themes and modules
- Updating Drupal
- Backing up and restoring your database
- Updating themes and modules
- Configuring your site

The Drupal community frequently comes out with updates. To make sure everything on your Drupal site runs smoothly, you need to keep your software up to date. In this chapter, we show you how to keep your site protected by upgrading when necessary. Also, there are many administrative features discussed in this chapter that extend your control over your site and allow you to monitor what visitors do when they come to your site, which can help you fine-tune your content.

Consider this chapter the next level in understanding how Drupal works.

Adding New Themes and Modules

One of the best things about Drupal is that developers are constantly contributing new themes and new modules. You can extend Drupal's functionality in incredible ways by adding new modules. You can create an extremely professional-looking site in minutes by finding the right theme.

With Drupal 7, there are now two ways to add modules and themes to your site. You may either download the file and install it manually, or tell Drupal where the file is on the web and make Drupal do most of the work. While it's easier to let Drupal do the heavy lifting, it's good to know how to do it yourself so you understand how it works. This section shows you both ways. We start with the big steps involved in automatically adding new modules and themes, and then drill down into each step.

Here are the major steps you take to download and add new contributed modules and themes to your site automatically:

1. Locate a new module or theme you want to use on your site and copy the URL.
2. Give Drupal the URL for the file.
3. Enable the new module or theme on your Drupal site.
4. Customize your new module or theme as desired.

The first step for both techniques is to find new modules and themes.

Locating themes and modules

For new modules and themes, head over to `http://drupal.org` and click the Download & Extend link on the top right corner of the page to browse around (see Figure 10-1).

Click the Modules or Themes tab to use a form to browse or search through the available files (see Figure 10-2).

For both Modules and Themes, select 7.x from the Filter by Compatibility drop-down list to make sure you see only modules or themes that are compatible with your Drupal 7 installation.

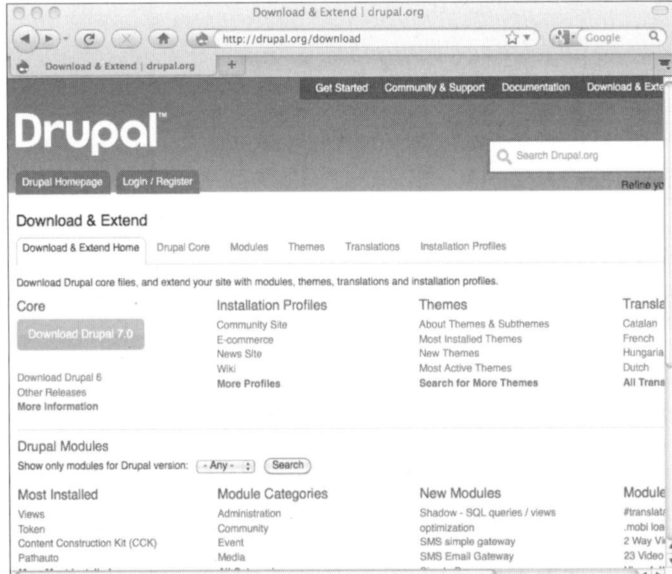

Figure 10-1: Drupal.org has links to user-contributed modules and themes.

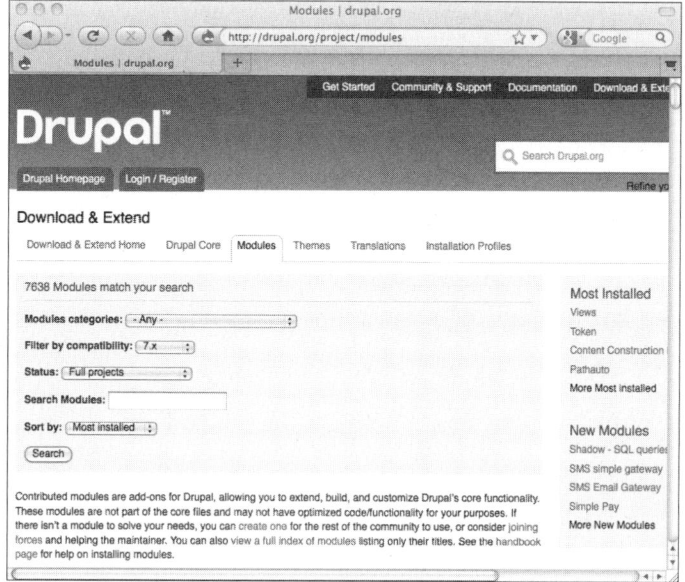

Figure 10-2: Search or browse through modules and themes.

You can find especially popular modules and themes on drupal.org by selecting Most Installed from the Sort By drop-down list when using the search form on the Modules and Themes pages. This lists the modules or themes in order of the most frequently downloaded to the least.

Chapters 16 and 17 list some great sites to visit to find new modules and themes.

Copying module or theme URLs

After you find a module or theme you want, look for a link to download it, a `.tar.gz` file. You don't need to download the file, but you do need the URL to it. To get the URL:

1. **Right-click (or Control-click the Mac) the link to the `.tar`, `orgz`, file.**
2. **In IE, choose Copy Shortcut. In Firefox, choose Copy Link Location.**

   The URL has now been saved to your Clipboard.
3. **Using Notepad or other word processor, choose Edit⇨Paste and paste the URL.**

   You need this URL to tell Drupal to download and install the theme or module, as described in the next section.

You should take a look at the documentation for the new module or theme. This documentation is generally available on the page with the Download link; it may contain detailed help to get the new theme or module up and running.

Automatically installing modules and themes

After you have the URL at which your module or theme file is located, you need to tell Drupal where to find it.

To direct Drupal to install a module, follow these steps:

1. **On your Dashboard menu bar, click the Modules link.**

   This opens the Modules page.

2. **Click the Install New Module link.**

   The Install form appears, as shown in Figure 10-3.

3. **Paste the URL to your new module or theme in the Install from a URL text box by pressing Ctrl+P or ⌘+P.**

4. **Click the Install button.**

   Your module is now installed.

It's possible that, some web hosts will kick out a nasty error when you click Install. The error message will look something like this:

```
The specified file temporary://filename could not be copied, because the
destination directory is not properly configured.
```

To fix this problem, browse to Configuration. Find the section called Media and click File System. Then change the Temporary directory from `/tmp` to `~/tmp`.

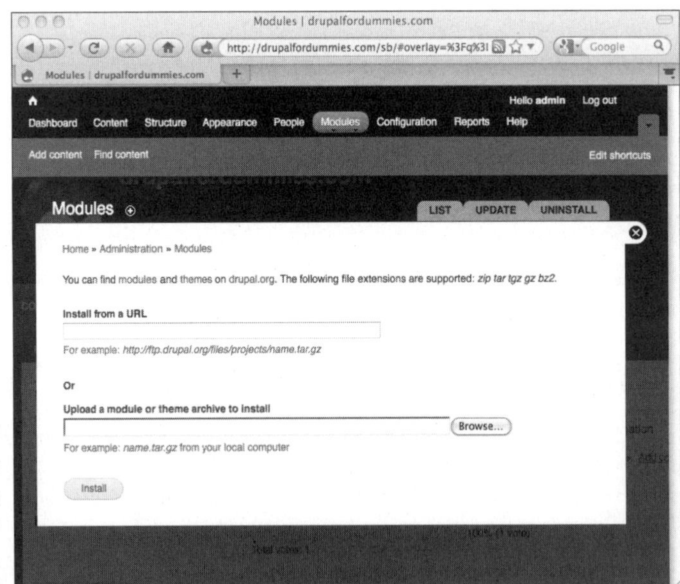

Figure 10-3: Install form for new modules.

To direct Drupal to install a theme, follow these steps:

1. **On your Dashboard menu bar, click the Appearance link.**

   This opens the Appearance page.

2. **Click the Install New Theme link.**

   The Install form appears.

3. **Copy and paste the URL to your new theme in the Install from a URL text box by pressing Ctrl+P or ⌘+P.**

4. **Click the Install button.**

   Your theme is now installed, but still needs to be enabled.

Enabling themes and modules

After you install your new theme or module, Drupal will see it and display it in your theme list or module list. After Drupal downloads and installs the theme or module, however, you still have to enable it before you can use it on your site.

For example, we downloaded the Marinelli theme from a link on the drupal.org site under Themes. We then automatically installed it.

To enable a theme, follow these steps:

1. **On your Dashboard menu bar, click the Appearance link.**

   The themes are in alphabetical order; disabled themes are at the bottom of the page, so our new one, Marinelli, is near the bottom of the list (see Figure 10-4).

2. **Click the Enable and Set Default link under the new theme.**

   The new theme is now being used.

To enable a new module, click the Modules button at the top of the Dashboard menu bar. Because you can run multiple modules at once, there is no default option. Select the Enabled check box next to your new module and then click the Save Configuration button at the bottom of the page.

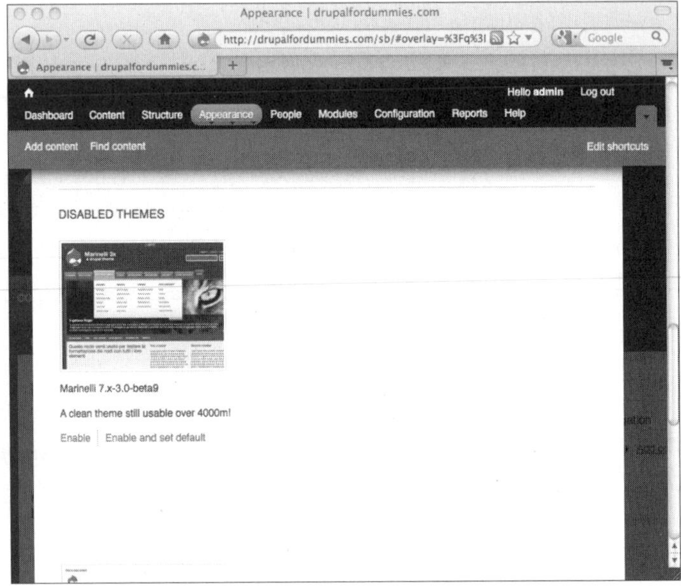

Figure 10-4: Enabling and activating a newly installed theme.

Manually installing themes and modules

Manual installation adds a few additional steps to the process. Here are the general steps:

1. Locate a new module or theme you want to use on your site.
2. Download the new module or theme to your local computer.
3. Upload the new module or theme to a specific folder on the web server where Drupal is running.
4. Extract the new module or theme file.
5. Delete the original `.zip` or `.tar.gz` file.
6. Enable the new module or theme on your Drupal site.
7. Customize your new module or theme as desired.

The following subsections take a closer look at downloading modules and themes.

Downloading modules and themes

After you find a module or theme you want, look for a link to download it. Most of the time the module or theme will download as a single compressed file (a `.tar.gz` or `.zip` file). Save this file to a directory you'll remember.

Installing modules and themes

Your module or theme comes as a single, compressed `.zip` file, but it actually consists of many files and folders. All of these files need to be located in a web directory under your Drupal directory on your web server.

The first time you install a new module or theme manually, you need to create the directory to store it. Create two new directories under your Drupal installation. One will be called `modules` and one will be called `themes`. Create these two under the directory `sites/all`. You will place new modules in the `sites/all/modules` directory and new themes in the `sites/all/themes` directory.

You can upload the single `.zip` file to either the `sites/all/modules` or `sites/all/themes` directory under your Drupal installation on most web hosting companies. You can extract the files after you've uploaded the `.zip` (this way, you don't have to upload a bunch of individual files).

In Chapter 2, when you install Drupal, we show you how to upload using a program called Fileman. Your web host may have a different-but-similar program that handles file management. If you know how to use an FTP program, you may find that easier.

To upload the compressed file, follow these steps:

1. **Browse to the web host's site and log in.**

   You should have received an e-mail from your web host that has your username, password, and login information.

2. **Click the link to a file manager.**

   You need a file manager so that you can select the `.zip` file and put it in the correct directory on your web host's site. After you click the file manager, you'll see a screen that displays the files on your web host's web server.

3. **You should see a single folder or directory named `html`, www, or `htdocs`. Open this folder.**

   There may be several directories, but the one for your website should be easy to spot. This is where all your web pages belong — and where you need to install the new theme or module.

4. **Browse to `sites/all`. If you see a folder named `modules` and one named `themes`, click the appropriate one.**

   This means that Drupal is installed in the root directory of your site.

5. **If you didn't see the `sites/all/modules` and `sites/all/themes` directories, look for a directory named `Drupal`. Click the `Drupal` directory and browse to `sites/all`.**

You should now see the `modules` and `themes` directories. If this is the first time you've installed a module or theme, you will need to create these directories.

6. **If you downloaded a module, click the `site/all/modules` directory to enter it; if you downloaded a theme, click the `site/all/themes` directory.**
7. **Click the Upload link on your file manager.**

   You should see an upload form with a Browse button.
8. **Click Browse and select the module or theme `.tar.gz` or `.zip` file you downloaded, and then click Upload.**

   Your file is now on your site and in the correct folder. But you still need to extract it.

Extracting module or theme files

The file extensions `.zip` or `.tar.gz` indicate that many files are compressed into a single file. File managers can extract your compressed file for you. Following is an example of how it works. (Your version may differ, so contact your web host for help if you can't find the same functions on your file manager.) Follow these steps to extract compressed files:

1. **Find the module or theme `.tar.gz` (or `.zip`) file you uploaded to the `modules` or `themes` directory and select it. Click the filename to open the file.**

   You see a list of files that are stored inside your `.zip` file. They will all be selected.
2. **You should see an option to uncompress your files. Leave the selection box set to Uncompress All and click the Go button.**

   This uncompresses your single `.zip` file into a folder with the same name. You now see both the compressed file (for example, `supercool-module.tar.gz`) and the uncompressed files in a new directory (for example, a folder named `supercoolmodule`).
3. **Select the original `.tar.gz` or `.zip` file on your web server and delete it.**

   Be careful to delete only the compressed file that the new module or theme came in — and nothing else.

Take a look inside the folder containing your new theme or module. If you see files named `INSTALL.txt` or `README.txt`, there may be more steps you have to follow for that specific module or theme. You need to read the instructions in that file. You may be able to view it through the file manager on your web server. If not, the file manager can send a copy of the file to your desktop so you can open it in Notepad (Windows) or TextEdit (Mac).

Disabling themes and modules

To disable a module, deselect the Enabled check box on the Modules page. To disable a theme, click the Disable link on the Appearance page.

Keeping Drupal, Modules, and Themes Up to Date

Updating a module or theme is an easier task than updating the Drupal software. Still, you need to know how to accomplish both. We start by showing you how to find out what you need to update. We show you how to back up and restore your database — a necessary step before any updates. We then show you how to update themes and modules. Finally, we go through how to update the Drupal software itself.

Knowing when you need to update

By now, you may be seeing a warning message on your site that says

```
No update information available. Run cron or check manually.
```

Drupal is designed to automatically check for updates. You don't have to allow automatic updates, and by default, Drupal may not be able to perform the updates. You have two options:

- The first option is to click the Check Manually link in that warning message. This tells Drupal to check for updates for the main Drupal software, as well as for updates to installed modules and themes.
- The second option is to set up an automated process to check for updates, known as a *cron.* Drupal is designed to check for updates frequently, because there are frequent updates you need to be aware of and install.

Drupal uses the cron for more than just checking for updated software. It is also for syndicating information from your site at specific times and retrieving syndicated RSS feeds from other sites or any process that has to happen at specific times. As you add new modules, some of them will use a cron to operate correctly.

You can control how frequently cron runs by choosing Configuration⇨System⇨Cron. This opens a form that lets you set the interval for cron to run (see Figure 10-5).

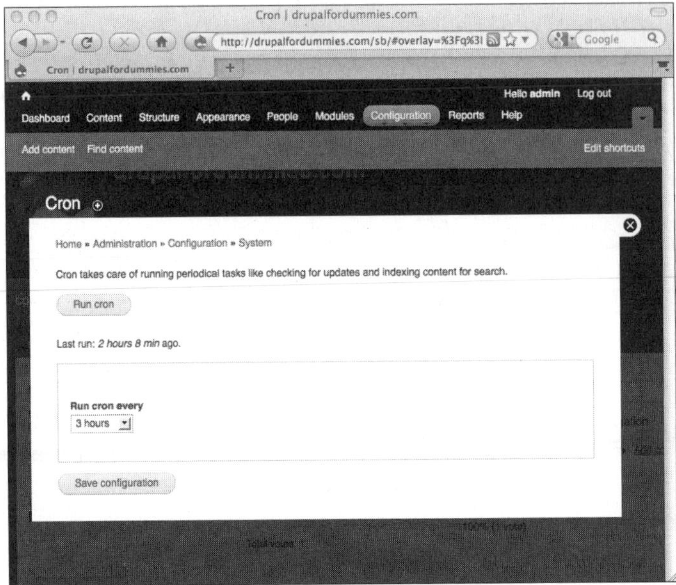

Figure 10-5: Set the cron interval.

Finding available updates

Drupal updates can come out every few weeks or even months. That applies to the main Drupal software, which includes the Core modules. But as you add more contributed modules and themes, you're likely to need to perform updates on the individual modules and themes more frequently.

It all begins by discovering what's out of date. Fortunately, that part is easy. Choose Reports➪Available updates. This page shows you the status of your Drupal software, as well as individual listings for every extra module and theme you've installed (see Figure 10-6).

Even better, when your software is out of date, links to the newer versions appear on this page.

Protecting your database

Before you update anything, you need to back up the database that operates behind your Drupal site. By doing so, you safeguard all the work you've done on your site. Your database contains:

- **All text content you've put on your site.**
- **Settings for everything you've customized.**
- **All user information, including logins and passwords.**

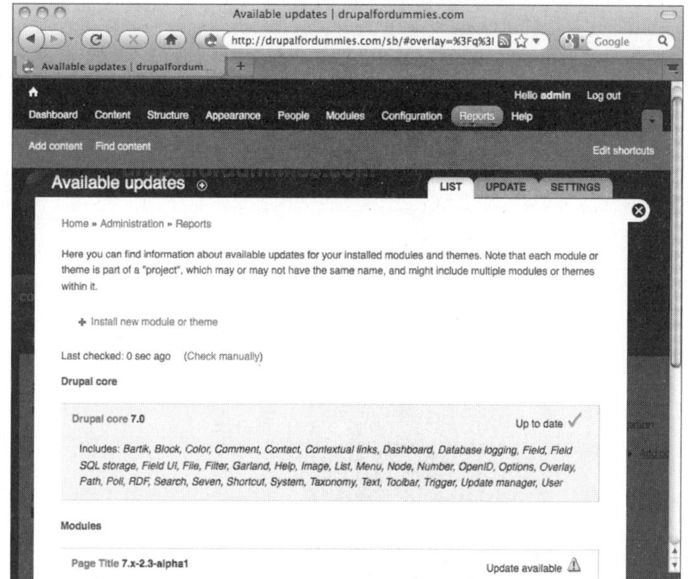

Figure 10-6: Status of all installed modules and themes.

Backing up your database

To back up your database, follow these steps:

1. **Log in to your control panel, provided by your web host.**
2. **Click the phpMyAdmin icon.**

   You see the phpMyAdmin interface (see Figure 10-7).

   Although phpMyAdmin is extremely common, not every web host has it. If you don't have the phpMyAdmin application, contact your web host and find out what resources it provides for backing up your database manually.
3. **Click the Export tab.**

   This opens the Export database screen shown in Figure 10-8.
4. **Under the Export section, select the Drupal database.**

   There may be more than one database in your list. The Drupal database may be named with your username on your web host site, or it may have Drupal in the name.

   Chapter 2 shows how to create a database for Drupal. The database name you use for the database you create is the one to choose in this step.

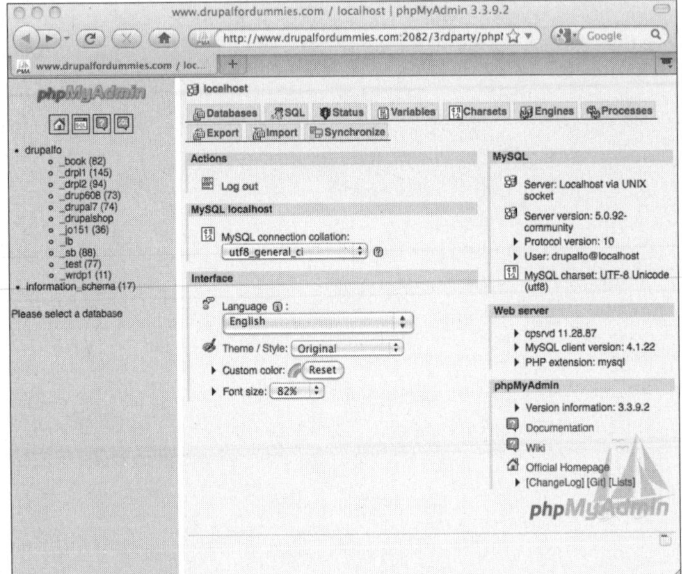

Figure 10-7: The phpMyAdmin interface.

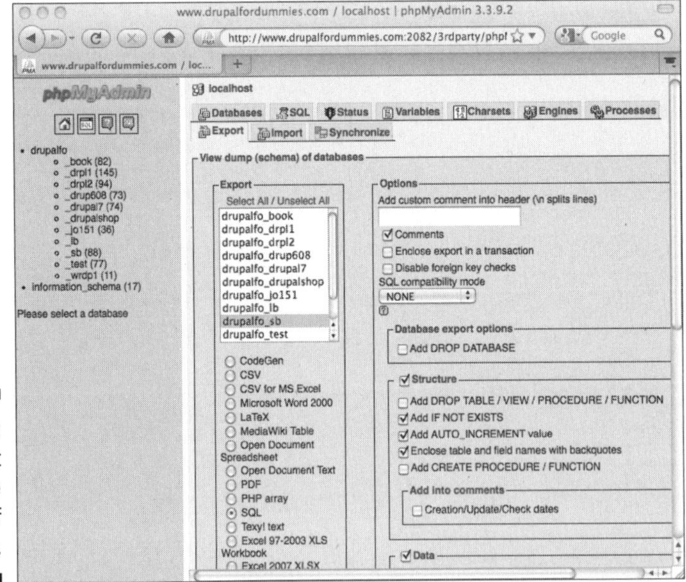

Figure 10-8: The Export database screen of phpMyAdmin.

5. **Under the database name, select the SQL radio button.**
6. **Under Options section, select these check boxes: Structure, Add IF NOT EXISTS, Add AUTO_INCREMENT Value, and Enclose Table and Field Names with Backquotes.**

7. **Also under the Options section, select these check boxes: Data, Complete Inserts, Extended Inserts, and Use Hexadecimal for BLOB Export Type.**
8. **At the bottom of this page, click the Save as File button.**
9. **For compression, select the Zipped radio button.**
10. **Click the Go button.**

    You may have to wait for a few minutes, but you'll be prompted to save a file (see Figure 10-9). This file is your database backup file, which you'll need if you ever have to restore your database.

By default, this file has a generic name, such as `localhost.sql.zip`. Rename this file so you'll recognize what it is later on; then save it in a location you'll remember. You may want to use the date as part of the filename so you can always select the most recent backup if you do have to restore your database.

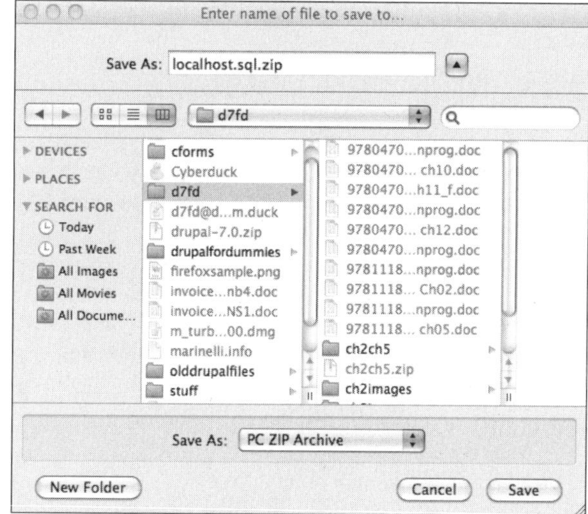

Figure 10-9: Download your database backup file.

Restoring your database

Should you ever lose your data and have to restore your database, this section provides the basic steps for that restoration.

We strongly recommend you consult your web host's documentation for specific instructions on restoring a database. There's a good chance that you won't have the appropriate permissions, and the following instructions won't work for you. If you do have the appropriate permissions, follow these steps:

1. **Using the phpMyAdmin application, choose the Drupal database from the list of database names in the left pane.**
2. **Click the Operations tab.**
3. **Type a name into the Rename Database To text box and click Go.**

   Your new database will have the same name as your old one, so you need to save your old one with a new name. You'll delete the old database when you're done.

   Your web host may have restricted you from deleting databases. If this is the case, this step will fail. Be sure to contact your web host's support staff to let them know that you need to restore your database — and send them the backup file.

4. **Click the Import tab.**
5. **Browse to the location of the database `.zip` file containing your Drupal database backup and select it. Click Go.**

   Your database is restored.

Updating themes and modules

Suppose you want to upgrade a module or theme you've installed. The Available updates page in Figure 10-6 shows any modules that are out of date, along with the link to download the new version right there on that page.

To upgrade a module or theme, follow these steps:

1. **Click the Modules link (or the Appearance link, if you're updating a theme).**
2. **Scroll to the bottom of the page and deselect the Enabled check box next to the module, or click the Disable link next to the theme.**
3. **Click the Save Configuration button.**
4. **Find the old module or theme to be upgraded on the web server using some kind of file manager program.**

   This may be through a control panel on your web host's site. If you're comfortable using FTP, it will also work. For example, a module called Author Pane would be located in the Drupal directory at `sites/all/modules/authorpane`.

5. **Back up these old files by copying them to your desktop computer.**

   The idea here is that you want to keep a copy just in case something goes wrong with your upgrade so you can restore the old files.

6. **After you make a copy of these files, delete the ones on your web server.**

   Be *extremely careful* that you delete only the files inside the folder of the module or theme you're upgrading.

7. **Delete the now-empty folder on your web server.**

   For example, we delete the `authorpane` folder.

8. **If possible, follow the steps in the "Automatically installing modules and themes" section. If you can't install automatically, use the "Manually installing themes and modules" sections.**

There's one last step. You need to run the `update.php` file.

Running update.php

Any time you upgrade a module — or (for that matter) update your Drupal software — you need to run a program called `update.php`. Before you do so, however, make sure you're ready to upgrade: Make sure you've done these three tasks:

- **Back up your database.** See the section "Backing up your database," earlier in this chapter, for instructions.
- **Back up your code.** For this step, you make a copy of your entire Drupal directory on your web server.

  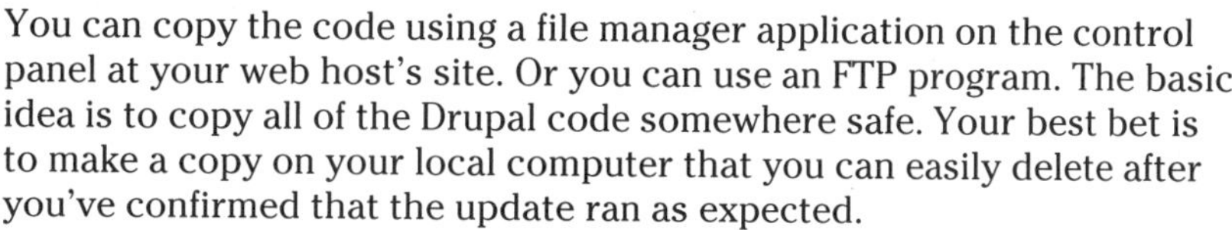

  You can copy the code using a file manager application on the control panel at your web host's site. Or you can use an FTP program. The basic idea is to copy all of the Drupal code somewhere safe. Your best bet is to make a copy on your local computer that you can easily delete after you've confirmed that the update ran as expected.
- **Put your site in maintenance mode.** Choose Configuration➪Development➪Maintenance mode and select the Put Site into Maintenance Mode check box. Click Save Configuration.

When you're ready, updating is a pretty straightforward process: You log in as administrator and browse to the `update.php` file on your website. (It will be located at `http://`*`yourwebsitename`*`.com/update.php`. For example, ours is at `http://drupalfordummies.com/update.php`.) You'll see a page listing the steps you need to follow next (see Figure 10-10).

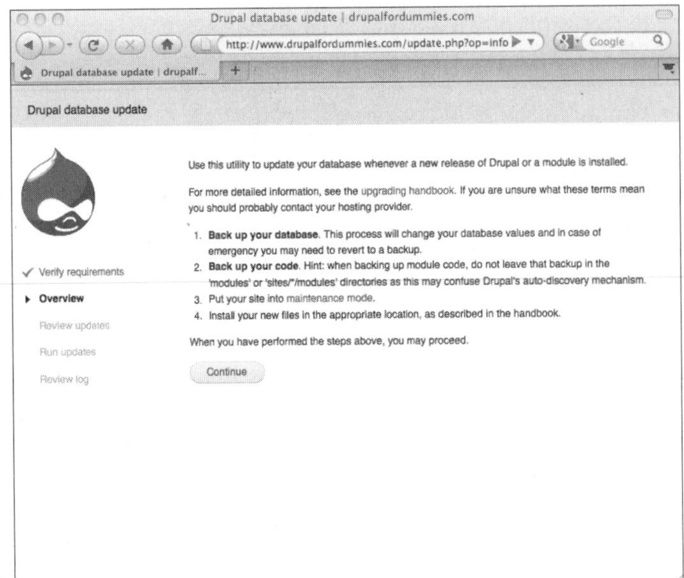

Figure 10-10: Steps to follow before running update.php.

Now you're ready to run `update.php`. Follow these steps:

1. **Browse to your site's `update.php`. Click Continue.**

   This screen shows you any available updates for the current version of Drupal, modules, or themes you've installed (see Figure 10-11).

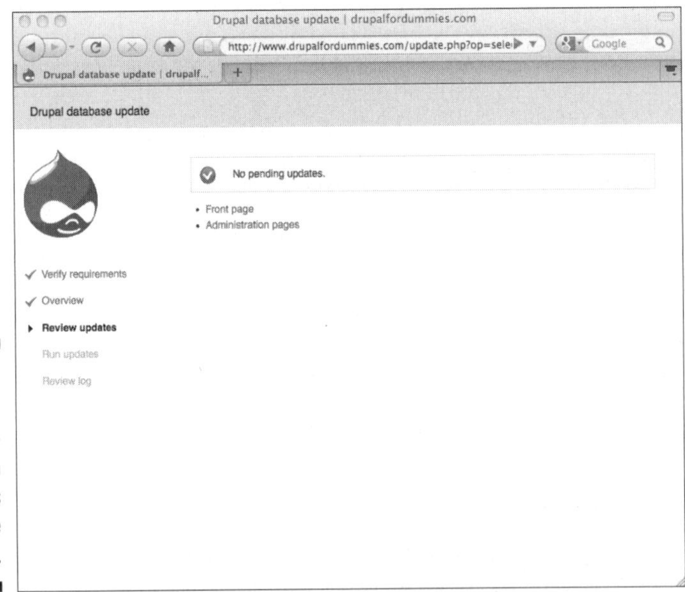

Figure 10-11: The update.php program finds available updates.

2. **Click Update.**

   Any updates you chose on the last screen will be made.

3. **Choose Configuration➪Development➪Maintenance mode and deselect the Put Site into Maintenance Mode check box.**

4. **Click Save Configuration.**

Updating your Drupal software

We cover two of the big pieces involved in updating Drupal software earlier in this chapter: backing up the database and running `update.php`. In this section, we put it all together for you.

Before updating, you need to decide which of these applies to you:

- **You installed Drupal using Softaculous or Fantastico. You have not installed any contributed modules or themes.**
- **You installed Drupal using Softaculous or Fantastico. You've installed contributed modules or themes.**
- **You installed Drupal yourself by getting a copy from drupal.org.**

The following subsections describe each of these approaches to installation.

Installed Drupal with Softaculous or Fantastico, no additional modules or themes

The simplest scenario is that you installed Drupal with Softaculous or Fantastico, and you have not added modules or themes. Because you haven't installed any additional modules, Softaculous or Fantastico can easily update your site for you.

There is often a delay between when a new Drupal update comes out and when Softaculous or Fantastico can upgrade for you. You may have to wait a few days and check periodically.

To find out whether you can upgrade, visit the control panel on your web host and click Softaculous or Fantastico. If you can update your Drupal installation, you'll see a message to that effect (see Figure 10-12).

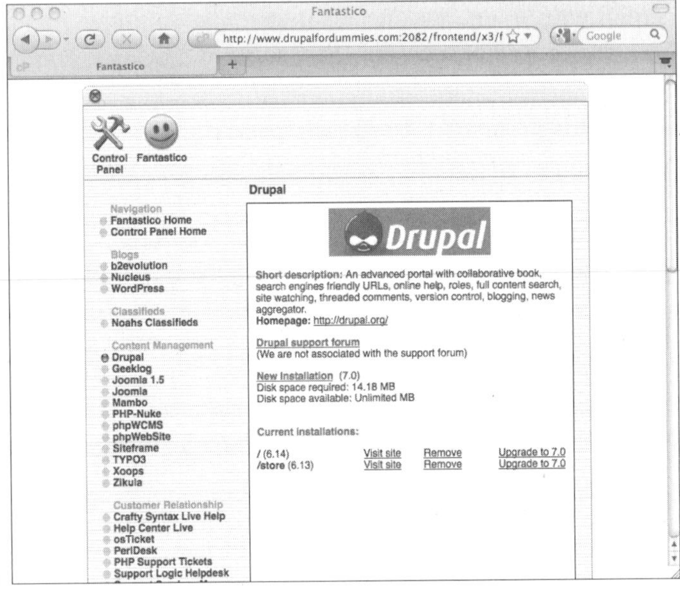

Figure 10-12: Fantastico message indicating Drupal software upgrade.

After you click the Update link, you'll see this message:

> If you have modified the files, languages, themes, or if you have added any third-party modifications to this installation of **Drupal,** it is possible that you may need to re-install your themes and/or reapply your custom changes after using Fantastico to upgrade. We take no responsibility for the integrity of custom modified installations after Fantastico upgrades them.

We recommend that you make your own backup of your database and script directory before proceeding — even though Fantastico will make one automatically before upgrading.

Softaculous or Fantastico will work well if you haven't done much with your site. After you begin customizing things, however, Softaculous or Fantastico may not be able to restore a previous state after you make changes. For this reason, you need to back up your database.

Installed Drupal with Softaculous or Fantastico, added modules or themes

After you add modules or themes, Softaculous or Fantastico may no longer be able to adequately manage updates to your Drupal software. Instead, you'll have to begin managing your updates manually. Follow the directions under the next section, "Installed Drupal by yourself."

Installed Drupal by yourself

To update Drupal, follow these steps:

1. **Back up your database.**

   See the section, "Backing up your database," earlier in this chapter, for instructions.

2. **Copy your entire Drupal site to another location.**

   Don't make a copy of your Drupal site and store it *inside* your Drupal site. Make sure your backup copy is outside of your entire Drupal directory — preferably not even on the same web server. You can always upload the copy back to the web server later if you need to.

3. **Choose Configuration⇨Development⇨Maintenance mode and select the Put Site into Maintenance Mode check box.**
4. **Click Save Configuration.**
5. **Click Modules and deselect any contributed modules. Leave the Core module settings as they are.**
6. **Click Appearance and choose one of the themes that was installed with Drupal originally, such as Garland.**
7. **Get the new version of Drupal from drupal.org.**
8. **Use a file manager or FTP program to copy the new files to your Drupal directory, with the exception of the `sites` folder.**

   Do not overwrite or copy over this folder with the new files.

   Transferring files is very much the same process you follow when you install Drupal in the first place. Take a look at Chapter 2 for specific instructions on getting your files on your web server.

   If you browse to your site right now, you'll see the original installation script we discuss in Chapter 2 when you install Drupal. *Do not run this program.* You're updating, *not* installing — and running an installation can destroy information stored in your database.

9. **Browse to the `update.php` on your website and click through the installation screens.**
10. **Choose Appearance, and then choose your desired theme.**
11. **Choose Modules and enable any contributed modules you want to use. Leave the Core module settings as they are.**
12. **Browse to the `update.php` on your website and click through the installation screens again.**

    It's important to run `update.php` every time you install a contributed module. Because this is the first time this new Drupal codebase is using the modules, it treats them like a new installation.

13. **Choose Configuration➪Development➪Maintenance mode and deselect the Put Site into Maintenance Mode check box.**
14. **Click Save Configuration.**

Configuring Your Site

In previous chapters, we briefly mention many of the Drupal site configuration options. After you have the basic Drupal concepts down, many of these configuration options will make more sense. In this section, we take a closer look at a few of them.

Triggering actions

An *action* is some event that happens in response to something. For example, when a new user registers on your site, sending him an automatic e-mail is considered an action. The Actions section under the System section of the Configuration page shows you a list of available actions and allows you to create custom actions.

The missing piece here is a way to actually use these actions. Behind the scenes, Drupal has code built-in that *triggers* these actions; for example, in the code for new users registering is a trigger that fires off the e-mail action.

The way you can use actions without having to write the code to trigger them is to use the Trigger module — which is an optional Core module that must be enabled before you can use it.

Here's a basic example of how to create a trigger to display a custom message to a user who signs in. You must first create a custom action by following these steps:

1. **Choose Configuration➪System➪Actions.**
2. **From the Create an Advanced Action drop-down list, choose Display a Message to the User and click Create.**
3. **In the next screen (see Figure 10-13), type your message in the Message text box.**

   For example, we typed: `Hi [user:name], it's good to see you. Let's do lunch sometime.`

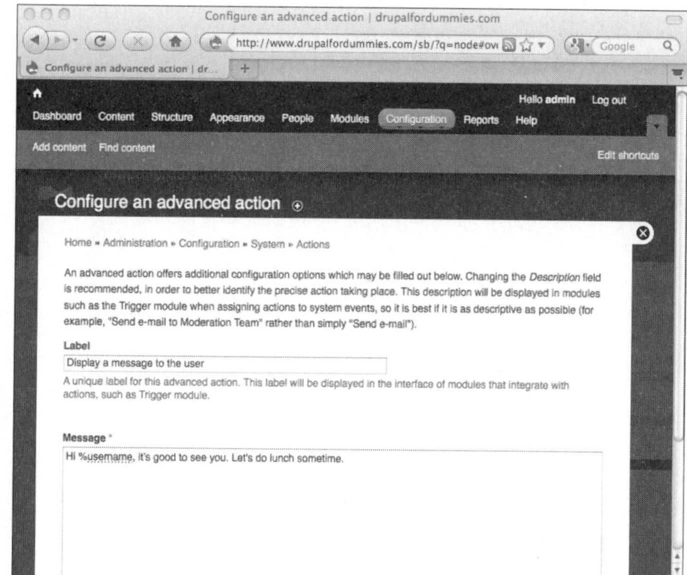

Figure 10-13: Configure an advanced action page.

The [user:name] is a stand-in for the name of the user who just logged in. In other words, if a user with the username Elmer logs in, after you trigger this action, that user will see the message, *Hi Elmer, it's good to see you. Let's do lunch sometime.*

4. **Click Save.**

   The other half of this operation is to set up a trigger to fire off this action when a specific user logs in.

5. **Enable the Trigger module from the Modules page.**

6. **Choose Structure⇨Triggers.**

   The Triggers page has five tabs along the top. These correspond to the types of activities that happen on your site.

7. **Click the User tab.**

   Because you want something to happen when a user signs on, the trigger you want is under the User tab (see Figure 10-14).

8. **Under the trigger After a User Has Logged In, select Display a Message to the User from the drop-down list.**

9. **Click the Assign button next to the drop-down list.**

Now when a user logs in, he or she will see the message, with the correct username substituted for the [user:name] you put in the action.

To delete a trigger, click the Delete link next to it.

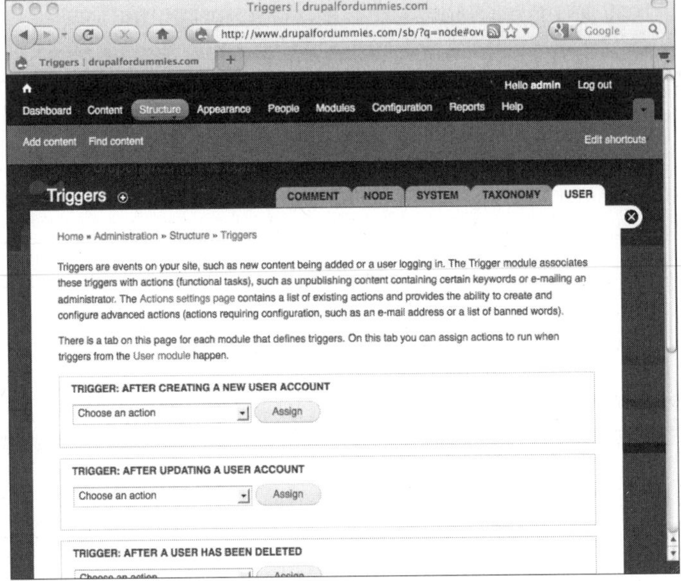

Figure 10-14: The User tab of the Trigger module.

Setting an administration theme

As you customize the theme for your particular site, you may find it unsuitable for using when you administer your site. You can set a theme to be used only on administration pages. To do so, follow these steps:

1. **Choose Appearance and scroll down to Administration Theme.**
2. **Choose a new theme from the drop-down list.**
3. **Optionally, select the check box to use the administration theme when creating or editing content.**

   Now, when you choose Create Content and create one of the content types, the administration theme will be in effect.
4. **Click Save Configuration.**

Creating clean URLs

Drupal automatically creates URLs for the content you add to the site. The format of these URLs is controlled by Configuration⇨Search and metadata⇨Clean URLs.

If this option is off, the URLs will be not be as simple — and will contain ? and = characters. For example, a URL without this setting might look like this:

```
http://drupalfordummies.com/?q=node/21
```

With clean URLs, the URL will be shorter and simpler. It looks like this:

```
http://drupalfordummies.com/node/21
```

Controlling Page Not Found errors

Sometimes visitors to your site attempt to browse to a page that doesn't actually exist. This is known as a *404 error.* Instead of displaying an ugly page that says `Page Not Found`, by default Drupal sends the visitor to a special page that reports this error.

If you have pages on your site that only logged-in users can see, and unregistered visitors try to go to one of those pages, Drupal redirects them to a page-not-found page.

The settings that control this behavior are found at Configuration➪Site Information➪Error Pages (see Figure 10-15).

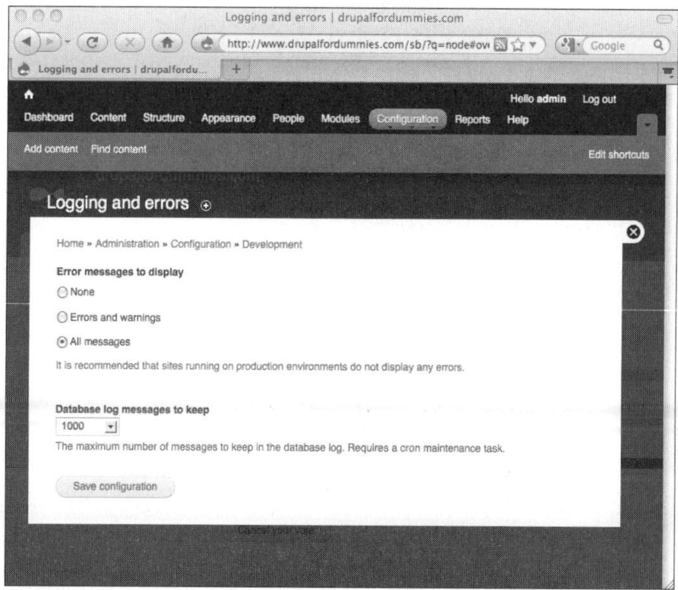

Figure 10-15: Settings for error reporting.

On this form, you can change the pages to which visitors are sent when they try to browse to a page that doesn't exist — or when an unregistered visitor tries to browse to a page that only logged-in users can see.

If you're curious, you can see what pages your users are trying and failing to reach. To see logged error messages, choose Reports⇨Recent Log Messages. Clicking Filter Log Messages allows you to sort through the messages and locate precisely the ones you're interested in. On the left are the types of errors; on the right are the levels of severity.

Chapter 11
Customizing Themes

In This Chapter

- Adding a new theme
- Understanding theme structure
- Modifying a theme
- Installing your theme
- Customizing your site's appearance

In this chapter, we take you through the anatomy of a simple theme. We show you how to change things to make your site more distinctive. A single chapter on creating a custom Drupal theme can't *possibly* cover all the details, but you can create a unique and custom site by taking an existing theme and making a few relatively small changes to it.

Drupal 7 themes have made tremendous strides in allowing you to customize your site from the admin interface. Prior to Drupal 7, if you wanted to make some basic changes to a theme, you had to know CSS or HTML. To make bigger changes, you had to have some understanding of PHP code. And while you still need all that knowledge if you're going to truly customize and create a new and unique theme, you can do an enormous amount without ever touching the code. In this chapter, we take a look at what files go into a theme and explore the options that new Drupal 7 themes give you for customization.

Adding New Themes

You can change the appearance of your site with just a few clicks when you add a new theme. Drupal 7 makes installing new themes so easy, there's no reason not to go find several and install them.

Finding new themes

New themes, like modules, are located at `http://drupal.org`. To find Drupal 7-compatible themes, follow these steps:

1. **Choose Appearance⇨Install New Theme.**

   This opens the theme installation form with a link to the themes directory on drupal.org (see Figure 11-1).

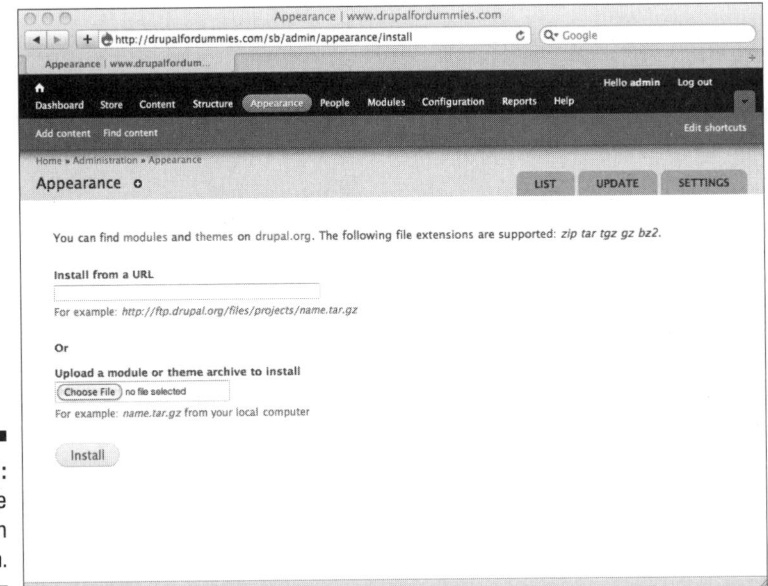

Figure 11-1: The theme installation form.

2. **Click the Themes link.**

   This takes you to the theme search form (see Figure 11-2).

3. **Choose 7.x from the Filter by Compatibility drop-down list and click Search.**

Find some themes you like and copy the paths to their `.zip` files, just as if you were installing modules. At the time of this writing, there aren't very many Drupal 7 themes available, but some you may want to try are

- **Acquia Marina:** `http://drupal.org/project/acquia_marina`
- **Marinelli:** `http://drupal.org/project/marinelli`
- **Danland:** `http://drupal.org/project/danland`
- **Zero Point:** `http://drupal.org/project/zeropoint`

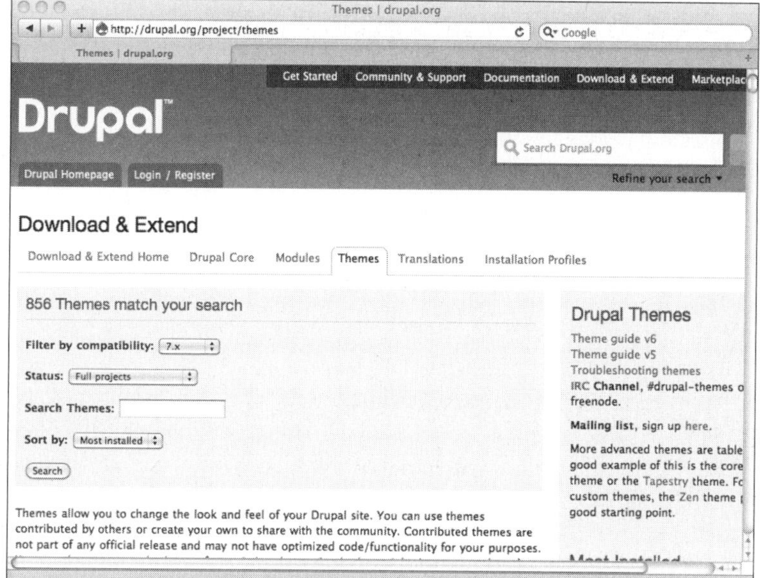

Figure 11-2: The theme search form on drupal.org.

Installing themes

If you've decided to install the themes mentioned in the previous section, you should have the URLs to four `.zip` files:

- `http://ftp.drupal.org/files/projects/acquia_marina-7.x-1.0-rc1.zip`
- `http://ftp.drupal.org/files/projects/marinelli-7.x-3.0-beta9.zip`
- `http://ftp.drupal.org/files/projects/danland-7.x-1.0.zip`
- `http://ftp.drupal.org/files/projects/zeropoint-7.x-1.1.zip`

Keep in mind that the filenames will change as themes undergo more development. By the time this book is in your hands, these `.zip` files may be out of date. Visit the themes' home pages to get the latest file URLs.

To install each of these themes, follow these steps:

1. **Choose Appearance⇨Install New Theme.**
2. **Paste one of the `.zip` file URLs in the Install from a URL text box.**

3. **Click Install.**
4. **Click Enable Newly Added Themes link and repeat Steps 1–3 for the rest of the `.zip` URLs.**

Your new themes now appear at the bottom of the Appearance page (see Figure 11-3).

Themes you add are disabled by default. To try a new theme out, click the Enable and Set Default link underneath its thumbnail.

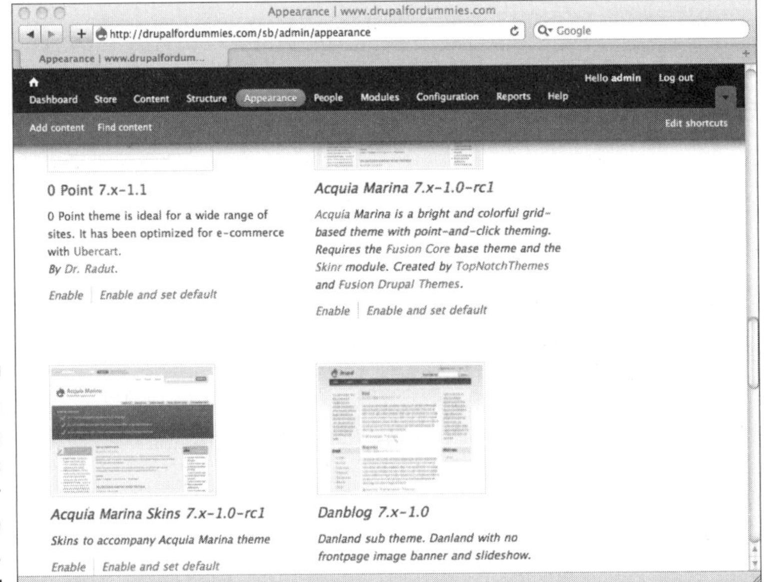

Figure 11-3: New theme thumbnails on your Appearance page.

Dissecting a Theme

Before you begin changing a theme, it's good to know how themes are structured. In this section, we show you the basic structure of a Drupal theme. We use the Garland theme because it contains all of the essential parts of a theme.

You can use FTP or your ISP's file manager to look in the `themes` directory under `Drupal` and see the files that make up each theme. Look at the `garland` folder in the `themes` directory (see Figure 11-4).

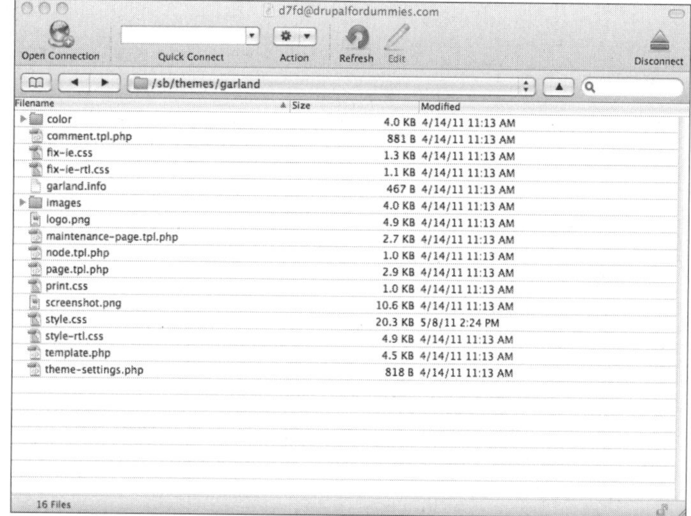

Figure 11-4: The Garland theme files.

To follow the discussion better, enable the Garland theme and activate the main menu (not visible by default with this theme). Follow these steps:

1. **Click Appearance.**
2. **Locate the Garland theme and click Enable and Set Default.**
3. **Choose Structure⇨Blocks.**
4. **Click the Garland tab at the top-right.**
5. **Find the Main menu item in the list and drag it to the top of the Sidebar second section.**
6. **Scroll down and click Save Blocks.**

Theme file types

The four types of files in the Garland theme are

- **CSS:** The information in CSS (Cascading Style Sheet) files controls all the colors, font sizes, font styles, margin widths, and much more.
- **INFO:** A very small text file containing theme-specific information.
- **PHP:** These files contain lots of HTML code and some PHP code. They are responsible for displaying all the content that appears on the various content type pages such as comments and blocks.
- **PNG:** Image files.

Theme code files

This chapter focuses on showing you how to modify and customize an existing theme. To do that, you need to understand what each file in the theme controls. Garland contains eight files containing code:

- `style-rtl.css`: Unless you're creating a site for a language that is read from right to left, you can ignore this file. This is used to help make right-to-left running languages more readable.
- `style.css`: This is the file to which you have to pay the most attention. This controls practically everything to do with the appearance of your site.
- `garland.info`: This file contains the information Drupal needs about this theme.
- `node.tpl.php`: This file controls the appearance of all the content types that appear in the blocks of the Garland theme. All your articles and blog posts are contained in nodes, for example.
- `page.tpl.php`: The page template is the biggest file. It builds a complete page, including menus, all the blocks, and all the content. This defines where everything goes on the page. If, for example, you wanted the content in the Left Sidebar to shift to the right, this is the file you would change. The appearance of pages in Garland is managed by this file. (See Figure 11-5 for a page in Garland.) The appearance of the content types in blocks within a page is managed by `node.tpl.php`.

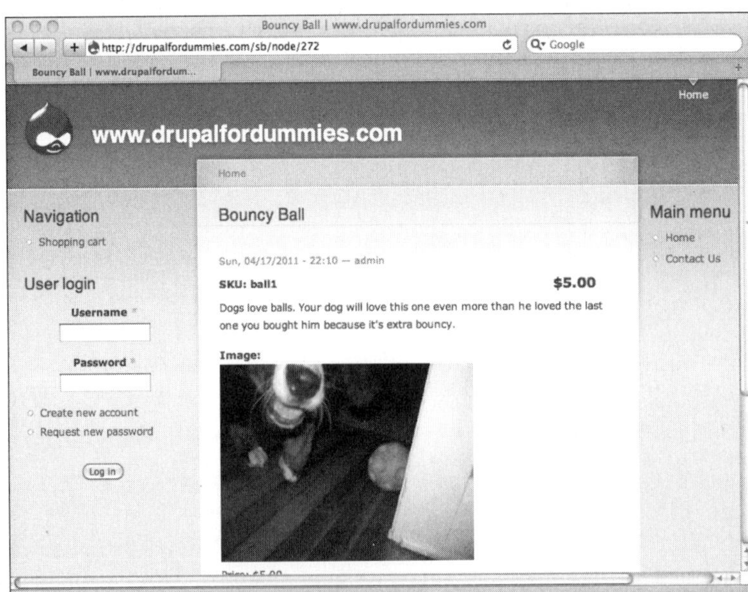

Figure 11-5: Page view with content in Garland.

- `comment.tpl.php`: The comment template pulls in and structures an individual comment. Optionally, it can include a user photo and signature block. Figure 11-6 shows a comment form in the Garland theme.
- `template.php`: The node template controls the structure of content. All your stories and blog posts are contained in nodes, for example.
- `theme-settings.php`: This controls what settings are available for this theme.

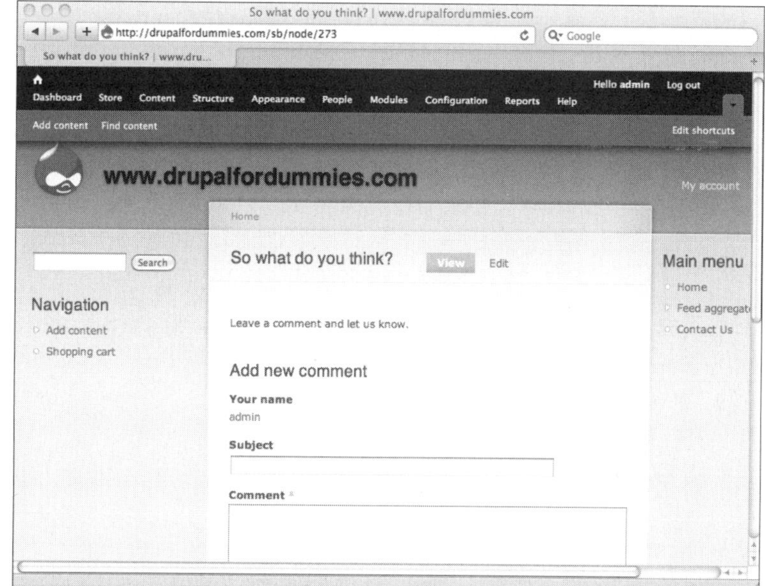

Figure 11-6: Adding a comment in the Garland theme.

Theme image files

Garland has a number of image files, but only two in the main directory:

- `logo.png`: The Drupal logo that appears in the upper-left corner of this theme.
- `screenshot.png`: The image preview of the theme.

Customizing Themes by Hand

It's far easier to duplicate and rename an existing theme and use it to build your first theme than to build one from scratch.

The first step is to install the theme you want to modify. Then make a copy of the theme directory on your computer. Use this local copy to make your changes, and then upload the modified copy to your `site/all/themes` directory on your web host. This section gives you a quick idea of how this works.

To edit the files in a theme, you need some sort of text editor:

- On a Windows machine, you can use the NotePad text editor.
- On the Mac, TextEdit will work, although be sure to choose Format➪Make Plain Text.

To create your own version of a theme, follow these steps:

1. **Rename the folder to a distinctive name you want to use for your theme.**

   The name may only contain lowercase letters, numbers, and underscores. We choose `drupalfordummies`.

2. **Open this folder and locate the `.info` file. Rename this file with your new theme name.**

   In our case, we use `drupalfordummies.info`.

   Make sure you rename the info file. Don't copy it with a new name. You only want one info file in your theme directory, and the name needs to match the name of your theme.

3. **Open the `.info` file in a text editor (see Figure 11-7).**

4. **Change the first line of this file to simply**

   ```
   ; $Id$
   ```

5. **Change the `name =` line to use your theme name.**

   In our case, we change it to `name = Drupal For Dummies`.

   This will be the name that shows up on the module selection page. It can contain spaces.

```
garland.info
; $Id: garland.info,v 1.10 2010/11/07 00:27:20 dries Exp $
name = Garland
description = A multi-column theme which can be configured to modify colors and switch between fixed and fluid width layouts.
package = Core
version = VERSION
core = 7.x
stylesheets[all][] = style.css
stylesheets[print][] = print.css
settings[garland_width] = fluid

; Information added by drupal.org packaging script on 2011-01-05
version = "7.0"
project = "drupal"
datestamp = "1294208756"
```

Figure 11-7: The contents of the .info file.

6. **Change the description text to describe your theme.**

   We change ours to `description = Yellow and Black Theme.`

7. **Save this file using the new name you gave your theme.**

   We name ours `drupalfordummies.info`. You can delete the original `.info` file.

   Your `.info` file should now look similar to Figure 11-8.

```
garland.info
; $Id$

name = Drupal For Dummies
description = Yellow and Black Theme.
package = Core
version = VERSION
core = 7.x
stylesheets[all][] = style.css
stylesheets[print][] = print.css
settings[garland_width] = fluid

; Information added by drupal.org packaging script on 2011-01-05
version = "7.0"
project = "drupal"
datestamp = "1294208756"
```

Figure 11-8: The modified .info file.

8. **Open the `template.php` file in a text editor, use FIND and REPLACE to find the name "garland" and replace it with your theme's name (for example, *drupalfordummies*). Save your file.**

9. **Repeat Step 8 for the `theme-settings.php` file.**

Installing Modified Themes

You haven't made any actual changes to the appearance of the theme yet, but it is a good time to get your theme installed to make sure the `.info` file is correctly configured. Use FTP or your web host's file manager program to move the folder containing your new theme into the Drupal `sites/all/themes` directory on your web server. In our case, this means copying the entire `drupalfordummies` folder — with all our theme files — into the directory under `sites/all/themes`.

You may find it easier to zip your theme folder, transfer it to your web server's `sites/all/themes` directory, extract it, and then delete the original zip file.

If you have correctly changed the theme folder name, the name of the `.info` file, and the information inside the `.info` file, you will see your theme in the list when you choose Appearance (see Figure 11-9).

You see your theme, your theme's description, and a thumbnail for your theme.

Click the Enable and Set Default link. This will make it easier for you to see the changes to your theme as you make them.

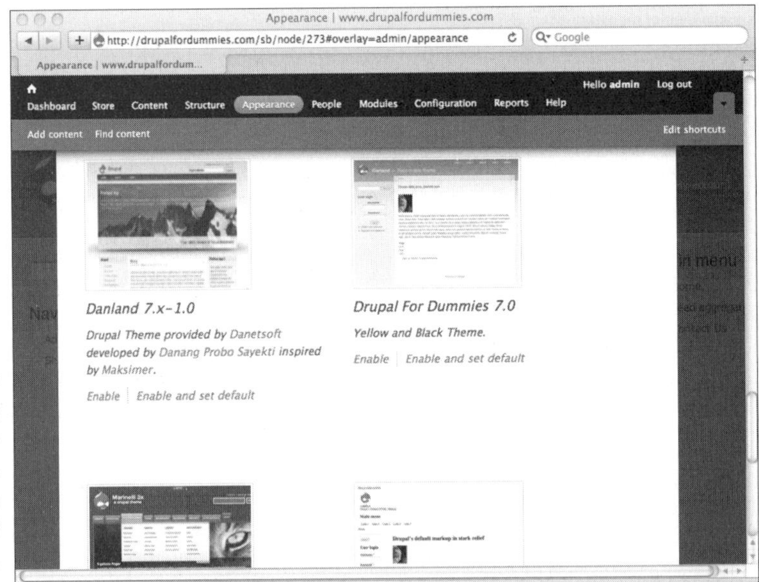

Figure 11-9: Your new theme shows up in the list of themes.

Naming colors

To change the colors used by your theme, you need to understand how colors are used in CSS code. Colors are described using hexadecimal numbers, rather than names. For example, suppose the header block of a theme is a light blue color. But instead of saying "light blue" in the code (which you will see in a moment), the value `#06090C` is used instead. This kind of number is known as an RGB value. RGB stands for Red-Green-Blue. The number `#6699CC` represents how much red (66), green (99), and blue (CC) to use.

Sometimes you will see only three digits, such as `#69C`. This one is the same as `#6699CC`. If you ever see a three-digit version, realize that it's simply leaving out duplicate numbers. Two colors you will see often are black (`#000` or `#000000`) and white (`#fff` or `#ffffff`).

Also, when you see letters, it doesn't matter whether they are upper- or lowercase. So `#fff` is the same thing as `#FFFFFF`.

Don't let this throw you. You don't have to come up with these numbers; you can use a tool to help you. Here are some websites that show you colors and the numbers that correspond with them:

- `www.colorschemer.com/online.html`
- `http://htmlhelp.com/cgi-bin/color.cgi`
- `www.yellowpipe.com/yis/tools/hex-to-rgb/color-converter.php`

Because some themes don't display the main menu by default, your theme may not either. To display your main menu links, follow these steps:

1. **With your theme enabled and set as default, choose Structure⇨Blocks.**
2. **Click the tab at the top-right with your theme's name.**
3. **Find the Main menu item in the list and drag it to the top of the Right Sidebar section.**
4. **Click Save Blocks.**

Right now, your main menu links are titled *Main menu* on your site. If you want to remove that title, choose Structure⇨Blocks. Click the Configure link next to Main menu. In the Block Title text box, type **<none>** and then click the Save Block button. That's it.

Changing your theme's appearance

At this point, you can enable your new theme and set it as the default. It looks exactly like the original because you haven't changed anything yet. You can now make changes to your theme.

There's simply not room in this book to cover the ins and outs of CSS coding. The point of this chapter is to show you the possibilities and a few of the simpler, although still dramatic, changes you can make to customize your site.

Changing colors

In our case, we want to begin with the colors used by our theme. In the previous version of Drupal, we had to open the `style.css` file on a desktop computer, make the changes, and then upload the altered `style.css` to the `Drupal/sites/all/themes/drupalfordummies` folder on our web server. It's much improved now, with most themes having a built-in interface to change color settings. For example, we can manipulate the colors in the Garland theme as follows:

1. **Go to Appearances and select Garland as the default theme.**
2. **Click the Settings link next to Garland.**

   This opens the settings page, as shown in Figure 11-10.
3. **Change the setting in the Color Set drop-down list.**

   For example, we select Citrus Blast. This changes the theme's colors. Scroll down to see a preview.
4. **Change individual colors on your site by clicking the section you wish to change and clicking the color wheel to the right.**

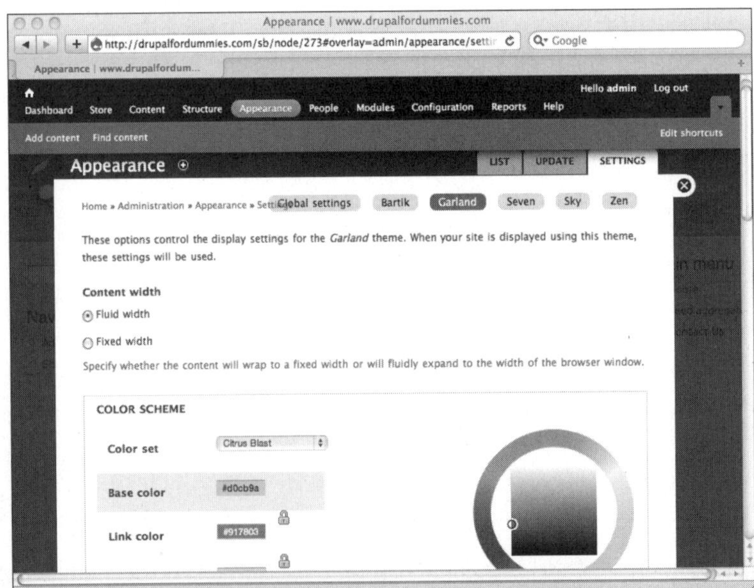

Figure 11-10: Garland theme settings page.

5. **Play around with the settings until you're happy with the result, and then click Save Configuration.**

If you know the hexadecimal value for the color you want to assign, you can also change colors by typing the hex values into the text boxes.

Understanding the style.css file

Using the settings page for a theme allows you to change some colors, but you are limited in what you can modify. In general, a theme's `style.css` file contains the values for all the colors on your site. The key to customizing your site's colors is to understand how this file is structured and to know what colors the hex values in this file stand for. The tricky part is that each theme is different — and there's very little consistency in where, for example, the header text color is controlled in this file. That being said, it's worth taking a closer look. You can also find tools that can help you track down the code that controls the specific colors of things.

Everything in the `style.css` file is divided into chunks of code. Each chunk consists of some names or labels, an open curly bracket, lines of code called rules, and a closing curly bracket. For example, the body section of the file might look like this:

```
body {
  margin: 0;
  padding: 0;
  color: #000;
  background-color: #fff;
}
```

For the moment, you only need to notice that this is the body section, and it has a background color defined in it, `#fff`.

Changing colors

When you know how to change `style.css` and upload it to your web server, you can start experimenting. If you see a color setting and don't know what it controls, change it to a crazy color, such as hot pink (`#FF00FF`). When you reload your site, you'll see what changes.

Here's a rundown of a few major color settings sometimes found in `style.css` files that you may want to change (though these colors may occur, they don't reflect the colors used in the example site):

- `body { background-color: #fff; }` — Controls the color behind the main content area. In this example, it's set to white.
- `a:link { color: #39c; }` — This is the color of web links on your site. #39c is a bluish color.

- `a:visited { color: #369; }` — This is the color of a web link a visitor sees after he or she has clicked it.
- `a:hover { color: #39c; }` — The color of a link when a cursor is over it.
- `body { background-color: #ddd; }` — The background color.

  You may notice that there already was a bit of code labeled *main* with a background color. In CSS code, you may have multiple rules that set the same color for some part of your site. *The last one is the one that shows up on a page.* In this case, the second body tag has the color that actually shows up on the page.

- `#main { background-color: #fff; }` — This controls the color behind your main content area.
- `#sidebar-left, #sidebar-right { background-color: #ddd; }` — The Left and Right Sidebars are set to a gray color.
- `#header { background-color: #FFFE01; }` — This is the main header background color.
- `.site-name a:link, .site-name a:visited { color: #000000; }` — This is the site name in the header.
- `.site-name a:hover { color: #369; }` — When a cursor is moved over the site name, it changes to this color.
- `#mission { background-color: #369; color: #fff; }` — The mission statement appears just below the header and has two color settings. The first is for the background color; the second is the color of the text in it.
- `#footer { background-color: #eee; }` — This is the footer color.
- `.title, .title a { color: #777; }` — These are the titles above various sections of your site. In our case, this affects *Who's new* and *Who's online* in the Right Sidebar and the username in the Left Sidebar.

Changing fonts

The `style.css` file also contains the rules for the color, style, and size of fonts. Here's a rundown of some of the coding used to control the appearance of fonts that you see in `style.css`:

- `font`: This tag appears only once in `style.css` and specifies the font to use for the entire site.
- `font-size`: Controls how large or small the text is.
- `font-weight`: Used to set text to bold.
- `font-style`: Primarily used to set text to italic.

- `text-decoration`: Controls whether a link is underlined.
- `color`: Sets the color of text.

The following code lines show a few major text settings in `style.css` that you may want to change.

```
body { font: 76%/170% Verdana, Arial, Helvetica, sans-serif; color: # 000000;}
```

Two things are going on in this line. The attribute `color` controls the text color for the entire site, setting it to black. If no other rules change the color later in this file, it shows up as black on the site. This specification controls the color of all the content text all over the site.

The font setting, `76%/170% Verdana, Arial, Helvetica, sans-serif`, sets both the text size and font. If you want to use a different font and larger text, you can change this line to read as follows:

```
font: 100% Times New Roman, Georgia, Serif;
```

This changes the font for the entire site, as you can see in Figure 11-11.

The font is larger — and is now Times New Roman instead of Verdana. We prefer the smaller font size and Verdana for the style, so after experimenting, we change this line back to `font: 76%/170% Verdana, Arial, Helvetica, sans-serif;`.

```
a { text-decoration: none; font-weight: bold; }
```

The `text-decoration` controls whether links on your site are underlined. In this case, they are not. The `font-weight` makes the site links boldface.

```
a:hover { text-decoration: underline; }
```

When you move your mouse cursor over one of the links on the site, the underline appears. When you move your cursor off, it disappears. Any time you see `hover`, it's referring to the cursor being moved over something and paused there.

```
#branding { color: #000; }
```

If we change `color` to `#000`, the color becomes black and looks better against the yellow background (see Figure 11-12).

When changing CSS code, be careful to keep the punctuation marks exactly as they are. For example, make sure each line in the block of code ends with a semicolon.

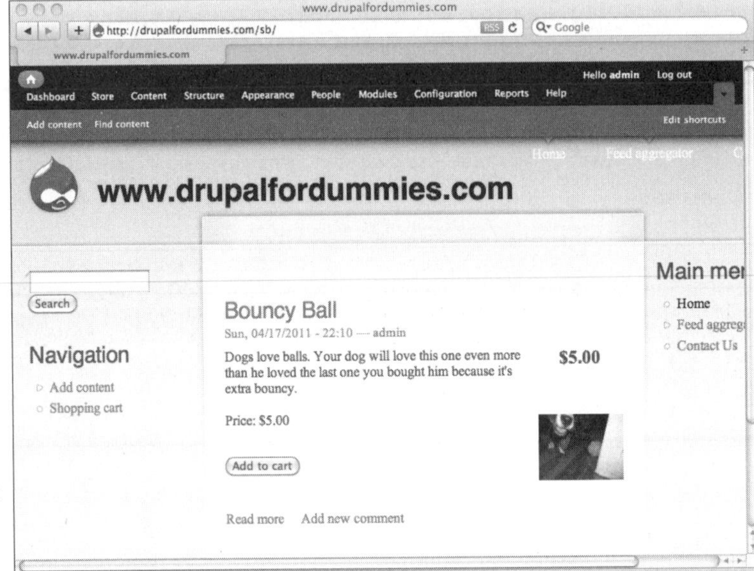

Figure 11-11: Using the Times New Roman, Georgia, Serif font family set to 100%.

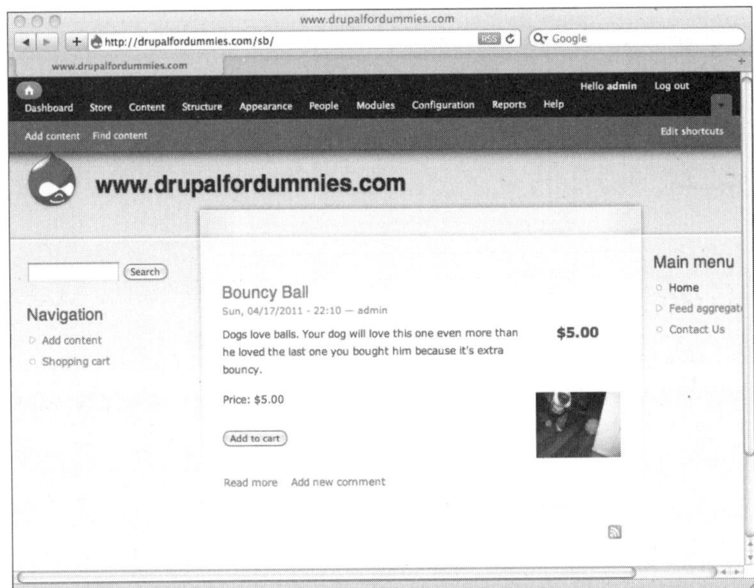

Figure 11-12: Site header text size set to black.

Trial and error is one way of figuring out what styles in the `style.css` belong to what elements on your site. But there's an easier way. We recommend you use the Firefox web browser and install the add-in called Firebug. Doing so opens a pane in the web browser and shows you what styles the elements on your web page are using. In Figure 11-13, you see which line in `style.css` is controlling the appearance of the site name in the header. At the bottom-right of the browser, you can see where in the CSS code the formatting is set. Find out more about Firebug at `http://getfirebug.com`.

You can tweak lots of other details and make modifications to themes. `http://drupal.org/theme-guide` is an extremely thorough guide.

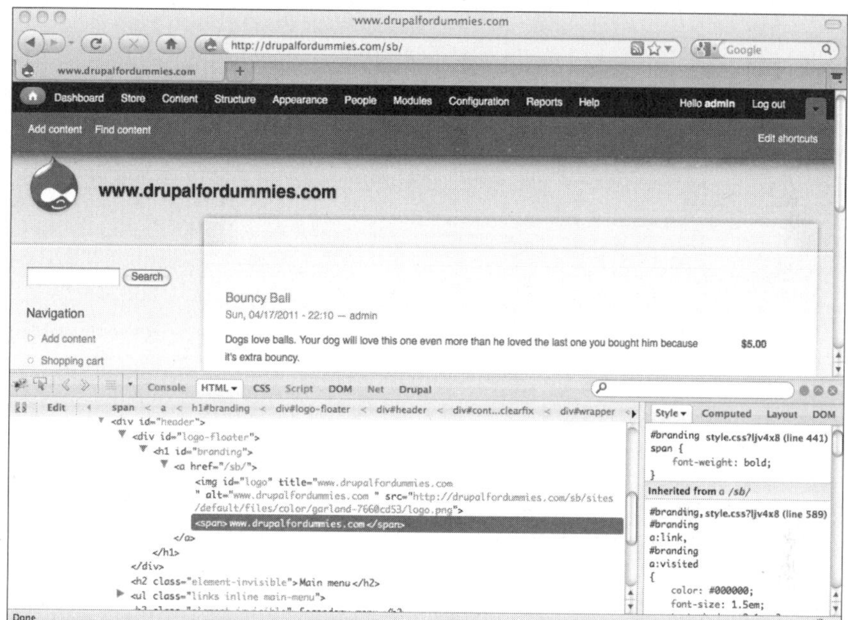

Figure 11-13: Firefox browser with Firebug.

Using graphics

You should now be able to change any color on your site. But suppose you want to use an image as a background for one of the areas. Say, for example, that you want to use a background image for the Left and Right Sidebars, or you want to change the logo. The following sections show you how.

Adding a background image

You can add a background image to the Left and Right Sidebars to spruce them up. For example, say you still want the text on top, but instead of gray, you want faint, diagonal pinstripes.

Follow these steps:

1. **Use FTP or your ISP's file manager to copy your background image to your web server. Put it in your theme's directory.**

For example, we have a background image called `stripes.gif`. We upload it to our Drupal site under `themes/drupalfordummies`.

2. **Open a copy of `style.css` in a text editor.**
3. **Locate a section of code that deals with the sidebars, such as:**

```
#sidebar-first, #sidebar-second {
  width: 16em;
  padding: 1em;
  margin-right: -18em; /* LTR */
  background-color: #ddd;
}
```

4. **Add the following line inside the curly brackets:**

```
background-image:url('stripes.gif');
```

5. **Save and upload your file.**

   Now when you look at the site, the stripes show up on the sidebars.

   Unfortunately, the bottom parts of the sidebars don't have the background. Only the portions of the sidebars with actual content blocks are filled in. You need one more line of code. Coming right up.

6. **In the body section of `style.css`, add the same line of code:**

```
background-image:url('stripes.gif');
```

7. **Save and upload your file.**

   Your background is now visible all the way to the bottom of the page.

Changing the logo image

The logo on the site still leaves something to be desired. You can easily replace it with one that looks better. Best of all, there's no coding involved.

To change the logo, follow these steps:

1. **Choose Appearance. Click the Settings link next to your theme.**
2. **Scroll down to the Logo image settings.**
3. **Deselect the Use the Default Logo check box.**
4. **Click Choose File to select and upload your new logo.**
5. **Click Save Configuration.**

   Your logo appears.

Between replacing the logo, changing the built-in theme settings, and modifying the code in the theme files, you can customize most themes to make your site look exactly the way you want.

Part IV

Taking Drupal to the Next Level

"Okay, well, I think we all get the gist of where Jerry was going with the site map."

In this part . . .

Building a basic site in Drupal is child's play to you now. Blogs? Simple. Forums? A piece of cake. Controlling user permissions? Pshaw.

You yearn for more features. You want to do more. The chapters in this part show you how use Drupal Gardens to create a website astonishingly quickly, build your own complete online storefront, and even display your Twitter and Facebook updates on your site. And lots more.

Chapter 12

Creating a Robust Website

In This Chapter

- Determining the purpose of your site
- Adding modules to enhance your site
- Enabling visitors to contact you
- Enhancing user profiles

To create something more than a generic website, you must take a close look at what you want to accomplish and discover which specific modules and techniques suit your needs. This chapter will help you figure out the purpose of your site — and show you some steps you can take to ensure that your site is effective and your message is getting across to your audience.

Planning Your Drupal Site

To figure out which Drupal modules features to add to your site, you need to have a clear idea of its purpose. Knowing this will help you pick the right features for your site.

Getting a clear picture of your site

Understanding the purpose of your site is the first step in creating it. Your site probably falls under one or more of these categories:

- **Blog:** Blogs allow you to share your view of the world on some particular topic. They're also good advertising tools for getting news out about a company. They're often one part of a larger site.
- **Brochure:** These sites are largely static advertisements or information about a business or service.

  An example of a brochure site is `www.thealamo.org`. While this site does have a calendar and gift shop, its main purpose is to serve as a brochure with rarely modified information (see Figure 12-1).

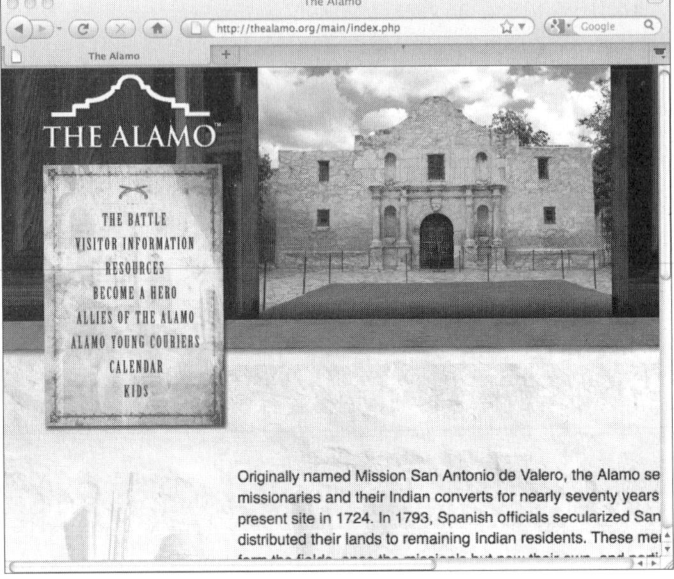

Figure 12-1: The Alamo website is primarily a brochure site.

- **Community:** These sites exist to attract people with something in common. They typically encourage discussion of a topic with forums. `www.drupalfordummies.com` falls under this category.
- **Image gallery:** Now that most people have digital cameras, photography has never been more popular. You may want to build a site (or portion of a site) devoted to showcasing your images.
- **Information or news:** You want to send out frequent news updates about a topic. You may also want to aggregate information from other websites. (Chapter 14 shows how to pull content from other websites with a technology called RSS.)
- **Storefront:** You have a product to sell and need an online shopping cart system to allow site visitors to order your goods. (Chapter 15 shows how to build a storefront using the Ubercart module.)

Your site may fall under several of these categories. For example, you might want to sell things and also blog about your company to let your visitors know about sales or new products. Or you may want to create a community site that allows members to post images.

Knowing your audience

As you create your site, keep your audience in mind. People visit websites for a variety of reasons, and the content of your site should be presented in a way to attract the visitors you want.

There are lots of good books about website interface design and designing for particular audiences. One book that provides a very quick and entertaining overview of the most important principles of site design and great insight into how visitors to a site will probably react to it is *Don't Make Me Think*, by Steve Krug.

Types of visitors to your site include

- **The random visitor:** Some people will visit your website by accident. A compelling main page may draw them into your site, but in general these visitors won't be inclined to buy your products, join your community, or be interested in your services.
- **Researcher:** These folks found you by using a search engine. Your site was in their search results and may or may not be what they're looking for.

  To boost the number of satisfied researching visitors to your site, focus on setting up your site to be found by search engines. This is a practice called *search engine optimization (SEO),* and it focuses on making sure the content on your site is presented in ways that search engines such as Google will find and index it. SEO is an entire subject worthy of its own book; we recommend a Drupal module (described in Chapter 16) as a good starting place.

- **Direct user:** This is someone who's part of your main user base; these visitors arrive at your site knowing what they'll find there. A friend or a link on another site may refer them to your site. These are the users you most want to please with your site layout. If your site is a community site, for example, you should make the link to your forums prominent on your main page. Or if you have a storefront, you might want to feature your most popular products on your main page.

You may also have to consider the technology your site visitors have available to them. For example, you may be creating a site that will be frequented by people with older computer equipment and slower connections. You may want to limit your use of Flash movies and large images to allow your site to load faster.

You should also consider the demographics of your audience. Perhaps you are trying to build a community for mothers, for example. That site would be very different from one built for video gamers.

Take your site design cues from sites that are successful. We're not suggesting that you steal designs from other sites, but you can definitely learn something by studying how they use their primary links, or from how much (or how little) content they provide on their pages.

Choosing your features

Your choice of features depends on the purpose of your site, as well as your user base. Here's a sampling of site types and site features to consider:

- **Blog:** Obviously, if you have a blog site you need the Blog module. But you may want to provide a page about yourself, a contact form, and a page with archives of previous blogs.

  Consider adding advertising blocks to your site as the number of visitors to your sites increases.

  If your site consists of blogs about a set of topics, you might want to create a submenu with links to these topics. A good example (and also a site that sometimes offers Drupal tips) is `www.smashingmagazine.com` (see Figure 12-2).

  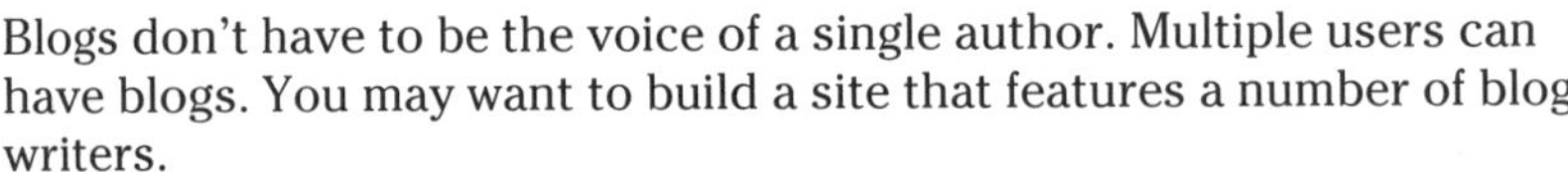

  Blogs don't have to be the voice of a single author. Multiple users can have blogs. You may want to build a site that features a number of blog writers.

- **Brochure:** Brochure sites are largely informational, and the information on these sites doesn't change very often. Generally, they contain
  - A main page
  - A contact page
  - Directions
  - Sub-pages containing more information

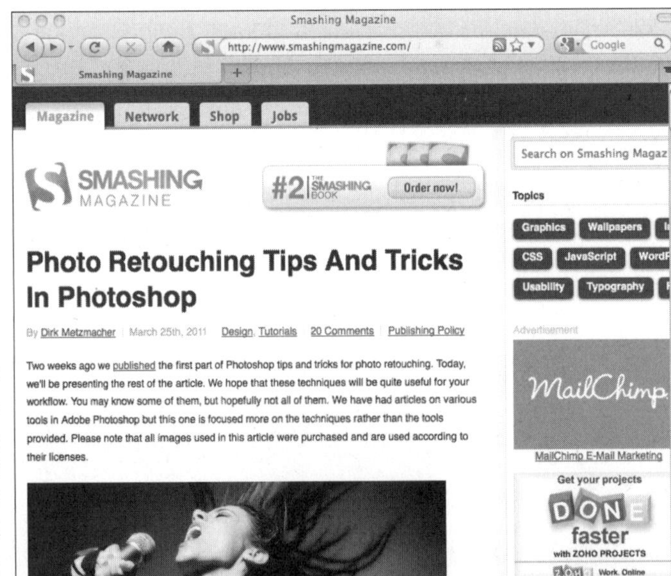

Figure 12-2: Smashing Magazine is an example of a blog site.

A good example of a brochure site is the National Park Service's Grand Canyon site (`www.nps.gov/grca`). It almost looks like a printed brochure that has been turned into a site. Very little information on this site ever changes.

- **Community:** A website for which its members provide the content is considered a community site. Community sites are often sponsored by a company and used to advertise, while providing a valuable resource for users of a product or participants in some activity. Most community sites are part of a larger site and primarily consist of forums. You will often see advertisements and company branding, as well as links back to the other sections of the site, as shown on the community forums at Frommer's, a travel book series (see Figure 12-3).
- **Image gallery:** Image galleries abound on the web. They may contain images from a single source or allow registered users of a site to contribute the pictures. You've probably seen Flickr (`www.flickr.com`), a site that combines both image gallery and community website features. An image gallery can be extended to become a media gallery, offering videos, podcasts, or PDFs. The idea behind the site is to serve as a repository for files, allowing them to be previewed online, and under certain conditions, downloaded by visitors to the site. These sites need a form to allow files to be uploaded to the site.

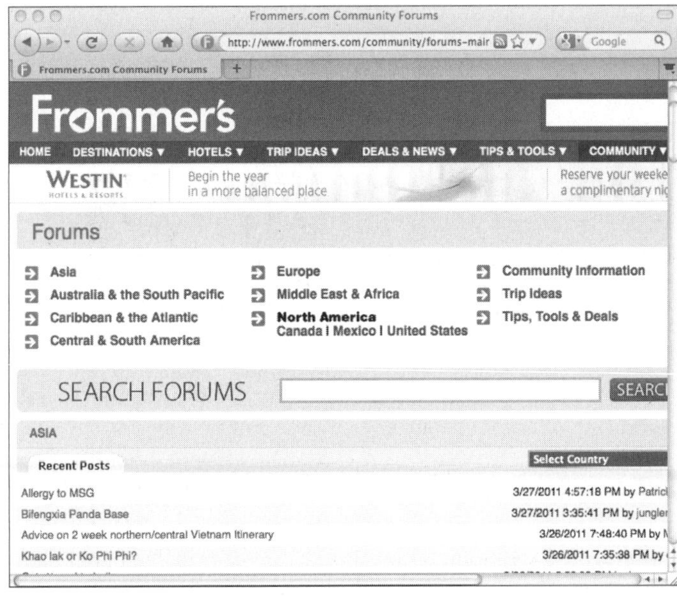

Figure 12-3: Frommer's community forums.

- **Information or news:** These sites are almost the opposite of brochure sites because their content frequently changes. The focus is on publishing blurbs that visitors click to read the full story. An example of this sort of site is `www.news.google.com`. Every time you visit the page, the news headlines have changed. News is acquired or aggregated from a variety of sources. News sites are typically very busy and don't have many other features beyond the headline links. New headlines may also be accompanied by thumbnail images.
- **Storefront:** From brick-and-mortar stores like PetSmart and Target to online-only retailers such as Amazon.com, storefront sites abound on the web. Storefronts exist to sell, and usually focus on doing that. You don't see many bells and whistles on shopping sites. As you can see in Figure 12-4, they have links to the products prominently displayed, a link to a shopping cart, and often a Search box to help visitors quickly find products they are seeking.

Figure 12-4: Storefront website for Design Within Reach.

Search boxes are great additions to most types of sites. They don't take up much room, and they save visitors to your site lots of frustration when they are looking for one particular subject, item, or article. Drupal has a preinstalled module for adding one to your site. We show how to enable and set it up in the next section.

Additional Modules to Install

Drupal comes with many preinstalled modules worth enabling. There are also many more contributed modules. You can also download and add many more contributed modules to your Drupal program that extend the features of your site.

In this section, we take a closer look at three preinstalled modules that can add useful features to your site. The first is the OpenID module that allows people who already have accounts on other sites to log in to yours without registering. The second is the Poll module that lets you set up questions for your registered users to vote on. Finally, the Search module allows you to place Search boxes on pages of your site for visitors to easily locate content.

OpenID module

So many sites expect users to create accounts. The idea behind OpenID is to allow a user who has already registered on a major website (for example, `www.google.com`) to log in to your site using his Google account information instead of creating a new account on your site. OpenID supports a number of major website logins. A user can also create a master login at `www.openid.net` that will allow him to log in at any site that allows OpenID.

If you turn on the OpenID module, you open your site to users you haven't personally verified. This doesn't matter if your site is mainly informational or if you want a large user base. But if you allow your users lots of privileges — such as posting unmoderated content to message boards — you may not want to use this module.

To activate the OpenID module, follow these steps:

1. **Click Modules on the Dashboard menu bar.**
2. **Select the OpenID check box.**
3. **Click Save Configuration.**

The next time a visitor arrives at your home page, she will see the normal login form and a link to use an OpenID login. If she clicks that link, the login form changes to prompt for her OpenID (see Figure 12-5).

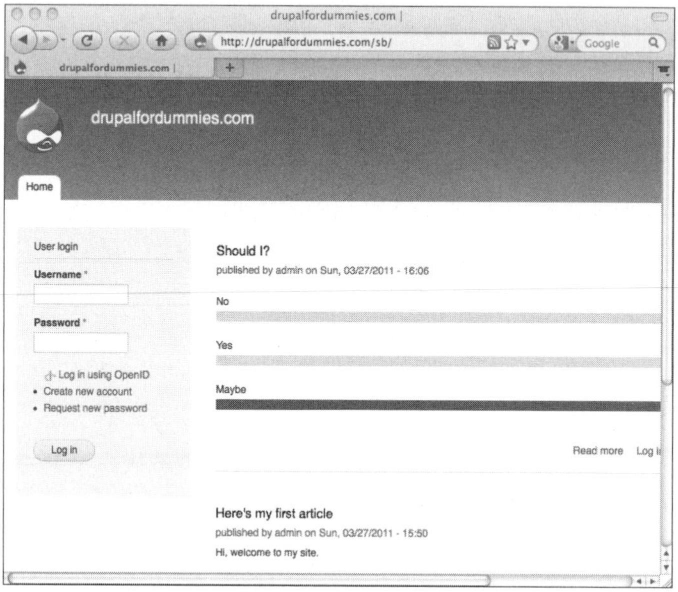

Figure 12-5: Login form with OpenID module enabled.

Poll module

Polls are great for community sites because they get people involved. You can also collect valuable information if you use them to query your users about directions your site should take. To activate the Poll module and set up a poll, follow these steps:

1. **Click Modules on the Dashboard menu bar.**
2. **Select the Poll check box.**
3. **Click Save Configuration.**
4. **Choose Content⇨Add Content⇨Poll to set up a new poll.**

   Figure 12-6 shows the Create Poll form.
5. **Enter a poll question in the Question text box.**
6. **Enter one of the possible answers in the first Choice text box.**
7. **Enter another possible answer in the second Choice text box.**
8. **If you want more than two choices, click the More Choices button. Enter the new choice in the third Choice text box.**
9. **Make sure the Active radio button is selected under Poll Status.**

   If the Closed radio button is selected, the poll and the voting results will be visible, but no more voting will be allowed.
10. **Click Preview to see your question. When you're happy with it, click Save.**

Figure 12-6: After enabling the Poll module, you can access the Create Poll form.

The poll question will now be published on the front page of your site (see Figure 12-7).

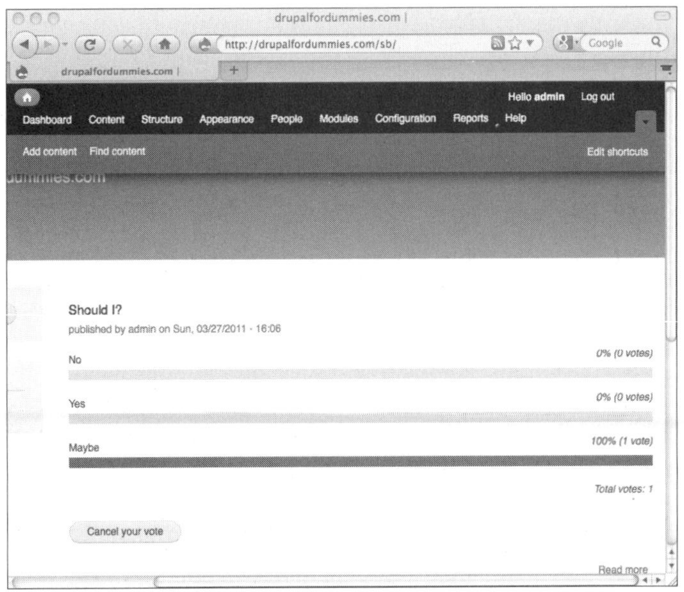

Figure 12-7: Poll published to the front page.

After a user clicks a choice, he sees the voting results. He can also cancel his vote if he chooses.

The Create Poll form (refer to 12-6) also controls a few other poll settings:

- **Poll publishing options:** As with a new post, your poll shows up as the top item on your home page. This can be changed for an individual post by changing the Publishing Options section of the Create Poll page by deselecting the Promoted to Front Page check box.

  If you never want your poll to appear on the front page, you can control the behavior for all polls. Follow these steps:

  1. *Choose Structure⇨Content Types.*
  2. *Click the Edit link next to the Poll type and deselect the Published To Front Page check box under Publishing Options.*
  3. *Click Save Content Type.*

- **Comments about poll:** By default, your poll allows registered users to comment. You can change this by modifying the Comment settings section of the Create Poll page. Your choices are Open or Closed.
- **Location of Poll:** You can control in which block your poll appears. Follow these steps:

  1. *Choose Structure⇨Blocks.*

     The item Most Recent Poll appears near the bottom of the page under the Disabled section.

  2. *Change the drop-down list or drag it to the region of your choice.*
  3. *Click Save Blocks.*

Search module

As you and your registered users add more content to your site, be it blog entries, forum posting, or news posts, visitors to your site will want to be able to find content of interest. Drupal has a Search module that displays a Search box and returns a list of links to content that matches the search terms entered in the box.

To set up the Search module, follow these steps:

1. **Click Modules on the Dashboard menu bar.**
2. **Select the Search check box.**

   If the Search module is already selected, that means it's already active on your site and you don't need to change anything.

3. **Click Save Configuration.**

4. **Choose Structure⇨Blocks.**

   The entry Search form now appears in this list. If you had to enable it, it will show up under the Disabled section.

5. **Drag the Search form to the region of your choice.**

   You can drag the items in each region to control the order within the block. For example, you can drag the Search form item to the top of the Sidebar first section to make it appear near top-left on every page of your site.

6. **Click Save Blocks.**

   Your search form will now appear on your site. When users search for a word, links to content containing that word appear (see Figure 12-8).

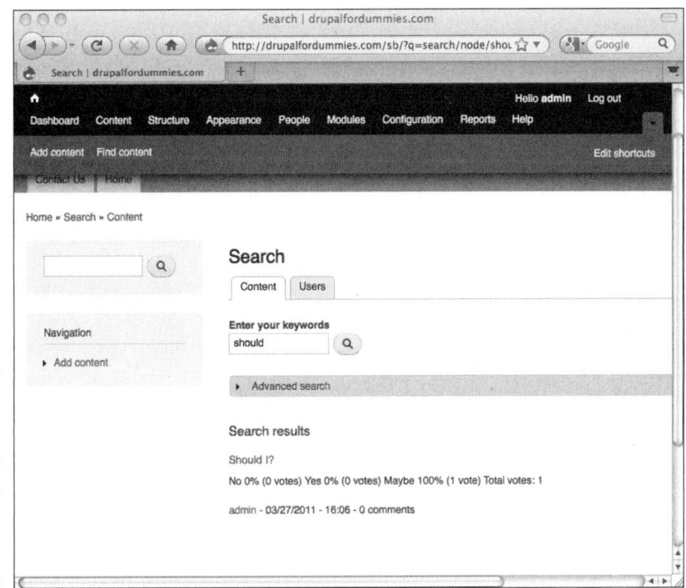

Figure 12-8: Search form in Left sidebar and search results.

By default, the search form appears as text box and a Search button. If you want to change the appearance, follow these steps:

1. **Choose Structure⇨Blocks.**
2. **Click the Configure link next to Search Form.**
3. **In the Block Title text box, enter any text you want for a title. If you want no title, enter** <none>**.**

   Be sure to include the angle brackets.

4. **Click Save Block.**

You can use this same technique to remove the title from any block component. You can add or remove the title of any block by choosing Structure➪Blocks, click the Configure link next to the block you want to modify, enter **<none>** for the title (or add a title), and click Save Block.

The Block form also lets you control in which region a block should appear based on which theme you are using. All your currently enabled themes appear in the Region settings. Region settings appear for each block, not just the Search block.

Adding a Contact Form

An important addition to most websites, especially ones offering products or services, is a contact form. This allows site visitors to ask for more information without having to locate an e-mail address on your site and send you a message.

Contact forms can also be constructed to allow certain types of messages to be sent to specific people on your staff. The contact form has a Category drop-down list that allows visitors to select from a list of topics. For example, if you have a storefront and an employee in charge of shipping, you can create a contact form that, when submitted, sends the contents directly to the right person on your staff. The same contact form can be sent to your website administrator.

To create a contact form, follow these steps:

1. **Click Modules on the Dashboard menu bar.**
2. **Select the Contact check box.**
3. **Click Save Configuration.**
4. **Choose Structure➪Contact Form.**
5. **Click the Add Category tab.**

   This opens the Contact Form overlay shown in Figure 12-9.
6. **For category, enter a subject that you think someone would like to contact you about.**

   For example, enter **Product Information**. You'll have the chance to enter more categories later.
7. **In the Recipients text box, enter the e-mail addresses, separated by commas, of everyone you want to receive the results of this form when a user submits it.**

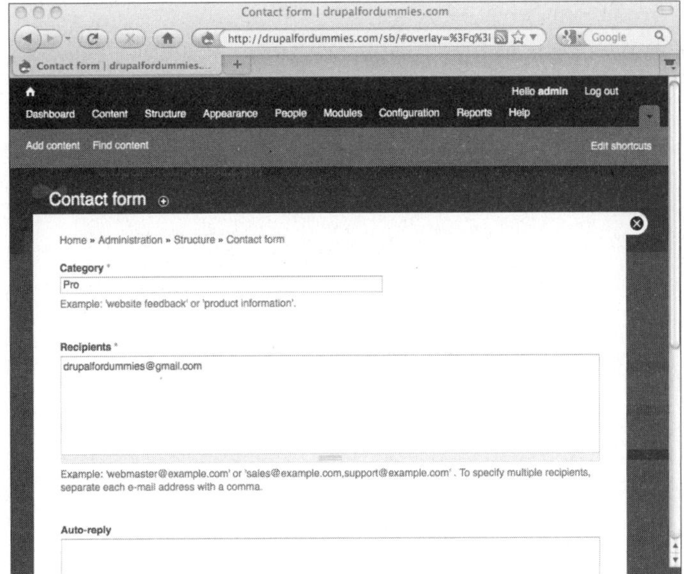

Figure 12-9: Adding a category to a contact form.

8. **If you want users to be sent a message after they submit the form, fill in the Auto-Reply text box.**
9. **If you think the category you entered in the Category text box is the most common one users will choose, select Yes in the Selected drop-down list.**
10. **Click Save.**

    You return to the Contact Form list page.

To add more categories or subjects to your contact form, repeat Steps 1 through 10.

You now have a contact form (see Figure 12-10).

To view yours, go to `http://yourwebsitename.com/?q=contact`. For example, ours is located at `http://drupalfordummies.com/?q=contact`.

The last step is to provide visitors to your site with a link to this form. To add a link to your Main menu, follow these steps:

1. **Choose Structure➪Menus.**
2. **Click List Links to the right of Main Menu.**

   You will see a list of your current main links. You need to add a new one for the contact form.

3. Click Add Item.

This opens the Add Item form, as shown in Figure 12-11.

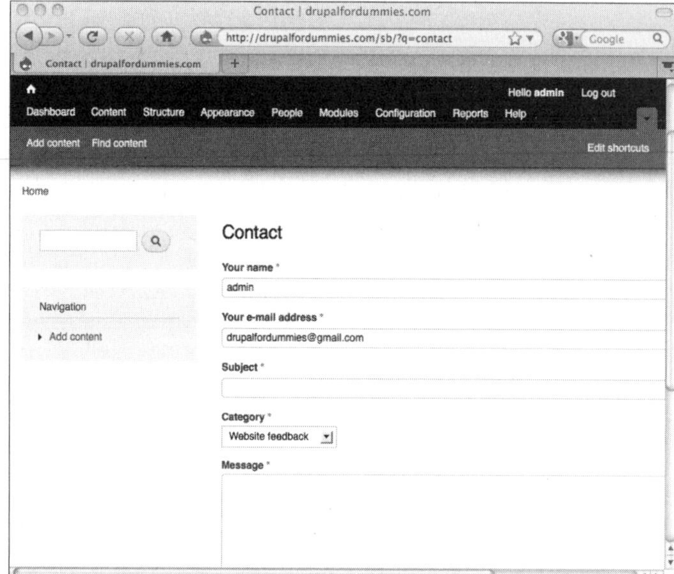

Figure 12-10: Contact form with Category drop-down list.

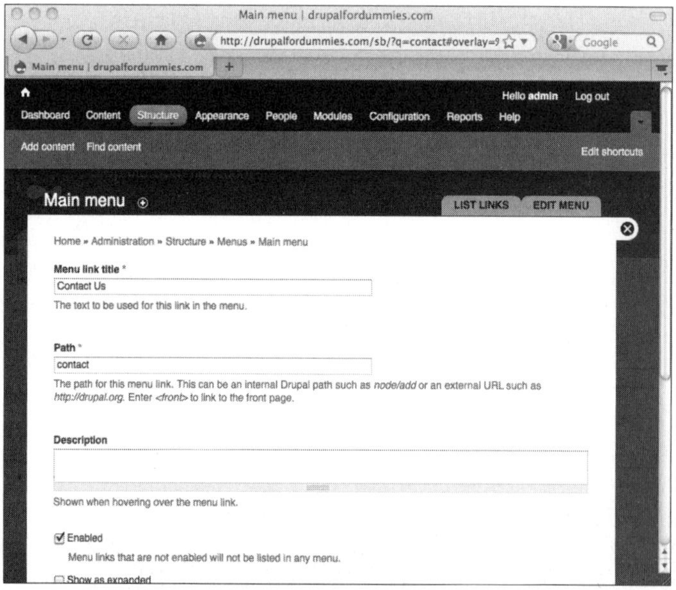

Figure 12-11: The Add Item form for the Main menu settings.

4. **In the Path text box, enter** contact.
5. **In the Menu Link Title text box, enter the text you want to appear in your primary menu as the link to the contact form.**
6. **Click Save.**

Your contact form will now be available to registered users.

If you want to make your contact form available to both registered and unregistered users, you need to change the permissions:

1. **Click People on the Dashboard menu bar and then click the Permissions tab.**
2. **Locate the Contact module and select the Use the Site-Wide Contact Form check box under the Anonymous User column.**
3. **Click Save Permissions.**

Enhancing User Profiles

Another good choice for increasing the community feeling of a site is to allow users of your site to add more details about themselves to their profile pages. Drupal 6 used the Profile module, but Drupal 7 has removed it and added this functionality to the Account Settings page (found by choosing Configuration⇨People⇨Account Settings). Figure 12-12 shows an example of a custom user profile form that users can fill out.

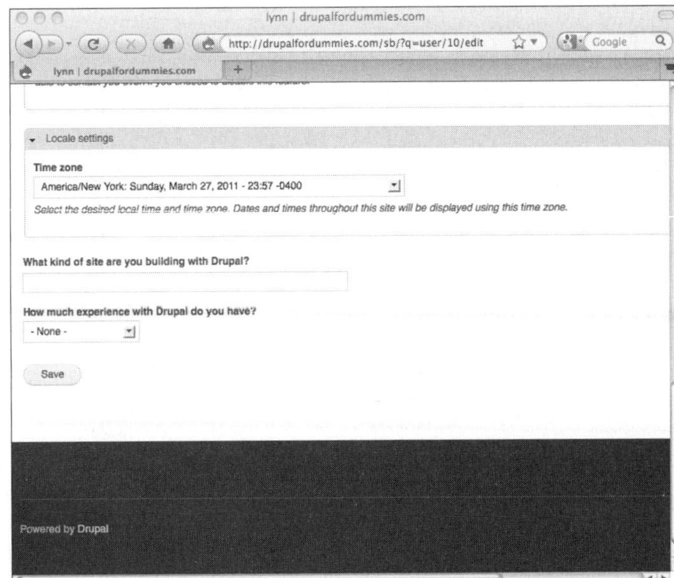

Figure 12-12: Profile form that asks for more user profile information.

The information a user enters on this form will show up when anyone clicks the username for that user.

Creating a personal information form

To create a form that your users can fill out and add more information to their profile pages, follow these steps:

1. **Choose Configuration⇨People⇨Account Settings.**
2. **Click the Manage Fields tab.**

   You have to create all the form fields that your users will answer using the Add New Field section of the form, as shown in Figure 12-13.
3. **In the Label text box, enter the question you want the user to answer.**

   This should tell the user what kind of information you want him to enter in this text box — for example, **What kind of site are you building with Drupal?**
4. **In the Name text box, add a distinctive name with underscores instead of spaces.**

   Drupal uses the name to keep track of this text box, but it will never be seen by you or the users filling out the form. We add to the word `field` that was already in the text box and end up with `field_about_your_site`.

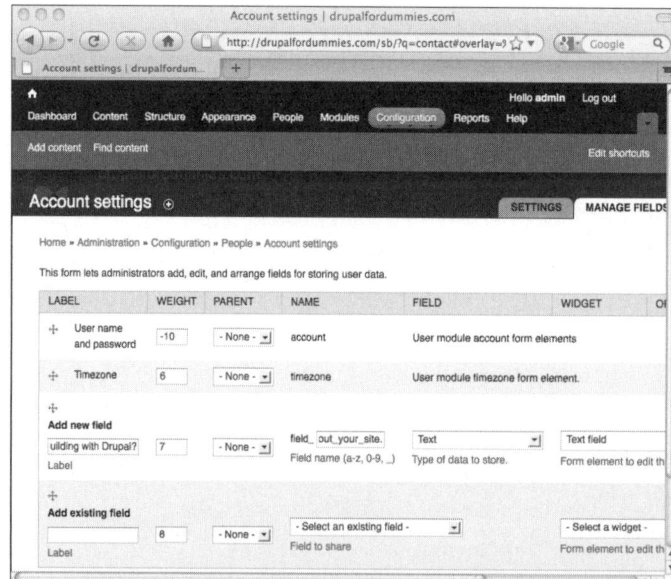

Figure 12-13: Form to create a new text box for a user profile form.

5. **From the Field drop-down list, select a field type.**

   In our example, choosing Text makes the most sense.

6. **From the Widget drop-down list, choose the type of form element that makes sense.**

   Text makes the most sense in our example. You can also use the widget to create a multiple-choice drop-down list by choosing Select List.

7. **Click Save.**

   Now, when users sign up or click the My Account link, they'll see the Personal Information tab. Clicking that tab displays any form fields you created under the Personal Information category.

To create a drop-down list, follow these steps:

1. **Choose Configuration⇨People⇨Account Settings.**
2. **Click the Manage Fields tab.**
3. **In the Label text box, enter the question you want the user to answer.**

   This time, make it a multiple-choice question such as, **How much experience with Drupal do you have?**

4. **In the Name text box, add a distinctive name with underscores instead of spaces.**

   An example is **profile_experience**.

5. **From the Field drop-down list, select a field type.**

   This time, choose List (Text); it makes the most sense.

6. **From the Widget drop-down list, find List (Text) and choose Select List.**

   You're prompted to enter drop-down list options.

7. **Click Save.**

   The Field Settings form appears.

8. **Enter the possible answers to the question, one per line.**

   For example, to answer "How much experience with Drupal do you have?", we might enter options such as these:

   - None
   - Less than 6 months
   - About a year
   - More than a year

   See Figure 12-14 for what the result looks like.

9. **Click Save Field Settings.**

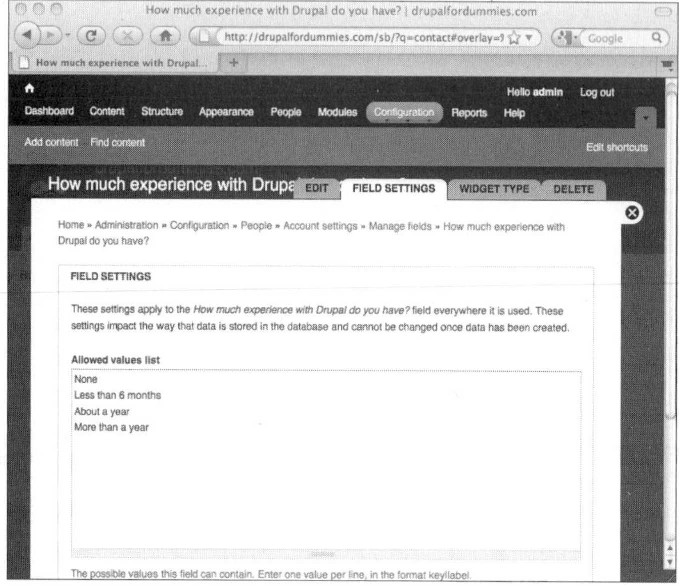

Figure 12-14: Field Settings form with list of options.

Now, when a user browses to her My Account page, she will see an Edit link that takes her to the form with the fields you just created.

Enabling registered users to view profiles

By default, Drupal only allows administrators to see everyone's user profile. You need to allow registered users and, if you choose, anonymous users to see them by changing the permissions. To give registered users permission to view other people's user profiles, follow these steps:

1. **Click People on the Dashboard menu bar, and then click the Permissions tab.**
2. **Select the check boxes next to View User Profiles.**

   You can choose to allow unregistered users to view them if you want.
3. **Click Save Permissions.**

Every username visible on your site will now link to that user's profile. Usernames show up in blog, comment, and forum postings. Figure 12-15 shows what a registered visitor to a site sees if he clicks a username.

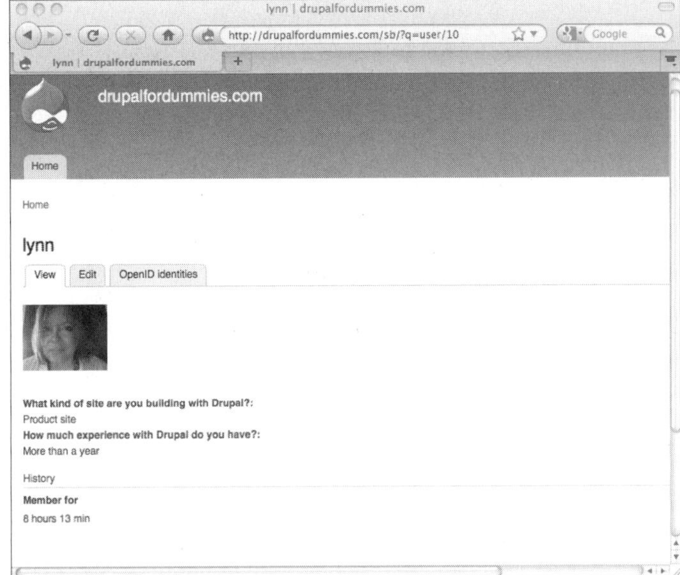

Figure 12-15: User profile page with custom Personal Information text boxes.

Enhancing profiles with user images and signatures

You can allow your registered users to upload an image that will show up on their profiles. By default, this image is turned on, but to modify its settings or turn it off, follow these steps:

1. **Choose Configuration➪People➪Account Settings.**
2. **Scroll down to the Pictures section.**
3. **Select the Enable Signatures check box.**

   This setting allows your users to create blocks of text that appear beneath every post or comment they write on your site.
4. **Select the Enable User Pictures check box.**

   More options appear beneath it (see Figure 12-16).

   You don't need to change any of these settings. The Picture Directory text box controls where the user images will be stored under the Drupal directory on your web server. The Picture Display Size drop-down list controls the size of the profile image. It defaults to Thumbnail, which is 85 pixels by 85 pixels. The Picture Maximum File Size drop-down list defaults to 30 kilobytes.

5. **Click Save Configuration.**

   Now, when a registered user chooses My Account⇨Edit, she will see a Picture section on the Edit form where she can select a photo to upload. This photo will appear on her user profile. She can also create a signature block.

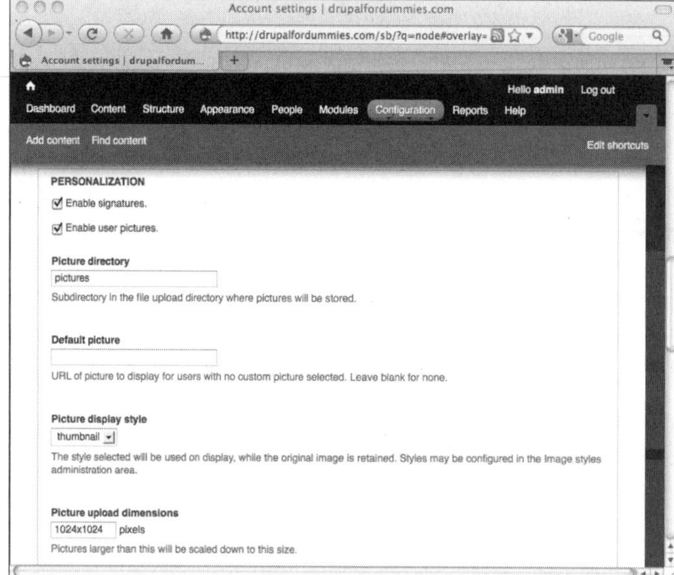

Figure 12-16: The Pictures settings to allow users to add profile pictures.

Chapter 13
Using Drupal Gardens

In This Chapter

- Walking through Drupal Gardens
- Creating an account
- Building a site with Theme Builder
- Managing your site's users

If you've found yourself stumbling through Drupal, still unsure whether it's for you, Drupal Gardens may be exactly what you're looking for. Drupal Gardens is a commercial website where you can find Drupal preinstalled for you, great documentation, and nifty features that make building and customizing a site incredibly easy. You don't need to deal with web hosting companies, file managers, or MySQL databases. It's all done for you. In fact, this chapter takes you from setting up your account to having a complete website online and ready for visitors in just an hour or two.

And the best thing is that most of what you learn about Drupal in this book still applies to Drupal Gardens sites. The same administration menu and the same controls we discuss in this book work on Drupal Gardens.

Ready? Get set! Go build an entire Drupal Gardens site, from start to finish, in record time.

Getting a Drupal Gardens Account

A basic Drupal Gardens website is free, and with onc, you can follow along in this chapter to create a complete site. We show you how to set up an account here. Also in this section, we discuss the other options available to you if you need a big site and if you want your own domain name. We start by showing you how to sign up for a free site.

Creating a free site

Signing up for a site is easy:

1. **Browse to `www.drupalgardens.com`.**

   This is the Drupal Gardens website (see Figure 13-1).

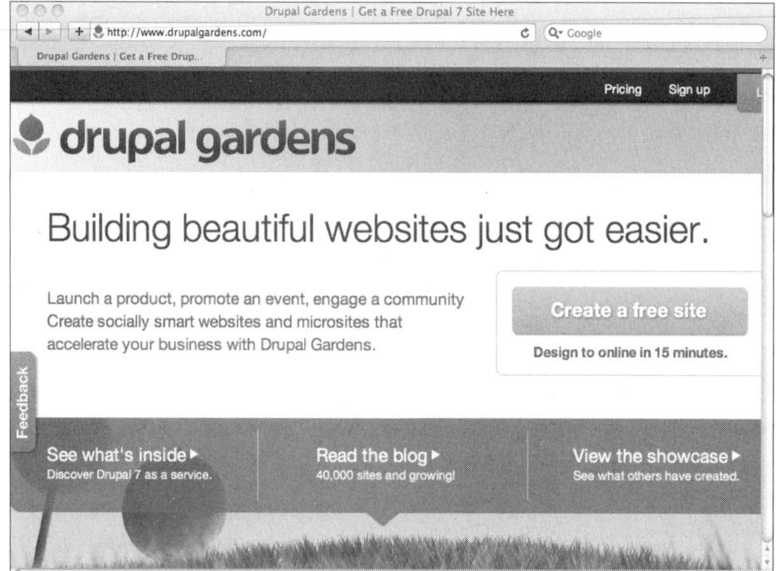

Figure 13-1: The Drupal Gardens website.

2. **Click the Create a Free Site button.**

   The Create the Next Social Phenomenon page appears, where you enter your contact information and basic information about your site (see Figure 13-2).

3. **In the Site URL text box, enter a name for your site.**

   The Site URL will be the address people browse to when they visit your site. In our example, we use `lynnwrites.drupalgardens.com`.

4. **Enter a username and password in the Username and Password text boxes, respectively.**

5. **Enter your e-mail address in the Email Address text box.**

6. **In the Word Verification text box, type the letters you see besidc the text box.**

7. **Click Continue.**

   At this point, you have to choose a template or pick specific features, pages, and blocks that you want on your site (see Figure 13-3).

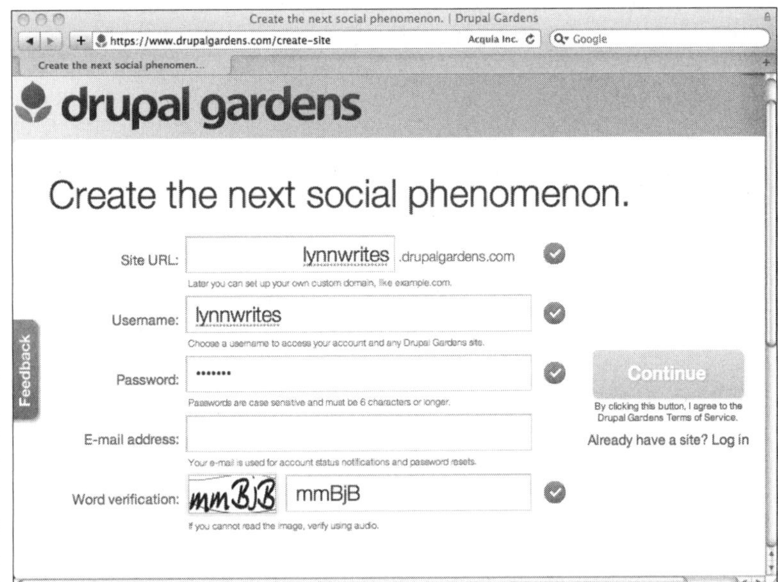

Figure 13-2: Register for your free Drupal Gardens site.

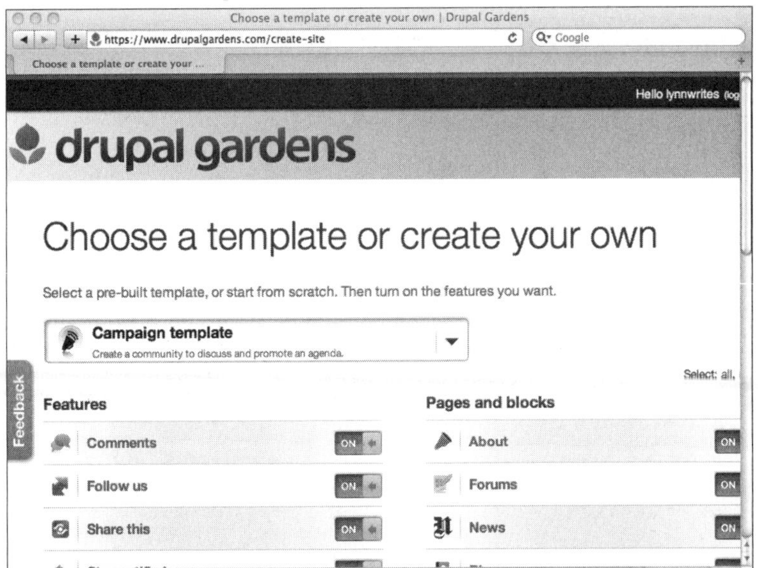

Figure 13-3: Choose a template for your new site.

The following list describes the available templates you can choose from. You can always change your mind later, but this tells Drupal Gardens about the basic things that should appear on your site. The types of templates are

- **Campaign:** If you're trying to build a community to talk about an idea or thing, this is a good choice. The Campaign template includes lots of features, such as mailing lists, for getting your message out there to other people. It also includes ways for your users to follow and share your content, as well as comments and forums. For example, if you are creating a site devoted to your hobby of collecting toilet seats used by famous people, this is the kind of site you want, where other toilet-seat collectors can join you to discuss this obscure hobby. Figure 13-4 shows you the settings for the Campaign template.
- **Product:** Say you manufacture the best zombie protection kits, ever. You know there's a market, and you want your site to advertise your kits for you. Choose the Product template. This template gives you excellent tools for spreading the word about your kits before the zombie apocalypse arrives. It includes product specific goodies, like Testimonials, Customers, and Product Feature blocks (see Figure 13-5).

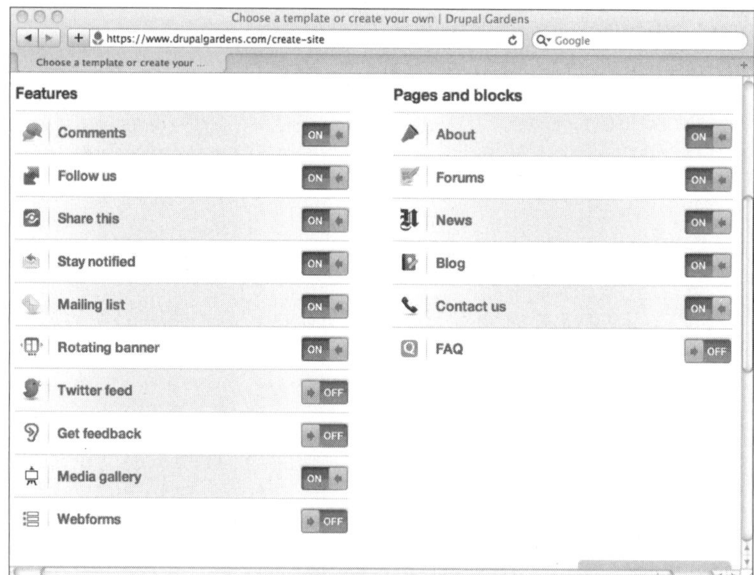

Figure 13-4: The Campaign template settings.

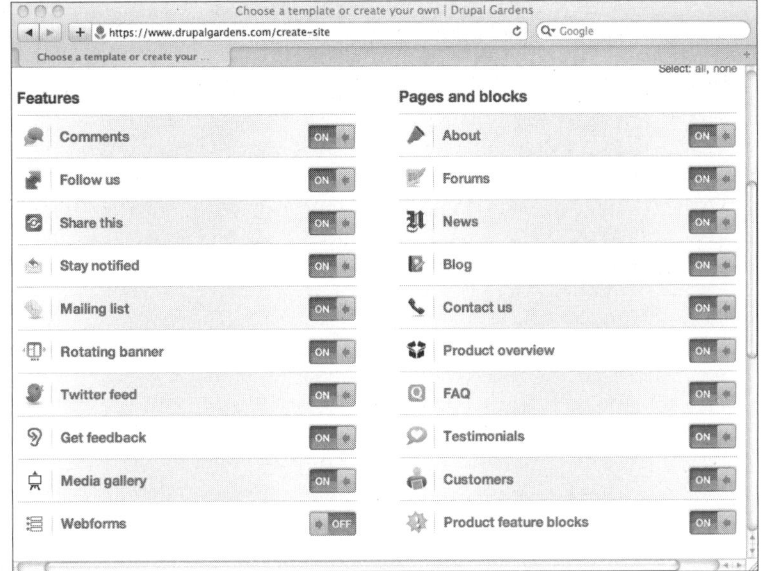

Figure 13-5: The Product template settings.

- **Blog:** Unless you've never used the Internet (and we assume that you have, since you're reading this book), you know what a blog site is. Typically, a blog is content about a topic that is frequently updated, sometimes daily. Blog entries range from personal stories to corporate reports on breaking news about something that affects their business. To work, blogs require three features:
  - An easy way to post information
  - Tools to let readers spread the word
  - Places for site visitors to express their own opinions on the blog topics

  Drupal Gardens blog templates feature social media "spread the word" tools (see Figure 13-6).
- **Create your own template:** Are you creating something that doesn't fit in any of the three categories listed here? Are you creating a product site where you sell your matchboxes, but you also want it to be a site where people can discuss matchboxes, and a blog where you can share your latest matchbox acquisitions? Choose Custom. This displays features, pages, and blocks that are all turned off. Turn on the ones you want on your site (see Figure 13-7).

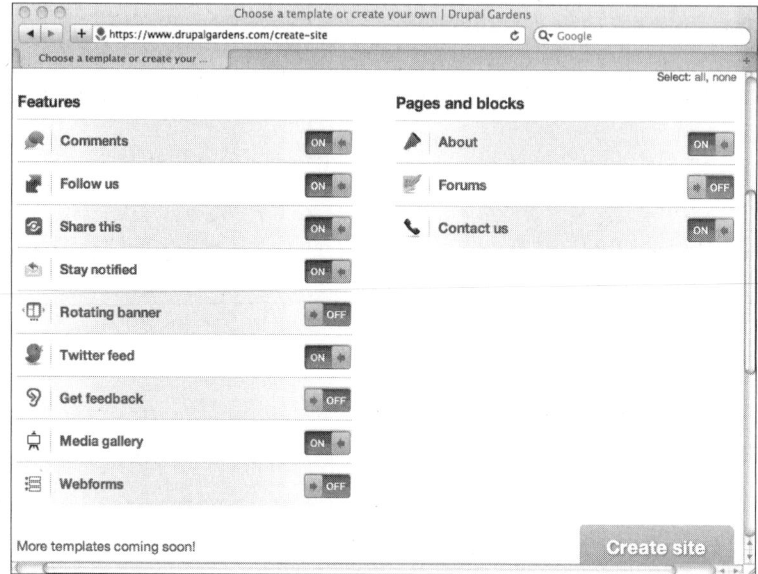

Figure 13-6: The Blog template settings.

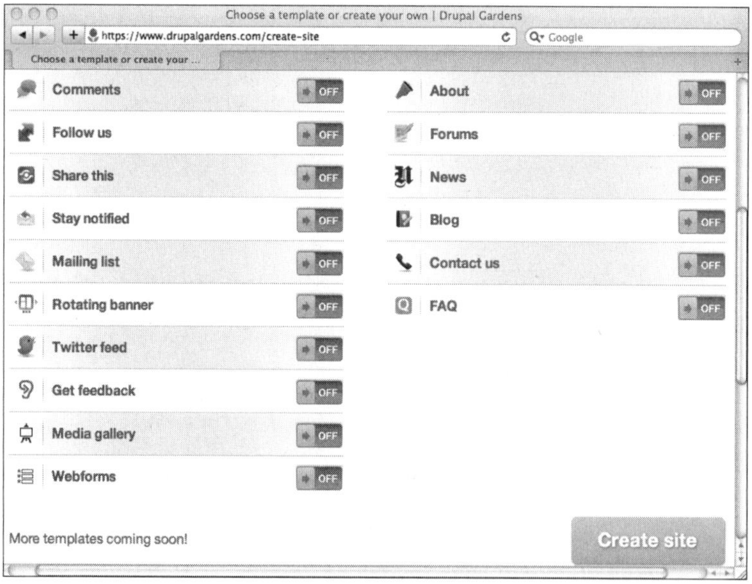

Figure 13-7: The Create your own template settings.

To get started, choose the blog template and click Create Site. As soon as you create your site, you'll get an onscreen warning that says:

```
Check your e-mail to complete registration. An e-mail has been sent to
youremailaddress@youremailaccount.com.
Click the link in the message by [date] to avoid having your account and
site deleted.
```

Be sure you confirm that you created this account by going to your e-mail account, opening the message, and clicking the Confirmation link.

Congratulations! Your site is now live and online. If you browse to your URL, you will see sample content that Drupal Gardens has posted to your site (see Figure 13-8).

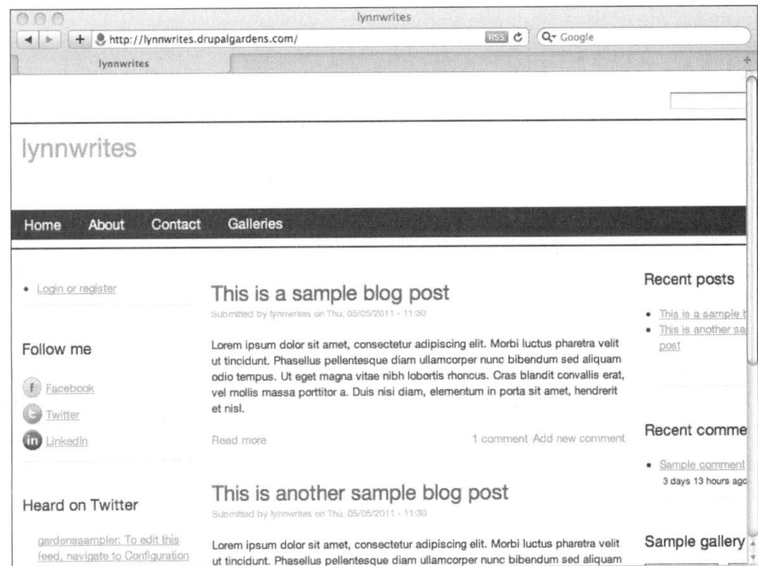

Figure 13-8: Your new Drupal Gardens site is live.

Use the same content-editing techniques used in Chapter 5 to edit or delete these sample content blocks. Add new content with the Add Content link.

You now have a basic site. You should recognize the administration links shown across the top of the page. They're the same ones you've seen throughout this book, and for the most part, operate the same way. We show you how to fine-tune your site with the administration links later in this chapter.

Upgrading your account

Your free site allows you 5GB of bandwidth per month, 50MB of storage, and five members. You might (of course) find this arrangement inadequate for your needs. The nice thing about using Drupal Gardens is that you can create your site for free, figure out whether it suits your purposes, and then purchase a higher-level account when your site takes off. The prices (shown in Figure 13-9) are reasonable, with $99 per year getting you your own domain name and ten times the storage and bandwidth you get with the free site.

If you want to upgrade, all you need to do is log in to the Drupal Gardens site with your e-mail and password. You'll see your Site Manager, which lists all sites you've created. Click Upgrade to select and pay for your package.

Drupal Gardens pricing plans | Drupal Gardens

https://www.drupalgardens.com/pricing

	Free	$11.95/mo	$19.95/mo	$39.95/mo	$79.95/mo
Limited time offer! Pay annually & save up to 37%		$8.25/mo $99/year	$12.42/mo $149/year	$24.92/mo $299/year	$49.92/mo $599/year
Bandwidth	5 GB	500 GB	1 TB	5 TB	Unlimited
Storage	50 MB	5 GB	1 TB	5 TB	Unlimited
Members	5	200	1,000	5,000	Unlimited
Webform responses	100/form	600/mo	3,000/mo	15,000/mo	Unlimited
Standard features	✓	✓	✓	✓	✓
Export site	✓	✓	✓	✓	✓
Custom domain		✓	✓	✓	✓
Duplicate site		✓	✓	✓	✓
Remove "Powered by Drupal Gardens"			✓	✓	✓
Support tickets			✓	✓	✓
Priority support				✓	✓

Figure 13-9: Drupal Gardens package prices.

Getting your own domain name

If you want to create a domain name that maps to your Drupal Gardens site, you have to upgrade to at least the Basic package. You will also need to purchase the domain name from a domain registrar such as 1&1 (`http://1and1.com`) or Namecheap (`www.namecheap.com`).

You only need to purchase the domain name. Because Drupal Gardens will host the name for you, don't buy any kind of hosting service from the domain registrar.

The registrar from which you buy the domain can give you the information you need to use the domain name on the Drupal Gardens site. Drupal Gardens provides in-depth instructions on this page (see Figure 13-10):

```
www.drupalgardens.com/documentation/custom-domains
```

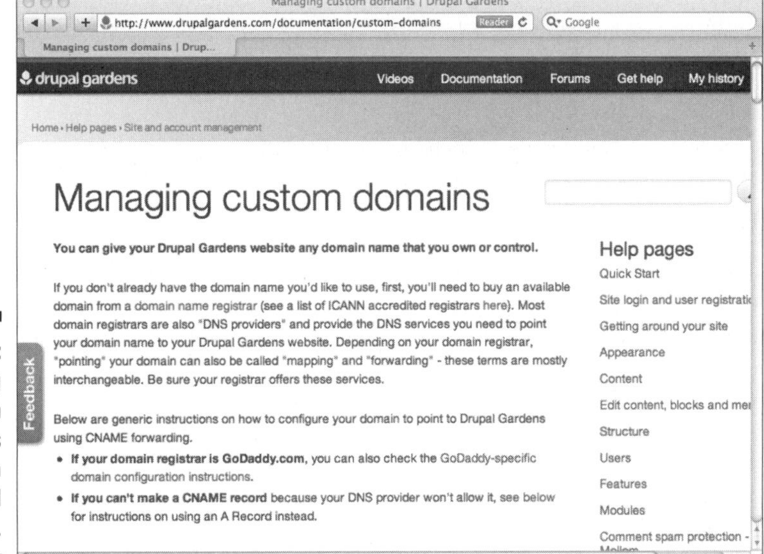

Figure 13-10: Managing custom domains page on Drupal Gardens.

Using Theme Builder

After you have the Drupal Gardens setup out of the way, you can start to have some fun and play with themes on your site. Controlling the appearance of your site with the Drupal Gardens Theme Builder is the major way it differs from installing your own copy of Drupal. But you're not missing much because the Theme Builder offers you tremendous flexibility and a great interface.

There isn't room in this single chapter to take you through all the Theme Builder options The following steps show you some of the highlights:

1. **Log in to your Drupal Gardens site and click the Appearance link.**

   This opens the Drupal Gardens Theme Builder (see Figure 13-11).

2. **Click the right arrow next to the theme thumbnails and scroll through the available themes. Click the theme you like.**

   For example, we clicked the Sparks theme. You now see a preview of your site behind the Theme Builder, using the theme you selected (see Figure 13-12).

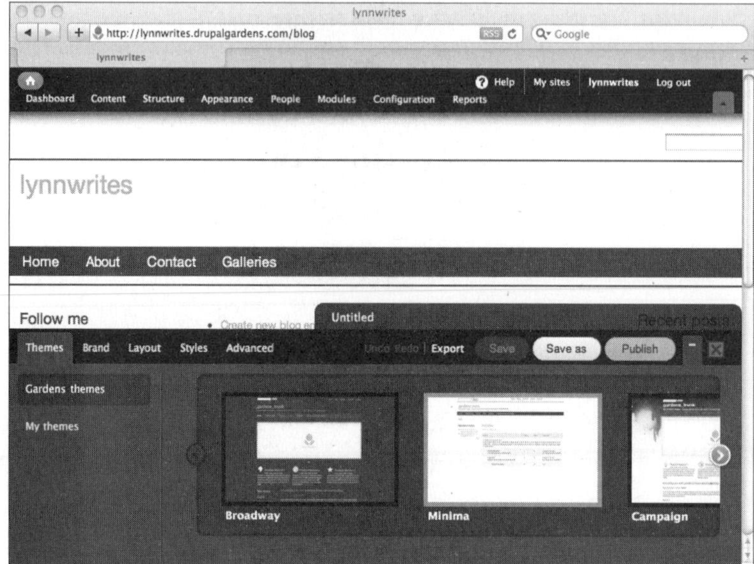

Figure 13-11: The Drupal Gardens Theme Builder.

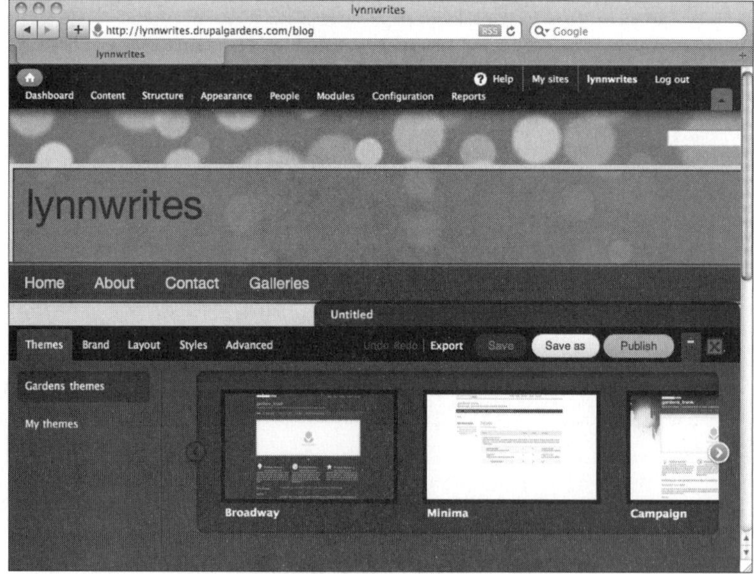

Figure 13-12: A website with the Sparks theme selected.

3. **Click the Publish button to make this theme show up on your site.**
4. **(Optional) Type in a name you will remember for this theme and click OK.**

The Theme Builder applies this theme to your site and saves this named theme under the My Themes tab on the left. You can have many different customized themes that are stored here.

5. **Click the Brand tab and click the palette you like.**

   We clicked the Spring Rain palette on the bottom right.

6. **Click Save.**

   This changes the colors your site uses and saves the changes to your saved theme.

7. **On the Brand tab, click the Logo link on the left. If you have an image you want to use as a site logo, click Browse and upload it.**

8. **Click Save.**

   You can also modify the favicon here. (The *favicon* is the small icon that appears in the browser's address bar next to your site's URL when someone visits your site.)

9. **Click the Layout tab.**

   These are the options for how the content in your site will be arranged on the page (see Figure 13-13).

10. **Click the layout thumbnail you like, and click Save to save your selection.**

11. **Click the Styles tab, and then click the Font link on the left.**

12. **Click the title of your site (in our case, it's *lynnwrites*) and change the font.**

    The Styles tab is interactive. Anything you click in the preview page behind the Theme Builder is changed when you modify the Styles settings. A blue line shows up around the element you've currently selected. For example, if we click the menu bar and change the font to Georgia and click Save to save our changes, the text for these menu items all over the site will change. You can control the font color, the style, the alignment, and the size in the Font section.

When you're changing styles, you're not stuck with only the part of the page that's visible. If you use your browser's scroll bar, you can scroll down your page while leaving the Theme Builder visible to make changes to things farther down on the page, such as the footer.

13. **Click the Borders & Spacing link on the left under the Styles tab and click the gray border that surrounds the header.**

    The border style currently being used for this element is displayed. We can turn it off by choosing the Style drop-down list on the right and selecting None (see Figure 13-14).

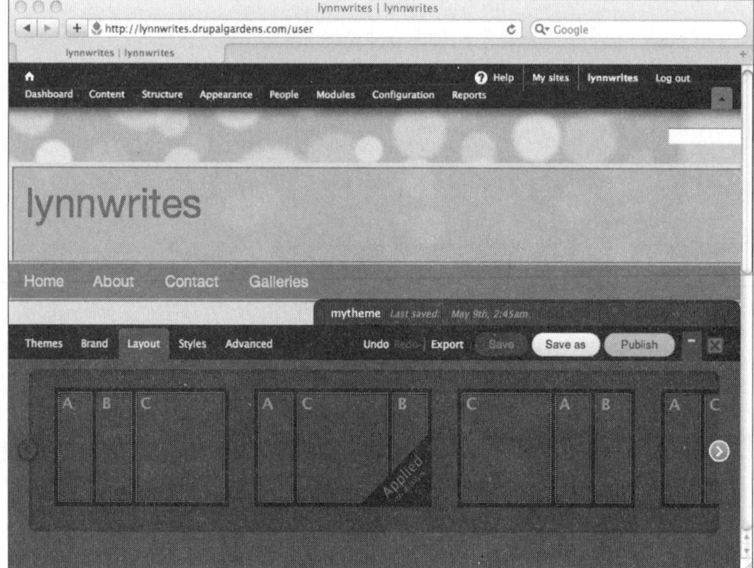

Figure 13-13: The Theme Builder Layout tab choices for your page layout.

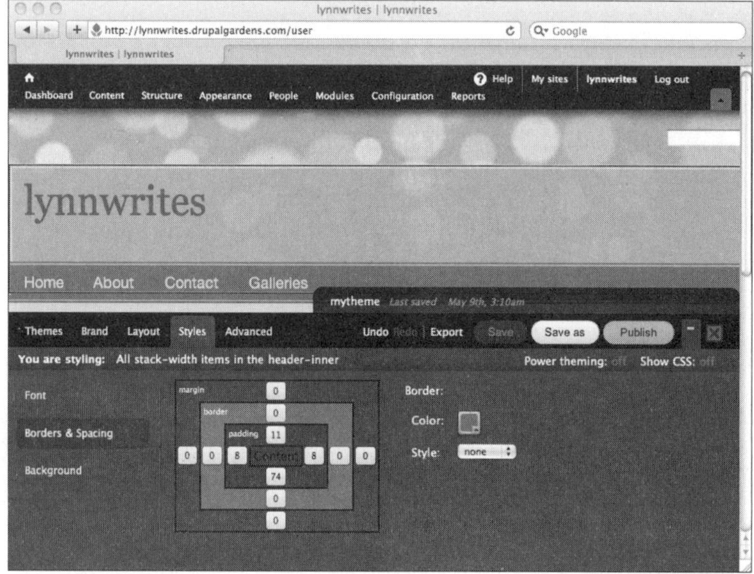

Figure 13-14: The Theme Builder Borders & Spacing page.

14. **Click the Background link on the left to change the styling of the background image.**

15. **Click the Advanced tab if you want to add your own CSS code to your theme.**

Theme Builder simply offers too much to cover everything about it in this chapter, but hopefully this quick walkthrough will encourage you to dive in and customize your own site. There's an excellent online resource from the Drupal Gardens folks here:

```
www.drupalgardens.com/documentation/appearance/theme-builder
```

Understanding features

When we created our site at the beginning of this chapter, we chose the Blog template. This installed some of the available features but not others.

To give you a chance to view and play with all the Drupal Gardens features, you can create another new site and choose the Custom option:

1. **Make sure you're logged in, and then click the My Sites link.**

   Doing so opens the Drupal Gardens Site manager.

2. **Click Create a New Site and enter a site name. Click Continue.**
3. **Choose Create Your Own Template from the Template drop-down list.**

   The Features list displays all possible features, all turned off (see Figure 13-15).

4. **Click each feature in the list to see more information about it.**

The available features and the modules that control them are described in the following list:

- **Comments:** Allows site visitors or registered users to comment on your site's content. This is the same functionality as turning on the Comments module.
- **Follow Us:** Adds social networking links to your content. This feature is the same as the Follow module.
- **Share This:** Allows visitors to share links to your site's content across their social networks.
- **Stay Notified:** Provides e-mail notification of comment follow-up when comments are posted. This feature is the same as the Comment Notify module.
- **Mailing List:** Creates a form where users can sign up for your mailing list. This feature is the same as the Mailing List module.
- **Rotating Banner:** Adds banners to your site that rotate between images. Banners are created as blocks. This feature is the same as the Rotating Banner module.

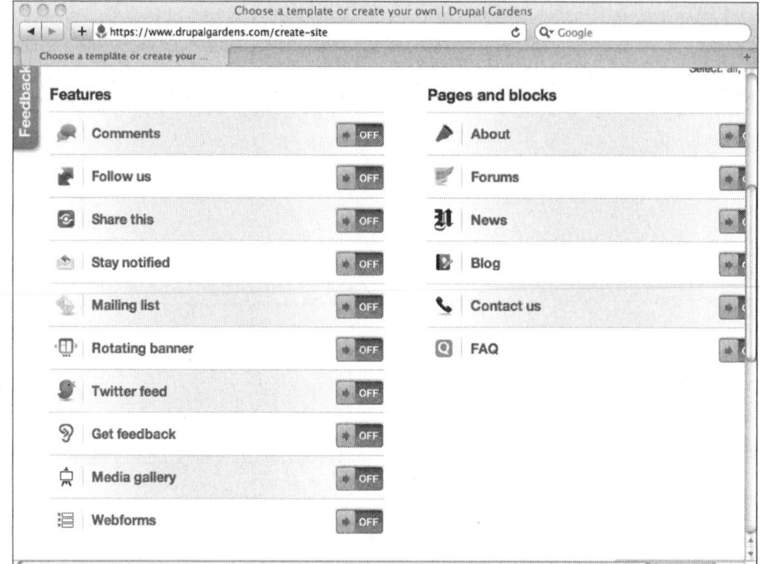

Figure 13-15: The available Drupal Gardens features.

- **Twitter Feed:** Adds a widget containing your recent Twitter posts to your site.
- **Get Feedback:** Provides a fixed feedback link on the side of site to let users provide feedback to you. This feature is controlled by the Gardens Feedback module.
- **Media Gallery:** Allows you to create galleries of images and videos with lightbox preview and slideshows. This feature is the same as the Media Gallery module.
- **Webforms:** Creates forms for your website. The Webforms feature lets you design custom forms for your site and collect the information your visitors submit.

If you didn't turn on one of these features when you created your site, or didn't choose a template with one of these features on by default, you can still turn them on by using the Modules administration link. Figure 13-16 shows the Drupal Gardens modules page, with some of the Drupal Gardens modules visible.

If there's a downside to Drupal Gardens, it's that you can't install new modules. You're limited to modules that are already available. We've contacted the company, and they assure us that over time they'll add new modules as more modules with stable, well-tested code bases become available.

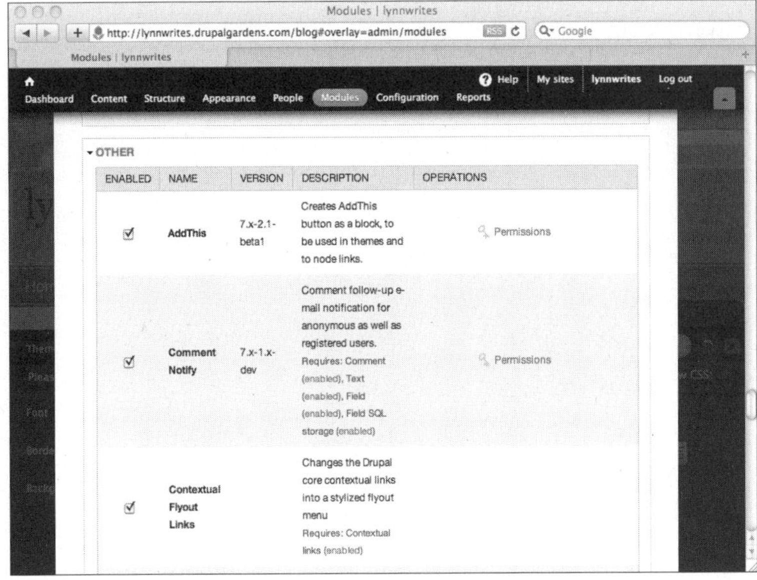

Figure 13-16: The available Drupal Gardens modules page.

Using pages and block

As with the Features list, when you first create your Drupal Gardens site, you can choose which preinstalled pages and blocks you want to appear on your site. Pages and blocks are exactly what you think they are: web pages or content blocks that serve some specific purpose (for example, Contact Us or Frequently Asked Questions). Figure 13-17 displays a site with all possible blocks and pages active.

Here are the available blocks and pages:

- **About:** Creates a page where you can enter information about your site. Figure 13-17 displays this page and its Edit tab. Editing content on Drupal Gardens pages is the same as on an installed Drupal site.
- **Forums:** Installs and enables the Forum module.
- **News:** Displays news items. News items are a specific content type you can create when you click Add Content. News items are intended for frequently updated and time-sensitive content.
- **Blog:** Posts a new blog entry on the Blog page.
- **Contact Us:** Creates a page containing a form for site visitors to contact you (see Figure 13-18). The submitted information is e-mailed to you.
- **FAQ:** Anticipate and answer the questions visitors to your site commonly ask.

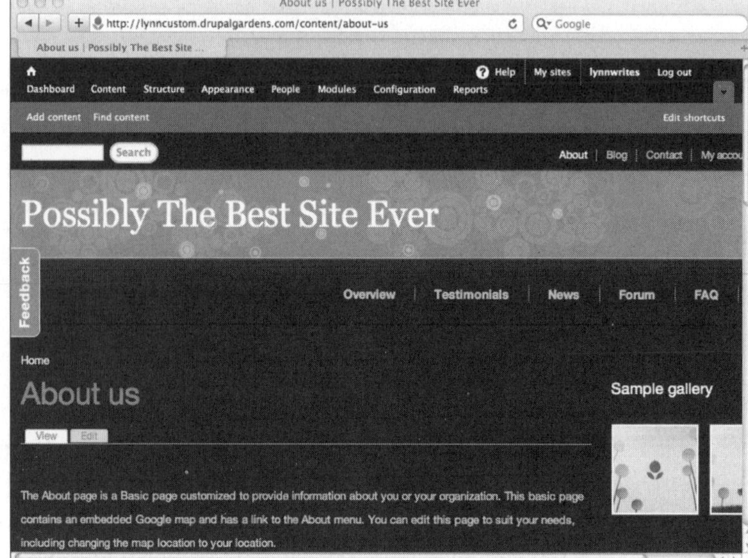

Figure 13-17: The available Drupal Gardens pages and blocks turned on.

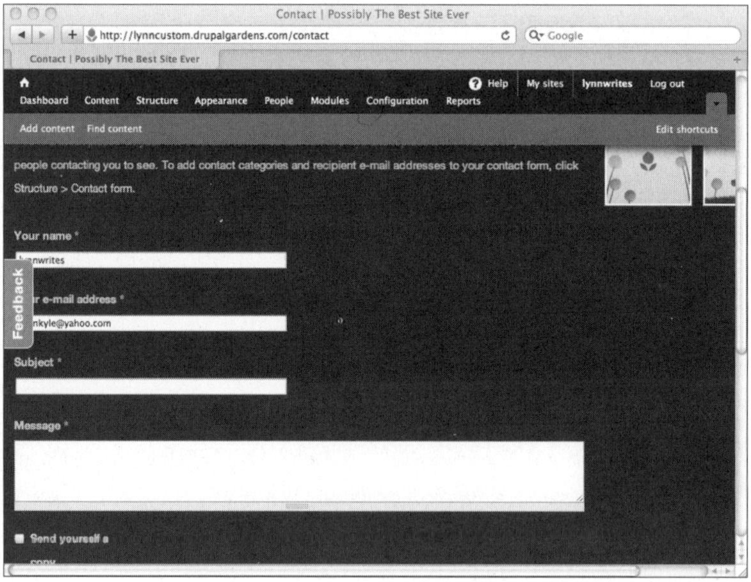

Figure 13-18: The Contact us page with form.

There are some additional Product template specific pages and blocks:

- **Product overview:** A block where you can display an overview of your product's details.
- **Testimonials:** A page where you can add customer testimonials.
- **Customers:** A block that displays the names and logos of your most impressive corporate customers.
- **Product Feature blocks:** Blocks where you can list three products or the benefits of a product.

If you want a site with every possible feature page and block available to you, choose the Product template and turn everything on.

Controlling the site structure

The Structure page (see Figure 13-19) is where you manage many of the features, pages, and blocks.

Some of the specific features, blocks, and pages you can control from this page include Contact forms, Forums, and Mailing lists. You can also manage the features that appear in blocks by using the Blocks page.

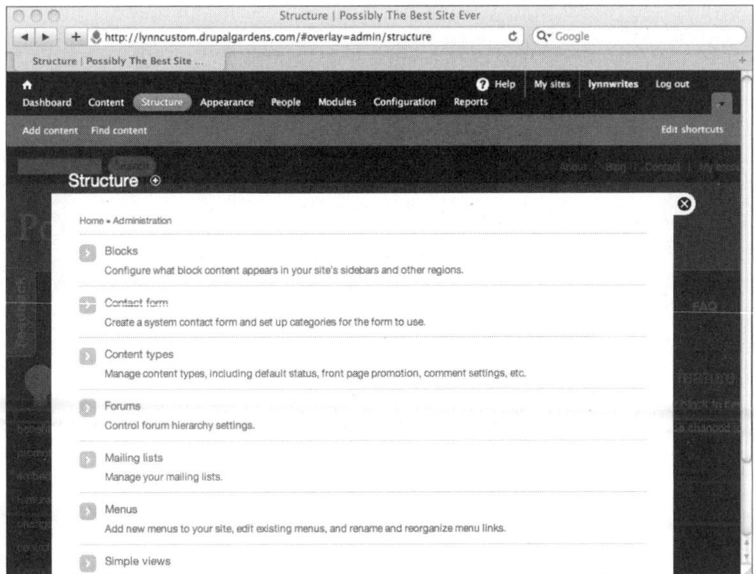

Figure 13-19: The Structure page.

Suppose you've created a Drupal Gardens site with all the bells and whistles. But you've decided that you really don't like that rotating banner or you don't want to use the media gallery just yet. To manage the content that currently appears on your site, follow these steps:

1. **Make sure you're logged in, and then click the My Sites link.**

   This opens the Drupal Gardens Site manager.

2. **Click the site you want to manage.**
3. **Choose Structure⇨Blocks.**
4. **Find the block you want to remove, and choose None from the Region drop-down list to the right of it.**

   For example, we removed the Rotating Banner block by selecting None from the Region drop-down list.

5. **Click Save Blocks.**

   The block you removed will no longer appear.

Managing Users

The People page lets you control users, just as you would in a regular Drupal installation. You can find users, block and unblock, delete, and assign roles. Click the People link to manage users. The List tab helps you locate existing users, and the Permissions tab allows you to create roles and manage user permissions.

After your site is up and running, you might want to invite users to join your site. To send an invitation, follow these steps:

1. **Click People.**
2. **Make sure the List tab is selected, and then click Invite People.**

   This opens the Invite People form.

3. **In the Enter E-Mail Addresses for People You Would Like to Invite text box, type in e-mail addresses, separated by commas.**
4. **(Optional) Customize the message that you will be sending by clicking View/Edit Invitation Message; edit the text in the text box as desired.**

   The default message is shown in Figure 13-20.

5. **Click the Send Invitations button.**

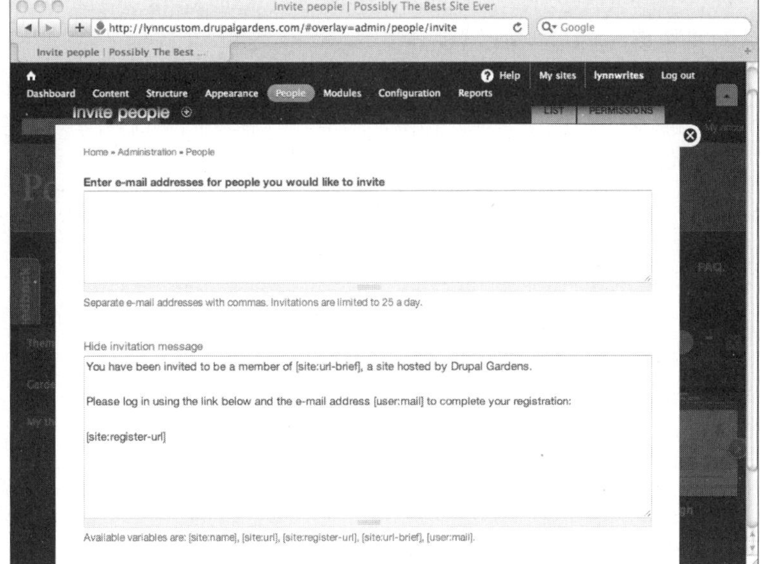

Figure 13-20: The form you use to invite users to your site.

Chapter 14

Interacting with Other Sites

In This Chapter

- Pulling in Twitter and Facebook statuses
- Displaying YouTube videos
- Aggregating and sharing RSS feeds

Getting people to visit your site is all about social media and pulling content from other sites. You're developing a community for your users with interactive features and timely information. But until now, all the content on your site has come from you, with a little help from your users.

Your site doesn't have to exist in a vacuum. Lots of modules for Drupal let you pull in information from other sites and push out content from your site. In this chapter, we take a look at a few nifty modules that let you tie in content from other sites — including such favorites as Twitter, Facebook, YouTube, and Amazon.

Working with Activity Stream

Activity Stream is a Drupal module that lets you publish your social media content on your own website. With Activity Stream, every time you Twitter, post a link on Digg, or receive a Facebook notification, you can view that information on your Drupal site. Many add-on modules for popular social media sites and services extend the Activity Stream module. Here are a few of them:

- **Facebook:** The current front-runner in the social media wars.
- **YouTube:** Post video streams directly from YouTube.
- **Qik:** Allows you to share live video from your mobile phone.
- **Identi.ca:** A Twitter-like status update site with a few more features.
- **Blogger:** Online blogging service.
- **Goodreads:** A place to research and compare notes on books.
- **IMDB:** All about movies and entertainment information.

Each registered user on your site can have his own set of activity streams. By default, they appear under the user profile section. Later in this chapter, we show you how to put your activity stream in a block and place it in the Right Sidebar.

Installing Activity Stream

The Activity Stream module should be available via a link on the `http://drupal.org` website.

As of this writing, you can't copy the URL of this module. You will need to download the file to your local computer and then upload it to your Drupal site. But first, go to `http://drupal.org/project/activitystream` and see if you can get the URL of the file from there. If not, follow these steps to download the file:

1. **Browse to `https://github.com/kylebrowning/activitystream`.**
2. **Click the Downloads button (see Figure 14-1).**
3. **Click the Download button to download this module.**
4. **Save this file to a directory you'll remember easily.**

   This module downloads as a single compressed `.tar.gz` or `.zip` file.
5. **Log in to your control panel on your web host's website or use an FTP client.**
6. **Find and click the link to a file manager.**

   After you click the file manager, you will see a screen that displays the files on your web server.
7. **You should see a single folder or directory named `html`, `www`, or `htdocs`. Click its name to open it.**

   There may be several directories, but the one for your website should be easy to spot.
8. **If you see the Drupal directory, click it, and then click the modules directory. If not, locate the modules directory and click it.**
9. **Click the Upload link on your file manager.**

   You should see an upload form with a Browse button.
10. **Click Browse and find the Activity Stream module file you downloaded. Click Upload.**

    The compressed Activity Stream module file is now on your site in the correct folder and ready to be extracted.

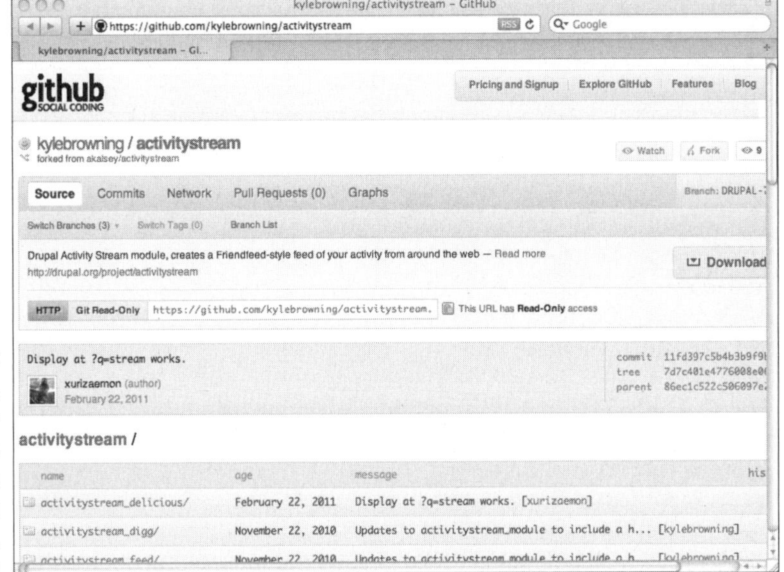

Figure 14-1: The Activity Stream module download page.

11. **Click the Activity Stream file to select it.**

    You see a list of files that are stored inside your compressed file, all selected.

12. **You should see an option to uncompress the files. Leave the All check box selected and click the Go button.**

13. **Select the original Activity Stream module `.tar.gz` or `.zip` file on your web server and delete it.**

Installing additional modules

Depending on which services you use, you can download and install some additional modules. The Activity Stream page at `http://drupal.org/project/activitystream` has a list of links to add-ons.

Follow the steps you used to install the Activity Stream module. The additional modules you might want to install are

- **Activity Stream for Facebook:** `http://drupal.org/project/activitystream_facebook`
- **Activity Stream for YouTube:** `http://drupal.org/project/activitystream_youtube`
- **Twitter Search Feeds:** `http://drupal.org/project/twitter_search_feedsporations`

Enabling Activity Stream modules

After you download and install modules, the new modules appear in the module list (see Figure 14-2).

To enable these modules, follow these steps:

1. **Click Modules on the Dashboard menu bar.**

   The new modules are located in the Activity Stream section.

2. **Select the Enabled check box next to all the modules in the Activity Stream section.**

3. **Click Save Configuration.**

   The new modules are now enabled.

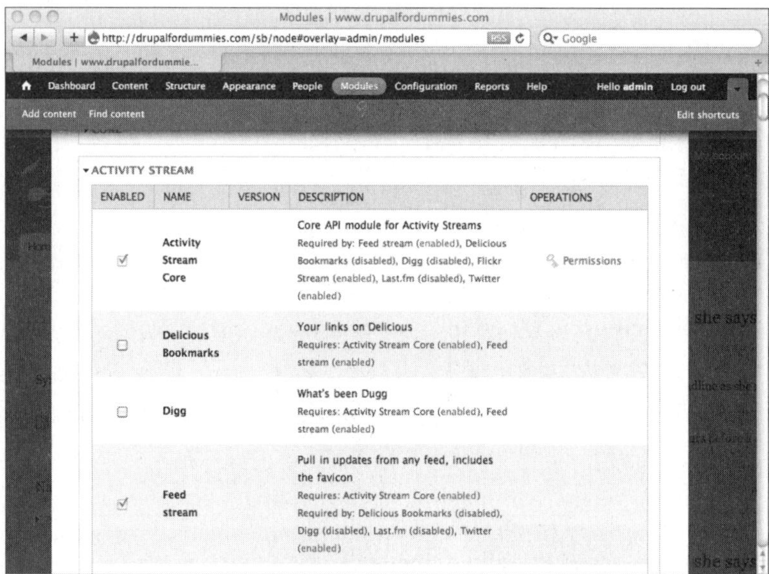

Figure 14-2: The Activity Stream modules.

Pulling in social media

After you enable the Activity Stream and related modules, you can begin pulling in content from other sites. Activity Stream is based on an individual user. To set it up for use with a particular user, follow these steps:

1. **Click People on the Dashboard menu bar.**
2. **Locate the user account for which you want to set up an Activity Stream. Click the Edit link to the right of the user's name.**

   In our case, we add it to the admin account.

   If you are adding the Activity Stream to the user account you are currently using, you can choose My Account➪Edit➪Activity Stream.
3. **Click the Activity Stream link under the Edit tab.**

   This opens the Activity Stream setup page (see Figure 14-3).

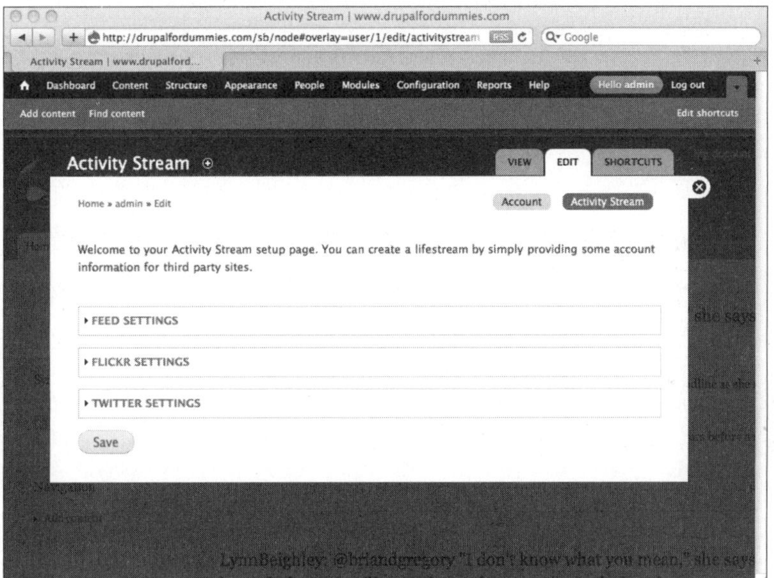

Figure 14-3: Activity Stream settings page.

This form has blanks for specific websites and a large box for Rich Site Summary (RSS) feeds. (We discuss RSS feeds later in this chapter.) With the exception of the Facebook text box, the text boxes on this page are simple to fill out. Del.icio.us, lastfm, Digg, Twitter, Flickr, and YouTube need your username on those sites.

4. **Enter your username for the particular website you want to include in your Activity Stream output and click Save.**

   Your streams update automatically at intervals, but to make it update immediately so you can see the new data, you need to run your cron program to make Drupal go out and get your information from the websites.

5. **Choose Reports➪Status Report.**
6. **Under the listing Cron maintenance tasks, click the Run Cron Automatically link.**

You can now view your Activity Stream page by choosing the View tab of the user's profile. In our case, we choose the admin account. The Activity Stream appears on the View tab (see Figure 14-4).

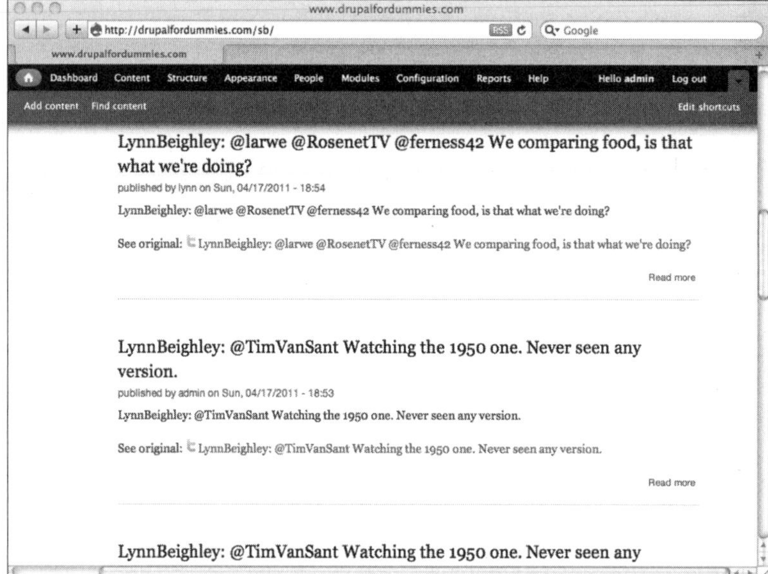

Figure 14-4: Activity Stream output on the profile page.

To activate your Facebook feed is a little trickier. Facebook requires a URL that you have to dig around a bit to find. Follow these steps:

1. **Log in to your Facebook account.**
2. **Navigate to `www.facebook.com/notifications.php`.**

   This opens a page with a list of your notifications (see Figure 14-5).
3. **Click the Via RSS link near the top of the page.**

   This opens a page with a URL similar to

   ```
   http://www.facebook.com/feeds/notifications.php?id=575826921&viewer=
   575826921&key=AQAZLhFMIqnd8WLZ&format=rss20
   ```
4. **Copy this URL to Notepad or another word processor.**

5. **In your copy of the URL, change the word *notifications* to *status.***

   This is the URL you paste into the Feed Settings on your Activity Stream setup form.

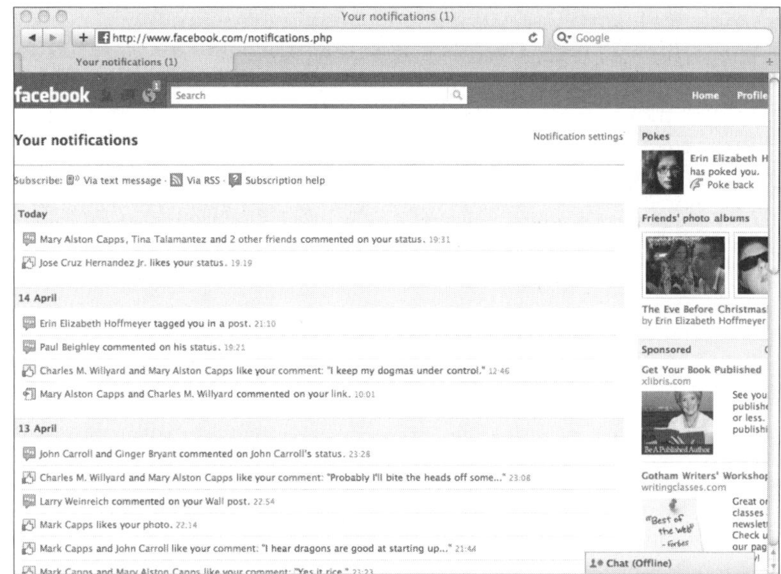

Figure 14-5: Facebook notifications page.

6. **Click People on the Dashboard menu bar.**
7. **Click the Edit link to the right of the username.**
8. **Click the Activity Stream link under the Edit tab.**
9. **Paste the URL in the Feed URL text box under the Feed Settings section.**
10. **Click Save.**

To see the Facebook feed immediately, you have to run your cron program. Otherwise it may take an hour or more to appear on your user profile page.

The Activity Stream module only has one setting you can change, the title. By default, the title is *Activity Stream.* This appears above your pulled-in content. To change it, choose Administer➪Site Configuration➪Activity Stream. Change the text in the Title box and click Save Configuration.

As of this writing, unregistered users can see your Activity Stream. The Activity Stream module doesn't permit you to allow only registered viewers to see it.

Posting YouTube Videos

You can post YouTube videos to any content type — article, blog post, or page — by first visiting YouTube to gather information about the video and then posting it on your site. Here's how it works:

1. **Locate the video you want to post on the YouTube site and open its page.**

   We open a video located at `www.youtube.com/watch?v=7EYAUazLI9k` (see Figure 14-6).

2. **Click the Share button under the video, and then click the Embed button.**
3. **Click the text in the Embed text box. Select all of the code and copy it.**
4. **On your Drupal site, click Add Content and select the content type where you want to post this video.**

   We choose Article.

5. **Paste the code you copied from the YouTube Embed text box into the Body box on your Drupal Create Content form.**
   - You can put text above or below the video if you want. Type any text you want above or below the section of code you just pasted into the Create Content form Body text box.
   - Don't forget to give your posting a title by entering text in the Title text box of the Create Content form.
6. **Select the Full HTML for Text format.**

   This is what allows the code you pasted in the Body text box to be interpreted correctly by the Drupal software. If you don't do this, Drupal will simply ignore the code and your video won't show up.

7. **Click Save.**

   Your video is published on your site (see Figure 14-7).

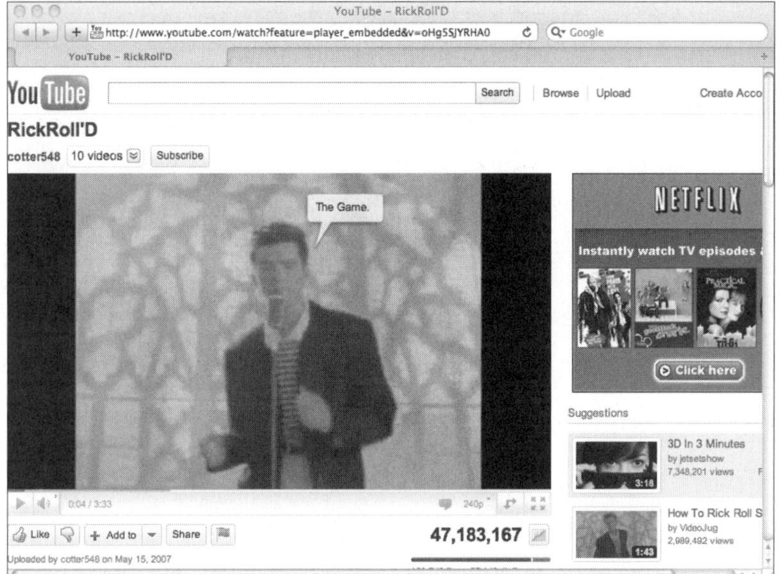

Figure 14-6: Individual video page on YouTube.

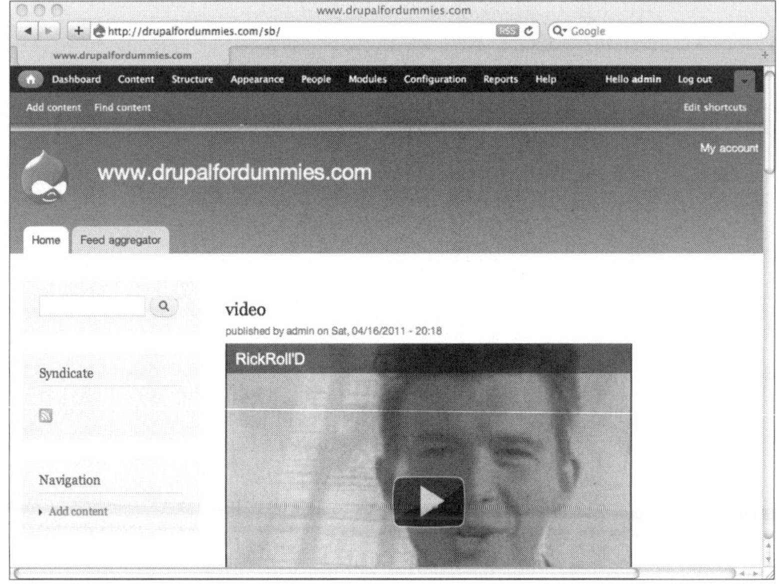

Figure 14-7: YouTube video on your Drupal site.

Sharing Content with RSS

RSS, or Really Simple Syndication, is a specific format for content that can be read by web applications written for that purpose. Sites with frequently updated content (such as news) often provide versions of their content in an RSS format.

If your browser understands how to interpret RSS-formatted content, and most modern browsers do, you can preview RSS feeds by browsing to them. These feeds use web addresses, so you can paste them into your browser to preview them. For example, you can see a feed by browsing to `http://drupal.org/node/feed`. This is a dynamic list of items from drupal.org.

Just as you can add your tweets, Facebook status, and YouTube videos (described earlier in this chapter), you can add a set of feeds to your website. But you have to find good feeds first.

Finding feeds can be tricky. Most major websites with content that frequently changes provide feeds. Lots of blog sites have feeds as well. If you want a feed from a specific site, hunting around and looking for a link to a feed is your best bet. The easiest way we know to find feeds is to use Google Reader to get the address of feeds of interest to you.

Finding feeds with Google Reader

You can find feeds about particular topics by using a feature of Google Reader.

You need to have a Google account to be able to use Google Reader and find feeds with it.

Follow these steps:

1. **Browse to `www.google.com/reader` and log in to Google.**
2. **Click Add a Subscription on the upper left.**

   Doing so opens a small search box.
3. **Type a search term and click Add.**

   We search for the word *dogs.* A list of feeds appears on the right (see Figure 14-8).

   Each item in the list shows the URL of the feed as green text beneath the description.
4. **Copy a feed you want to use and paste it in the address bar of a browser window to preview the content (see Figure 14-9).**

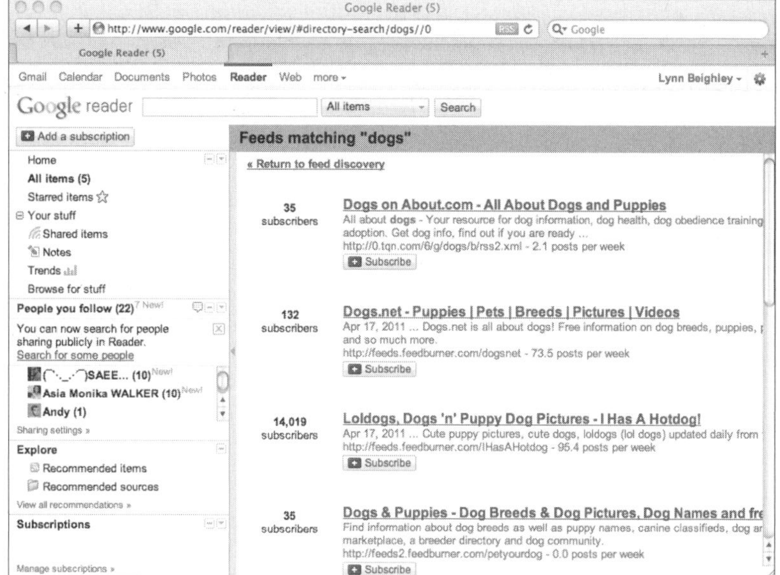

Figure 14-8: Google Reader list of feeds about dogs.

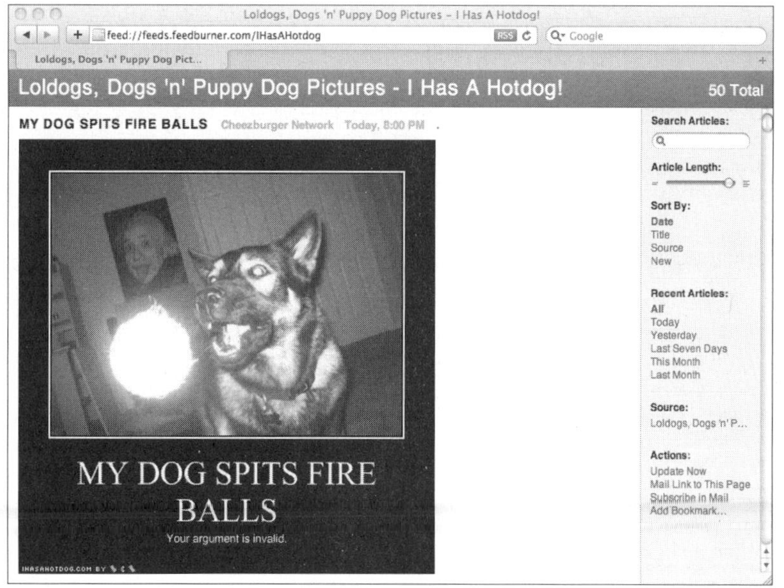

Figure 14-9: A single feed in a browser.

This is a roundabout way to find feeds, but it works fairly well. You can use the Add a Subscription button again and again, refining your search terms, until you find feeds on the subjects you want.

Using the Aggregator module

You can use your feeds with the Activity Stream module by pasting them, one per line, in the Feed URL text box. But if you're already using that to publish content from your social media sites, you may want the content from the feeds to go somewhere else on your site.

A simpler solution is to use the included Core module called Feed Aggregator. To enable and use the Aggregator module, follow these steps:

1. **Click Modules on the Dashboard menu bar.**
2. **Click the Enabled module next to the Aggregator module under the Core section.**
3. **Click Save Configuration.**

   The Aggregator is now active and a new link to Feed Aggregator appears in the Navigation menu. This will be where all your feed content appears.
4. **To add a feed, choose Configuration➪Feed Aggregator.**
5. **Click the Add Feed tab.**

   This opens the Add Feed form (see Figure 14-10).

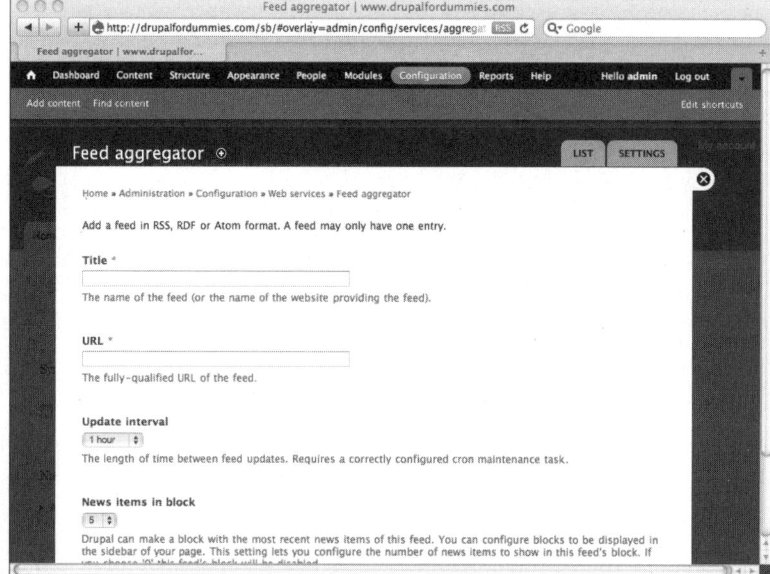

Figure 14-10: The Feed Aggregator's Add Feed form.

6. **Give your feed a title in the Title text box.**

   For example, we use a feed from the drupal.org site and call this **Drupal.org**.

7. **Paste or type the URL of the feed in the URL text box.**
8. **Click Save.**

Your feed will update every hour. To get the feed to appear immediately, run cron by choosing Reports⇨Status Report. Choose Run Cron Manually next to Cron maintenance tasks on the right.

You can view your new feed by choosing Navigation⇨Feed Aggregator.

To move the Feed Aggregator from the Navigation menu, and to give it a different Link title, follow these steps:

1. **Choose Structure⇨Menus.**
2. **Click List Links next to the Navigation menu.**

   This opens a list of links currently in your Navigation menu (see Figure 14-11).

3. **Locate Feed Aggregator in the list and click the Edit link.**
4. **If you want to change the link's title, type the new title in the Link Title text box.**

   Ours will be used to aggregate feeds about Drupal, so we change our title to **Drupal News**.

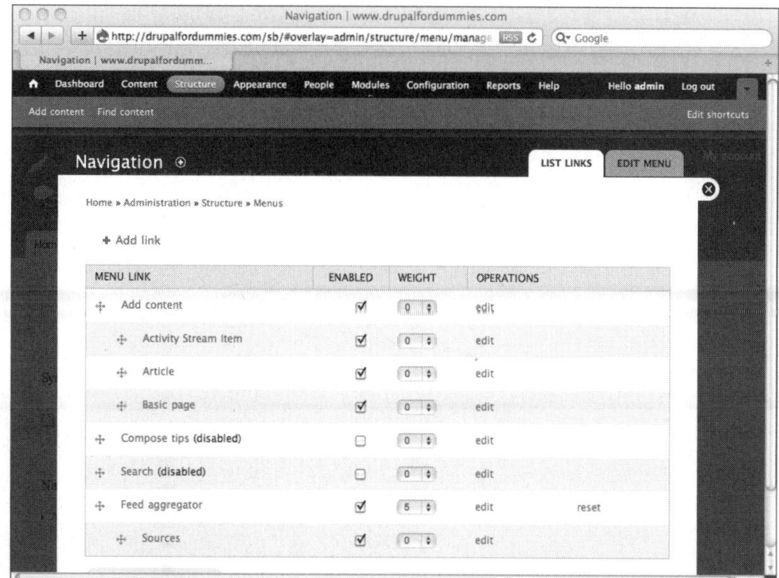

Figure 14-11: Links in the Navigation menu.

5. **Change the menu by clicking the Parent Item drop-down list and choosing a different menu.**

   We select `<Main menu>`.

6. **Click Save.**

   The Drupal News link is now the last link in our Main menu. We want it to come before the Contact Me link. We're already on the right page to do it (the List items under the Main menu).

7. **To move the position of the link, click and drag it to the new position.**
8. **Click Save Configuration.**

   The Feed Aggregator now appears in the Main menu (see Figure 14-12).

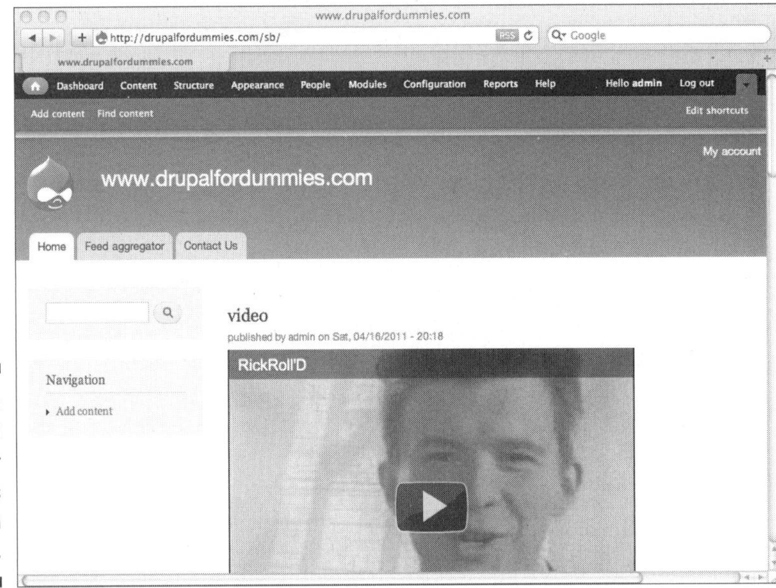

Figure 14-12: The Feed Aggregator tab appears in the Main menu.

Creating a feed for your site

Not only can you pull in RSS feed content from other sites, but you also can create your own RSS feed for other sites to pull content from you. Behind the scenes, Drupal has already created a feed; you just give your site visitors a link to it. Follow these steps:

1. **Choose Structure➪Blocks.**
2. **Find Syndicate in the list under the Disabled section. Move it to the location you want.**

   We drag ours to the bottom of the Sidebar first.
3. **Click Save Blocks.**

   You now have a Syndicate block on your site, with a small logo (see Figure 14-13).

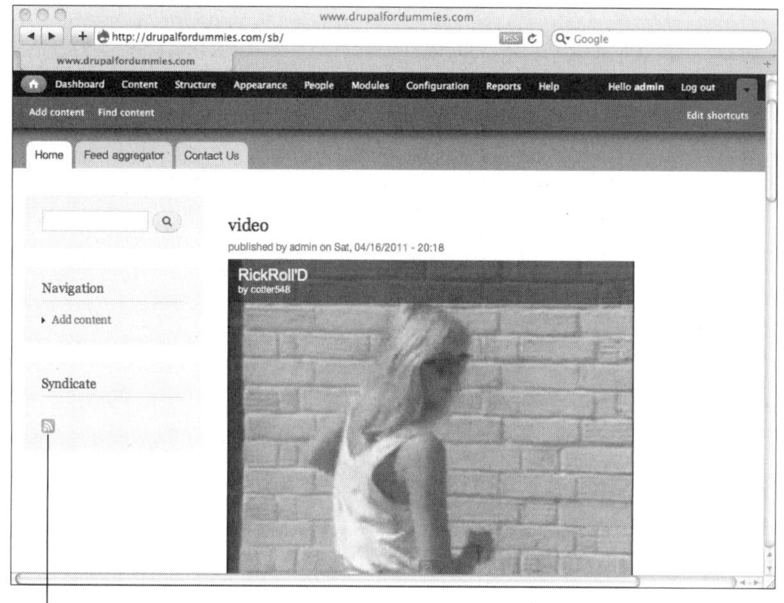

Figure 14-13: The Syndicate block and RSS feed logo in the Left Sidebar.

This logo is used all over the web to represent RSS feeds. You can click it on a site with a feed you want to use, copy the URL from the address bar of the page that opens, and use it with Feed Aggregator.

4. **You can remove or change the title of the Syndicate block by clicking the Configure link next to it on the Blocks page.**
5. **Type a new title — or, if you don't want a title, type** <none>.
6. **Click Save Block.**

   Clicking this logo opens your feed page. In our case, it looks like `http://drupalfordummies.com/rss.xml` (see Figure 14-14).

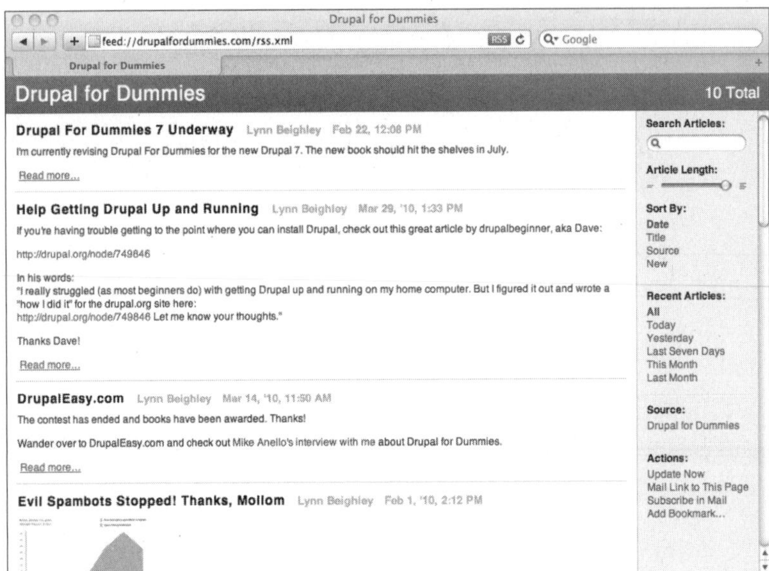

Figure 14-14: The RSS feed page for a site.

Chapter 15

Building a Storefront

In This Chapter

- Putting up a storefront with Ubercart
- Tweaking storefront configuration settings
- Showing off products with images and a catalog
- Accepting online payments
- Keeping your store tidy with fulfillment modules

If you've decided you want to sell products online, the Ubercart module is an easy-to-use, robust option. You can have your items online in minutes, complete with a shopping cart and an online order form that collects the necessary customer information. Additional modules allow you to add more robust product listings, automatically figure sales tax, and of course, accept credit card payments.

In this chapter, we discuss the parts of an online storefront. You find out about Ubercart and how to install it. Then we show you how to build and customize your own storefront, fetch order information, enhance your product listings, and finally how to accept payments.

Understanding Storefronts

At their most basic, storefronts are made up of products for sale, a shopping cart, and a form that a customer can use to provide information and purchase items by placing them (virtually) in his or her cart:

- **Product listings:** An individual page with product information and a button for the shopper to click to add an item to her cart.
- **Shopping cart:** A form that displays all the products a user has clicked to purchase.
- **Order form:** A form the shopper fills out to finish making his order. It collects information and saves it for processing.

Figure 15-1 shows a basic storefront with product listings.

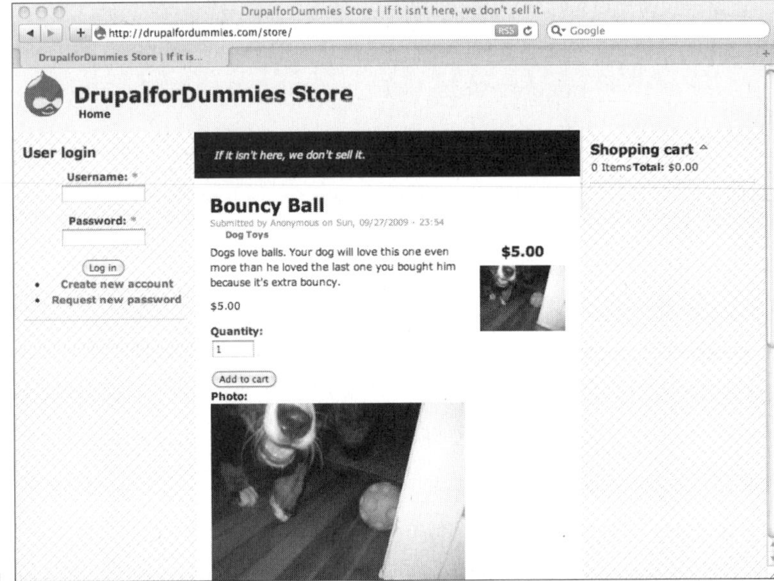

Figure 15-1: Basic Drupal product listings.

Storefronts can have lots of other features. Take a look at the Amazon.com website (see Figure 15-2).

Figure 15-2: Amazon.com storefront.

Amazon.com includes these additional e-commerce features:

- **User accounts:** To buy something from Amazon, you can set up an account. Amazon saves your address and credit card information so you don't need to provide it each time you buy something.
- **Order tracking:** Along with having an account, you can log in to view the status of orders you've placed.
- **Wish lists:** If you want to save an item listing so you can find it again later but not purchase it right away, you can save it in a wish list.
- **Product catalogs:** This is a collection of product listings grouped into categories.

The Ubercart module allows you to easily implement all these functionalities, with the exception of wish lists.

Getting Started with Ubercart

Ubercart is a single download composed of a number of modules. Ubercart also depends on several other modules that must be downloaded and installed. In this section, we go through the steps to download and install Ubercart and the other modules it requires.

Ubercart works best when users can register for your site automatically. Because you can post a link to a shopping cart in a block on your site, you may want to devote an entire Drupal site to being a store rather than adding Ubercart to your existing site. In our case, we created a new Drupal installation at `http://drupalfordummies.com/store`. We then created a link on the main site to the store, and vice versa, making the Primary navigation match both sites. We used the same theme on both sites to help with branding.

Getting Ubercart and additional modules

You can install just the minimum necessary modules, or the complete system.

We recommend you download and install all the modules for the full system. That way, even if you don't want to use all the features, you can have them available for future enhancements.

For the full installation, you will need the latest Drupal 7 modules from each of these sites:

- **Ubercart:** `http://drupal.org/project/ubercart`
- **Rules (7.x-2.0-alpha5 or later):** `http://drupal.org/project/rules`
- **Views:** `http://drupal.org/project/views`
- **Ctools:** `http://drupal.org/project/ctools`
- **Entity API:** `http://drupal.org/project/entity`
- **Entity tokens:** `http://drupal.org/project/entity`
- **Colorbox:** `http://drupal.org/project/colorbox`
- **Google Analytics:** `http://drupal.org/project/google_analytics`

Installing Ubercart and additional modules

The next task is to install the modules you've downloaded. For each module, complete the following steps:

1. **Right-click (or Control-click for the Mac) the link to the `.tar.gz` or `.zip` file and choose Copy Shortcut (in Internet Explorer) or Copy Link Location (in Firefox).**

   The URL has now been saved to your Clipboard.

2. **Using Notepad or another word processor, choose Edit⇨Paste and paste the URL.**

   You will need this URL in a moment.

3. **On your Dashboard menu bar, click the Modules link.**

   This opens the Modules page.

4. **Click the Install New Module link.**

   The Install form appears.

5. **Copy and paste the URL to your new module in the Install from a URL text box.**

6. **Click Install.**

   Your module or theme is now installed.

Take a few minutes to look at the documentation about the new module or theme. This documentation is generally available on the page with the download link and may contain detailed help to get the new theme or module up and running.

Your new modules appear on the Modules administration page on your site.

Enabling the basic Ubercart installation

In this section, we walk you through enabling the appropriate modules to create a basic storefront website.

Don't enable all the new modules at once. There's a specific order that Ubercart recommends.

To enable a basic storefront, follow these steps:

1. **Choose Modules from the Dashboard menu bar.**
2. **Under the Core section, select the Path check box.**
3. **Under the Ubercart – Core section, select the Cart, Order, Product, and Store check boxes.**
4. **Under the Rules section, select the Rules check box.**
5. **Under the Other section, select the Entity API and Entity Tokens check boxes.**
6. **Click Save Configuration.**

Your site has now been configured to allow you to create product listings and take orders.

Creating Your First Storefront

After you install Ubercart, you're ready to add product listings to your site and test the ordering process.

Creating product listings

With Ubercart, product listings are a type of content. To create your first product listing, follow these steps:

1. **Choose Add Content➪Product.**

   This opens the form shown in Figure 15-3.

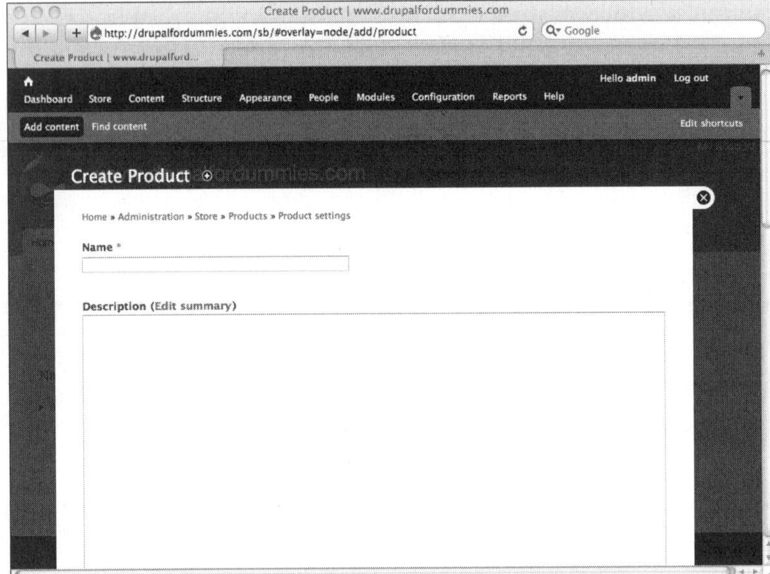

Figure 15-3: The Create Product form.

2. **Enter a name for your product in the Name field.**
3. **Enter a description of your product in the Description field.**
4. **In the Product Information section, enter the SKU number for it or a unique description for your product.**

   SKU stands for *stockkeeping unit.* It's a unique number or combination of numbers and letters that represents a particular product. The SKU allows a product to be tracked for inventory. An SKU is associated with a particular item in a store or catalog. For example, a dog toy of a particular style and size might have an SKU of 1234-M, meaning Style 1234, size medium.

5. **In the List Price field, you can optionally enter the manufacturer's suggested list price.**
6. **In the Cost field, you can optionally enter the cost you paid for the item.**
7. **In the Sell Price field, enter the cost of the item for shoppers to purchase it.**

8. **If you need to know the weight of an item to figure shipping costs, enter the weight of the item in the Weight field.**

   You can modify the value in the Unit of Measurement drop-down list as needed.

9. **Enter the dimensions of the item in the Length, Width, and Height fields.**

   Change the Unit of Measurement drop-down list as needed.

10. **Enter the number that you can fit into one box in the Maximum Package Quantity field.**

11. **Change the List Position to control how high or low this item will show up in a list of items.**

12. **The rest of the options are the same as used in any content item.**

    Change them if you want.

13. **Click Save.**

Your first product listing is created. By default, it's posted on the main page of your site. Repeat this process to add more products. Each one will be added to your storefront.

If you don't want your products to appear on the main page of your site by default, modify the Publishing options setting by deselecting the Promoted to the Front Page check box.

Clicking a product name opens the product information page (see Figure 15-4).

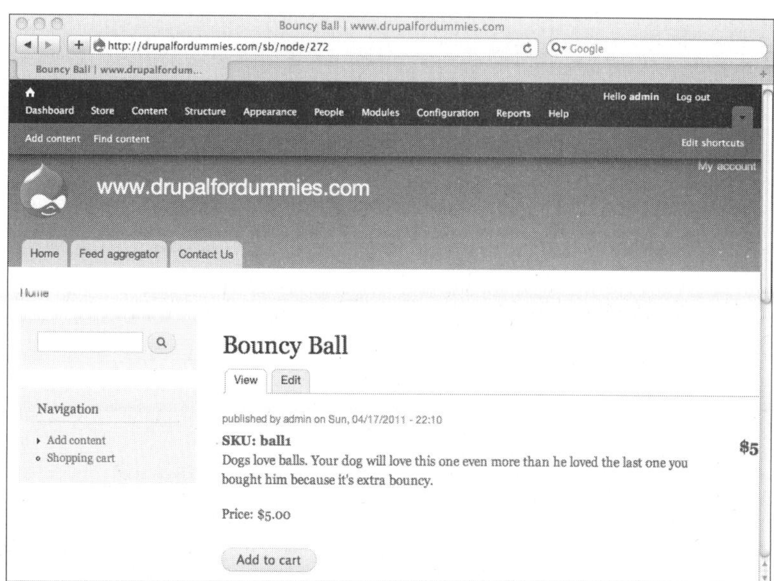

Figure 15-4: Individual product listing.

Testing the ordering process

To see how your storefront works, you should test it. At this point, you have no payment mechanism tied into your store. When someone adds products to her cart and checks out, she is presented with a form to gather information. When she finishes, she is sent a confirmation e-mail, you're sent an e-mail notifying you of the order, and the order information is saved on an administration page on your Drupal site. To test it for yourself, follow these steps:

1. **Log out as Administrator by clicking the Log Out link.**

   You should now see any products you added on the main page of your site.

2. **Click the Add to Cart button for one of the products.**

   This opens the Shopping cart form (see Figure 15-5).

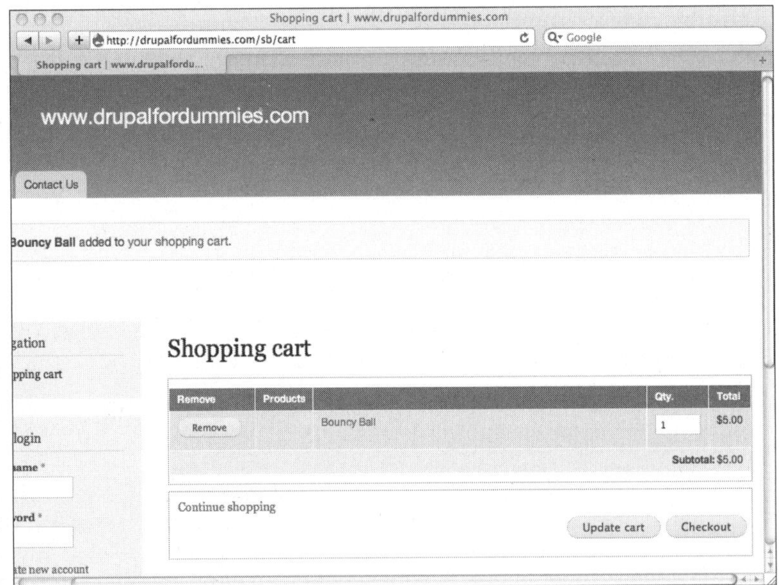

Figure 15-5: The Shopping cart with a product added to it.

   The shopping cart lists all the items a shopper has added and the total cost. This form also allows him to update or remove items.

3. **Click the Checkout button.**

   This opens the Checkout form (see Figure 15-6).

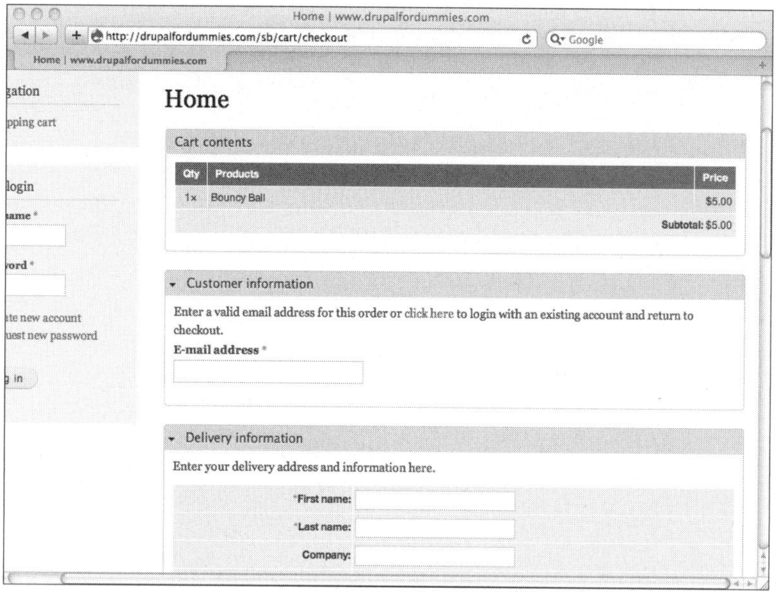

Figure 15-6: The top part of the Checkout form.

4. **Fill in a valid e-mail address in the E-mail Address field.**

   This is where the order confirmation will be sent after a shopper completes this form.

5. **In the Deliver Information section, fill out the required information in these text boxes: First Name, Last Name, Street Address, City, Country, State/Province, and Postal Code.**

6. **Select the My Billing Information Is the Same as My Delivery Information check box.**

   This handy box pulls the information from the Delivery Information section automatically and enters it into the Billing Information fields.

7. **Click Review Order.**

   This opens a confirmation page with the information the shopper has entered. At this point, the shopper can click Back to change the order, or click Submit Order to finalize it (see Figure 15-7).

8. **Click Submit Order.**

   An Order Complete message appears.

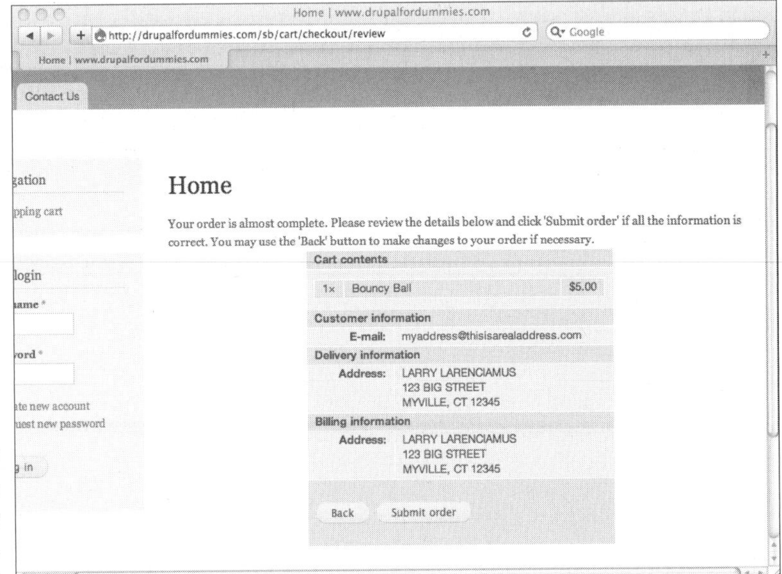

Figure 15-7: Review order page.

If the user had no account on your site, a new one is created for her automatically.

Managing orders

An e-mail is sent to you automatically when a new order is made. You can see all the orders made on your site. To review orders, follow these steps:

1. **Choose Store➪View Orders.**

   This opens a list of orders that have been placed on your site (see Figure 15-8).

2. **Click the View Order icon next to one of the orders.**

   Each order has icons on the left of the order ID:

   • *View* allows you to see the order details.

   • *Edit* allows you to make changes to the order and send an invoice to the customer.

   • *Delete* deletes the order.

Each order has a status that indicates whether the order has been fulfilled. As you get more orders, you may have to filter them by status. For example, if you only want to see completed orders, select Completed from the View by Status drop-down list.

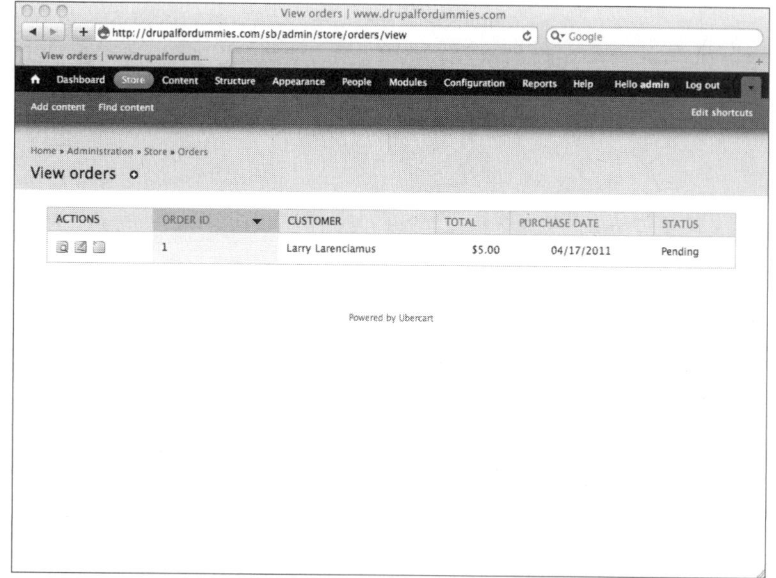

Figure 15-8: List of orders and current statuses.

3. **You can change the order status for an individual order at the bottom of the order View screen.**

   Currently the status is Pending. As you go through each stage of handling an order, you can change the status to Processing, Completed, Canceled, or In Checkout.

In addition to changing the status of an order, you can modify an existing order. Follow these steps:

1. **Click the Edit button next to the order you want to change.**
2. **Make sure the Edit tab is selected.**
3. **Make any desired changes on this form.**

   You can modify any information the shopper entered; add, edit, or delete the products that were ordered; and add private Admin information about the order (which the shopper never sees).

4. **When you're finished, click Submit Changes.**

You can use the Orders section of your site to send out invoices by e-mail or create a printable invoice that can be mailed to your customer. Follow these steps:

1. **Click the Edit button next to the order you want to change.**
2. **Click the Invoice tab.**
3. **You can view, print, or e-mail an invoice by choosing the appropriate link at the top of the Invoice page.**

As you make changes to the customer's order, such as changing the status or e-mailing an invoice, Ubercart keeps track of them for you automatically. Click the Edit button next to an order, and then click the Log tab to see activities related to that order.

Configuring Your Storefront

While Ubercart is practically ready to work after you add products, you also have some ways to customize your site.

Adding a shopping cart block

Most major storefronts give shoppers a link to their shopping carts. This way, they can easily check what they've selected to purchase. To add a link to the shopping cart on your site, follow these steps:

1. **Choose Structure⇨Blocks.**
2. **Locate the Shopping Cart block under the Disabled section.**
3. **Drag this block to the location you want it to appear.**

   We move ours to the top of the second sidebar.
4. **Click Save Blocks.**

   Not only is the Ubercart Shopping Cart block a link to the cart, but it also keeps a running total of the cost of items added to it.

Using the Configuration settings

There are more than 100 configuration options buried under the Store⇨Configuration menus. In this section, we highlight some of the most important ones to know.

Cart settings

Cart settings control how the shopping cart behaves. To modify them, choose Store⇨Cart Settings. Here are the ones you're most likely to change:

- **Minimum Order Subtotal:** Use this to set a minimum order amount a shopper must meet before the order can be submitted.

- **Cart Lifetime for Anonymous Users:** If a shopper adds items to his shopping cart, but isn't signed in on your site, this duration controls how long the items in his cart will remain there. If he browses to a different site but returns within four hours, his items will still be in the cart.
- **Cart Lifetime for Authenticated Users:** If a shopper adds items to her shopping cart, and is logged in, items in her cart will remain for a year. Each time she logs in, she can click the shopping cart link and see them.

Checkout settings

Checkout settings control the checkout process. To modify them, choose Store⇨Checkout settings.

- **Enable Checkout:** Located on the Basic settings of the Checkout settings screen. If you eventually use a third-party vendor to manage the transaction, you need to deselect this option.
- **Instruction Messages:** Under Instruction Messages, you can customize the text of the Checkout Instructions and Checkout Review Instructions the shopper sees during the checkout process.
- **Completion Messages:** Under Completion Messages, you can customize the text of a number of different messages the shopper sees after he completes the checkout process.
- **Address Fields:** Click the Address Fields tab. You can modify the Title of any of the fields in the address section of the checkout form. You can also specify whether they're enabled and if they are required.

Country settings

Country settings allow you to set up the checkout form for other countries. To modify them, choose Store⇨Country Settings. You can import countries into your list.

When a shopper reaches the Contact form, he or she chooses a country from a drop-down list. The Country settings control which countries appear in that drop-down list. After the shopper changes the country, the values in the State/Province drop-down list change accordingly.

Order settings

Order settings control what happens to the order after the checkout is completed. To modify them, choose Store⇨Configuration⇨Order Settings.

- **Number of Orders on Overview Screen:** Controls the number of orders you see when you choose Store⇨Orders.
- **Order Statuses:** Under the Workflow tab, you can customize the text of the order statuses. You can also add custom ones.

Product settings

Product settings control the appearance of the information on product listings pages. To modify these settings, choose Store➪Product Settings, and then click the Edit tab near the upper-right of the screen.

- **Display an Optional Quantity Field in the** *Add to Cart* **Form:** Selecting this check box places a quantity field on the product listing pages. We recommend selecting this check box. Click Save Configuration to enable this option.
- **Product Fields:** You control which fields show up on the product listing pages. If the products you sell should display their dimensions or weight, here's the place to add them. Select the appropriate check boxes and then click Save Configuration.

Store settings

The Store settings page controls many of the overall store settings. To modify these settings, choose Store➪Configuration➪Store Settings (see Figure 15-9).

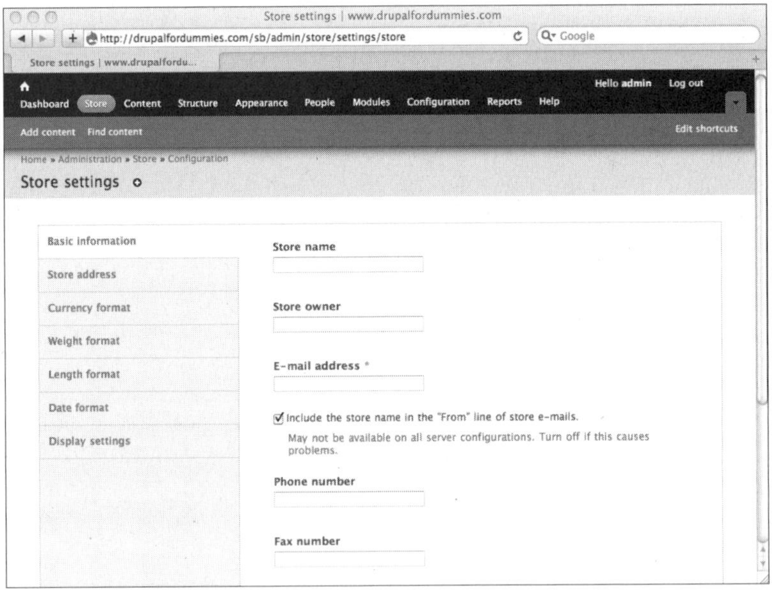

Figure 15-9: Store settings Overview page.

- **Basic Information and Store Address tabs:** There are a number of fields you should enter data into on these forms to give shoppers more information about your store. If possible, provide contact info for your store on the Store Address tab.
- **Footer Message for Store Pages:** Click the Display Settings tab to find this option. You can remove the Ubercart messages, although if you don't have to, it's nice to leave them at the bottom of your site.
- **Currency Format tab:** This form allows you to change the default currency.
- **Weight Format, Length Format, and Date Format tabs:** You can change the units of measurement for weight and length, and the date format.

Enhancing Product Listings

The basic product listing from Ubercart includes a field for photos, which can enhance your listing. The product listings aren't organized into catalogs, but should be. These are important features that will make your site more professional, and they are worth spending a few minutes to add.

Using images

Your products won't sell if the product page doesn't have any pictures displaying the product. To add images to your product listings, follow these steps:

1. **Choose Store⇨View Products.**
2. **Click the product to which you want to add an image.**
3. **Click the Edit tab.**
4. **Scroll down to the Image section of the form and click Browse.**

   This opens the File browser shown in Figure 15-10.

   Keep the image a relatively small height and width if possible. A reasonably good size is 250 x 250.

5. **Click Save.**

Follow the preceding steps for each additional image you want to include for the same product.

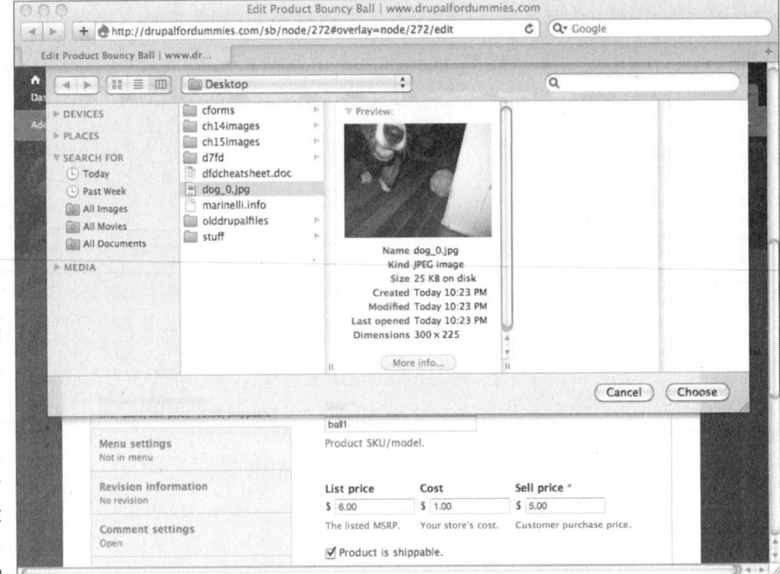

Figure 15-10: Locate the image you want to add to your product listing.

Adding a catalog

To add catalog pages and organize your products by type, follow these steps:

1. **Click Modules on the Dashboard menu bar.**
2. **Under the Chaos Tools Suite section, select the Chaos Tools check box.**
3. **Under the Views section, select the Views check box.**
4. **Under the Ubercart – Optional section, select the Catalog check box.**
5. **Click Save Configuration.**
6. **Choose Structure⇨Taxonomy.**
7. **Click Add Terms next to Catalog.**

   This opens the Add Term form (see Figure 15-11).
8. **Enter a product category in the Name field.**

   For example, if you had an online pet store, you might use Dog Toys or Cat Food for a term name.
9. **Click the Browse button to locate and upload a small image and add a description in the Description text box if you want.**
10. **Click Save.**
11. **Repeat Steps 7 through 10 until you've created all the categories you need.**

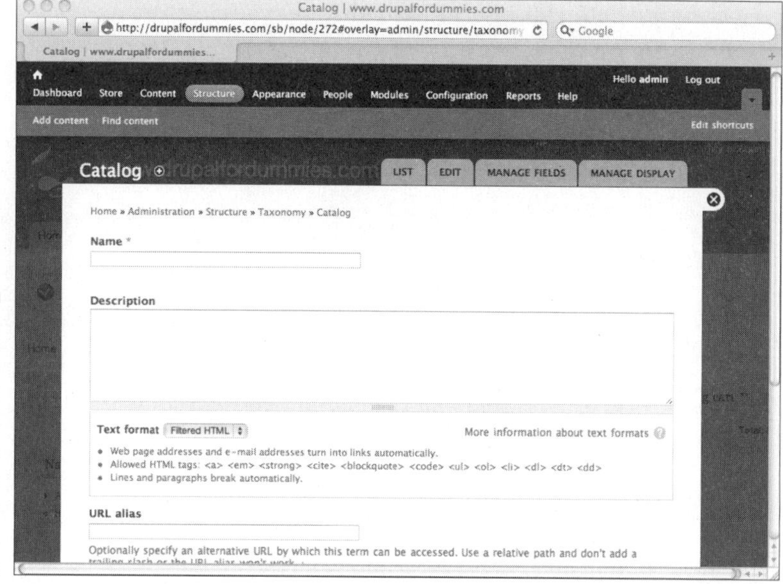

Figure 15-11: The Add term form is used to create categories for your catalog.

Now you're ready to add products to your catalog. You see a box on your Add Content⇨Product forms with all of the product categories you just created. Choose the appropriate one for the product you're adding. You can also put a product into more than one category by pressing the Ctrl or ⌘ key while selecting categories.

To see your catalog, browse to `/catalog` on your site. For example, `http://yourdrupalsitehere.com/catalog`. Ours is shown in Figure 15-12.

You can add a description to your catalog by choosing Structure⇨Taxonomy. Click Edit Vocabulary next to Catalog. Enter a description in the Description field. You can also change the name of your catalog by changing the Vocabulary name on this form. For example, you might want to call it Our Products.

You can create a primary navigation link so shoppers can find your product catalog. Follow these steps:

1. **If you haven't done so, move your Main links to a block on your site by choosing Structure⇨Blocks.**
2. **Move your Main links to the region of your choice.**

   We choose the Header region.
3. **Click Save Blocks.**
4. **Choose Structure⇨Menus.**
5. **Click Add Link next to Main menu.**

6. **In the Path text box, enter** catalog.

7. **In the Menu Link Title text box, enter** Catalog.

8. **Click Save.**

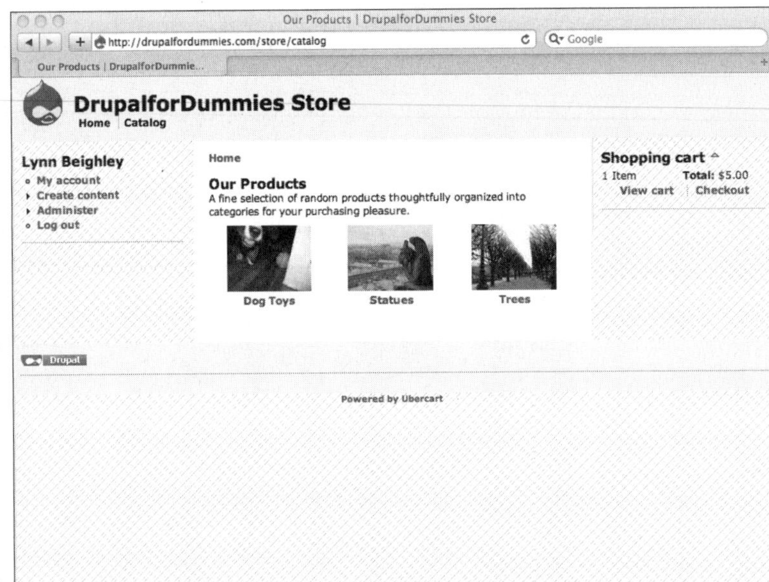

Figure 15-12: A simple catalog page with a description and three categories.

Getting Paid

Before you can accept credit cards, you need to

- Make sure your site is hosted on a secure server, which protects the credit card information your users enter on an order form.
- Activate additional modules.
- Sign up for an account with a company that can process your credit card orders for you, such as PayPal or Google.

You have a number of options for third-party merchant services you can use to handle the credit card transactions on your site. In this section, we discuss activating the modules that allow interaction with these sites and let you accept payment. We focus on Google Checkout specifically, but other companies operate in a similar fashion. First you have to enable the Payment module, and then set up — and use — a Google Checkout account.

To give you an idea of the process involved in setting up one of these accounts, we walk through setting up a Google Checkout account. Unfortunately, sites and processes change all the time, so your best bet is to visit the site and read the documentation for the correct processes to follow.

Choosing a credit card service

Before adding the modules to accept payment, you should create an account with the service you intend to use. Some of your options are

- **2Checkout:** `http://2checkout.com`
- **Authorize.net:** `http://authorize.net`
- **PayPal:** `http://paypal.com`
- **Google Checkout:** `http://checkout.google.com/sell`

All these services take a small fee for each transaction they process. Check with the specific company for details.

Setting up Ubercart to accept credit card payments

When you've chosen a company to work with to process your transactions, you need to enable the correct modules and set your site to process payments with that merchant. To set Ubercart to accept payment, follow these steps:

1. **Click Modules on the Dashboard menu bar.**
2. **Under the Ubercart – Core (optional) section, select the Payment check box.**
3. **Under the Ubercart – Payment section, select the Google Checkout check box (or select the check box for your particular vendor).**

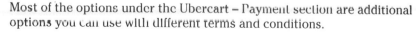

   Most of the options under the Ubercart – Payment section are additional options you can use with different terms and conditions.
4. **Click Save Configuration.**

Turning on payment

All of the configuration options for setting up payment are found under Store⇨Payment Settings. To set Ubercart to use your payment method of choice, follow these steps:

1. **Choose Store⇨Payment Settings.**
2. **Click the Payment Methods block.**
3. **Click Payment Methods.**

   You see the list of payment methods you enabled (see Figure 15-13).

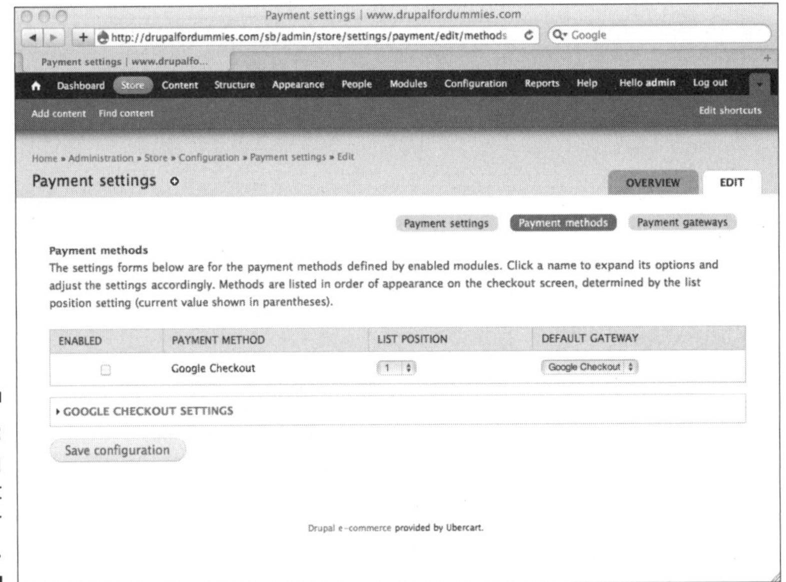

Figure 15-13: Enabling Payment methods for Ubercart.

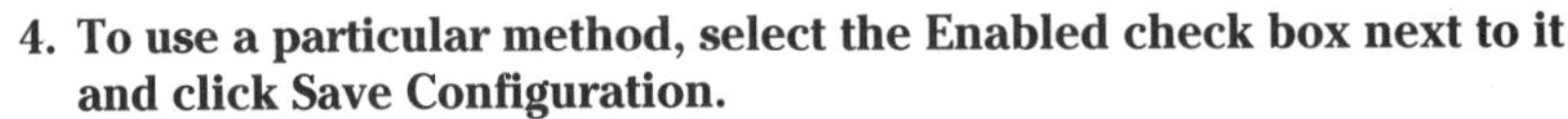

4. **To use a particular method, select the Enabled check box next to it and click Save Configuration.**

You won't be able to select a method until you've configured its settings.

Setting up a Google Checkout account

To set up a Google Checkout account, follow these steps:

1. **Browse to `http://checkout.google.com/sell`.**

   If you don't already have a Google account, you need to create one.

2. **Fill out a form to gather business information for your account (see Figure 15-14).**

3. **After you complete the form, click the Settings tab to get the Merchant ID you will need for your site.**

   It's in the Private Contact Information section next to Merchant ID.

4. **On your site, choose Store⇨Payment Settings⇨Payment Methods⇨ Google Checkout Settings.**

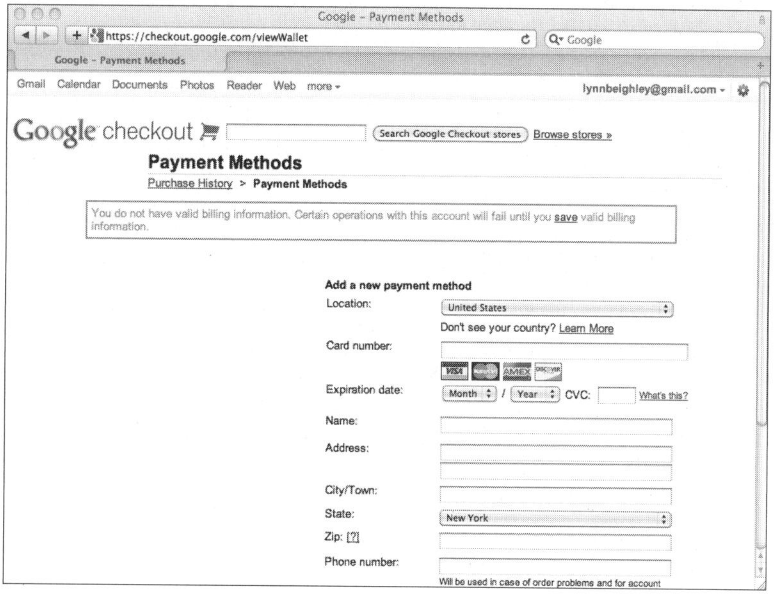

Figure 15-14: Google Checkout new merchant form.

5. **Click the Account tab.**

6. **In the instructions, copy the URL it tells you to enter on the Google Checkout Merchant Center site.**

7. **In another window, browse to `http://checkout.google.com/sell` and log in if necessary.**

8. **Click the Settings tab, and then click the Integration link on the left. Enter the URL from step 6 in the API callback URL text field.**

9. **Copy the Google merchant ID number. Click Save.**

   Press Ctrl+C (Windows) or ⌘+C (Mac).

10. **In the browser window with your Drupal site open, choose Administer⇨Store Administration⇨Configuration⇨Google Checkout Settings.**

11. **Click the Account tab, and paste the Google merchant ID number into the Merchant ID field.**

    Press Ctrl+P (Windows) or ⌘+P (Mac).

12. **Go back to the browser window with the Google Checkout page, and copy the Google merchant key.**

13. **Repeat Steps 10 and 11, but paste the merchant key into the Merchant Key field.**

Enhancing Your Store

When you installed all the Ubercart and related modules, you added in lots of functionality you haven't yet turned on. This section is a quick look at the best of the other parts of Ubercart you haven't yet seen.

Using the fulfillment modules

Not only does Ubercart manage the products, catalog, shopping cart, and order forms for you, but it also has the capability to handle shipping cost calculations. To use the fulfillment modules, follow these steps:

1. **Click Modules on the Dashboard menu bar.**

2. **Under the Ubercart – Core (optional) section, select the Shipping Quotes check box.**

3. **Under the Ubercart – Fulfillment section, select all four check boxes.**

4. **Click Save Configuration.**

5. **Choose Store⇨Shipping Quote Settings.**

6. **Click the Quote Methods tab, and then the General settings link (see Figure 15-15).**

7. **Select the Enable check box(es) for the shipping type(s) you use.**

   Depending on which type you choose, clicking the appropriate link can give you more options for providing account information.

8. **Click Save Configuration.**

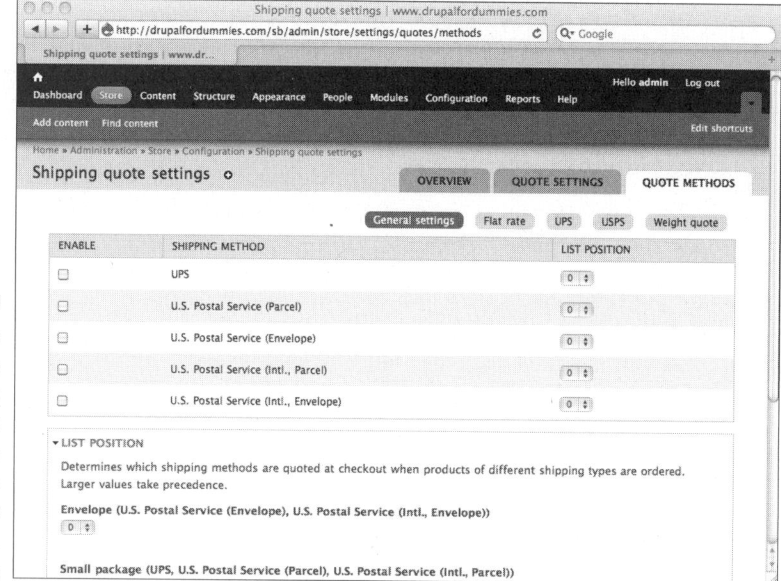

Figure 15-15: The Shipping Quote Settings allow you to select types of shipping.

Taxing your customers

It's not a fun thing to think about, but it's necessary for many online merchants to collect tax on the goods they sell. Three modules can help. Follow these steps:

1. **Click Modules on the Dashboard menu bar.**
2. **Under the Ubercart – Core (optional) section, select the Reports, Tax Report, and Taxes check boxes.**
3. **Click Save Configuration.**
4. **Choose Store➪Tax Rates and Settings.**
5. **Click the Add a Tax Rate tab (see Figure 15-16).**
6. **Enter a name for the tax in the Name text box, and then enter the tax rate as a percent or decimal in the Rate text box.**

   The name you enter appears on the customer's checkout form.
7. **Click Save Configuration.**

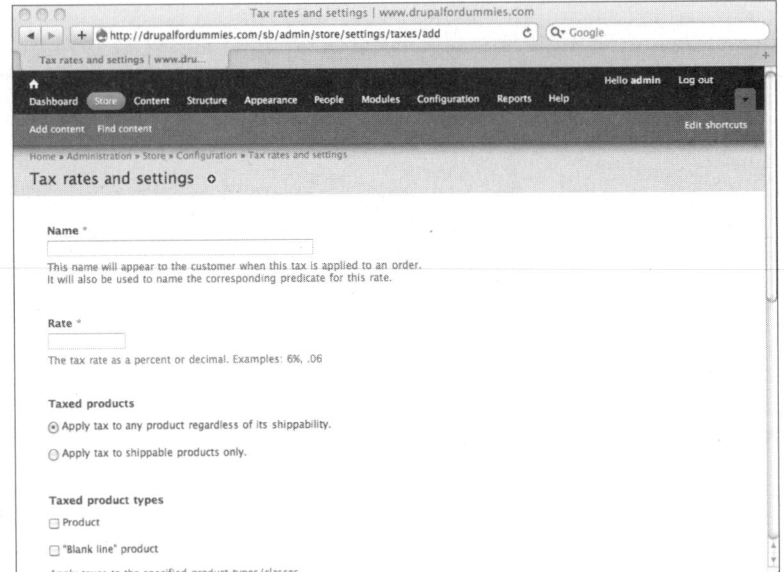

Figure 15-16: The Add a Tax Rate tab sets up automatic taxation of purchases.

When you installed the Reports module, you gained access to a Sales Tax report, located at Store⇨Reports⇨Sales Tax Report. There are a number of other valuable reports in this same area of your site:

- **Customer reports:** Presents the total orders, products, sales, and average order totals for each customer.
- **Product reports:** Shows every product listed in the store, how many have sold, how many times it has been viewed, revenue, and gross profit.
- **Sales reports:** Displays sale summaries for the last two days, average monthly sales, and projected sales.
- **Sales Tax report:** A handy report that shows you the sales tax you've collected for a particular period.

Part V

The Part of Tens

"Ooo–wait! That's perfect for the clinic's home page. Just stretch it out a little further ... little more ..."

In this part . . .

You've built a tremendous website, but you want more. More modules, more themes. These two chapters each consist of ten nuggets — ten more modules and themes for Drupal and ten websites that let you connect with other users to garner even more knowledge about Drupal. Because after you've built one site using Drupal, there's no reason not to build more.

Chapter 16

Ten Must-Have Drupal Modules and Themes

In This Chapter

- Finding useful modules
- Gathering lovely themes

Drupal sites can be extended with hundreds of additional modules available for free download. In this chapter, we point out five that'll help you make your Drupal site even more usable and inviting to your users than it already is. We also provide you with a peek at five awesome free themes available from Drupal.org to help you personalize your website.

CAPTCHA Module

If you plan on rocking a site with an active forum or open account registrations, you will want to download the CAPTCHA module sooner than later. CAPTCHA (Completely Automatic Public Turing Test to Tell Computers and Humans Apart) provides a random question to site visitors that they must answer to prove they're humans. CAPTCHA questions come in three basic forms:

- A small graphic image that contains a printed word. The word in the image has to be typed into a form before a user can complete some action on a site.
- A basic math question; for example, your visitor has to type in the answer to 10 + 8.
- A string of text about which the visitor is asked a question; for example, "What is the first word in the phrase *ofomom isulul iki udev uquse*?"

Using CAPTCHA keeps spammers from being able to use programs to spam your site with lots of fake comments that are actually advertisements for prescription drugs, online casinos, or other questionable services.

While using CAPTCHA is a good idea, it doesn't stop humans from posting spam. It only prevents *automated* spamming — those obnoxious programs that locate Drupal sites and root through them looking for places to add spammy comments. We highly recommend you moderate all comments in addition to using the CAPTCHA module. This may seem like overkill, but CAPTCHA limits the amount of spam you have to wade through so you have a manageable number of comments to moderate. Trust us, the legitimate users of your site will thank you for your efforts.

After you have uploaded and activated the module, you can configure where CAPTCHA questions appear in your site by looking to your Dashboard menu bar and choosing Configuration➪People➪CAPTCHA (see Figure 16-1).

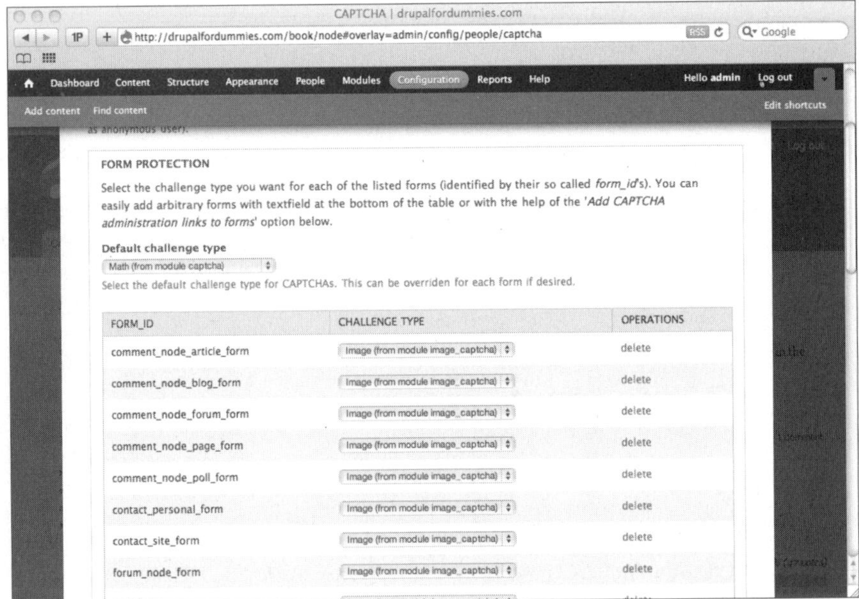

Figure 16-1: CAPTCHA interface.

You will see a list of form types on your site and a drop-down list that allows you to select which of the three CAPTCHA types — text, image, or math — that must be answered before a form can be successfully submitted.

The Image CAPTCHA tab gives you some options to control the image CAPTCHA. You can specify font size, which font to use, what characters should be used, and what colors to use. The Distortion and Noise section lets you control the appearance of the text by adding noise and distorting the letters. If you do distort the text in your image CAPTCHA, make sure you test it a few times to ensure that it's still readable.

Hacker techniques grow increasingly sophisticated all the time. Image CAPTCHAS work best when they are a little difficult to read. Optical character recognition programs, the same algorithms used to allow scanned documents to be output as text, can easily scan CAPTCHA images and extract the text, so adding a bit of noise or distortion can help foil them.

The Text CAPTCHA tab allows you to create and use your own phrase for visitors to answer rather than the random gibberish it produces.

TinyMCE – WYSIWYG HTML Editor Module

Proving that size really doesn't matter, TinyMCE is a small but powerful module that allows you and your users to easily create formatted content, much like a word processor produces. It places a framework of formatting commands on top of any large text entry fields (see Figure 16-2).

In order to add TinyMCE to your Drupal installation, you are first required to download and install a module called WYSIWYG HTML Editor. (What's a WYSIWYG? That's geek-speak for *what you see is what you get.*

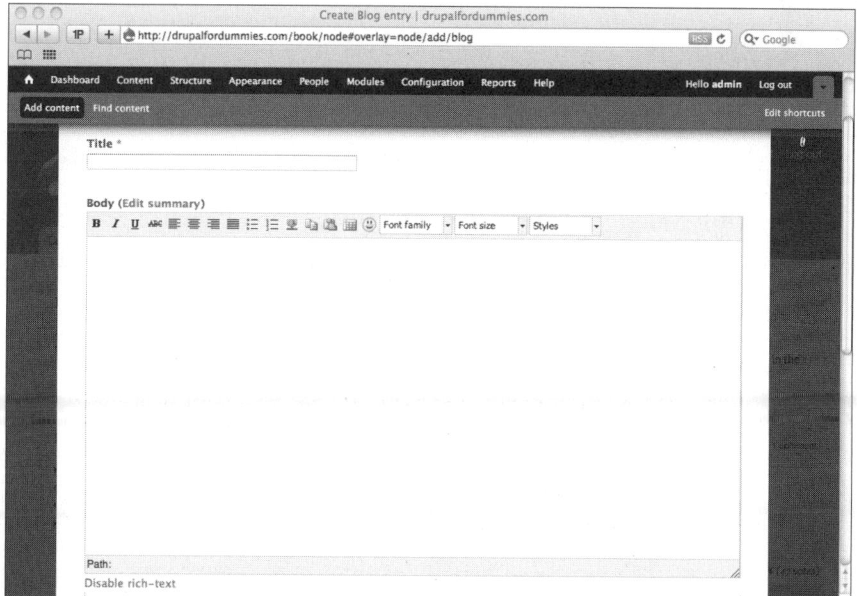

Figure 16-2: TinyMCE embedded in Drupal site.

Unlike a true word processor, TinyMCE formats text with HTML code behind the scenes. In the case of fonts, this means you have a limited set available through this panel. The font you use on a web page will show up only for your users who also have that same font on their computers.

Not only does TinyMCE modify your text, but it also allows you an easy way to include images and Flash movies in your posts. You can also control the color of your text and the background color behind your post.

TinyMCE can offer as many or as few options to your site's users as you want. To change the number of WYSIWYG editing options available to your users when they create content on your site, click Configure on your Dashboard menu bar and then select WYSIWYG Profiles, found under the Configuration page's Content Authoring pane. You will be presented with a wide variety of options for TinyMCE, as well as an explanation for each. The WYSIWYG profiles configuration page can also help you to install other HTML editors, should TinyMCE not be a perfect fit for your site.

TinyMCE can be set up to allow the upload of media files such as images and video. Although software creators do their best to ensure the security of their applications, malicious people constantly work hard to exploit weaknesses. In general, when using a module that allows users to upload files or customize content, be cautious. We recommend that you only allow people in highly trusted roles access to this module — or any other modules involved in content creation.

Mollom Module

If you find that, in spite of using the CAPTCHA module, you still have spam, Mollom is your best bet. Mollom is more than a module; it's also web service. Mollom.com knows how to detect spam from a variety of sources. When a new comment is entered on your site, Mollom.com checks it to see if it's spam. If Mollom thinks it may be, the user who entered it is shown a CAPTCHA.

Fortunately, you don't have to do anything. Your Drupal software, thanks to the Mollom module, automatically sends the user information to the Mollom.com server, checks for spam, and then, if the CAPTCHA challenge is not passed, the comment never even reaches your website. It's estimated that Mollom blocks up to 99.7 percent of all spam messages.

One of the great things about Mollom is that users don't see the CAPTCHA unless they are suspected of creating spam. This means that most legitimate users don't have to go through the trouble of answering a CAPTCHA. A recent study showed that a significant number of users will not bother filling out a CAPTCHA, and they don't end up writing their comments on your site. That's great news if you're an isolationist, but it's lousy if you want to build a sense of community and inclusion for your site's visitors.

For all its sophistication, Mollom is relatively simple:

1. **Browse to `http://mollom.com` and set up an account there.**

   You're walked through a process in which a Public key and Private key are created for your site.

2. **From your Dashboard menu bar, choose Configure⇨Content Authoring⇨Mollom.**

3. **Enter the Public and Private keys from the Mollom site in the Public Key and Private Key text boxes.**

4. **Click Save Configuration.**

   See Figure 16-3.

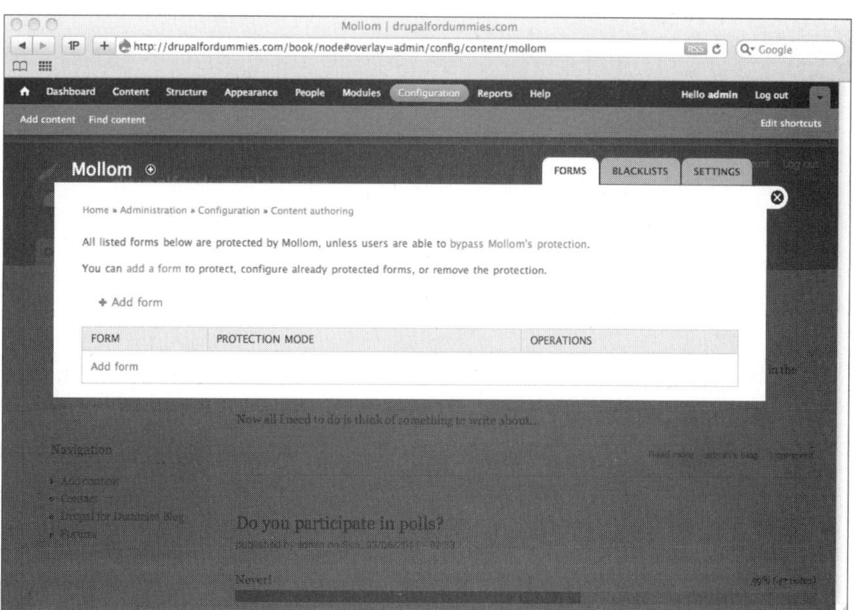

Figure 16-3: Mollom configuration.

That's all there is to it. Each time you browse back to Administer⇨Site Configuration⇨Mollom, you see a report of spam that Mollom has stopped. This same location can be visited to select which forms on your site are protected by the module.

Mollom has another nifty feature. Suppose you have a spammy comment on your site. With Mollom installed, every time you delete content, you are presented with a form that asks you if you want to report the content to Mollom as spam. This is part of how Mollom keeps its data up to date and is able to detect new types of spam. You can even classify what kind of spam it is (for example, violent content, taunting, or simply unsolicited advertising). Reporting the content is optional, which is good because sometimes you delete comments that are not spam.

Printer, E-mail, and PDF Versions Module

By downloading and installing the Printer, E-mail, and PDF Versions module to your site, your visitors can print, e-mail, and create PDF versions of your content.

After the module has been downloaded and installed, you control its settings by choosing Modules⇨Printer, E-mail, and PDF Versions. There are three rows: PDF Version, Printer-Friendly Pages, and Send by E-mail (see Figure 16-4). Each of these options can be configured.

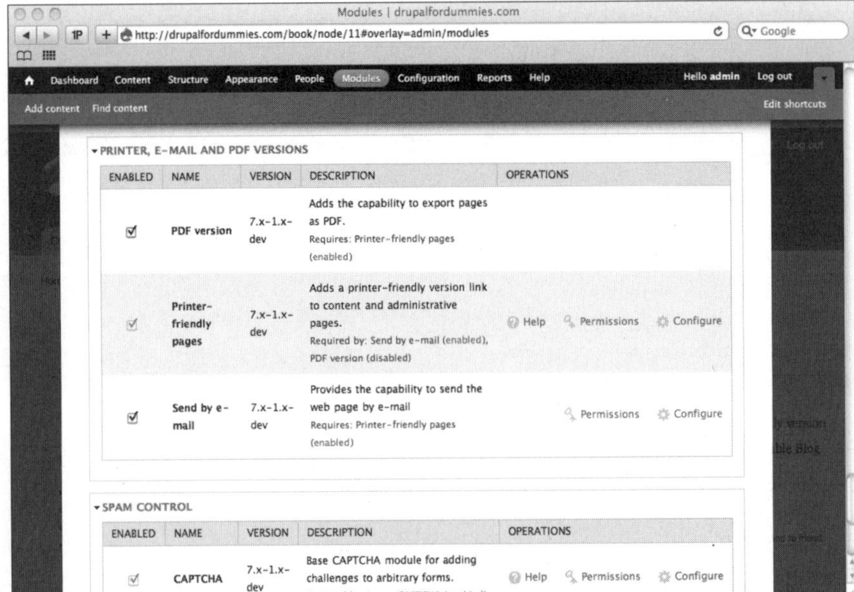

Figure 16-4: Setting the printer, e-mail, and PDF version in the content creation form.

This module gives you nearly complete control over its appearance and behavior. For example, you can specify the text or logo to be used to produce the print, e-mail, or PDF output. With the e-mail output, among many other options, you can control how many e-mails a user can send out in an hour.

By default, no basic pages or articles on your site will have the print, e-mail, or PDF links. You have to activate them. After you install the module, each time you create content, you will see a Printer, E-Mail and PDF Versions tab on the content creation page. This controls whether this content can be output, and in what fashion.

When you publish your content, Print, E-mail to a Friend, or Create a PDF links will appear. By default, they show up after the Add New Comment link at the end of the content.

Site Map Module

As your site grows, it's important that visitors be able to find the information they are seeking. Creating a site map can help, and the Site Map module automatically creates one for you. To create one, choose Configuration➪Search & Metadata➪Site Map. This opens the Site Map form, shown in Figure 16-5.

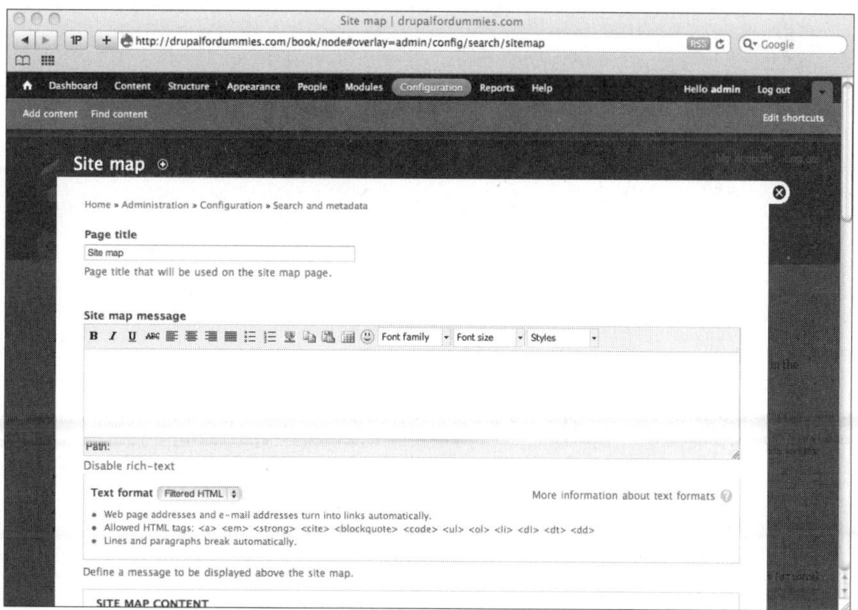

Figure 16-5: Site map configuration.

The form allows you to enter text to appear at the top of the page. You can specifically include menus and front-page content if you like. Click Save Configuration to generate your site map.

Before your site map will work, you have to enable it. To do this, follow these steps:

1. **Click Modules on the Dashboard menu bar.**
2. **Scroll down to Site Map module and select the Enable check box on the far left side of the module's row.**
3. **Click Save Permissions.**

The newly created site map is located on your site at `yourdomainname.com/sitemap`. For example, ours is at `http://drupalfordummies.com/sitemap`. You can link to the site map as you would any other page by adding a link in one of your menus.

BlogBuzz II Theme

BlogBuzz II (Figure 16-6) is a theme designed with bloggers in mind. Its clean lines and minimal feature set allow a site's administrator and users to focus on content creation, instead of spending their time endlessly tweaking settings.

Figure 16-6: The BlogBuzz II theme in action.

That's not to say BlogBuzz can't be tinkered with — far from it. In addition to being able to select from four different color palettes, an administrator can also insert a personalized site logo, redeploy menus and modules to a number of areas within the theme, and control how user information appears on the site.

Jackson Theme

Did you build your website in a fever? Is it hotter than a pepper sprout? Then you've been waiting for Jackson ever since Drupal 7 came out! Johnny Cash references aside, Jackson (as shown in Figure 16-7) is an ideal theme to consider if you're creating a web presence for your small business or a community organization. Clean and professional in appearance, a site dressed up by this winning theme will no doubt garner the respect and credibility that your endeavors deserve.

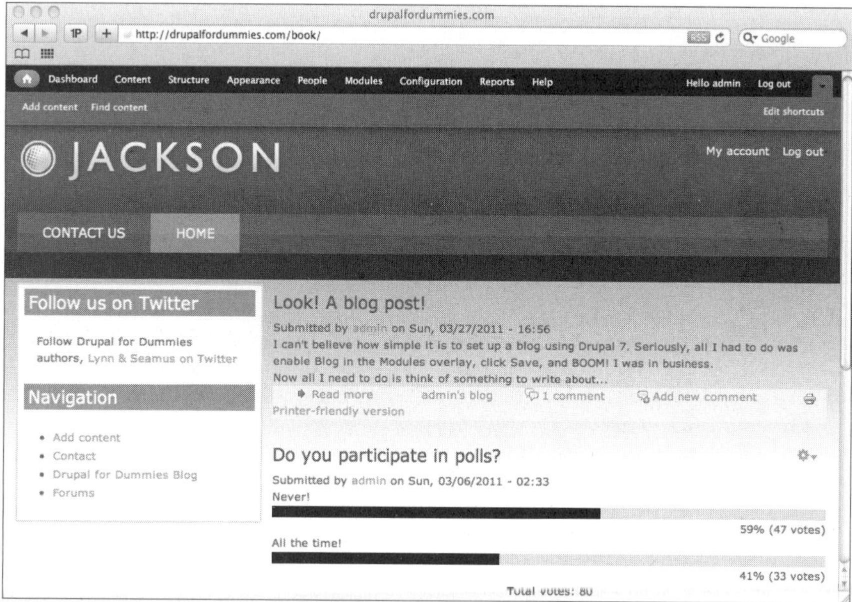

Figure 16-7: The Jackson theme in its default format.

BlueMasters Theme

BlueMasters started life as a popular WordPress CMS theme before being ported over for use with Drupal by the open source community. Aside from being relentlessly blue, the theme offers a number of features that will appeal to individuals seeking to build a magazine or portfolio style website, including built-in social media connectivity, a slick slideshow-style image gallery, twelve block regions, and options to implement a two- or three-column layout. As you can see in Figure 16-8, even in the theme's default form, it's definitely a looker.

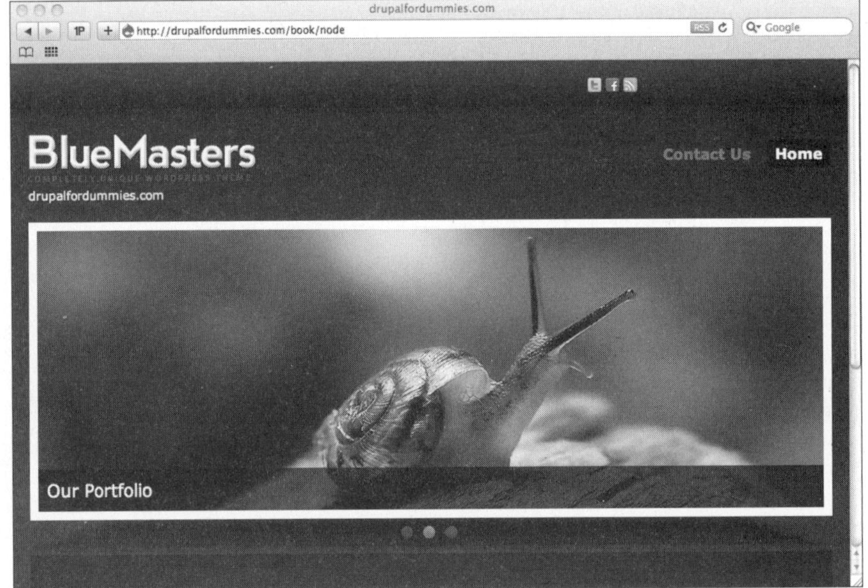

Figure 16-8: The Blue Masters theme.

Zen Theme

If you're a designer charged with rolling out a Drupal site for your client in record time, you're going to absolutely love Zen. A standards-compliant theme, Zen (shown in Figure 16-9) is pretty bleak insofar as aesthetics are concerned. That's because the theme wasn't designed to look pretty. Instead, Zen was created to act as the backbone for the development of complex PHP-

and CSS-enabled sites. So instead of having to build a one-in-a-million Drupal theme from scratch, you can load the Zen theme and use it as a framework to build something utterly unique in half the time. It's bursting at the seams with options and flexibility; you'll want to consider using Zen for your site, or for those of your clients, if you have a strong background in design and the ability to churn out Cascading Style Sheets in your sleep.

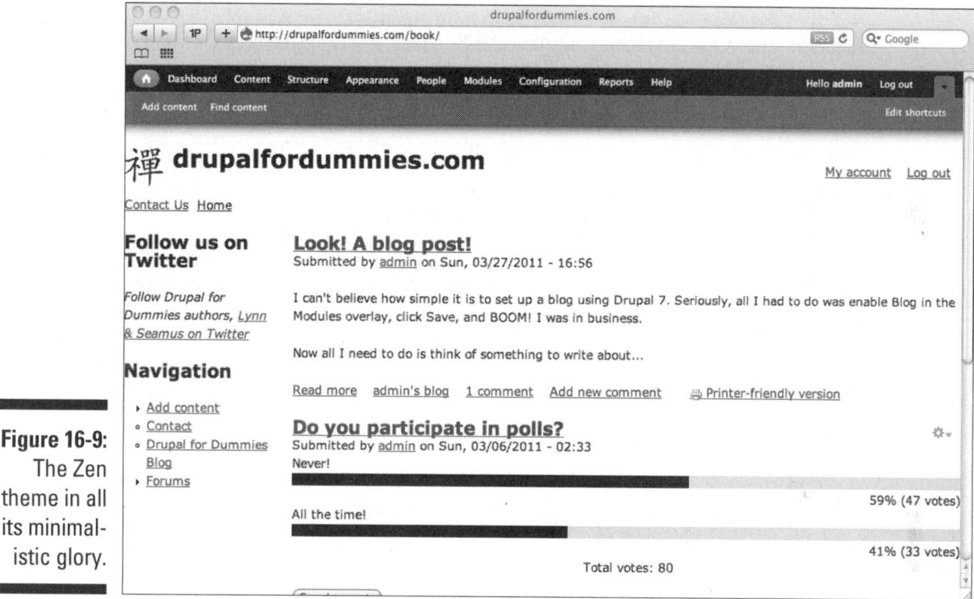

Figure 16-9: The Zen theme in all its minimalistic glory.

Marinelli Theme

Boasting a three-column layout, a generously-sized customizable image banner, and easy-to-locate tabs for your site's primary links, Marinelli is a great theme choice for anyone who wants a clean, visitor-friendly look for a site. Marinelli is compatible with most modern browsers and boasts some really nice interface touches, including front-end drop-down lists, eight collapsible regions, and support for rotating banners. As you can see in Figure 16-10, Marinelli is one good-looking theme.

Figure 16-10: The Marinelli theme in action.

Chapter 17

Ten Places to Help You Do More with Drupal

In This Chapter

- Getting more help
- Finding new themes
- Meeting other Drupal users

There are many great resources where you can get help, download new themes, and meet other Drupal users. This chapter contains ten great resources to help you get the most from Drupal.

Drupal.org Forum

When in doubt, go to the source! The Drupal.org website has a great user forum (see Figure 17-1) full of people from around the world willing to share their expertise. To access the forum, browse to `http://drupal.org/forum`.

You don't need an account on the Drupal.org site to read the forum, but you do need an account to post your own questions. Having an account also enables you to receive notifications when your questions get responses, as well as other news about Drupal.

Twitter

Twitter may seem an unlikely source for Drupal help and information, but it's worth a bit of attention. You can screen for tweets about Drupal topics by typing **#drupal** in the search box located on the right side of the Twitter home page (see Figure 17-2). Many of the resulting tweets point you at new themes, Drupal sites, and Drupal developments.

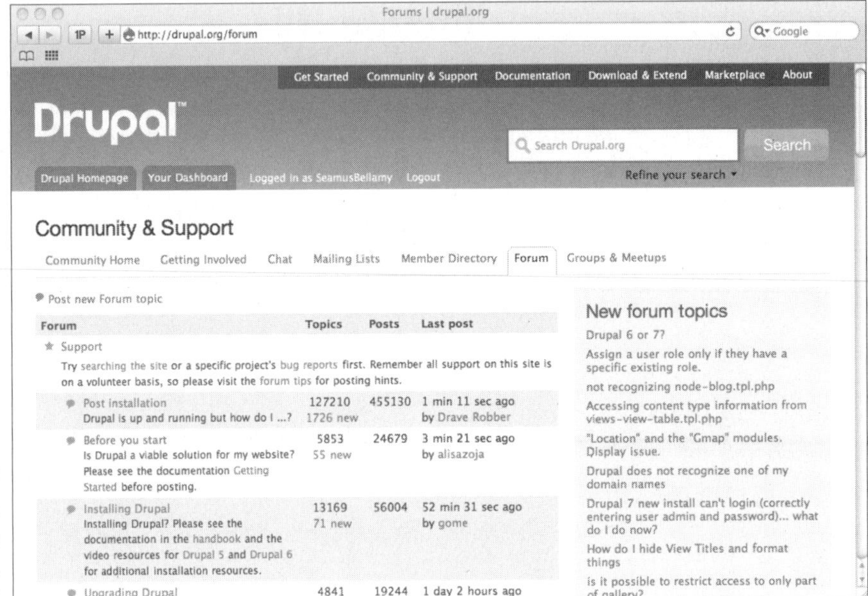

Figure 17-1: Drupal.org user forum.

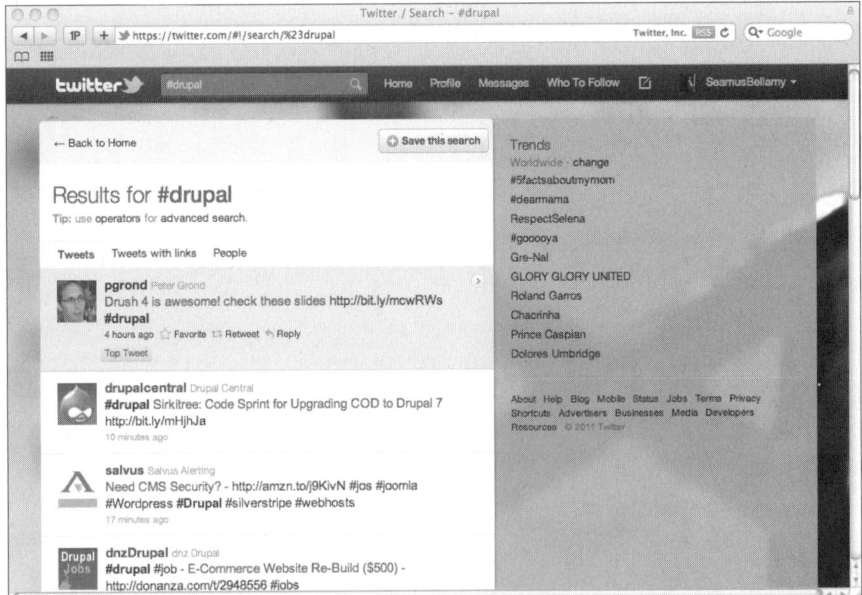

Figure 17-2: Twitter search of #drupal.

Facebook

Facebook may seem like another unlikely resource for Drupal news or help, but the Facebook Drupal group is a great place to get help and ideas (see Figure 17-3).

To join the group, you need a Facebook account (go to www.facebook.com to sign up). After you have an account, click the small groups icon on the bottom right of the screen. You can also browse directly to www.facebook.com/pages/Drupal/8427738891.

Learn By The Drop

If you like video demonstrations, Learn By The Drop (http://learnbythedrop.com), shown in Figure 17-4, is a good site to visit. This site contains a number of video and written tutorials for Drupal.

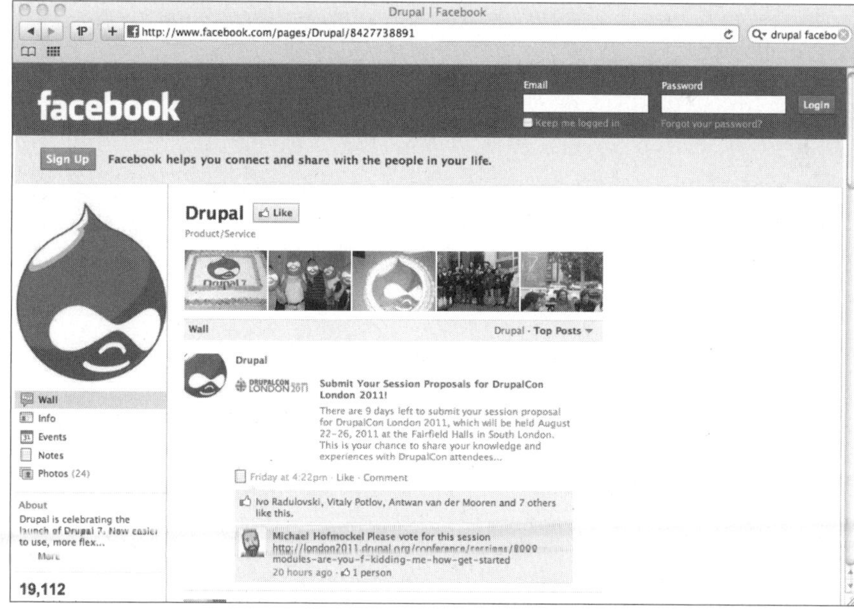

Figure 17-3: Facebook Drupal group.

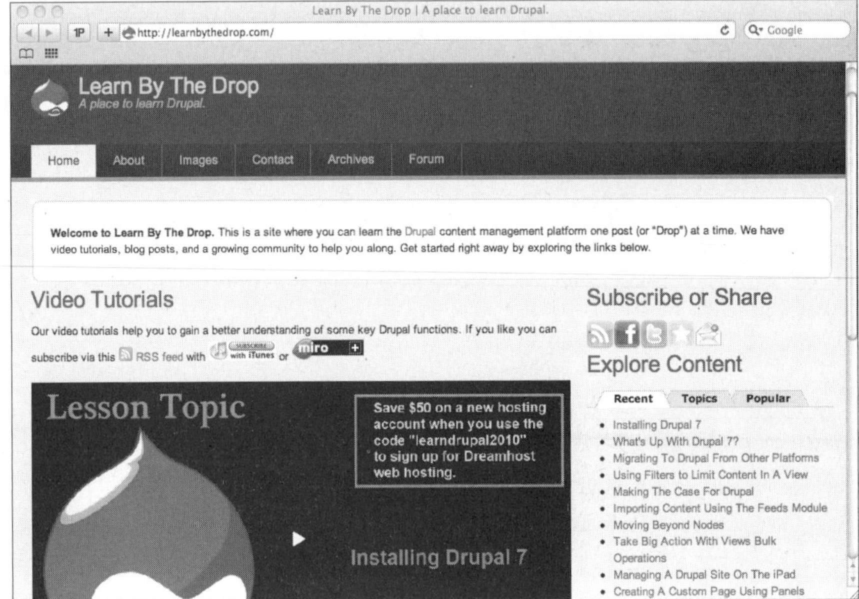

Figure 17-4: Learn By The Drop is a Drupal tutorial site.

GotDrupal.com

Another tutorial site with videos is GotDrupal.com at `http://gotdrupal.com` (see Figure 17-5). The videos are created as the site is being developed, and it's a bit like watching a house being built.

Drupal.org Mailing Lists

It's a good idea to stay informed of Drupal news. The Drupal.org site offers a number of mailing lists (see Figure 17-6). These are located at `http://drupal.org/mailing-lists`.

We recommend signing up for these lists:

- **Support:** A list for support questions.
- **Development:** A list for Drupal developers.
- **Consulting:** A list for Drupal consultants and Drupal service/hosting providers.

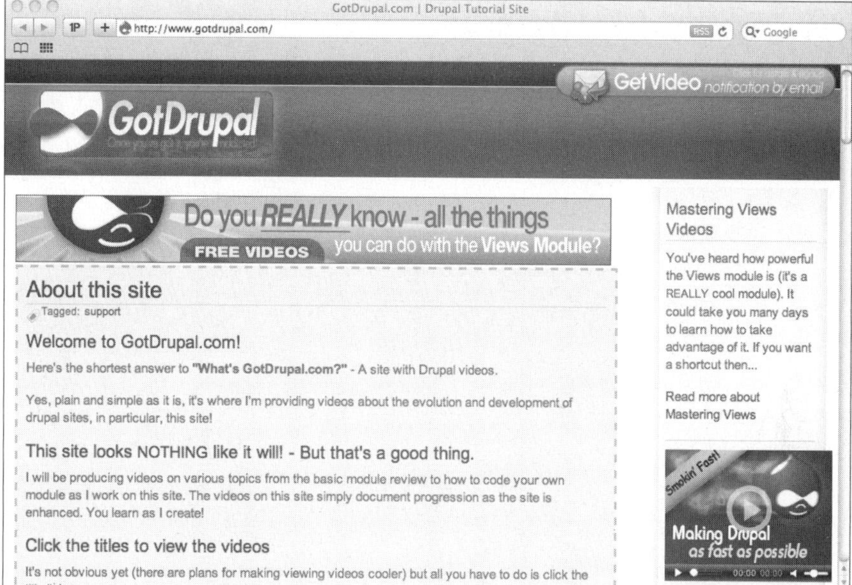

Figure 17-5: GotDrupal.com contains videos about Drupal site construction.

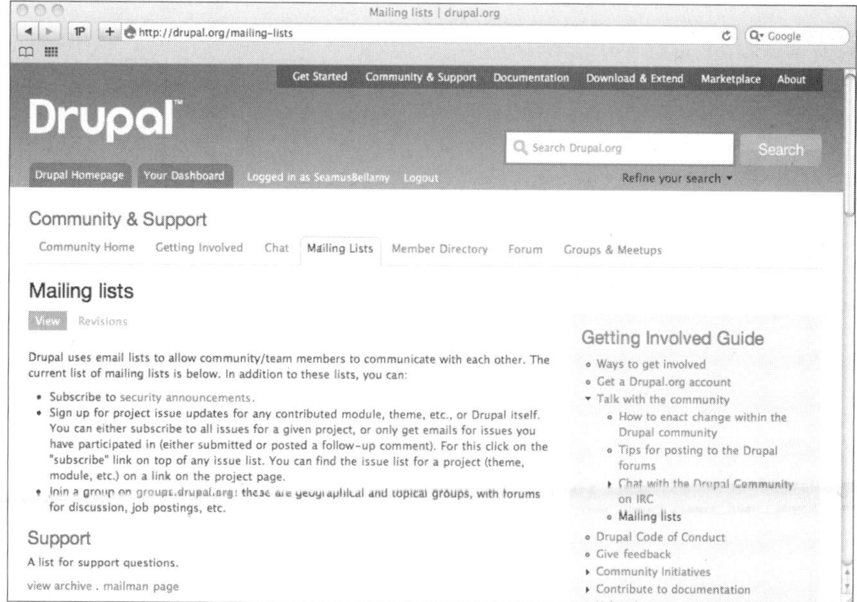

Figure 17-6: Drupal.org mailing lists.

Drupal.org Themes

Once again, the Drupal.org site is a great place to turn and has links to newly developed themes (see Figure 17-7). You can find them at `http://drupal.org/project/themes`.

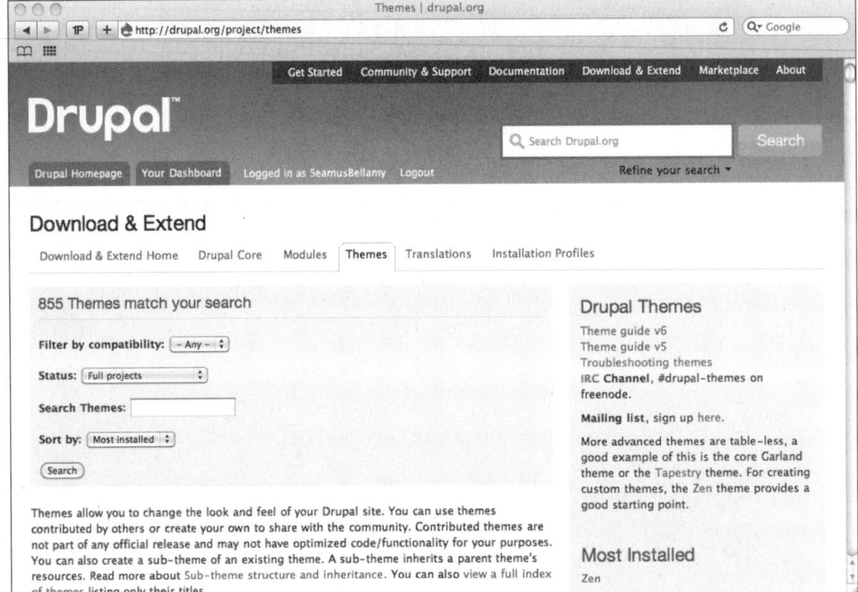

Figure 17-7: Drupal.org themes.

Drupal2U.com

Another site with great new themes is Drupal2U.com at `http://drupal2u.com` (see Figure 17-8).

Drupal.org User Groups

The Drupal.org site keeps a list of local Drupal user groups. These groups can be a great place to meet other Drupal users and site administrators, pool information, learn new site development skills and network (see Figure 17-9). To access the directory of groups, visit `http://groups.drupal.org/groups`.

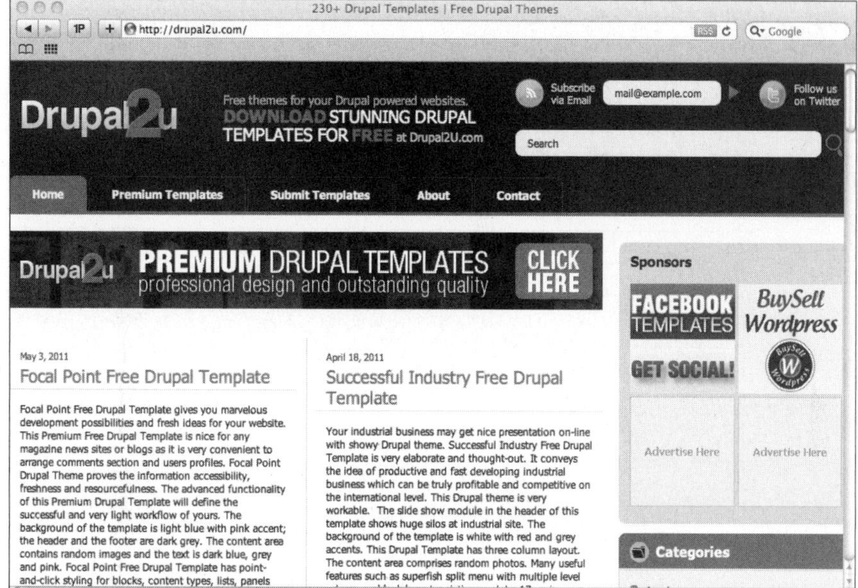

Figure 17-8: Drupal2U.com contains additional Drupal themes.

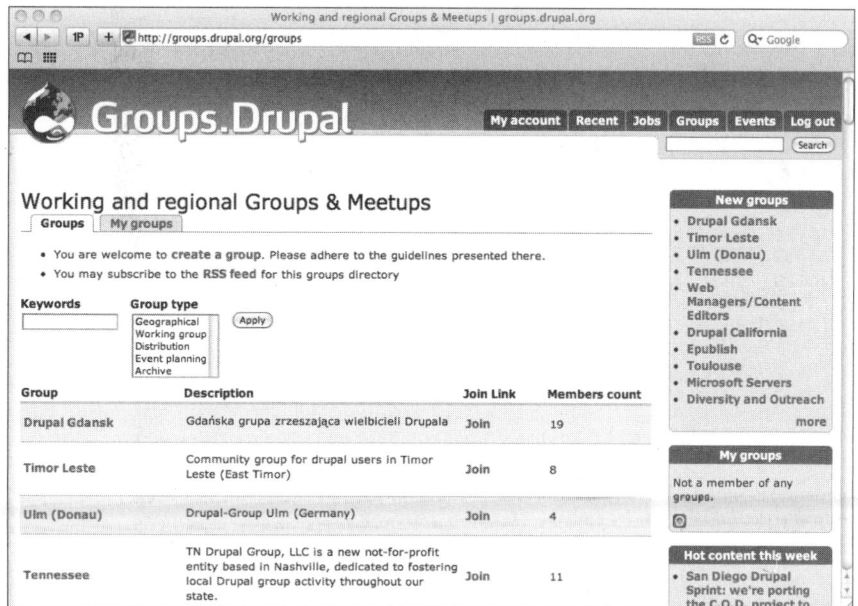

Figure 17-9: Drupal.org list of user groups.

Meetup.com

Meetup.com is a great place to find other people in your area who are building Drupal sites (see Figure 17-10). Just like with Drupal user groups, meetups are a great way to meet other Drupal users and share information. To find a local Drupal Meetup group, visit `http://drupal.meetup.com`.

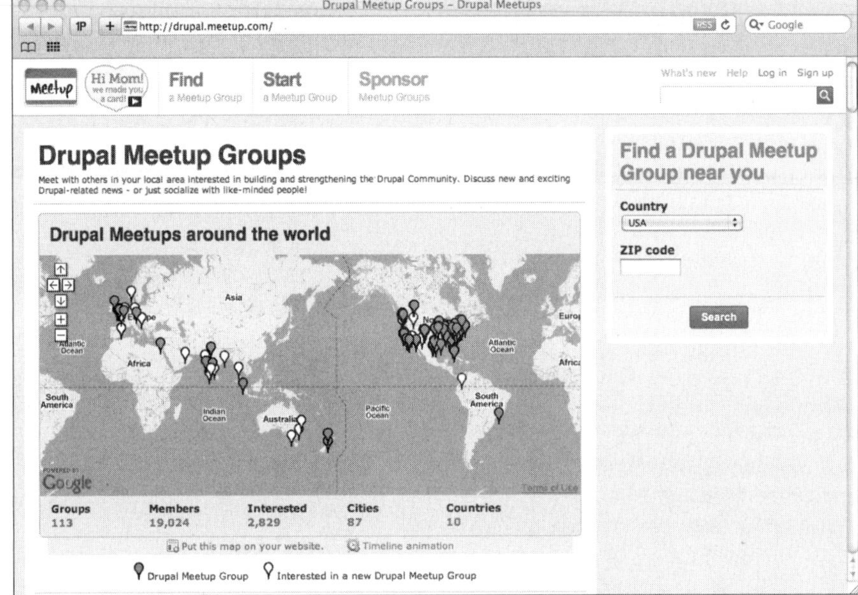

Figure 17-10: Meetup.com map of local Drupal user groups.

Index

• B •

• C •

• D •

• E •

• F •

• G •

• H •

• I •

• J •

• K •

• L •

• M •

• N •

• O •

• P •

• S •

• T •

• U •

Apple & Macs

iPad For Dummies
978-0-470-58027-1

iPhone For Dummies, 4th Edition
978-0-470-87870-5

MacBook For Dummies, 3rd Edition
978-0-470-76918-8

Mac OS X Snow Leopard For Dummies
978-0-470-43543-4

Business

Bookkeeping For Dummies
978-0-7645-9848-7

Job Interviews For Dummies, 3rd Edition
978-0-470-17748-8

Resumes For Dummies, 5th Edition
978-0-470-08037-5

Starting an Online Business For Dummies, 6th Edition
978-0-470-60210-2

Stock Investing For Dummies, 3rd Edition
978-0-470-40114-9

Successful Time Management For Dummies
978-0-470-29034-7

Computer Hardware

BlackBerry For Dummies, 4th Edition
978-0-470-60700-8

Computers For Seniors For Dummies, 2nd Edition
978-0-470-53483-0

PCs For Dummies, Windows 7 Edition
978-0-470-46542-4

Laptops For Dummies, 4th Edition
978-0-470-57829-2

Cooking & Entertaining

Cooking Basics For Dummies, 3rd Edition
978-0-7645-7206-7

Wine For Dummies, 4th Edition
978-0-470-04579-4

Diet & Nutrition

Dieting For Dummies, 2nd Edition
978-0-7645-4149-0

Nutrition For Dummies, 4th Edition
978-0-471-79868-2

Weight Training For Dummies, 3rd Edition
978-0-471-76845-6

Digital Photography

Digital SLR Cameras & Photography For Dummies, 3rd Edition
978-0-470-46606-3

Photoshop Elements 8 For Dummies
978-0-470-52967-6

Gardening

Gardening Basics For Dummies
978-0-470-03749-2

Organic Gardening For Dummies, 2nd Edition
978-0-470-43067-5

Green/Sustainable

Raising Chickens For Dummies
978-0-470-46544-8

Green Cleaning For Dummies
978-0-470-39106-8

Health

Diabetes For Dummies, 3rd Edition
978-0-470-27086-8

Food Allergies For Dummies
978-0-470-09584-3

Living Gluten-Free For Dummies, 2nd Edition
978-0-470-58589-4

Hobbies/General

Chess For Dummies, 2nd Edition
978-0-7645-8404-6

Drawing Cartoons & Comics For Dummies
978-0-470-42683-8

Knitting For Dummies, 2nd Edition
978-0-470-28747-7

Organizing For Dummies
978-0-7645-5300-4

Su Doku For Dummies
978-0-470-01892-7

Home Improvement

Home Maintenance For Dummies, 2nd Edition
978-0-470-43063-7

Home Theater For Dummies, 3rd Edition
978-0-470-41189-6

Living the Country Lifestyle All-in-One For Dummies
978-0-470-43061-3

Solar Power Your Home For Dummies, 2nd Edition
978-0-470-59678-4

Available wherever books are sold. For more information or to order direct: U.S. customers visit www.dummies.com or call 1-877-762-2974. U.K. customers visit www.wileyeurope.com or call (0) 1243 843291. Canadian customers visit www.wiley.ca or call 1-800-567-4797.

Internet

Blogging For Dummies, 3rd Edition
978-0-470-61996-4

eBay For Dummies, 6th Edition
978-0-470-49741-8

Facebook For Dummies, 3rd Edition
978-0-470-87804-0

Web Marketing For Dummies, 2nd Edition
978-0-470-37181-7

WordPress For Dummies, 3rd Edition
978-0-470-59274-8

Language & Foreign Language

French For Dummies
978-0-7645-5193-2

Italian Phrases For Dummies
978-0-7645-7203-6

Spanish For Dummies, 2nd Edition
978-0-470-87855-2

Spanish For Dummies, Audio Set
978-0-470-09585-0

Math & Science

Algebra I For Dummies, 2nd Edition
978-0-470-55964-2

Biology For Dummies, 2nd Edition
978-0-470-59875-7

Calculus For Dummies
978-0-7645-2498-1

Chemistry For Dummies
978-0-7645-5430-8

Microsoft Office

Excel 2010 For Dummies
978-0-470-48953-6

Office 2010 All-in-One For Dummies
978-0-470-49748-7

Office 2010 For Dummies, Book + DVD Bundle
978-0-470-62698-6

Word 2010 For Dummies
978-0-470-48772-3

Music

Guitar For Dummies, 2nd Edition
978-0-7645-9904-0

iPod & iTunes For Dummies, 8th Edition
978-0-470-87871-2

Piano Exercises For Dummies
978-0-470-38765-8

Parenting & Education

Parenting For Dummies, 2nd Edition
978-0-7645-5418-6

Type 1 Diabetes For Dummies
978-0-470-17811-9

Pets

Cats For Dummies, 2nd Edition
978-0-7645-5275-5

Dog Training For Dummies, 3rd Edition
978-0-470-60029-0

Puppies For Dummies, 2nd Edition
978-0-470-03717-1

Religion & Inspiration

The Bible For Dummies
978-0-7645-5296-0

Catholicism For Dummies
978-0-7645-5391-2

Women in the Bible For Dummies
978-0-7645-8475-6

Self-Help & Relationship

Anger Management For Dummies
978-0-470-03715-7

Overcoming Anxiety For Dummies, 2nd Edition
978-0-470-57441-6

Sports

Baseball For Dummies, 3rd Edition
978-0-7645-7537-2

Basketball For Dummies, 2nd Edition
978-0-7645-5248-9

Golf For Dummies, 3rd Edition
978-0-471-76871-5

Web Development

Web Design All-in-One For Dummies
978-0-470-41796-6

Web Sites Do-It-Yourself For Dummies, 2nd Edition
978-0-470-56520-9

Windows 7

Windows 7 For Dummies
978-0-470-49743-2

Windows 7 For Dummies, Book + DVD Bundle
978-0-470-52398-8

Windows 7 All-in-One For Dummies
978-0-470-48763-1

Available wherever books are sold. For more information or to order direct: U.S. customers visit www.dummies.com or call 1-877-762-2974. U.K. customers visit www.wileyeurope.com or call (0) 1243 843291. Canadian customers visit www.wiley.ca or call 1-800-567-4797.

DUMMIES.COM®

Wherever you are in life, Dummies makes it easier.

From fashion to Facebook®,
wine to Windows®, and everything in between,
Dummies makes it easier.

Visit us at Dummies.com